# The Avoidable War

Pierre Laval

VOLUME 2

# The Avoidable War

## Pierre Laval & the Politics of Reality

**1935-1936**

J. Kenneth Brody

Transaction Publishers
New Brunswick (U.S.A.) and London (U.K.)

This book is printed on acid-free paper that meets the American National Standard for Permanence of Paper for Printed Library Materials.

Library of Congress Catalog Number: 98–49011
ISBN: 1-56000-375-8 (cloth); 0–7658–0622–3 (paper)
Printed in the United States of America

Library of Congress Cataloging-in-Publication Data

Brody, J. Kenneth.
The avoidable war / J. Kenneth Brody.
p. cm.
Contents: v. 2. Pierre Laval and the politics of reality, 1935-1936
Includes bibliographical references and index.
ISBN 1-56000-375-8 (v. 2 : cloth : alk. paper). — ISBN 0–7658–0622–3 (v. 2 : paper : alk. paper).
1. Europe—Politics and government—1918–1945. 2. World War, 1939–1945—Causes. 3. World War, 1939–1945—Diplomatic history. I. Title.
D727.B655 1999
940.5—dc21 98-49011
CIP

For Sandra

Who Shares My Life

"There are, however, some situations in which
one is only offered a choice of two evils,
one greater and one less."

—Sir Eric Drummond

# Contents

# Acknowledgments

One of the most rewarding aspects of the creation of this history has been the generosity of eminent scholars who have reviewed the manuscript. Their commentaries, criticism, corrections and suggestions have embellished and enriched this work and its companion volume. For all this I extend my gratitude to the following: Professor Henderson Braddick of Lehigh University, Professor Bernard V. Burke of Portland State University, Professor Maurice Cowling of Cambridge University, Professor Gordon A. Craig of Stanford University, Professor George W. Egerton of the University of British Columbia, Professor John F. Naylor of the State University of New York at Buffalo, Professor Alberto Sbacci of Atlantic Union College, Professor Donald E. Shepardson of the University of Northern Iowa, and Professor Gerhard L. Weinberg of the University of North Carolina.

For their help and suggestions in a variety of contexts I am indebted to Professor Donald C. Birn of the State University of New York at Binghamton, Professor Martin Gilbert of Oxford University, Townsend W. Hoopes, and Professor Joachim Remak of the University of California at Santa Barbara.

My non-academic reviewers were Arthur Levinson, Herbert W. Park and Alfred H. Stoloff. Each made a signal contribution to the work.

I am deeply grateful to Richard Abel, longtime publisher and bookman, to Ambassador Walter J. P. Curley, and to Comte Rene de Chambrun, historian and history maker, for their indispensable help in achieving publication of this work.

Natasha Kern of the Natasha Kern Literacy Agency led me by the hand across the convoluted pathways of the publishing world.

Professor Irving Louis Horowitz, Chairman of Transaction Publishers, had the vision to see two separate but companion works in a very large manuscript. To him, and to Transaction President Mary Curtis and editor Laurence Mintz I am deeply indebted for their significant contributions and for their encouragement and unwavering support of this work and its companion volume.

Much of the work was done in the excellent facilities and with the help of the staff of the Portland State University Library. I am grateful, too, for the resources and help of the New York Public Library and the Sterling and Seeley Mudd Libraries at Yale.

The original manuscript was prepared by Joanne Castles. The revisions were done by Rebecca L. Peer. Their competence, patience and good humor kept the project on track and a continuing pleasure. The software wizardry and support of Richard F. Crall kept the manuscript apace with technical developments.

Grateful acknowledgment is made to the Public Record Office for permission to use extracts from British Cabinet papers and to H.M. Stationery Office for permission to use materials from Documents on British Foreign Policy, Second Series. Crown copyright, including material in the Public Record Office, is reproduced with the permission of the Controller of Her Majesty's Stationery Office. Extracts from its Survey of International Affairs for the years 1932, 1934, and 1935 and Documents on International Affairs for the years 1933 and 1935 are used by permission of Oxford University Press which is gratefully acknowledged.

The dedication of this volume and its companion volume record my heartfelt gratitude to my wife and daughter for their loving support and never failing encouragement.

# Author's Note

Ethiopia is an African state with a long and colorful history. For much of that history it was known as Abyssinia. In the period covered by this book and its companion volume, both Ethiopia and Abyssinia were used but Abyssinia predominated. For clarity and uniformity, Abyssinia is used throughout this work except as required by direct quotation.

# 1

# The Summer of the Dictators

The summer of 1935 was the summer of the dictators who occupied center stage in Europe when Europe was the center stage of the world. Incontestably, the most dynamic force was Adolf Hitler, who had become German Chancellor in January, 1933.

In newsreels, on magazine covers, the lank, dark lock that traversed his forehead, the hypnotic stare, the mini-mustache, half comical, half sinister, were familiar to audiences across the world. They knew, too, in pictures, moving or still, the searchlights and torchlights, the massed bands and banners, the phalanxes of brown-shirted storm troopers and steel helmeted soldiers that were the background for his strident proclamations. They did not have to know German to catch on their radios the hatred, the savagery of his tone, the cadences rising in swelling tides from passion to hysteria. They could hear and they could feel the thunderous responses: Sieg Heil! Sieg Heil! Sieg Heil! They well knew the cruel persecutions that Hitler's hatreds had unleashed. A few apologists aside, the sinister nature of the Nazi regime was known and understood across the world.

Hitler had never accepted Germany's defeat in 1918 and the peace settlement at Versailles that followed it. His immediate goals were to eliminate all of the servitudes of the Treaty of Versailles which had almost totally disarmed Germany and most importantly had demilitarized the critically strategic Rhineland, the banks of the Rhine, and the lands between the Rhine and the French border. To achieve these goals meant building a mighty new army and air force, and this is what Hitler proceeded to do in defiance of treaties and the condemnation of the other nations of Europe and the League of Nations. Hitler noted that such condemnations in no way altered the accomplished fact.

If these were his immediate goals, Hitler's long-term program was more ambitious. One blood, Hitler proclaimed, demanded one Reich. A Greater Germany must include all Germans meaning those who lived in Hitler's birthplace, Austria, in the borderlands of Czechoslovakia and Poland and the lost territories of the East. But that was not all. For Germany to be the preeminent world power, the German sword would make way for the German plow to acquire the land needed to sustain world power, and it was in Russia that this land would be found. These were the doctrines Hitler laid out in *Mein Kampf* early in his career, which he preached ceaselessly in the years of struggle before he attained power and which, as Fuhrer, he proceeded, as circumstances allowed, and with growing confidence, to turn into reality.

Another dictator occupied center stage in the same year. Benito Mussolini had been in power for more than a decade. His power was absolute. If he stood for law and order, the emphasis was on order and the law was strictly Fascist, that is to say, Mussolini's law. Yet he cultivated a more benevolent image than Hitler. He was associated with draining marshes, removing beggars from the streets, and famously making the trains run on time. His outthrust chin and bulging eyes were as universally recognizable as Hitler's mustache though his penchant for theatrical costumery (for he was an actor at heart) far outshone Hitler's sober brown shirt and swastika armband. Mussolini had over the years garnered the good opinion of many notable people and where Mussolini stood and how he would respond to the crises the year would bring were questions to ponder.

The danger posed by Hitler's Germany was clear to Mussolini. He knew something about dictators and dictatorship and he saw sooner than most the menace of the Nazi state. When in 1934 his friend and protégé, the Austrian Chancellor Dollfuss, was assassinated in an abortive Nazi putsch, Mussolini was shocked and appalled. He railed at the Nazis as criminals and degenerates and did not hesitate to point his finger directly at Hitler. He sent his troops to the Brenner Pass and proclaimed himself the defender of Austrian independence. Something had to be done about the menace of Nazi Germany, he said, and done quickly. If it were not, Europe would face a Germany of eighty millions, its hegemony stretching from Berlin to the Bosphorus.

He looked to Italy's allies of 1915–1918, Britain and France. There had been longstanding issues with France. They revolved around Italy's claims to territory on the coast of the Adriatic which the 1919 peace treaties had assigned to France's ally, the new state of Yugoslavia, and Italian claims in the French protectorate of Tunisia. In January, 1935, Mussolini entered into accords with France resolving these issues. But the primary goals of these accords were the defense of Austria and, equally important, a firm stand against further treaty violations by Germany. The treaty violation that France feared most was the remilitarization of the Rhineland.

Amid the changing governments of the French Third Republic, Pierre Laval was a familiar figure. He was now both Prime Minister and Foreign Minister. His goals were the eternal goals of France–Frenchsecurity against the German threat, precisely as Foch and Clemenceau the victors of 1918, had proclaimed. In population and economy, Germany, the vanquished in 1918, was incomparably stronger than France. Nothing was more critical to France than the demilitarized zone of the Rhineland. It was an open door to Germany, enabling France to come to the aid of its Central and Eastern European allies. And it denied to Germany the jumping-off place for the attack on France. Not only did Laval enter into the Rome accords with Mussolini but he also entered into a pact with the Soviet Union, a basic goal of which was to contain Germany in the East.

In all this Great Britain played a critical role. With its vast empire, it was seen as the greatest of the great powers, especially since the United States had retired into isolationism and the Soviet Union remained aloof from the affairs of Europe.

Britain was far from unaware of the menace of Nazi Germany. Its diplomatic and military representatives abroad had reported in accurate and chilling detail on the character of the Nazi regime, its headlong thrust for rearmament, and its ultimate goals. The challenge was to craft a suitable response. A series of problems impeded the effort.

Depression had concentrated people's minds on domestic issues. Memories of the suffering and losses of the war of 1914–1918 were fresh and poignant and the root of widespread disillusionment. It was not only the war losses of the past but the fear of immeasurably larger losses from weapons of mass destruction in wars to come that led thoughtful people to wonder if civilization could survive another general war.

In these circumstances peace movements flourished and disarmament was seen by many, the Labour Party included, as a practical policy. It was this outlook that braked and limited the modest steps the Government could take to rearm in the face of Hitler and his regime.

Together with Italy, Britain was a guarantor of the 1925 Locarno Treaty under which with Italy it would come to the aid of France if France were attacked by Germany and of Germany if Germany were attacked by France. By this treaty Germany had confirmed and ratified the provisions for the demilitarization of the Rhineland which had been contained in the Versailles Treaty. But, aside from Locarno, Britain was increasingly wary of any continental commitments.

Fearing Germany, Mussolini wanted to associate Britain with France and Italy in the defense of Austria and treaty obligations. To that end he convened a conference of the three powers at Stresa on Italy's Lake Como in April, 1935. There France and Italy strove to propound concrete answers to concrete cases of German treaty violations. Unhappily, in this effort, Britain's hands were tied. Its Cabinet, meeting on January 14, 1935, had determined that the Rhineland was not a vital British interest and it was this secret that led the British representatives at Stresa to dilute the firmness with which France and Italy wished to confront Germany and to deflect any action which would imply a British commitment.

Far from wishing to join France and Italy in confronting Nazi Germany's treaty violations and rapidly growing armed forces, British leaders persistently strove to arrive at an understanding with Germany. Thus, the British Foreign Secretary, Sir John Simon and his youthful aide Anthony Eden had met the March, 1935 announcement of Germany's new army and air force in outright violation of the Versailles Treaty not with protests and remonstrances but with a friendly visit to Hitler. They then proceeded to compound the situation by entering into a naval agreement with Germany in June, 1935, undisclosed to France and Italy till it was fait accompli, which released Germany from the naval limitations of the Versailles Treaty.

Mussolini's fundamental aim was to contain the threat of Nazi Germany, but he had other goals. Like Germany, Italy had felt aggrieved at Versailles. Italy had not received the colonial booty to which she believed she was entitled. In the summer of 1935, Mussolini had his eyes firmly fixed on the ancient empire of Abyssinia, Africa's only truly independent state. An affray between Italian and Abyssinian troops at the desert waterholes of Wal Wal in December, 1934, had furnished a pretext. Mussolini was determined to build a new Roman Empire in Africa and while Abyssinia moved through the lengthy conciliation procedures of the League of Nations, Mussolini continued his single-minded buildup of the attacking forces.

There were complications here, but Mussolini believed he could accomplish his goals in Africa before Nazi Germany became strong in Europe and that there would still be time, if he moved swiftly and decisively in Africa, to confront and contain the growing menace of Nazi Germany. He did not wish to act against the will of his French and British allies in the containment of Germany. He believed that by his January, 1935 accords with France he had obtained tacit French approval of his Abyssinian adventure. In early 1935 he had signaled directly to Britain that he threatened no British interest. But Britain remained silent and this silence Mussolini took for consent. Nor had Britain raised the Abyssinian issue at Stresa.

There was one British commitment which went beyond Locarno and beyond Europe. This was Britain's membership in the League of Nations of which it had been a founding member. What that commitment meant was far from clear. From the inception of the League in 1919, France had always championed a powerful League executive and League armed forces to enforce the Covenant. Britain, to the contrary, saw the League as an organ of conciliation, not enforcement, and was wary of any commitment to participate automatically in enforcing the League's mandates.

Greatest among British champions of the League of Nations was Lord Robert Cecil, son of a Victorian Prime Minister, co-founder with Woodrow Wilson of the League. He had watched in alarm the growing power of the dictators, the failure of the 1933 Disarmament Conference, the failure of the League to halt Japanese aggression in Manchuria, and the systematic destruction by Germany of the limitations and restrictions of the Versailles Treaty. He believed that foreign policy must have a moral basis, and its governing force must be public opinion. This was in contrast to the balance of power operated in the dark corridors of traditional diplomacy and power relations.

Lord Cecil was not content to philosophize. He was a man of action. He resolved to put a series of fundamental issues of foreign policy to the British public in the conviction that their response would guide the British Government to a policy that would preserve the peace and make the League of Nations the dominant force in international relations.

This was the Peace Ballot of 1934–35, a great national referendum on issues of war and peace. It asked the British people whether Great Britain should remain a member of the League of Nations. It asked whether they were in favor of the all-round reduction of arms and the abolition of national military and naval aircraft by international agreement and whether the manufacture and sale of arms for private profit should be prohibited by international agreement. Finally, it asked, if one nation insisted on attacking another, whether other nations should combine to stop it, first by economic means and second, by military means.

It will be noticed that each of the questions the Peace Ballot asked was phrased as a statement of principle detached from any specific case. They did not address the question of what British interests might be at stake. They did not ask practical questions about what membership in the League of Nations really meant and what would happen if some nations (Nazi Germany came readily to mind) declined to disarm and instead rearmed. What in fact were economic sanctions, by whom adopted and by whom enforced, and how effective they might be, and whether economic sanctions could succeed in the absence of military sanctions were questions inherent in the Peace Ballot, but to which it could suggest no answer.

Nevertheless, by superb organization, shrewd publicity, and the devoted services of a half million volunteers, the Peace Ballot became a meteoric phenomenon of public opinion and political influence. Its first returns came in December, 1934, the same month that the conflict at the waterholes of Wal Wal gave Mussolini the pretext for launching his plans of Abyssinian conquest. Though Lord Cecil had initially looked for a modest response of a half-million votes, in the end the Peace Ballot returns measured eleven and one-half million people, more than had ever voted in a Parliamentary election.

The results were overwhelmingly in favor of British membership in the League of Nations, in favor of international disarmament by international agreement and against the private manufacture of arms. There was a decisive vote in favor of halting aggression by internationally agreed economic sanctions. But the vote in favor of a military response to aggression got little more than a majority of the voters taking abstentions into account.

The results were announced on June 14, 1935. Faced with so overwhelming a display of public opinion, the British Government, hitherto so wary of the League and of continental commitments, promptly capitulated and Prime Minister Stanley Baldwin proclaimed that the Covenant and the League of Nations would be "the sheet anchor of British policy." Anthony Eden, dashing and popular, the newly appointed Minister for League of Nation Affairs, vigorously seconded his Prime

Minister's declaration. This was indeed far different from the policy of reticence and distance from both Europe and the League that had been such pronounced features of British policy as recently as at Stresa.

So it was in the summer of 1935 that Europe faced the crisis of threatened Italian aggression in Abyssinia. Britain and France ran the risk of totally disaffecting their Italian ally and associate in the containment of Nazi Germany if, as the undisputed leaders of the League of Nations, they sought to curb or defeat Italy through the operation of economic or military sanctions. Indeed, it was clearly recognized that to come down on the side of the Covenant and of the League might well push an angry and embittered Mussolini into Hitler's waiting arms.

To Pierre Laval, the risk was clear. The interests of France lay in Europe and not in Africa, in Austria and the Rhineland and not in Abyssinia. Something must be done to avoid the breakup of a combination he and his predecessors had so carefully constructed to contain Germany, now Nazi Germany.

But the British people had spoken. There would be a General Election soon and the Government was in no position to ignore the voice of eleven and a half million Peace Balloters and the Delphic responses they had given to the questions of the Peace Ballot. This then was what Sir Samuel Hoare, the new British Foreign Secretary, called in a masterpiece of understatement "a most inconvenient dilemma."

# 2

# A Most Inconvenient Dilemma

*"Any sound political thought must be based on elements of both utopia and realism."*
—E.H. Carr [1]

## Duce and Negus

Amid thunder and showers, poised on a gun carriage, Mussolini harangued troops leaving for Africa:

> We have entered upon a struggle which we as a Government and a revolutionary people have irrevocably decided to carry to its conclusion.
>
> Remember that black troops have always been defeated by Italians, and that Adowa, owing to the enormous difference in the proportion of forces, 14,000 Italians against 100,000 Abyssinians, was a glorious object of Italian heroism....
>
> All Italy is behind her sons who are leaving for Africa and Italians prefer a life of heroism to one that is insipid. Italians today are protagonists of a glorious history, and all the world must recognize this will and the spirit of Fascist Italy.[2]

The Duce's history may have been dubious, but another announcement the same day evidenced his sincerity. Vittorio Mussolini, eighteen, and his brother, Bruno, had volunteered for service as flyers in East Africa. At seventeen, Bruno would be Italy's youngest pilot.

Haile Selassie replied in kind. He reviewed his troops; then seated on a gilt and silk embroidered chair under an orange umbrella, he told his Parliament on the morning of July 18 that Abyssinia rejected a mandate or protectorate of any kind. Abyssinia would stand against Italian aggression:

> Soldiers when you have heard that in the battle fire a loved and respected chieftain has fallen, do not weep or despair. The man who dies for his country is happy. Blind death destroys in peace as well as in war. Better die free than to live as slaves. Remember your fathers who fell.[3]

A week later, the Emperor celebrated his forty-fifth birthday amid scenes of antiquarian pageantry. The streets around the Great Gebbi, the Emperor's palace, were thronged with riflemen on foot and chiefs mounted on mules carrying velvet flags. The steps of the throne room were decorated with spears, lions' manes and embossed shields.

The Emperor received his ministers and counselors on the Alga, the bed throne, which was caparisoned in scarlet. His black cape, too, was embroidered in scarlet, set off by the Golden Collar of Solomon.

The ceremonies were followed by the *geber*, the feast of the Emperor and his warriors. He sat at the high table with his commanders, but today the customary veil that separated him from the masses was set aside. The soldiers kept their swords, their pistols and their rifles at their sides. Their fare was tef, an Abyssinian mead, and whole oxen and sheep from which the warriors hacked off choice portions with their knives and swords. The more tef they quaffed, the more heroic were the tales of martial glory they rose to tell. It was amid such scenes from another era of mankind's history that Abyssinia prepared to wage a twentieth century war.[4]

## Anglo-Saxon Attitudes

Britain's Foreign Secretary, Sir Samuel Hoare, had spoken with truth, feeling and understatement when he told the cabinet on June 19, 1935 that England was being placed "in a most inconvenient dilemma." He described it with precision:

> Either we should have to make a futile protest which would irritate Mussolini and perhaps drive him out of the League into the arms of Germany, or we should make no protest at all and give the appearance of pusillanimity.[5]

The League of Nations Union was plagued by no such doubts. It adopted a resolution on July 11 noting both Baldwin's declaration that the League was the sheet anchor of British policy and Eden's strong pro-League statement at East Fulham. The resolution pointed to the growing danger of war, and expressed confidence that the Government's policy would indeed be based on the Baldwin and Eden declarations. The LNU assured the Government "of the warm support of public opinion for any measures, however drastic, which they may consider wise and effectual to safeguard the peace of nations and maintain the supreme authority of the League in international affairs."[6]

The dilemma that Hoare described was the classic dilemma of expedience versus principle. The spectacle of incipient Italian aggression against a primitive African state, the contrast between Mussolini and Haile Selassie, the stark exemplification, as it seemed, of right and wrong, raised moral issues which gained in importance as the crisis developed. The Peace Ballot had posed principles, not cases. The 500,000 workers had been animated by a love of peace, of justice, and a desire to see the precepts of morality applied to international relations. The peace societies, the women's societies, the labor unions and the churches who had been so prominent in the effort had, like Lord Cecil, combined the practicality of their organized effort with a moral fervor for the result.

Writing to the Times in August, the Archbishop of York said:

> We are bound by the Covenant of the League. It is reassuring to be told that adherence to the League of Nations is 'the keystone of British policy' but it is more than this: it is a clear moral obligation. To fail now in loyalty to the League because that loyalty might have grave consequences would be sheer wickedness involving indelible disgrace.[7]

In the same vein, Canon R.F. Barry told the congregation in Westminster Abbey on August 25, 1935 that support of the League was a moral obligation, even if it meant the sacrifice of British possessions or British sovereignty.[8]

In an October newspaper interview, the Archbishop of Canterbury instructed the French in these terms:

> We are animated by moral and spiritual considerations.... It is...no egoist interest that is driving us forward and no consideration of interest should keep you behind.[9]

It all seemed plain to the celebrated historian, Professor Arnold Toynbee, when he wrote the history of the Italo-Abyssinian war a year later. It was, he said, a tale of sin and retribution. The sin of aggression, he went on, had become mortal instead of merely venial and no adult observer, certainly no responsible statesmen, could be excused for not recognizing this.[10]

In *The Gathering Storm*, Winston Churchill looked back and agreed:

> Mussolini's designs upon Abyssinia were unsuited to the ethics of the twentieth century. They belonged to those dark ages when white men felt themselves entitled to conquer brown, black, or red men and subjugate them by their superior strength and weapons. In our enlightened days when crimes and cruelties have been committed from which savages of former times would have recoiled, or of which they would at least have been incapable, such conduct was at once obsolete and reprehensible.[11]

Here was a good measure of the change in British attitudes. Churchill had not always felt this way. As a bloodthirsty youth he had eagerly joined the Spanish in pursuit of Cuban rebels. He had served under Sir Bindon Blood with the Malakand Field Force on the Indian frontier, narrowly escaped death at Omdurman, campaigned against the Boers in South Africa, and written enthusiastically and colorfully about it all.

In those days he had glorified Britain's colonial campaigns:

> Year after year, stretching back to an infinite horizon, we see the figures of the odd and bizarre potentates against whom British arms continually are turned. They pass in a long procession: The Aknund of Swat; Cetewayo, brandishing an Assegai as naked as himself; Kruger singing a psalm of victory; Osman Digna, the Immortal and Irretrievable; Theebaw, with his umbrella; Lobengula, gazing fondly at the pages of *Truth*; Prempeh, abasing himself from the dust; the Mad Mullah on his white ass; and, latest of all, the Khalifa in his coach of state. It is like a pantomime scene at Drury Lane.[12]

Vintage Churchill, but all this had become in 1935 "obsolete and reprehensible." Anthony Eden agreed. He was especially concerned for the preservation of moral authority of the League and feared any solution of the crisis which would, as he said, be unjust, unworthy, or would rob Britain of its good name.[13]

Like all dictators, Mussolini was infuriated by opposition. What infuriated him most was opposition based upon moral claims. He told a French correspondent:

> I think for Italy as the great Englishmen who have made the British Empire have thought for England, as the great French colonizers have thought for France.[14]

What made it more excruciating was the fact that, thanks to his efficient intelligence service, Mussolini had acquired a copy of the Maffey Report, which the British Government had commissioned to gauge the extent of British interests in Abyssinia and probably read it even before it had been circulated to the British Cabinet. He read it in the simplest and most direct sense: Britain had no vital direct interests in Abyssinia and it should be a matter of indifference on the African scene if Abyssinia remained independent or became an Italian colony.

Yet this same Britain had acquired a quarter of the globe. "We have got her the same," Kipling sang of Queen Victoria, "by the sword and the flame." To these had been added guile, treachery, economic and technological superiority, and the vast disparities in resources and power between the British Empire and the "lesser breeds without the law."

Mussolini was not likely to be impressed by British claims that the dispensation thus crudely obtained was part of the moral order of the universe and that any attempt by others to enlarge their estates reeked of sin and immorality. Instead, he put it down to Anglo-Saxon hypocrisy, which, viewed in another light, was the British talent amounting to genius to convince themselves that virtue and morality inevitably coincided with British interests.

Such pretensions could be as exasperating to friends as they were to adversaries. One day in September Laval cried out to Anthony Eden that "morals were one thing; the interests of a country are another." It was a difference in viewpoints which made collaboration difficult and true alliance impossible.[15]

There were others who were moved by practical considerations. Their champion was Sir Robert Vansittart, Permanent Under Secretary at the Foreign Office, and Vansittart had Hoare's ear. To Vansittart, the issue never varied. The choice was between Austria and Abyssinia and he chose Austria because "it was the first point of Hitler's expansion which, once permitted, would be boundless."

Mussolini was forcing the choice. Vansittart said,

> I hated it and him for driving a wedge between me and Eden, since I necessarily appeared less wholehearted than he for justice. To me that was injustice. I had full sympathy for the League but, even when I lost most at racing, I never backed a horse when I knew from form, jockey and trainer that it could not win.... The real crux was that the Leaguers were anti-Italian while I was anti-German. Doubtless I was lopsided about Germany, but I persistently saw an end if ever Hitler was sure of his southern flank.[16]

Concern about Germany was a question of ultimate ends. Any attempt to coerce Italy had to take into account the question of means.

The League had no military force. If the Covenant were to be enforced, it was the Royal Navy that stood between Italy and East Africa. How had it been affected by the ten-year rule, by the limitation of cruisers which Cecil had championed, how well armed and ready was it for war? The issue could not be viewed in the context of an Anglo-Italian confrontation alone. Whatever the result, the ultimate issue was how the Navy would emerge from the conflict and what, if any, margin of security it could provide the British Empire against the obvious challenges of Germany and Japan.

## Hoare's Policy

Hoare had been left to sign a controversial naval treaty with Germany that his predecessor, Sir John Simon, had negotiated. He now found himself at the center of a major international crisis. The issues of British principles and British interests were sharply defined externally between the League, of which Britain was the champion, and Italy. The same division wracked the British Parliament and the Cabinet. Above it all there loomed the eleven and a half million votes of the Peace Ballot, which Hoare must interpret as best he could and ignore only at his peril and that of his Government.

He was by nature a cautious and careful man, with a taste for compromise. When he reported to the Cabinet on July 3, 1935, he did not minimize the gravity of the Abyssinian crisis. The Covenant, the Kellogg-Briand Pact, and the 1906 Treaty were all involved. He reviewed several possible courses of action. He reminded the Cabinet that economic sanctions were likely to lead to war.

It seemed prudent, therefore, to ask the Committee of Imperial Defense for its report and opinion on the application of Article 16 of the Covenant and the possible closing of the Suez Canal.[17]

Hoare was prudent, too, on July 11, 1935 in his first report to the House of Commons as Foreign Secretary. He ably defended the naval pact. He expressed British interest in an Eastern European Pact without, of course, any British commitment. He also expressed sympathy but no commitment for Austria. He pushed for an air pact.

But the principal topic was Abyssinia and here Hoare staked out two positions to which he would adhere during his tenure as Foreign Secretary. He pronounced firmly for collective security—the settled policy of the British government—subject to a proviso. Collective security had to be shared: "You cannot have collective security without not only contribution, but proportional contribution."

To this he added:

> As things are, and as long as there is an effective League and a system of collective security, we are ready and willing to take our full share of collective responsibility. But when I say collective responsibility, I mean collective responsibility.

Here was a clear warning that the world could not expect Britain to enforce the Covenant singlehanded.

Hoare defended the Zeila offer whereby Britain had proposed, by way of settlement, to offer a part in British Somaliland to Abyssinia while Abyssinia granted a portion of the Ogaden Province to Italy. He admitted Italy's need for expansion. This led to Hoare's second position. Could not Italy's needs and complaints be peacefully adjusted without war?

> We have surely found in the past that it is possible to adjust demands and differences of this kind without recourse to war, and I am not prepared even now to abandon any chance that may present itself for averting what I believe will be a calamity, whether it be through the machinery of the 1906 Treaty or whether it be through the machinery of the League, or whether it be through both....
>
> We stand for peace and we will not abandon any reasonable chance that may offer itself for helping prevent a disastrous war [cheers].[18]

The League's, then, was not to Hoare the exclusive machinery of conciliation or enforcement. What mattered was to avoid war, however that might be accomplished.

The League's Conciliation Commission, meeting at Scheveningen had also been searching for a peaceful solution to the quarrel. But it had once more deadlocked. One potential mechanism for a negotiated settlement, was a three-party conference under the 1906 Abyssinian Treaty to which Italy, France and Britain were parties.

A suggestion to that effect made by M. Avenol, Secretary General of the League, was promptly conveyed to Pierre Laval and eagerly taken up. Laval counseled precision in defining the objects of the meeting and secrecy enabling realistic discussions in search of a compromise. First he suggested a preliminary inquiry to Mussolini by Sir Eric Drummond, the British Ambassador in Rome. But Laval had a penchant for more direct methods. He picked up his phone and spoke to Mussolini, then reported Mussolini's opinion: Such a meeting was useless and could be dangerous unless (interestingly enough) it was known precisely what would be discussed. If this was not encouraging, at least the proposal had not been rejected out of hand.[19]

Hoare now pressed hard for the three-party meeting. Otherwise the League Council would meet at the end of July and the issue would have to be faced.

In Rome, the French Ambassador tackled Mussolini, who was not coy. He reminded the Ambassador how he had earlier pointed out on the map his demands to Eden, telling him what parts of Abyssinia he would take and what part he would leave to the Emperor.

The Ambassador displayed a large envelope. If this is what you require and you could get two thirds peaceably, he asked, would you accept? Mussolini turned cryptic. "Well," he said, "it would depend on what exactly the two thirds represented."[20]

Drummond now presented the proposal for a three-party conference to Mussolini. Had Mussolini read the debate in the House of Commons on July 11? It represented the general public opinion of the country that Britain would be compelled on grounds of honor to stand by its League obligations at Geneva. Mussolini nodded assent. He had read it. He fully realized, he said, British fidelity to the League.

Again Mussolini referred to his earlier talks with Eden. He would not risk the security of Italy's colonies. As to the League meeting set for July 25, he had a proposal. If it were agreed to limit the inquiry solely to the cause of the Wal Wal incident, excluding the issue whether Wal Wal was within the Abyssinian frontier, he would agree to break the deadlock by naming a fifth member of the Conciliation Commission. This was modest progress in British eyes.[21] To Abyssinia it represented the pattern of continuing proceedings outside the League without result while Italy finalized its war preparations.

The Italians were being difficult but Hoare was hopeful. If only Italy would attend the meeting of the League Council on July 25, it was not impossible, he told Drummond, that a solution could be reached that was at the same time favorable to Italy and not inconsistent with the principles of the Covenant.[22]

A three-party conference naturally appealed to Laval. He instructed the French Ambassador in Rome to deliver a forceful warning to Mussolini not to misunderstand the French position. France wanted to live in the spirit of the Rome accords. It would do all it could *legitimately* to facilitate a solution favorable to Italy. But Mussolini must however bear in mind first and foremost that France remained loyal to the League of Nations on which her whole European policy was based. Such a message, Sir George Clerk, the British Ambassador in Paris, told Hoare ought to dispose of any belief that Laval had given Mussolini a free hand in Abyssinia.[22]

The British Cabinet was not as forthright as Laval had been when it confronted the issue on July 22. It considered a variety of proposals, the first of which was that Eden, en route to the meeting of the League Council in Geneva, should call on Laval and inform him "in the privacy of negotiation, but not in public, that the British Government was prepared in the last resort to fulfill its engagements under the Covenant and would eventually have to announce that this had been its attitude."

This, it was suggested, would be consistent with the present trend of public opinion in the country. There was an interesting proviso ("though not necessarily later on if it led to war"). Was this, then, the answer to questions 5a and 5b of the Peace Ballot and did they indeed mean all sanctions short of war?

The cabinet thought it unlikely that France would participate in sanctions. A second suggestion was that Eden should intimate to Laval as a personal opinion that Britain would be compelled to announce its willingness to enforce the Covenant.

The third was to press Laval for his own solution, the fourth was to hold a conference with France, the fifth to examine financial sanctions which might not involve belligerent rights and hence the risk of war, and the sixth to warn France of the consequences of a war in Abyssinia on the natives of the British and French African empires.

The Cabinet was more fertile in suggestion than resolution and in the end only resolved to adjourn the issue to another day.[24]

When the Cabinet next met on July 24, 1935, they had before them a dispatch from Clerk to Hoare confirming French loyalty to the League, French insistence on the sanctity of the Covenant and at the same time the keen French desire for a three-power conference.

With the meeting of the League Council imminent, the Cabinet had to define a British position. Hoare suggested that this be done in a dispatch to Laval defining the basis of talks in Paris and Geneva. The minutes of the meeting brilliantly illuminate the extreme distaste of the Cabinet for clarifying its position.

> In this Dispatch, he [Hoare] proposed to deploy the whole case as to the dangers to European peace and security involved in an Italo-Abyssinian war, and to end on the note that the two governments ought to agree on a policy for averting war.

So much was clear; not what follows:

> His aim was to avoid crude questions being put by either side as to whether they were prepared to carry out their obligations under the Covenant. The underlying assumption would be that both Powers realized their obligations and were therefore jointly interested to find a way out of the difficulty.[25]

What was the "crude question" that Hoare wished to avoid? Long years of association with France and intimate knowledge that France's paramount concern was Germany made this too obvious to articulate. Were Britain to ask bluntly for French enforcement of the Covenant in Abyssinia, the French would reflexively and spontaneously ask the dreaded question: was Britain prepared to enforce the Covenant—and the Locarno Treaty—on the Rhine?

Having muddled its position on enforcement of the Covenant, the Cabinet next agreed that it should be on its guard against any settlement unacceptable to Abyssinia and outside the general framework of the League.

It was on this basis that it was vaguely resolved that the Foreign Secretary should press Italy to modify its attitude and that Eden should follow the same policy at the meeting of the League Council.

Hoare followed through with a note on the same day from Drummond, his Ambassador in Rome, to Mussolini. Drummond recounted in his note Eden's visit to Mussolini to offer the Zeila compromise and Mussolini's territorial claims, stating that such claims were inconsistent with the Kellogg-Briand Pact, the Covenant of the League of Nations, and the 1906 Treaty. Britain would facilitate a peaceful solution. But, there was anxiety:

> Deliberate disregard of the Covenant of the League of Nations and of the Pact of Paris would strike at the root of public law and international security and would be so viewed by public opinion in the United Kingdom.

Lord Cecil would have approved. But what would Britain do? The note begged Mussolini to give full weight to the considerations it set forth; but as to British action it offered no clue.[26]

The meeting of the League Council was now set for August 1, 1935. Hoare again outlined the difficulty of the situation in an informal meeting with the Dominion High Commissioners on July 29. Potential disaster lurked in every course of action. If Britain called for sanctions, it was possible that France would refuse to cooperate and Italy would leave the League. But if Britain concluded that enforcement of the Covenant was not a practical policy, "the shock to large sections of public opinion in this country and in very many parts of the Continent would be great."

If there were a war between Italy and Abyssinia, Austria would be weakened and Germany strengthened. No direct British interests were involved in Abyssinia. But there were constraints under which Hoare operated. His Government could accept no solution under which Abyssinia renounced her sovereignty or which was forced upon her without her consent. Short of this, he added significantly, there was no solution Britain was not prepared to consider.[27]

On July 30, Eden set forth for Paris to see Laval en route to Geneva. He carried the memorandum for Laval prepared by the Foreign Office as suggested by the Cabinet of July 22. In it Hoare detailed the adverse impacts of an Abyssinian war. The consequences would be bad if Italy won a short war, and emerged having successfully flouted the League and international law. They would be worse in the case of a protracted war, where Italian influence in Europe would wane to Germany's profit. Under any circumstances, the impact on the League of Nations would be wholly bad and this was the most important reason why France and Britain should cooperate to avoid war.

Hoare's memorandum now directed Laval's attention to a critical point. If Britain had to go to war in defense of the Covenant, it was essential to have the unanimous, or practically unanimous assent of the British people. Abyssinia was widely regarded as a test case. Collective security had to be truly collective and to maintain the support of the British people it must be seen as the defense against aggression from any quarter and not merely security against Germany alone.

It is hard to imagine a more undiplomatic approach to a French Prime Minister whose primary concern was Germany. Yet Hoare concluded his note by urging the necessity for Britain and France to act together, and speedily if disaster were to be averted.[28]

Having prepared this advice for Eden to convey to Laval, Hoare reported to the July 31 Cabinet meeting on proposals for the three power conference. What, it was asked, would the British delegates say if asked whether Britain was prepared to fulfill its obligations under the Covenant. To this the minutes note:

> It was explained that the Minister for League of Nations affairs would adopt the line of the Dispatch sent to Paris, as suggested at a meeting of the Cabinet, namely that both we and France had obligations that we should carry out and therefore were greatly concerned to see that the emergency did not develop to the point where the questions of their fulfillment arose.

Hoare now requested the Cabinet ministers to be careful not to convey the idea that the situation was hopeless but at the same time to be extremely cautious in any references as to what would or would not do in the event of an outbreak of hostilities.[29]

## Laval's Quiet Diplomacy

Pierre Laval had hardly been able to devote the whole of July to the international crisis. A more intimate crisis of the French economy absorbed his attention. During June he had forced a budget through Parliament, and in July issued a series of decree laws reducing government expenditure. This was difficult in an economy as centralized and government-dominated as France's. By way of compensation, other decrees reduced the cost of living—rents, fuel, and bread. By these measures Laval incurred the active hostility, not only of the right wing and the quasi-fascist leagues, but simultaneously the hostility of the civil servants, the labor unions, and the business community.

Laval was a survivor and the end of the month saw his fiscal program substantially in place. His tribulations had been eased during the month by an unusually happy family event.

Laval had boasted of being the manual lawyer. But before he had been a lawyer, he had been, as his wife always fondly said, a peasant. He hated society, preferred to be in bed by nine, and had resolutely refused to bring evening dress to the London meetings in February.

Laval simply was not made for evening dress, his wife cheerfully complained. No matter how carefully she arranged his shirt front, by the end of the evening it would have gone awry exposing an excessively hairy chest.[30]

Laval's manner and manners did not escape the critical comment of aristocratic British diplomats. A report to the Foreign Office portrayed Laval as they saw him:

> At all events he lunched at the American Embassy this morning when he was in great spirits, declaring that there would certainly be no war between Italy and Abyssinia as France would not tolerate it, in conclusion of which little speech he blew his nose on his table napkin.[31]

However proud of his origins, the self-made man rarely wishes his children to repeat his struggle. He was proud of his daughter and only child, Josée. Heredity had been generous; she was as elegant as her mother and as quick as her father whom she often accompanied on missions of state. On the first of July, there had been announced the engagement of Mlle. Josée Laval to M. René de Chambrun, son of General Comte de Chambrun who had commanded French forces in Morocco and Mme. de Chambrun, neé Clara Longworth of Cincinnati, Ohio, whose brother, Nicholas Longworth, had married Alice Roosevelt making the groom cousin to Franklin and Eleanor Roosevelt and grand-nephew of Theodore Roosevelt. The prospective groom was also the nephew of Charles de Chambrun, the French Ambassador to Rome, a descendant of Lafayette, by virtue of which he was a hereditary citizen of the state of Maryland, and a member of the New York Bar into the bargain.[32]

Pierre Laval never lacked for confidence. He had surmounted difficulties and could look back on July as a good month. He could in good heart and with high hopes take up the international crisis of August. His method had been tested: one issue at a time, one step at a time, and private, face-to-face negotiations whenever possible.

He met Eden on July 31. Eden had wanted a firm declaration from his own Government supporting the Covenant and this was precisely what he had not gotten. Instead he got the ambiguous British dispatch which he proceeded to read to Laval. Unerringly Laval fastened on its weakness. It described the dangers but offered no solution.[33]

France had clearly warned Italy, Laval said, referring to the French note of July 19, and Mussolini's response showed he had read it. From the start Laval counseled avoiding open condemnation in Geneva which might drive Italy out of the League. He was for a rare moment pessimistic, but agreed with Eden that the appointment of a fifth arbitrator and a three-power meeting offered hopes of a settlement.[34]

At Geneva on August 1 and 2, Laval and Eden labored privately with Pompeo Aloisi, Italy's delegate to the League, to avoid a full discussion by the League Council. It was Aloisi's burden to convey proposals to an unreceptive government in Rome. While these discussions continued, the British Ambassador in Rome received a reply signed by Mussolini to the British note of July 24. Mussolini reviewed the Zeila offer and the reasons for refusing it, reflected on the League's differing role in Europe and colonial realms, emphasized that the Stresa resolutions specified the peace of Europe, and denied any intent to injure the prestige of the League of Nations or to diminish Italian contributions to collective security which he interpreted to mean European collective security. In response to the British appeal, the Duce was obdurate. He had carefully considered the Abyssinian threat which, he said, Italy was determined to settle once and for all.[35]

It was Hitler's pattern to act violently and then speak of peace and conciliation. In contrast, Mussolini spoke violently but left open the corridors of conciliation. Essentially the Council marked time while the real work was done, as Laval preferred, in private. In the end there was a resolution in which everyone could claim some modicum of satisfaction.

By the League Council's unanimous resolution of August 4, the Commission of Conciliation would continue its labors, confined to the issue of what happened at Wal Wal, rather than under what sovereignty. A fifth arbitrator would be appointed if necessary. It was hoped that the issue would be determined by September 1, and in any case the parties would report to the Council on September 4.

It was a sacrifice, but Abyssinia accepted. Mussolini in turn was satisfied that the matter remained, until then, outside the League and confined to the Wal Wal incident.

Laval applauded the Council's resolution but added that the task of France was far from ended. As the London Times reported,

> With all of his force and in every possible thing he would contribute to the search for every means of conciliation. He would be faithful to the obligations of the Covenant and in response to the unanimous feelings of his countrymen he would fulfill his duty to the end, leaving no stone unturned to maintain peace.[36]

Eden followed Laval's lead, emphasizing, not enforcement of the Covenant, but conciliation:

> I will conclude by giving the Council the emphatic assurance that his Majesty's Government will devote every effort to securing a pacific settlement of this dispute in harmony with the principles of the Covenant.[37]

These speeches concluded, it was announced that the Three- Power

Conference under the 1906 Treaty would convene in Paris at the earliest possibly date.

Eden came home and broadcast a gloomy prognosis; the meeting of the League Council had been held under the shadows of a thunder cloud which, were it to burst, would have consequences no man could foretell.[38]

Laval remained cheerful, always keeping in mind that the ultimate solution for France would undoubtedly require him to do business with Mussolini. These very different viewpoints were reported in the Fascist press. It characterized Eden's remarks as singular and unhappy, at the same time praising Laval for his spirit of independence, his correct and cordial attitude to Germany, and his just vision of the European problem as a whole.[39]

## The Three-Power Conference

Hoare emphasized again to the House of Commons on August 2, 1935 on the one hand British intent to fulfill obligations under the Covenant while at the same time making every effort to find an accommodation. He emphasized, too, that collective security and proportional contribution were inseparable and vigorously denied that Italy had been given a free hand in Abyssinia.

On the same day, the Cabinet received the report of the subcommittee of the Chiefs of Staff, which it had requested in July. It was a thoughtful and measured document evincing a keen sense of responsibility and orderly procedure.

The subcommittee first concluded that economic sanctions were more than likely to lead to war. Italy might retaliate at any time. This is what Baldwin had often said. This was the probability that the Peace Ballot had neatly evaded by dividing question 5 into two parts, permitting a vote for economic but not military sanctions.

Any step taken to close the Suez Canal could lead to war, and shipping control in the Red Sea might necessitate the exercise of belligerent rights. This issue was known in other quarters as freedom of the seas and Britain and America had once fought a war over it.

Adequate naval and military preparations would be needed as well as preconcerted naval, military, and air arrangements with other powers. This meant French naval cooperation and the use of Greek and Turkish bases. There was a grave danger of embarking on sanctions until all this had been done.

The subcommittee concluded by saying that it had not considered the wider military implications and possible repercussions in Europe of steps taken against Italy. Those repercussions would involve, among others, Austria and Germany.[40]

The subcommittee's first concern was British naval strength vis-à-vis Italy. There were deficiencies of ships, equipment, and ammunition, but in general, British naval opinion never varied that Britain would decisively defeat Italy. This opinion was more than verified under far more difficult conditions in 1940–43.

But there was always the explosive and unpredictable Duce and the fear of, not traditional combat, but, in Vansittart's colorful words, a "mad dog" act—an act inflicting grave damage even without hope of success. Vansittart's coinage was more successful than many of his opinions and the mad dog thesis became a staple of the crisis.

The danger, of course, was in the long range where, as Vansittart pointed out to Hoare, there was no naval margin against the looming German and Japanese threats.[41]

Eden and Vansittart were designated to attend the Three- Power Conference. Baldwin and Hoare briefed them on August 6, 1935. The instructions were as vague as those Eden had carried to Geneva. He was to attempt to modify Mussolini's stance with a proposal for economic concessions that all knew would fail. If Eden was not given a carrot, neither was he given a stick, for he was instructed to avoid any mention of sanctions.[42]

No wonder Eden was downcast. He dreaded these conversations, he wrote to a friend: "vague instructions from home and a thieves' kitchen in Paris." He had little hope of a good result:

> My chief fear is that we should be led into taking part in some attempt to make the Abyssinians accept an unjust and unworthy settlement. This would rob us of our good name.[43]

This was an appreciation grounded on moral values and not a rigid analysis of where, in the proposed conference, British interests lay.

If Eden was reluctant, Haile Selassie was wistfully eager to attend the conference. Month after month, his pleas had been postponed, and his country and its fate left in the hands of adversaries and strangers, whose disinterestedness was suspect. He pleaded unsuccessfully for an invitation. Instead of participating, he was asked by Hoare what concessions he would make to preserve peace.[44]

Vansittart was as active as Eden was fearful. He sought to impress on Charles Corbin, the French Ambassador in London, that "the League represented the rallying point of all wise, moderate and instructed opinion in this country."[45] Corbin hardly needed to be told this. In a dispatch to Laval the preceding day, he had brilliantly analyzed the British press, British public opinion, and its leader, Lord Cecil. With Gallic precision he contrasted Britain and Italy. "Many think," he observed, "that Britain would accept a fait accompli. But, it ought to be remembered that

> the Anglo-Saxon public is always susceptible to be extremely moved when juridical principles and, no less moral principles, which touch the roots of the national temperament, are put in peril.

In Rome, on the other hand, they thought that if Italy made war in Abyssinia, the British response would be limited to "some sermons by Presbyterian bishops, some demonstrations in Hyde Park and the vengeful discourse of Lord Cecil." Corbin was not so sure. A sudden rush of public opinion, he hazarded, could force the British Government into positions which it would never take on its own. To engage in a colonial war without the tacit assent of Britain was a dangerous business. He hoped Mussolini would consider British opinion and profit from British desire for compromise.[46]

Vansittart told Dino Grandi, the Italian Ambassador to Britain, that, contrary to Italian opinion, Britain had no selfish interest in Africa. Britain's interest lay in the League. He promised "serious satisfactions" if Italy would abate her demands.[47] He reviewed naval problems with the First Sea Lord, Admiral Chatfield, who wanted to know what French support would be available and who reasonably observed, "War is not a light measure which we can go into blindfold trusting to luck."[48]

Eden and Vansittart met Laval in Paris on August 14, The alternatives were plain and grim. Once more they emphasized that the real issue was the League, "the one issue on which every British Government and the vast majority of the British people had been unanimous for the last fifteen years." This was a large claim. Was the influence of the Peace Ballot retrospective? Laval accepted this,[49] but in Eden's opinion, still hoped for a deal, not yet facing the consequences if the deal failed.[50]

The Emperor now made his contribution. Abyssinia would cede the Ogaden on the basis of the Zeila offer. It would offer territory in Aussa against financial compensation. It would complete arrangements foreseen in 1928 for a road from Dessie to Assab in Eritrea. Foreign officials selected by the League would oversee antislavery measures, frontier police, and the control of a League sponsored loan to Abyssinia for roads, communications, and administration. In exchange, Abyssinia would seek inclusion in a revised 1906 Treaty.[51]

When Laval met Aloisi in a preliminary session on August 15, Aloisi proposed that France and Britain recognize Italian economic *and* political preponderance in Abyssinia and declare their appreciation of Italy's need to expand, in which case Italy would cooperate at Geneva.

Laval resolutely refused. It amounted to a mandate, he said, and that was impossible. Instinctively he turned to what was possible. He proposed economic concessions, technical advisors, and rights of settlement which would give Italy in substantial part what she might gain by war. He was not precise, but he offered intriguing possibilities.[52] This was Laval's method—to induce negotiation and play by ear. Aloisi said that his instructions were uncompromising and that Mussolini's demands remained what he had outlined to Eden in Rome.[53]

The formal session took place on August 16. Laval faithfully reported to Aloisi British devotion to the League. Eden declared Aloisi's proposal of the day before unacceptable. But Laval had prepared an alternative plan.

By this plan, Abyssinia would appeal to the League for foreign collaboration and assistance in economic development. Such assistance could be international, most appropriately from Italy, Britain, and France. The program could include economic concessions, trade, financial reorganization, communications, public works, administration including justice and health, the suppression of slavery, and frontier policing.

The independence and integrity of Abyssinia would be maintained. Territorial adjustments could be made. In all these matters due regard would be had to the special interests of Italy—without prejudice to the specific rights of France and Britain.[54]

Aloisi immediately said Italy could not accept. Laval urged the program as a basis for discussion, subject to modification. He telephoned the French chargé d'affaires in Rome, instructing him that the French plan would shortly be on its way and urging him to warn Mussolini that the document represented the limit of his effort to find agreement. He offered to telephone Mussolini directly. He begged Mussolini to consider his proposal carefully, adding that if it were rejected, Laval would then be obliged to range himself on the side of his English friends.[55]

Laval's first concern as Foreign Minister had been to compose French differences with Italy and enlist Italy in a defensive front against Germany. This was his proud accomplishment to which the Soviet accord took second place. Laval's view was continental; the balance of forces on France's border was critical as was Italian support of Austria. Yet, at this stage of the negotiation, he had without hesitation made his choice. He chose Britain over Italy.

There was no meeting on August 17. Eden, anticipating refusal, reported pessimistically to Hoare that the Italians were probably only playing for time. As to France, "both Monsieur Laval and Monsieur Leger have been fertile but also firm in their endeavors. Indeed their attitude, from our point of view, has been perfectly loyal and satisfactory."[56]

The expected reply came from Mussolini on April 18. He expressed appreciation to Laval. There were no words of appreciation for Eden. The proposals were unacceptable. Ten months ago they might have been. They would only enhance Abyssinia—a menace to be destroyed—by raising her to the same level as the other three powers.

Had Mussolini any proposals, Eden asked Aloisi. None but those given Eden in Rome, Aloisi replied. This was, Eden thought, the end.[57] But Laval told him after the meeting that his resources were not exhausted and that he would again communicate with the Italian Government. A disinclination to take no for an answer or to regard any negotiation as totally foreclosed would be Laval's hallmarks as long as he remained in office.

At Laval's earnest request, Eden saw him on August 19 before leaving Paris. Could anything have been done to avert the breakdown, Laval asked rhetorically, and concluded there was not. Laval urged Eden to understand his position. He had made a treaty with Italy; without Italy he had no allies in Europe, for Russia was unreliable.

But, Eden interjected, there was Locarno. Yes, Laval replied, he appreciated this. But he knew, too, that Britain always found it difficult to state its position in advance.

He feared what Mussolini might do, including the bombing of Malta. "We must be very careful," he told Eden, "to act closely together in all we do." In any event, he thought some form of condemnation of Italy by the League when it met in September would be inevitable.

Eden again reminded Laval of the strength of British public opinion supporting the League. Laval in turn replied, that he had no interest in turning his back on the League or Britain's League policy. All he asked of Eden was to be aware of his own difficulties in dealing with Italy and to take those difficulties into account in the advice he gave his Government.[58]

## Vox Populi

In February and March, Italy had sounded Britain out on its Abyssinian ambitions tendering assurances that British interests would be respected and protected. The British government had ignored these feelers. It had resolutely at Stresa averted its gaze from the impending crisis in Abyssinia. It had supported initiatives to keep the issue outside the competence of the League of Nations, even though it was increasingly obvious that Italy was using the conciliation process not to arrive at a settlement but to cover its military preparations until the time came to strike. The Zeila proposal and the Three-Power Conference had failed. Having taken extreme care not to adopt a public position on enforcement of the Covenant, the Government, however earnestly it may have hoped for something to turn up, was now face to face with the problem. It had to take a stand.

This would not be done in a vacuum. The Abyssinian drama had engaged the rapt attention of the British public and the Government had little doubt as to what the public thought.

For the League of Nations Union, fresh from the triumph of the Peace Ballot, the issue was made to order. The votes of the Peace Ballot could be translated into support for the League and enforcement of the Covenant in what was clearly a test case. The Union had adopted resolutions in July referring to pertinent Articles of the Covenant and the duty of League members to uphold them. It pointed very specifically to the declarations of Baldwin in response to the LNU deputation that the League would be the sheet anchor of British Policy and Eden's at Fulham in the very same vein. The LNU resolutions ended "expressing…confidence that His Majesty's Government's policy in this matter will be based upon the principles laid down in the declarations of the Prime Minister and the Minister for League Affairs quoted above."[59]

The correspondence columns of the *Times* became the venue of a national hearing on Abyssinia and the League. Stephen King-Hall spoke for the 750,000 dead of 1914–18. "Peace needs a great victory," he wrote. The world was watching to see if Britain would boldly deter aggression and vindicate international law.[60]

To George Lansbury, leader of the Labour Party, the issue was, as always in its foundation spiritual. He appealed to the Archbishop of Canterbury and to the Pope to call for a Truce of God and bid the war spirit rest.[61] What policy with respect to the Covenant of the League this implied was nowhere made clear, but the message had its impact and quite clearly endorsed virtue as opposed to wickedness. In this posture of the issue, where virtue lay and where wickedness were not much disputed.

Charles Hobhouse recognized the costs of resolute enforcement of the Covenant: dislocation of trade, and the risk of war. He ably argued the long run; the risks were far greater if international cooperation ended and the League could not offer security. Finally, he said, to repudiate the Covenant would be what a repudiation of the Belgian guaranty would have been in 1914: to forfeit honor.[62]

Norman Angell, who had taught before 1914 that there was no profit in war, agreed that it was not Abyssinia but British security that was at stake. Britain would mobilize and fight to defend the smallest and meanest British possession—no doubt of that. How much greater, then, was her interest in the security of civilization?[63]

Lord Parmoor was crisp and to the point. Britain's decision would shape the future course of European history: "The powers vested in the League of Nations are amply sufficient, if loyally and effectively supported by the Government and people of Great Britain."[64]

There was not, and could not be unanimity. Lord Hardinge made three critical points. The issue in 1914 had not been exclusively one of principle. The German invasion of Belgium had directly threatened a vital British interest. In the present crisis, there was no direct threat to the security of Britain or any possession. Moreover, without the United States, Germany, and Japan, the League was not the League its founders had envisioned and thereby the power, the effectiveness, and the ability of the League to insure security had been gravely compromised. Finally, the purpose of the Covenant had been to prevent war. Was Britain morally bound, in a League far different from the original conception, "to punish a recalcitrant member by measures which may be described as political and material suicide and the destruction of a civilization which it had taken centuries to create?"[65]

This drew a prompt reply from Lord Cecil. He did not believe that sanctions inevitably meant war. Of course, certain sanctions could mean war; but if all the powers of Europe imposed sanctions, he was confident there would be no war. He did not suggest, indeed no one suggested, that Britain should act alone.

Lord Cecil's final appeal found widespread approval:

> If we leave Abyssinia in the lurch now, we shall be guilty of an impardonable breach of faith for which we shall unquestionably suffer in the near future.[66]

Lord Cecil again indicated his profound belief in the inseparable connection between moral values and practical consequences.

## A Policy for Britain

"Anthony," Vansittart told Eden the night of August 18, "you are faced with a first class international crisis. We have got to reinforce the Mediterranean Fleet."[67]

The crisis was equally apparent to Sir Samuel Hoare. In such case, no matter how large the Government's majority in Parliament, it was prudent to take all views into account and build the broadest base of support for the policy that would emerge. This was the firm advice of Austen Chamberlain, sometime Foreign Secretary and co-author of Locarno. He thought economic sanctions were unavoidable. British public opinion would demand action. If the Government failed to participate in collective action it would face the gravest consequence of all—a great wave of public opinion would sweep it out of power.[68]

Hoare now undertook to meet with the leaders of all parties and sectors of public opinion to achieve understanding, unity, and a broad-based course of action. He was a prudent man.

Sir Herbert Samuel, the Liberal Party leader, agreed with Austen Chamberlain that economic sanctions must be based on collective action and Anglo-French cooperation. Hoare confided to Samuel his chief concerns—that France would not back economic sanctions and that Mussolini would by a mad dog act precipitate a war for which Britain was totally unprepared.[69]

The advice of many leaders reflected their well-known positions. When George Lansbury met with Hoare, he pressed on him his perennial project for pooling the world's economic resources.[70]

To Winston Churchill, it was naval weakness in the Mediterranean that had encouraged Italy. He recognized France's difficult position because of its Italian treaty and German concern. Britain was justified, he said, in going as far with the League of Nations as it could carry France. But his chief preoccupation, like France's, was Germany.[71]

Lloyd George wholeheartedly agreed with Chamberlain that any failure to participate with France in truly collective action would bring down on the heads of the Government the overwhelming mass of public opinion.[72]

A discussion with the Dominion High Commissioners disclosed some perplexing issues. Stanley Bruce of Australia questioned the efficacy of purely economic sanctions. Would Britain, in blockading Italian ports, prevent U.S. shipments to Italy? Would Italy shrink from declaring war on Britain and France? Mussolini was totally unpredictable. Of course, Italy would be defeated, but what then of Germany? He posed the ultimate question. If sanctions were impracticable and dangerous, and if the League were limited to a moral gesture, ought not Britain to face the facts, rearm, and rely on its own strength to lend stability to a world in crisis?

As always, there was much talk of the great force of public opinion. But what did it mean? Sir James Parr declared firmly that public opinion strongly favored collective action and sanctions, but it did not consider war justified. But what if sanctions were not enough and carried a serious risk of war? Eleven and a half million Peace Balloters had failed to make this point clear.[73]

When Hoare met with Lord Cecil, Cecil offered the full support of the League of Nations Union in any efforts to enforce the Covenant. He wanted a prompt declaration that the Government intended to do just that. Such timing, Hoare parried, might be inopportune. Cecil yielded. The Government had to be free to decide when to announce, but carry out its obligations it must.[74]

August 21 had been a busy day for Hoare. After his talks with Samuel, Lloyd George, Lansbury, Churchill, Cecil, and the Dominion High Commissioners, he attended a meeting of ministers prior to the Cabinet meeting scheduled for the next day.

In attendance were Baldwin, MacDonald, Simon, Neville Chamberlain, Hoare, and Eden. Eden summarized the Three Power Conference and his postconference talk with Laval. Hoare reported that Laval had withstood every pressure the Italians had put on him. Eden reported Vansittart's view that France would indeed be prepared to take part in economic sanctions.

Hoare pronounced his conclusion. It was essential to follow the regular League of Nations procedure in the crisis. He had talked to leaders of the Opposition. He had been left with this impression: "There would be a wave of public opinion against the Government if it repudiated its obligations under Article 16 [of the Covenant]."

But what did Article 16 mean? In 1921 League resolutions had attempted to define it but had failed to pass for want of unanimity. If the League Council concluded that a state had been guilty of a breach of the Covenant, it would so advise the members of the League and invite them to act accordingly. But invitations may be declined. It had been further concluded that, in accordance with the spirit of the Covenant, the League should at the outset, attempt to avoid war, and to restore peace by economic pressure.

It was clear, said Hoare, that each member state must make its own decision. The League had no executive and no enforcement agency. That had always been true. The ministers now understood that the action of member states was purely voluntary. There was no automatic or binding obligation, no self-enforcing procedure. To ministers who agreed to a man, as did their opposition, that Britain must not act unilaterally, that collective security must be truly collective, this was a serious consideration.

Did the public understand this? Did the 97 percent who had voted in the Peace Ballot for continuing British membership in the League of Nations, did the 94 percent who had voted for economic sanctions understand this? Not only was this dubious in the extreme; to the contrary a large portion of the public believed quite the opposite: that the League was a competent power, that it could enforce the Covenant, and many believed that the enforcement would be without cost or obligation to them. This was a difference in perceptions which the Government needed to address.

What attitude would the United States take? Baldwin inquired if the President could bind the nation to sanctions.

Chamberlain summed up. Economic sanctions carried the risk of war. The armed forces ought to be put in order. Hoare added that in his present state of mind, Mussolini was not a normal man; almost anything Britain did could result in war. MacDonald reiterated the view that public opinion would be shocked if Britain took no action. There were no firm conclusions. These were reserved for the Cabinet the day following.[75]

When the Cabinet met on August 22, it reviewed a lengthly series of reports including (long after Mussolini had seen it) the Maffey Report. It "discussed the question in all its bearings, political (including British public opinion), international, military, and economic." It then arrived at these conclusions:

• That the British delegation to Geneva should be authorized to reaffirm statements made in Parliament as to British intent to fulfill its League obligations. This still did not say how.

• "That they should keep in step with the policy of the French Government, and, more particularly in the matter of Sanctions, they should avoid any commitment which France was not equally prepared to assume."

• That they should follow the procedures under the Covenant "not in any quixotic spirit and with due regard to the many difficulties," making it clear that each member had to examine cooperation with a view to collective action. They should, moreover, be on guard against the possibility that the other nations might not fulfill their commitments. And, with a collective sigh of relief, the Cabinet extended to its vaguely instructed representative "the usual latitude" in carrying out a "task which they recognized to be one of peculiar difficulty."[76]

Eight and a half months after the affray at Wal Wal, during which the Italian military buildup had been continuous and during which Mussolini had vocally and persistently stated claims that had been neither met nor compromised, the British Government had achieved a policy.

To the world the policy would be collective support of the Covenant. The unannounced limitation was French cooperation. The policy had not been arrived at by any deliberate calculation of British interests which had, indeed, on a direct basis been pronounced as unaffected by the competent report of the Maffey Committee. Nor had there been a long-range examination of the nexus between Britain's ultimate interests and the Covenant.

There was a moving force in arriving at the policy. That force was public opinion. It little mattered that Question 2 of the Peace Ballot, the all-round reduction of arms by international agreement, Question 3, the all-round abolition of civil and military air craft by international agreement, and Question 4, prohibition of the private manufacture and sale of arms were totally irrelevant to the crisis. What mattered was the response to Question 1, the 97 percent vote for the League, and the response to Question 5a, the 94 percent vote for economic sanctions which loomed like a brooding omnipresence over the deliberations of the British Government. However imprecise the questions may have been, however tangential to the real issues, and however contradictory, the Government did not think them so.

It was all painfully clear to Sir Samuel Hoare. He outlined the dilemma to his Ambassador in Paris:

> The general feeling of the country, fully reflected in the Cabinet, can, I think, be summarized as one of determination to stick to the Covenant and of anxiety to keep out of war. You will say that these feelings are self-contradictory. At present at least the country believes that they can be reconciled. Most people are still convinced that if we stick to the Covenant and apply collective sanctions, Italy must give in and there will be no war. You and I know that the position is not as simple as this and that the presumptions that, firstly, there will be collective action including full collective action by the French, and secondly, that economic sanctions will be effective are, to say the least, very bold and sanguine. None the less, whatever may develop it is essential that we should play out the League hand in September.[77]

Why was it necessary? The answer was purely political. Because, as politicians had opined, and as the press had broadcast, the Government would have been turned out of office if it had not.

Hoare continued:

> If it is then found that there is no collective basis for sanctions, that is to say in particular that the French are not prepared to give their full co-operation, or that the action of the non-member States, for example Germany, the United States and Japan, is so unhelpful as to make economic sanctions futile, the world will have to face the fact that sanctions are impracticable. We must, however, on no account assume the impracticability of sanctions until the League has made this investigation. It must be the League and not the British Government that declares that sanctions are impracticable and the British Government must on no account lay itself open to the charge that we have not done our utmost to make them practicable.[78]

Vansittart had once posed the question: Abyssinia or Austria? The answer was going to be Abyssinia. Britain would challenge Italy, plunging France into a dilemma, moving Mussolini away from Stresa and toward Germany. Hoare knew and feared all this.

No man could foretell the course of events and the worst of outcomes was not inevitable. Lacking arms, time is a weapon; "the only munition within the power of diplomacy" Vansittart had said.[79] Here again Hoare agreed. Perhaps the crisis could be managed to obtain the time to become strong and to reply to strength with strength. The plot had been sketched out, and rehearsals were in order before the curtain was raised at Geneva.

## America, France, Italy

Stanley Baldwin's inquiry concerning American participation in sanctions was soon answered. Averting its virtuous gaze from colonial rivalries and European power politics, Congress on August 23 and 24, 1935 passed the Neutrality Act embargoing as against both Italy and Abyssinia arms, ammunition, and other implements of war. The legislation was signed on August 31, 1935 by the President. He had broad power to define war material but in the first instance, did not include coal, oil, steel, and other necessities of war. Traditional diplomatic weapons were at the President's disposal: withdrawal of diplomatic representatives, refusal to recognize a conquest, and a variety of financial actions. It was nonetheless, increasingly clear that the United States was not about to become a de facto member of the League of Nations in operating economic sanctions and that this would be a large gap indeed in the cincture of enforcement.[80]

The British Ambassador in Paris duly explained Hoare's concerns to Laval. He described the League conviction held by the British public, conceding, nevertheless, that "there was a unanimous desire to avoid war."

Laval had heard all this many times. France's position, he replied, was more delicate than Britain's. Where would France be without the Rome agreements? And there sat Hitler, simply waiting to take the fullest advantage of the breakup of the Stresa front. Perhaps Mussolini had once been bluffing. Now he would not halt till the guns had sounded—a salvo or two and a victory at Adowa. Perhaps then there could be a reasonable discussion.[81]

The next day Laval met with the French Council of Ministers. For himself, he feared sanctions would lead Mussolini to retaliate against a Britain lacking real power. He wanted to moderate British attitudes and avoid a rupture with Italy.

Colonel Jean Fabry, the War Minister, agreed that sanctions, by ending the Italian alliance, could create grave military problems weakening France decisively. The other service ministers and Gamelin, Commander in Chief of the Army, agreed.

Edouard Herriot's Radical Party was the largest in the Assembly, an essential element of Laval's coalition. He disagreed. France must stand by the League and by Britain, he argued. He would back sanctions. That was a matter of principle. But he saw that it was not that easy. It was necessary, he said, to find sanctions that wouldn't result in the outbreak of a European war. Ringing declarations of support for the League, then, would not necessarily result in a happy conclusion.

Laval told the Council that he would never vote for sanctions. He agreed, however, that Herriot should accompany him to the League meeting at Geneva, free to speak as he wished.

To Mussolini, Laval showed another face. Good negotiators maintain friendly contact with the opposite party. They also establish positions from which they can move to settlement. On August 30, Laval wired Mussolini. He reaffirmed his warning of July 19, 1935. French policy was based on the League and Locarno and to these France would remain faithful. He had exerted every effort at reconciliation. He had used his influence with his British colleagues. He hoped his efforts had not been in vain.

Laval entreated Mussolini not to reject propositions which could lead to a peaceful solution. He had given Mussolini ample testimony of his friendship and hoped Mussolini would not make his task at Geneva more difficult. But in any case, France remained faithful, both to the pact of Rome and, as its traditional policy, to the League.[82]

There was no reply.

In Addis Ababa, on August 19, the Emperor attended mass at the Cathedral of St. George. Outside, riflemen filled the square. The Empress, who was accompanied by seventy ladies of the court, sat apart from the congregation behind iron gates, veiled in a cloth of gold. The Abuna, the Coptic Primate of Abyssinia, clad in a black cassock, cape, and purple hat, officiated at the mass. He was assisted by the Echege, the Prior of Debra Libanos, the chief monastery in the land.

After the bells and shouts of the mass had ended and the court chamberlains had cleared the church, the Empress and the Emperor remained. They sat beneath silk umbrellas; before each of them was a cross draped in silk because it was improper to touch the cross with naked hands. A priest recited passages from the Gospels; the court ladies wept.

Now the Emperor, the Empress, the Abuna, and the Echege moved to the four corners of the cathedral and prayed for world peace. The Abuna prayed that God would quench the fire of war. He gave thanks for the sympathy that peace-loving nations had extended to Abyssinia. After the benediction, the Emperor kissed the Abuna's cross; he donned his shoes, and left the church under a tasseled green umbrella, accompanied by his guards.[83]

The Emperor did not rely entirely on prayer. He reinforced piety with cunning. On August 30, 1935 the Emperor signed a concession giving the exclusive right for seventy-five years to explore and develop petroleum in the eastern half of Abyssinia to an American firm, a subsidiary, indeed, of Standard Vacuum Oil Company, though the promoter was an Englishman, Francis Rickett. The thought that Britain was interested only in promoting its own interests might be expected to arouse the ire of both France and Italy, confirming their worst suspicions. The British Government promptly disclaimed any interest and indeed urged the Emperor to withdraw the concession.

If the Emperor had hoped, by involving the United States, to discourage Italy, he was disappointed. The policy of neutrality was too firmly entrenched. The State Department urged Standard Vacuum to cancel the contract and in time it did. The Emperor was left to face the crisis alone.[84]

The arbitration proceeding continued far off the center stage. On August 20, M. Politis, the Greek minister to Paris and a recognized international lawyer, was named the fifth member of the panel, to act if agreement could not be reached. His services were called upon on August 29 when the commission once more arrived at deadlock. The importance of the arbitration proceeding lay not so much in the result it might produce. What was vital to Abyssinia was that it was the long-delayed prelude to the day when the League of Nations would finally confront the issue for it was upon the League that the Emperor placed his faith, his hopes, and his nation's destiny.

Italy could act decisively and quickly. The League could only act after deliberation and the nature of its action and its adherents could not be known. Abyssinia had to look to its own defense.

Lacking everything, the Emperor made strenuous efforts to prepare Abyssinia for war. The 1906 Treaty had severely limited its right to purchase and import arms. He struggled vainly to persuade Britain and France to lift these restrictions. Britain talked of principles and the League, but offered no practical help.

There was no letup in Italian military preparations as new troops were called up and ships departed Naples crowded with the manpower and impedimenta of war. It was a Mussolini family affair. His son-in-law, Count Galeazzo Ciano, joined his sons; he, too, would serve in the air force in Africa.

Mussolini was determined to act. But how, to what extent, and to what end? On August 25, 1935 he wrote to his commander in the field:

> This is the last letter I will write to you before the action.... I believe that after 10 September you should expect my word of command at any moment. By that time you will have in Eritrea two divisions of Blackshirts and another sixty airplanes. The forces are sufficient for the first rush and the winning of the established objectives. You will halt on the line conquered and take steps to organize the rear and await events on the international plane.[85]

The line conquered was a border territory. It included Adowa, and the territory from which Italy had been so humiliatingly ejected in 1896. It was far from the Amharic heart of Abyssinia.

Mussolini shouted defiance, but he practiced prudence. With a victory in hand—a victory he would know best how to dramatize—he could await the response of the League and of the world.

Perhaps the British would see, as clearly as the French, that Germany indeed was the issue; perhaps they would agree that Hitler was preparing for war and would make it as soon as possible, just as Mussolini had warned. In that case, he could proceed. If, on the other hand, the response was hard, unyielding, forceful and dangerous, he could, from a victorious position, minimize his exposure.

For Mussolini had taken out a policy of reinsurance. His ambassador in Berlin, Vittorio Cerutti, had detested the Nazis, especially Hitler. He was now sent to Paris. He was replaced by Bernardo Attolico, who was to become Germany's friend and champion. He told Bernhard von Bülow of the German Foreign Ministry on August 19, 1935 that his task was to improve relations between Germany and Italy. Von Bulow emphasized that Germany would remain neutral in the conflict. But this development must have been pleasing to Adolf Hitler who long ago, in the Landsberg prison, had written that to carry out his program Germany must first have an ally and that Italy ought to be that ally.

On August 28, 1935, Mussolini addressed his cabinet at Bolzano. Italy would attend the meeting of the League Council on September 4, he said. It would present a detailed statement of Italian grievances, of the condition of Abyssinia "in all its crude reality," demonstrating the need for an enlightened controlling power.

He pointedly declared that Britain had nothing to fear, that there was no threat to any British interest. Italy had an issue to settle with Abyssinia. This should not impact the European situation, unless there was a desire to unloose a new world war. Were the League to adopt sanctions, which Mussolini noted, had not been applied in earlier and, he thought, graver cases, the nations would place themselves on a slippery slope which might lead to the gravest complications.

But Italy would be ready. Mussolini announced a series of economic and fiscal decrees—limitations on dividends, a tax on interest, dividends and profits, conversion of foreign obligations into Italian state bonds and, significantly, the employment of substitute fuels.[86]

His military and economic plans were in place. He maintained close contact with France and offered new assurances to Britain. He would attend the League meeting and present his case. He prepared to enter into a new relationship with Germany. And he determined to limit his initial military thrust in order clearly and calmly to appraise the situation, its dangers and its opportunities.

Mussolini was cynical. He was an opportunist, but he was not, at this point, reckless. He knew from the offers already on the table that meaningful rewards were within his grasp, with or without war. The question for the statesmen of the world, and particularly for Britain and France was with whom in the end the Duce would do business, at what price, and when.

But, in the end, perhaps the decision would not be the product of sober evaluation and judgment. In London, on August 30, 1935, Grandi met with Corbin. Grandi was optimistic that many segments of British public opinion, Labour on the left, the Conservative right wing, the imperialists, the Navy, and the pacifists would oppose sanctions and war.

He did not think for a moment that the British Cabinet would permit the closing of the Suez Canal, contrary to treaties. It would be inhuman, he thought, to cut off an expeditionary force of 200,000 from its supplies and bases in Italy. Such humanitarian considerations did not extend to the Abyssinians; the supplies included poison gas against which they were defenseless.

Grandi realized, he told Corbin, the "infinitely delicate position of Laval." He admired the finesse with which Laval had maintained his good offices on all sides. He had neither spoken against Italy or given Britain the pretext that France had abandoned collective security.

Grandi echoed Mussolini. The Duce, he said, would be wise enough, after his initial success, to avoid a long colonial compaign. This, then, would be the hour of reconciliation, and then perhaps the entente Rome-Paris-London would emerge on a base more solid than ever. But, he added smilingly, without a new Fashoda.

Corbin was a veteran observer of British politics and British opinion. He warned Grandi against undue optimism. There would be a wave, he said, not only of indignation, but indeed of horror when the British public regarded the spectacle of a bloody victory over a primitive and ill-armed people thanks to the weapons of modern war. To expect the Stresa front to continue after Italy had violated the Covenant and the Kellogg-Briand Pact might be too much to expect. In that case, he told Grandi, it would be the British public which would decide and which would in the end impose its will on its Government.[87]

# 3

# The Die is Cast

*"It is quite clear that the National Government's decision to give unqualified support to the League was promoted by the public mood as expressed by the Peace Ballot and by the fact that the General Election was due before November, 1936."*

—Neville Thompson[1]

## At the Ready

The Arbitration Commission was in session. The meeting of the League Council was set for September 4. But the overwhelming reality was preparation for war.

Italian troops, eight divisions strong, marched past Mussolini and the King at Alto Adige on August 30, 1935. A motorized division climaxed the review. An additional 200,000 men would be called up in September, Mussolini told the troops, bringing effectives to a million:

> The world must know once again that so long as there will be talk, in an absurd and provocative manner, of sanctions, we will not give up a single soldier, a single sailor, a single airman; but we will bring to the highest possible level the power of the armed forces of the nation.[2]

Haile Selassie's forces were modest in comparison. The first large contingent passed through Addis Ababa on September 2, en route to the railway station. They marched silently, without bugles or drums. They were regular troops, but they were not in uniform. The soldiers carried goat skins filled with grain, waterbottles and gourds, blankets, lion-skin shields, and long knives. Ras Mulugeta, the War Minister, accompanied them on muleback; so did their commander, Dedjasmach Hapta Mickael, a veteran of Adowa.

They numbered some 1,200. As they silently boarded the trains, women wept in the streets of Addis Ababa.[3]

## Laval's Concern

En route to Geneva for the League Council meeting, Eden and Vansittart stopped in Paris on September 2 to coordinate policy with Laval. It would be necessary, Eden said, to report to the League Council on the outcome of the Three-Power Conference. Laval shrewdly observed that they ought not disclose the terms that had been offered to Mussolini in detail. That might inhibit the Duce in the future, and under other circumstances, from accepting what he had once declined.

It was important to gain time, Laval thought, and it would be wise to set up a League committee to recommend bases of settlement to the Council.

But what if war should break out? Where would France stand? Eden stressed the great weight of British public opinion behind the Covenant and the League.

Laval answered this question with a question. It was the question French statesmen had asked since 1918—the German question. Could Eden give France the assurance that in the future, Britain would be as firm in upholding the Covenant in Europe as she now was in Africa?

Eden said he did not hesitate to answer:

> If the Covenant was upheld in this instance and peace were in consequence preserved the authority of the League would be immensely strengthened and our own moral obligation to assist in supporting and enforcing the Covenant in the future would be correspondingly increased.[4]

On the other hand, were the League to fail, its future influence in Europe and elsewhere must be negligible.

That, said Laval, was the answer he had expected. It did not, he added, answer his question.

Years later Eden wrote:

> This may have been true, but the British government's wariness and the state of our defenses made it impossible for me to promise unconditional

support of the Covenant for the future, regardless of the outcome of the present dispute.[4]

Laval had asked for a specific assurance, which was one thing. He had received a statement of principle and morals, which, to him, was quite another.

In this question, which would later be formally put to the British government, lay the key to French policy in the Abyssinian crisis. Laval's concern was France, not Abyssinia; to him the threat was Germany, not Italy, his ally in the defense of France.

They talked of sanctions which Laval feared would lead to war. Eden thought they would be effective but he realized that much depended on the attitude of the non-League members.

If Laval's chief concerns lay in Europe, he did not close his mind to the imposition of sanctions. Beyond a moral condemnation, he could envision a ban on the export of arms to Italy, which could be expanded to cover vital minerals, rubber, and oil. He did not bar a prohibition against imports from Italy. On one point he was adamant. He would never consent to a naval blockade, which in Mussolini's state of mind, would lead to war.

What he wanted, he said, was to maintain his friendship with Italy without breaking the Anglo-French front. How to avoid a choice between Britain and Italy was the dilemma he clearly saw, and when the time came to make his choice, he would not hesitate.[5]

On August 30, Laval had charged his Ambassador in Rome to convey to Mussolini assurances of French friendship, particularly asking him not to limit the negotiating possibilities of the Italian delegation to the League Council and at the same time to recognize Laval's difficulties at Geneva. But, he had told Chambrun by way of preface, the policy of France rested entirely on the League of Nations, Locarno, and entente with Britain.[6]

Chambrun saw Mussolini on September 3. Mussolini thanked Chambrun for Laval's friendship. He would not, he promised, take any action in Abyssinia during the League meeting. His representatives there would listen to new proposals.

But economic concessions, Mussolini said, were valueless without some military control. He could not call 230,000 men back to Italy without glory. He urged Laval to oppose any sanctions or declarations which would force Italy to leave the League of Nations and which would threaten the peace of Europe. He asked Laval to do everything possible to avoid an armed conflict between Italy and Britain which would force Italy to denude the Brenner and give Hitler the chance he was waiting for—to effect Anschluss, the annexation of Austria; the first step, as Hitler had written on page one of *Mein Kampf*, in building a Greater Germany.[7]

On the same day, Grandi, pleaded with Hoare in London for British understanding and friendship. He emphasized what the Duce had said at Bolzano, that no British interest was threatened. If it came to war in Abyssinia, Britain and Italy would be better friends than ever when it was over. Hoare cautioned him that British public opinion might take another view.

One point Grandi wished to make clear. Britain had delayed unconscionably in answering the Italian inquiries of January. Britain had been silent at Stresa. For all the talk of British loyalty to the Covenant and for all the public clamor for sanctions, never once had Hoare uttered what he called "that dangerous word."

These things were demonstrably true. Nevertheless, Hoare warned Grandi, British silence must not be construed as consent.[8]

Fearing Germany, France sought Italy's friendship. Fearing Germany, Italy sought British understanding. If the Stresa partners could not resolve their differences, the result was not hard to foretell. The British Minister in Berlin wired Hoare on September 4 to describe the motives behind German neutrality."For if Italian ambitions (in Abyssinia) are frustrated," he concluded, "Italy is likely in any case to draw closer to the German camp."[9]

## The End of Arbitration

Italy's cynical and underhanded diplomacy was now rewarded by the Conciliation Commission. It announced its unanimous decision on September 3, 1935. Neither party had been responsible for the Wal Wal incident. Both had believed Wal Wal to be a part of their own territory, and Italy had occupied it continuously since 1930. The Italians at Wal Wal had taken precautions to avoid an incident. The attitude of the Abyssinian forces at Wal Wal might have been considered threatening. But neither country could be proved to have caused the incident.[10]

The Commission's decision promptly disposed of the Italian thesis, that the differences between Italy and Abyssinia were confined to the incident at Wal Wal. When the League Council met the next day, Italy took a very different stand. Far from acting the defendant, Italy took the offensive.

In a voluminous memorandum, Italy stated its case against Abyssinia. Abyssinia had disregarded its treaty undertakings with Italy; it had refused to delimit its frontiers with the Italian colonies; it had refused to proceed with the road between Dessie in Abyssinia and Assab in Eritrea which an annex to the 1928 Treaty of Friendship mandated, but instead had raised obstacles and obstructions to Italian economic activity in Abyssinia. Abyssinia had failed to grant to Italians the most favored nation treatment called for by the Treaty. The memorandum detailed incursions and attacks on Italian territory. All this, Italy complained, in spite of Italian efforts at constructive collaboration and development.

Chronic internal disorder, suppression of non-Amharic minorities, the persistence of the slave trade and the violation by Abyssinia of special undertakings to the League upon admission were familiar Italian charges.[11]

The memorandum contained many truths, frequent exaggerations, and a generous measure of special pleading. Italy was not without justifiable complaints. But the Council and the world understood the real issue: Did these complaints justify war? The question was all the more pertinent because the League was itself an appropriate forum for redress of Italian grievances.

Italy, cloaked in indignation and injury, now announced it would hold no further intercourse with Abyssinia and would, indeed, refuse to sit at the Council table while the representatives of Abyssinia spoke. Eden and Laval were face to face with the crisis which the British Government had been so reluctant to acknowledge and which both had striven to evade.

Eden told the Council of the last offers to Italy, which would afford Italy economic advantages, Abyssinia much needed reforms and would allow the League an effective role in resolving the conflict to the benefit of all. These had been rejected. He spoke eloquently of the hopes the League had inspired: "The machinery of the new order set up by the Covenant is here in Geneva. If its spirit is also here we cannot fail." Britain was prepared to fulfill its responsibilities to the League.

No specific British interests were involved. There was no dispute between Britain and Italy. Britain's sole interest was as a member of the League and as a signatory of the Kellogg-Briand Pact. Eden was careful to avoid offense. He did not speak of enforcement of the Covenant. Instead he emphasized that his government would do anything possible to arrive at a peaceful settlement.[12]

In London there had always been doubts as to what course Laval would take. He spoke briefly after Eden. He refused to believe a settlement could not be reached which afforded Italy legitimate satisfaction while still safeguarding Abyssinian rights and sovereignty. He now seized the opportunity for which French statesmen had waited so long—the opportunity to bind Britain to the Covenant.

> The Covenant is binding upon us all. You have just heard the United Kingdom representative state that his country is faithful to the principle of collective security of which the League is the symbol. No one feels greater satisfaction at that statement than the French representative. I do not intend to refer to the past, but I am entitled to say that no Government has put forth greater efforts than the French Government in the defence of this principle, on which all my country's international undertakings are founded.

Could the League successfully withstand this ordeal? It had succeeded in the Saar. It had settled the dispute between Yugoslavia and Hungary. It had so far avoided war. "I preserve," Laval said, "my entire belief in its future."[13]

When, on the following day, the Abyssinian representative presented his case, he was blunt: "The Italian government having resolved to conquer and destroy Ethiopia begins by giving Ethiopia a bad name."[14]

Aloisi left the room. M. Jeze then specifically asked the League to take action under Article 10 of the Covenant dealing with threats to the peace and Article 15, covering the duty of the League Council, in the event of a dispute between members not settled by arbitration, to make its report and recommendations. At long last the issue was firmly placed in the League's hands.

The League Council's first step was instructive; it formed a committee. This was the proposed Committee of Five, Britain, France, Poland, Spain, and Turkey. Italy objected strenuously.[15] Mussolini felt personally offended.[16]

Laval pressured Aloisi. It would be the Committee of Five, he said, or a committee of the whole Council. Privately he complained to Eden:

> It is foolish of them to behave like this for some day perhaps not so far distant they will have need of us both. Then if they go on this way they will find we are not there to help them.[17]

In the end, Italy yielded and the Committee met. Its terms of reference were that "it should be entrusted with an inquiry into all aspects of the relations between Italy and Ethiopia, *with a view to finding a peaceful settlement.*"

On September 8, the new Italian Ambassador to Berlin presented his credentials to Hitler. Both sides remarked on the mutual interest of the two countries. Bernardo Attolico took plains to outline his task—to strengthen bonds with Germany, and this Hitler welcomed with, he said, lively satisfaction.[18]

While Italy extended a hand to Germany, France looked to Britain. Laval explained his position with brilliant clarity in a dispatch to Corbin in London on September 8. He recalled the question he had posed to Eden in Paris: If France enforced the Covenant in Africa, would Britain enforce the Covenant in Europe? He wrote,

> We are justified in putting the indispensable question, in all clarity, to the British government in view of its hesitant policy of reticence in the past and its lack of solidarity with Geneva in a recent case (the revision of the German naval limitations). In what measure and under what guarantees can we be assured in the future of the immediate and effective solidarity of England in case of a violation of Treaty and a recourse to force in Europe?

He had to know that, he said, in order to fulfill his responsibilities. He now laid out France's continuing problem with Britain. The British Government had never manifested the interest in European security that it showed in the Abyssinian case. His comment was precisely in line with the opinions and frustrations of his predecessors:

> Since 1921, all the efforts of France and its friends to assure the effectiveness of a general system of mutual assistance have been frustrated by British disinterest or opposition.[19]

He cited chapter and verse. What France had to know was whether Britain was prepared to modify its policy to give the same guarantee in Europe, in any hypotheses and in the same conditions as the obligations it invoked today.

There was more. Laval and Mussolini had talked at Stresa of concrete cases. He now posed a concrete case. If sanctions against Italy caused an extension of the conflict to Europe, and if Germany sought to profit by absorbing Austria, what would Britain do? Would Britain give the guarantee of Austrian independence and integrity she had heretofore refused?

This was plain talk. Laval made it plainer still:

> I don't ignore the repugnance of the London government to found policy on hypotheses; but the case envisaged is so directly linked to today's crisis that we have the right to be informed with precision.[20]

This, then, was the precise tenor of the formal communication France addressed to the British Government on September 10.

At Geneva, the League Assembly met on September 9. It was understood that the Committee of Five was considering a joint League mandate over Abyssinia. Haile Selassie indicated that he was willing to accept foreign advisors, reserving to himself the decision to whom they should report and be responsible.[21]

To all this Italy was uncompromising. Instead, on September 10, Mussolini made a dramatic announcement. He would soon order a general assembly of the nation. All military, Fascist, and civil government forces would gather in full uniform, to the ringing of bells, the whistling of sirens, and the beating of drums, in every town, village, and commune of Italy. Ten million Italians would assemble in a gigantic display of unity and resolve. They would remain assembled till midnight, but the small boys of the Ballila would be permitted to go home at 9:00 PM.

In ancient times, the magistrate would gather the whole commune to participate in a dialogue, and at its end, submit a resolution to the people who would shout "Fiat, fiat"—Let it be done. No one doubted that the same response would greet the Duce's order of the day.[22]

## Hoare-Laval 1

Pressured by the fear of a wave of adverse public opinion, the Foreign Secretary had advised and the British Cabinet had agreed that when the Abyssinian affair came before the League, Britain must follow the League procedure. The British delegation was authorized to reaffirm statements already made that Britain would fulfill its Covenant obligations—provided, of course, that Britain kept in step with France, assuming no commitment France did not share. Britain would follow the procedures of the Covenant "not in any quixotic spirit and with due regard to the many difficulties."

Hoare prepared his speech to the League Assembly with care and with the help of Vansittart and Neville Chamberlain.[23] On the afternoon of September 5, Hoare visited Baldwin at Chequers. Over tea Baldwin perfunctorily approved Hoare's final text.[24] When he arrived in Geneva, Hoare showed his speech to Eden and to his junior colleague, Viscount Cranborne, who was Lord Cecil's nephew. Eden was surprised and impressed by its strength. It was firm, perhaps too firm, he thought, and broad in its general statements of readiness to support the Covenant. But it had, Hoare assured him, the endorsement of the Prime Minister and if Eden was surprised, the surprise was agreeable. The British Government, it appeared from the speech, had decided to face the issue squarely.[25]

There was one more essential step. Hoare had to concert his position with Laval. They met the morning of September 10. Laval had maintained his contacts with Mussolini. He reported that Mussolini had promised to refrain from any drastic action during the Geneva meeting. If some new element were brought into the picture at Geneva, perhaps the discussion could continue elsewhere. Again the Duce had pleaded—he could hardly bring 200,000 troops from Africa without glory. He had begged Laval to try to prevent talk of sanctions,and to prevent a conflict between Britain and Italy.

From all this, Laval concluded that Mussolini had not yet made his final decision; that there was still room for discussion:

> M. Laval's conclusion was that, as practical men, they would now have to see how far they could go in making a proposal to the Italian Government. It would be best to leave aside for the moment the moral issue. If negotiations failed, the moral basis for the attitude of the French and British Governments would remain.[26]

Hoare responded that his chief preoccupation was German rearmament the gravity of which the British public had only recently come to understand. Indeed, the German threat had impressed on the British public the need for collective security under the League.

This was a test case. If the Covenant failed here, Hoare said, it would fail with Germany in future years. Hoare saw perfectly clearly, he said, French difficulties. He knew what value France attached to Italian friendship. He had no wish to place France in an impossible situation. His Government would accept any solution that met Italian needs so long as the solution did not entail the destruction of Abyssinian sovereignty and was accepted by the members of the League, Abyssinia included.

Hoare now came down to cases. If there were to be sanctions, his Government thought it unwise to begin with extreme measures that would not be supported by all members of the League or by nonmembers. It was better to begin with milder measures commanding more general assent that might either stop the war or shorten it without—and this was a critical point—raising the issue of belligerent rights. What this meant quite simply was no military measures, no blockade.

Anything that was done, Hoare added, should be done in as unprovocative a way as possible. For an example, he did not himself use, or intend to use the word "sanctions" in his speech.

If indeed there was a mad dog attack, all should combine to resist it. Not that he expected such an attack; but taking this position openly would be a useful deterrent.

Hoare closed by asking Laval to make still another plea to Mussolini. The message Hoare wished to convey was strangely at variance with his mild proposals to Laval. He asked Laval to assure Mussolini that Britain was not bluffing, that the League was at stake, and that France agreed.

There was a curious addendum. Perhaps, Hoare said, Laval had noticed in the papers reports of movements of substantial elements of the Home Fleet to the Mediterranean. Britain had taken this major step without advising France, but Hoare assured Laval that the movements were unprovocative in character.

Laval was gracious. In similar circumstances, he said, France would have done the same thing. He thanked Hoare for both his loyalty and his moderation. He hoped for a solution; Hoare's moderation would facilitate the task. He read his telegram of August 30 to Chambrun, reinforcing his message of July 19. In both he had made it clear to Mussolini that France would stand by Britain, the League, and Locarno. In the latter message, he had assured Mussolini that he would do his best to protect Italian esteem and interests. But his task was difficult, and Mussolini would understand.

Laval had already taken concrete action. An Italian order for motors, ready for shipment, would not be delivered. He had signed a decree that war material could not be sent to Italy without permission of the Ministry of Foreign Affairs. He wanted control before, not after the fact. He denied the rumor that France had extended loans to Italy.

Laval expressed to Hoare his appreciation for British moves to rearm and advised Hoare of the formal inquiry that Corbin would soon put to Britain. They agreed to talk later in the day; and Hoare promised to give Laval a summary of the speech he intended to make.[27]

Hoare had been very much the moving party in proposing to Laval the kind of joint measures France and Britain might adopt. When they met again that evening, Laval was in a position to respond.

He had seen Aloisi in the afternoon who had inquired if Hoare's speech would be severe. Laval had assured him it would be "extremely reasonable." Hoare commented that it was moderate as regards Abyssinia, but firm in the will to remain faithful to the League. That indeed, Laval said, was what he had conveyed, plus the assurance Britain was engaged in no bluff.

Laval again reviewed the French position: faithful to the League and the Rome Pact, hopeful to reconcile the two. If they had to pressure Mussolini, they must avoid casting him out of the League and into the arms of Germany. Hoare agreed. He said he had read the remarks of the new Italian Ambassador to Berlin.

Laval said he had clearly understood Hoare's recommendations to apply the Covenant without provocation or useless damage to Italian amour-propre. He agreed. France would engage not to furnish arms and war materials, financial assistance, or minerals to Italy.

Hoare had spoken of German rearmament. Laval could not resist a passing reference to the Anglo-German Naval Treaty. It had been wrong, he said, conceding gallantly that it had been done in good faith. France had no wish to provoke Germany. Indeed a Franco-German rapprochement was essential to peace. But the most effective guarantee of peace would always be a common French-British front in German matters.

As to Abyssinia, it was wise to go as far as possible in concessions to Italy. If war broke out, prudence was required. Italy might not persist after an initial success; it might then be happy to accept French and British conciliation.

In the event of war, the Council must meet immediately and take appropriate steps to end it. Those steps, Laval said, must be in not one but two directions: economic pressure, but always the search for solutions. In any case, Britain and France must always maintain the closest collaboration.

Hoare agreed. He thought that one day they would need to consider a ban on exports from Italy. Laval responded that it would not be psychologically sound to menace Mussolini with an export ban. There would be time for that if Italy refused conciliation.

They discussed how materials of war might be defined. If coal and oil were included, economic pressure would be effective indeed. Nothing would be easy, Laval observed. Stopping exports raised issues of blockade. He had intense political problems and cutting off imports from Italy could cause economic hardships in France.

Hoare said that as a coal exporter to Italy, Britain would suffer:

> But none the less, if this form of economic pressure were the only one likely to be effective, he thought that His Majesty's Government would be prepared to face that kind of damage provided that it was collective and effective. What he was anxious to avoid was the adoption of any action which was not likely to have any effect, or any action which would raise the question of blockade or belligerent rights.[28]

Here Hoare underlined once more that there should be no military action, no blockade. What was most important, he said, was for France and Britain to maintain a united front.

Laval returned to his theme. There had to be a hierarchy of measures to apply, and in applying them, one could not be too prudent. The League had succeeded in Europe. The principle of equality of nations ought to be respected, but there was hardly a complete analogy between a European war and what Mussolini called a colonial campaign. The Covenant should be applied—but applied with prudence. The League had been created, after all, to prevent war. One ought not, by an excess of zeal, to arrive at just the opposite result. They must remember that in Italy one dealt not with public opinion, not with Parliament, but with one man whose opinions changed from day to day.

If certain measures were applied, Mussolini might reply by bombarding Malta and the fire would have been lit in Europe—with Germany standing by. You had to put pressure on Mussolini, Laval said, but not a knife to his throat.

These were consequences for which Hoare had no stomach either. Again he urged measures which were effective but not provocative. He relied more on hope, less on practicalities than Laval. But Laval was optimistic as well as practical. After Mussolini had avenged Adowa, perhaps he would wish to put an end to his campaign and make a deal.

They agreed to remain in close consultation. Laval spoke plainly. France wanted Italian friendship, but Britain was more important than Italy. Mussolini knew and was resigned to this. But Hoare should remember—the Fascist regime, and the person of the Duce himself, were at stake. A solution was not impossible. The important thing was not to stop trying.[29]

The policies thus arrived at Hoare and Laval followed as long as they were in office and neither afterwards ever regretted or apologized for them.

Eden, Britain's great champion of the League and Hoare's successor, sat through the meeting in near total silence.[30] Laval was clear and consistent. Between Britain and Italy, if he had to choose, it must be Britain. He looked to Britain for a lead. Hoare gave it. It was Hoare who proposed that sanctions should be mild and gradual, and that military measures and blockade should be excluded. Laval was happy enough with this. He saw the issue against a European backdrop, but he also saw it as a very personal negotiation with Mussolini. For this, it was important to proceed in a logical manner and use methods adapted to the Duce's peculiar psychology. It was a continuous process, and it would continue even after war had started.

In the event of war there must be sanctions. That was no problem for Laval so long as the sanctions were of a kind to pressure a settlement rather than to spread the war. In essence, then, there were two policies, or better stated, a double policy because to Laval pressure and conciliation were two aspects of the same policy.

It is important to understand that Hoare and Laval readily and fully agreed. This was no instance of a policy pressed upon a reluctant ally by its partner. Hoare later wrote that

> We both excluded the idea of war as too dangerous and double-edged for Europe. We also agreed that as we must, if possible, avoid provoking Mussolini into open hostility, any economic pressure upon which the League collectively decided should be applied cautiously and in stages, and with full account of the unescapable fact that the United States, Japan, and Germany were not Member States of the League.[31]

When Laval reviewed his policy in the French Parliament in December, he confirmed Hoare's stand:

> Without waiting for the official meeting of the Council, we discussed and examined—in that spirit of close cooperation which ought always to animate French and British statesmen—the grave situation with which the World was going to be confronted by the Italo-Ethiopian War. We found ourselves instantaneously in agreement upon ruling out military sanctions, not adopting any measure of naval blockade, never contemplating the clo-

sure of the Suez Canal—in a word ruling out anything that might lead to war.[32]

The pressure of public opinion had moved the British Government to support of the Covenant. The public demanded economic sanctions. Question 5a of the Peace Ballot had been proof of this. It had also implied that economic sanctions could succeed, independent of military sanctions, and without risk of war. If the Government perceived that the public overwhelmingly backed the Covenant and economic sanctions, it did not believe that the British public wanted or would support war for the Covenant.

## A Momentous Speech

September 11 was the eve of the Abyssinian New Year. It would be celebrated with brushwood torches and night-long singing and on the morrow, the singers would butcher a bull, a sheep, or a kid for the daylong feast which would be accompanied by copious quantities of tef. Flowers, especially roses, symbolized the New Year. At the Royal Palace, a great *geber*, or feast of raw meat, would take place and the Royal Band would welcome the New Year.[33]

More significant to Abyssinia, on September 11, Sir Samuel Hoare addressed the League Assembly. The crisis was the most critical, and the moment the most dramatic yet in the League's history.

With an effusion of self-congratulations that came so easily to the British in those days, Hoare accurately noted that the world often found it difficult to understand either the course of British foreign policy or the workings of the British mind. But in spite of occasional failings, "British public opinion has usually shown a sound instinct upon the big issues and has usually in moments of crisis expressed itself with firmness, justice, and common sense."[34]

He wanted it understood that Britain supported the League out of no selfish motive but instead was moved by a great ideal. Support of the League was the best way to insure peace.

He made it clear that the League was no superstate. The members were sovereign and acted through the League only by their own decision: "The League is what its member states make it." It would fail if the people of a nation did not support a League policy: "In a word public opinion matters to the League as much as it matters to every democratic government."

He now pronounced a clear limitation on the collective enforcement of the Covenant:

> The obligations of the Covenant remain; their burden upon us has been increased manyfold. But one thing is certain. If the burden is to be borne, it must be borne collectively by all. If risks for peace are to be run, they must be run by all. The security of the many cannot be ensured solely by the efforts of a few, however powerful they may be. On behalf of His Majesty's Government in the United Kingdom, I can say that they will be second to none in their intention to fulfil, within the measure of their capacity, the obligations which the Covenant lays upon them. The ideas enshrined in the Covenant, and in particular the aspiration to establish the rule of law in international affairs, have appealed, as I have already said, with growing force to the strain of idealism which has its place in our national character, and they have become a part of our national conscience.[35]

Hoare wished to be constructive. The prime causes of war, he said, were economic. There were nations that possessed immense resources, especially in their colonies. The obvious reference was to the disparity in British and Italian resources. The problem was economic, not territorial. The British Government stood ready to deal fairly and effectively with the problem. Here was another hand stretched out to Mussolini.

He bracketed this proposal by once more denying that Britain was animated by selfish motives. This was an illusion both unjust and dangerous:

> The attitude of His Majesty's Government has been one of unwavering fidelity to the League and all that it stands for, and the case now before us is no exception, but, on the contrary, the continuance of that rule. The recent response of public opinion shows how completely the nation supports the Government in the full acceptance of the obligations of League membership, which is the oft-proclaimed keynote of its foreign policy.
>
> To suggest or insinuate that this policy is for some reason peculiar to the present question at issue would be a complete misunderstanding. It is to the principles of the League, and not to any particular manifestation, that the British nation has demonstrated its adherence. Any other view is at once an under-estimate of our good faith and an imputation upon our sincerity.[36]

The recent response of public opinion was the Peace Ballot. Its impact can be gauged by Hoare's pronouncement that, just as in the Peace Ballot, it was the principle and not the specific case to which the nation had rallied.

Hoare now stated the principle with a vigor which astonished his audience:

> In conformity with its precise and explicit obligations the League stands, and my country stands with it, for the collective maintenance of the Covenant in its entirety, and particularly for steady and collective resistance to all acts of unprovoked aggression. The attitude of the British nation in the last few weeks has clearly demonstrated the fact that this is no variable and unreliable sentiment, but a principle of international conduct to which they and their Government hold with firm, enduring, and universal persistence.[37]

He always denied that he had meant to do it. But Sir Samuel Hoare, prim and precise, cautious and conservative, everyone's maiden aunt, had created a sensation. The Council greeted his speech with an enthusiasm verging on passion.

It would be difficult, the Deputy Secretary General of the League said, to exaggerate the effect of the speech:

> Once more it seemed, after four years of uncertainty, timidity, opportunism, the true voice of Britain was heard. Now that the test was at hand, she was ready to take her natural place as the leader of the League and all it stood for—the respect for treaty obligations, the rights of small nations, the prevention, or if need be the defeat of aggression, through collective action.[38]

Paul Heymans of Belgium thought that "The British have decided to stop Mussolini, even if it means using force."[39] The Czech delegate said to a League official, "that speech has changed the whole outlook and given hope of peace to Europe."[40]

Amid the intense excitement, only Aloisi stood aloof. The Abyssinian delegate, Tecle Hawariat wore that afternoon an unaccustomed smile.[41]

The impression that Britain meant to act was heightened the following day by the announcement that the garrison of the critically strategic island of Malta would be reinforced by three more infantry battalions.[42]

More impressive still was the arrival on September 17 at Gibraltar of imposing elements of the Home Fleet: the battle cruisers *Hood* and *Renown*, three cruisers of the Sixth Cruiser Squadron, and six ships of the Sixth Destroyer Flotilla. Britain now had in the Mediterranean six battleships, eleven cruisers, and forty-five destroyers.[43]

On that day, representatives of the smaller nations, heartened by Hoare's speech, rallied to the support of the League. They were led by Belgium, Holland, Norway, and Sweden.[44]

The *Times* declared Hoare's speech an authoritative and historic declaration of British policy: "Without doubt he had succeeded in expressing the views, not only of the Government, but of the Country as a whole."[45]

The Bishop of St. Albans was moved to quote the Fifteenth Psalm:

> He that sweareth unto his neighbors
>
> And disappointeth him not
>
> Even though it were to his own hindrance. Who so doeth these things shall never fail.[46]

To none did Hoare's speech afford a greater satisfaction than Lord Cecil and the League of Nations Union which of course, stood firmly for enforcement of the Covenant.[47]

Cecil had pressed the government for similar action and, in a moment of discouragement in August, contemplated a step scarcely credible for a lifelong Conservative and son of a three-time Tory Prime Minister—becoming a member of the Labour Party.[48]

It had been Lord Cecil's triumph to hear the Prime Minister, responding to the Peace Ballot in July, declare that the League of Nations was the sheet anchor of British policy. Lord Cecil now had the supreme satisfaction to hear that policy pronounced from the rostrum at Geneva in the League's moment of crisis.

He lauded the speech as opening a new and hopeful chapter in world history. Hoare and Eden, the LNU's monthly magazine reported, were inundated with messages of congratulations, like film stars, struggling with their fan mail.[49]

French opinion was impressed by Hoare's stand. But there were those who said it was late in the day, that a strong stand months and even years ago might have avoided the problems of the day. What would Britain do in Europe? The Paris correspondent of the *Times* captured this mood:

> What guarantees have we, is the question on every Frenchman's lips today, that this zeal, new in expression if not in fact, for the League over an African question will be found undiminished should a similar problem arise in Eastern Europe...?
>
> To the British reader the categoric terms of the British Minister yesterday should leave no doubt in any reasonable mind about the certainty that henceforth Great Britain is committed to upholding the League with undi-

> minished vigour so long as it remains an 'effective body.' To the Frenchman, with his passion for definiteness, his hunger for cast-iron assurances, this is not enough. Presumably M. Laval and his colleagues realize the full significance of what they heard yesterday. But he, like any other democratic statesman, draws both his strength and his weakness from public opinion. And public opinion, without a doubt, is calling for the assurance described.[50]

Perhaps the listeners would have been less euphoric had they considered some of the implications of Hoare's speech. He had said very plainly that the League had no power other than what its members contributed. An effective action had to be collective action, not simply the action of the few, however powerful. The world could not, then, look to Britain alone, or Britain and France. He had never once uttered the word sanctions.

Yet there it was, a clear and unequivocal statement of British commitment to the League, collective security, and collective resistance to acts of aggression, not simply in this context but as an invariable principle of British policy.

## Hoare-Laval 2

Later that afternoon, Hoare, Eden, and Strang again met Laval, Léger, and Massigli. Laval congratulated Hoare on his speech. He added wistfully his regret that such a speech had not been made long ago.[51]

They discussed the proposals being drafted by the Committee of Five. Laval was fertile in ideas. It was no use submitting the Paris proposals again. There had to be something new. Mussolini wanted some kind of police control in Abyssinia. Perhaps there could be two periods, the first when the police were international, yielding after five years to Italian predominance. He thought of further territorial concessions by France and Britain. He suggested that France and Britain consider loans to Italy to help in the development of Abyssinia.

Hoare turned to talk of sanctions. They were dangerous, Laval said; what was possible for Britain might be less possible for France and almost impossible for other members of the League.

"International morals were one thing," Laval said. "The interests of a country were another."

With economy of words and precision of thought, Pierre Laval had cut through Hoare's verbiage to the heart of the matter. Laval's whole duty and responsibility, as he saw it, was prescribed by the interests of France.

In putting a series of five questions to the British people, the proponents of the Peace Ballot had never asked where British interests lay. Hoare had imitated this exercise in abstract principle in his speech. He had disclaimed selfish interests; instead, he stated, the British people were deeply and genuinely moved by a great ideal.

He had mentioned the British interest in an effective League but it was his final, limitlessly broad statement that had caught the attention of the world. Britain, he said, stood for the maintenance of the Covenant in its entirety, against all acts of aggression as a principle of international policy that he characterized as "firm, enduring, and universal." This meant literally anywhere, at any time, quite irrespective of the degree to which British interests were involved.

Laval saw things differently. He would not hide, he said, the prudence with which he would approach the whole question of sanctions. Hoare explained to Laval why he had spoken so strongly. He had been thinking of Germany. His closing words has been chosen with care to show that this was a test case. If it failed, he feared Britain would lapse into isolation.

They turned to issues of disarmament. Hoare pressed Laval for his position on arms limitations, an air pact, and the Danubian pact.

Laval's reply was simple. He stood on the communiqué of February 3, 1935 when France, Italy, and Britain had rallied to the defense of Austria and pronounced unacceptable the unilateral revocation of treaties. That day, he had had a beautiful dream. It had been shattered by the Anglo-German Naval Treaty. But, what was done was done. As to arms control, his sentiments were well known. He had always sought a reconciliation with Germany and he would work with Hoare to that end.

"France will never attack Germany," he said. It's the most pacifist country in Europe even though the best armed. He warned Hoare: Germany respects Britain and France only to the degree that they face up to her if she tries to disturb the peace.[52]

Laval closed with the same plea: Franco-British collaboration was indispensable. France's sole concern was the organization of peace. He knew that England disliked alliances and looked to Geneva. But France and Britain must not leave the direction of European affairs to the dictators.

## An Enigma

On September 10, Hoare had proposed to Laval severe limitations on the response to Italian aggression. The next day he had spoken in the broadest terms of invariable opposition to not only that aggression but to any act of aggression. He was clearly riding two horses, a feat that can succeed only for brief periods of time and then only if the horses are going in the same direction.

In later years, Hoare pronounced himself as puzzled by the sensational effect of his speech. There was nothing in it, he observed, that he had not said to a thoroughly bored House of Commons.

But had he ever spoken to the House in the explicit terms of Geneva? Geneva, moreover, was not the House of Commons, and the occasion, far from being a routine Parliamentary debate, was a response to a world crisis. Hoare had said that foreigners find it difficult to understand the workings of the British mind. Perhaps he himself underestimated the degree to which more rational minds might take his words at face value.

The day before he had urged Laval to convey to Mussolini that he was not bluffing. He later admitted having determined to make "a revivalist appeal to the Assembly. At best, it might well start a new chapter of League recovery; at worst it might deter Mussolini by a display of League fervour. If there was any element of bluff in it, it was a moment when bluff was not only legitimate but inescapable."[53]

Eden, who had been at Hoare's side, disagreed. Mussolini, he said, was "a man to practice bluff, not to be its victim at faltering hands."[54]

The day after his speech, in a radio broadcast, Hoare emphasized conciliation, rather than firmness for the Covenant. His aim was, he said, a settlement which would do justice alike to Abyssinia's national rights and Italy's claims for expansion.[55]

## Pierre Laval

Hoare had spoken. Conscious of France's difficult position, her internal divisions, and her paramount concerns in Europe, the statesmen and peoples awaited the moment when Pierre Laval would speak for France.

When he spoke on September 13, Laval was blunt and concise. "France is loyal to the Covenant. She cannot fail to carry out her obligations."

This, he emphasized, was not a new policy:

> From the 1924 Protocol to the Conference for the Reduction and Limitation of Armaments, they have maintained and supported with the same zeal the doctrine of collective security. This doctrine is and will remain the doctrine of France. The Covenant is our international law. How could we possibly allow such a law to be weakened? To do so would be to deny our whole ideal and it would contrary to our interest to do so. The policy of France rests entirely on the League. All our agreements with our friends and allies are now concluded through Geneva or culminate at Geneva.[56]

France's inquiry as to British support for the Covenant in Europe had been formally lodged two days before. Laval was not one to miss the opportunity to brace his British friends.

Hoare's speech, he said, had combined lofty inspiration and a sense of the universal and this he defly turned to France's account:

> No country welcomed the words of the British Secretary of State with more satisfaction than did France. No country is better able to appreciate and to estimate the scope of such an undertaking. This partnership in responsibilities of all kinds, in all circumstances of time and place, a responsibility which is implied for the future by such a declaration, marks a date in the history of the League of Nations. I rejoice thereat with my country, for my country fully understands the need for close collaboration with the United Kingdom in the defence of peace and for the protection of Europe. As long ago as February 3 in London our two Governments had jointly drawn up a programme that was full of hope. The news of this event was welcomed throughout the world with real enthusiasm. Obstacles arose and have hindered its practical application. I had a splendid dream. Could that dream be on the point of realization?[57]

He now addressed soothing words to Mussolini, recalling the Pact of Rome and Stresa over which Mussolini had presided. France and Italy had the same interests in European solidarity and general peace.

He had spared no effort at conciliation which was his metier. He spoke with his accustomed confidence: "The task is doubtless a difficult one, but I still do not think it is hopeless." His closing was as emphatic as his opening: "Our obligations are inscribed in the Covenant. France will not shirk them."[58]

These were bold words in difficult circumstances. A substantial body of French opinion was deeply apprehensive of antagonizing Italy and equally concerned that Britain's new enthusiasm for the Covenant would not extend to Europe. The Front Commun on the left and the Front Paysan on the right, furiously antagonistic, were united in their antagonism to Laval's deflationary fiscal policy. Ten thousand farmers of the Front Paysan gathered at Chateaubriand on September 14 to protest high costs and low prices and to demand a moratorium on farm loans. At Blois a week later Communist demonstrations at a Front Paysan meeting exploded into violence.[59]

In 1935, the press was the dominant mass medium. Its reporters were international figures. They were perspicacious and well-informed. Reports appeared in the *Manchester Guardian* on September 13 that Laval had agreed to economic and financial but not military sanctions.[60]

The *New York Times* reported on September 15 that the sanctions would be nonbelligerent.[61] In his speech Laval had emphasized, in addition to French loyalty to the Covenant, friendship with Italy, and his ultimate belief in a negotiated settlement. At no time did he seek to keep secret the understandings he had arrived at with Hoare on September 10. Indeed, from time to time he suggested, unofficially and officially, that the substance of those conversations be made public. The limitations that he had agreed to then were an essential element of his point of view and of his policy.

## The Duce Responds

Sir Samuel Hoare had rallied the League to the Covenant. The Italian response was firmly negative. The Italian cabinet met on September 14. It pronounced itself unsurprised by the British and French stands, but noted with satisfaction Laval's cordial words confirming "a friendship that Italy intends to develop and strengthen, not only in the interest of the two countries, but also in the interest of European collaboration which cannot be broken by a conflict of a colonial character."

There could be no compromise, the communiqué said, with Abyssinia. But Mussolini still hoped to preserve the Stresa front.[62]

Suvich told Chambrun of Mussolini's views on September 16. As to Germany, Mussolini had adopted a position which would enable Italy to obtain economic aid in the event of sanctions. But he had not engaged in any political negotiations and relations between the two countries remained *sans amenité*—distant.

What Mussolini absolutely wished to avoid, Suvich said, was a conflict with England. The effect in Europe would be disastrous. Italy could not maintain positions in Abyssinia, on the Danube, and in the Mediterranean at the same time.

Mussolini's intransigence, he said, was a response to the anti-Fascism which was using Abyssinia to attack the regime. Mussolini did not wish to leave the League, but what ought he do if the proposals of the Committee of Five were unacceptable? Responding to English fleet movements and the threat of sanctions, he had effected certain reinforcements in Libya and in the Red Sea. He would readily renounce these if he were assured that there would be no military sanctions or economic sanctions which would threaten the life of the nation. Suvich even thought he would accept a vote of censure that did not inpugn national honor.

Chambrun urged Suvich to see that the proposals of the Committee of Five were given the most serious consideration and to convince Mussolini of his responsibility to avoid a conflict, the ultimate and disastrous consequences of which were very easy to imagine.[63]

Chambrun saw Suvich again the next day, at Suvich's request. Suvich envisioned a melancholy chain: the threat of sanctions, military preparations, sanctions, then war. Again he pressed Chambrun for a declaration that Britain and France would take no military sanction, no move threatening the life of Italy. Otherwise the risk of war was too great.

Laval told Eden all this in Geneva on September 19. He also reported on his talk the evening before with Aloisi. Italy should not object, Laval had told Aloisi, to economic sanctions. "After all," he said, "you cannot make [the] British buy gorgonzola and chianti if they don't want to."

What he did tell Aloisi was that he would seek an assurance to be given to Mussolini that Britain and France did not contemplate military sanctions or indeed any sanctions such as might involve war outside Africa.

Laval frankly asked Eden to ask for British approval of such a step. Would Britain assure Italy it would neither apply military sanctions, a blockade, or close the Suez Canal?[64]

Eden advised to the contrary. Though contemplating no more than economic and financial pressure, it was out of the question, he thought, for the British Government to give such an assurance. It would expose the Government to reproach that it was not acting as a loyal member of the League. Furthermore, "it would surely come as a shock to our public opinion to learn that we had come to terms with the transgressor and with a third party possibly to defeat the intention of the Covenant."[65]

Laval never departed from the view that the interests, not only of

France, but of Europe demanded a compromise with Italy. He firmly believed that no good would come of military threats, much less of hostile action; that to the contrary, to forswear them was the path to settlement. He had no desire to cloak in secrecy the understandings he had arrived at with Hoare on September 10. Quite the contrary, he believed it would smooth the path to settlement to proclaim them to the world.

The policy of Hoare was to shake the big stick, concealing the fact that neither he nor his electorate were prepared to wield it. Curiously, Laval's straightforward attitude gained him the reputation of being unreliable. This was the considered opinion of Vansittart, whose influence with Hoare was near its zenith.[66]

Mussolini still had hopes of British understanding. In an interview published in *Le Matin* on September 17, he had said,

> We have had a sincere and faithful friendship with the British people for many years, but today we find it monstrous that a nation which dominates the World refuses us a wretched plot of ground in the African sun. Many times and in every way I have given the assurance to Great Britain that her interests in Abyssinia would be scrupulously safeguarded. But the interests for which she is so strongly opposing us are other interests and she does not say so.... It is not a game of poker.... We shall go straight ahead.... Never from our side will come any hostile act against a European nation. But if one is committed against us—well, it means war. Italy does not want it, but she is not afraid of it. Instead of the losses involved in a colonial policing operating, such as England and France have carried out in turn, does one want millions of dead?"[67]

Clearly, the Duce found it hard to understand the British. He was, he thought, only taking a leaf from their book. This was vividly apparent in the same week. All summer long, hostile tribesmen had waged a lively little war on India's Northwest Frontier. Their leaders were the Fakir of Alingarh, the Haji of Turengzai and his son, Bakshah Gul. On September 17, a British force of 15,000, no longer relying on Kipling's horse, foot, and gun, but replete with aircraft, tanks, radio communications, and motor transport, as well as infantry, cavalry and artillery, advanced toward the Khpak and Nahakki Passes where tribesmen were reported in large numbers. This was the Mohmand Force, commanded by Sir Claud Auchinleck, who would one day face the Italians and their ally, Rommel, in the Western Desert. In a dramatic night operation, Indian troops of the Peshawur and Nowshera Brigades scaled the precipitous heights on either side of the Nahakki Pass and occupied the peaks while the Highland Light Infantry advanced under the covering fire of field batteries to secure the pass from which the tribesmen had vanished.

A road would now be built, which the Governor of the Northwest Province said, would hardly please the rebels; and Mohmand Force would remain in occupation until peace could be established which was permanent and not, as the Governor remarked, at the whim of some irresponsible leader.[68]

On September 18, the Committee of Five completed its report and recommendations to the parties. It had been guided by two principles: to preserve the independence and integrity of all member states and to insure good and neighborly relations among them. The League would offer its services to Abyssinia on a collective international basis, to improve the lot of the Abyssinian people, enhance economic development, and contribute to secure and friendly borders.

More specifically, the program envisioned international assistance in organizing a police force capable of suppressing slavery, regulating the trade in arms, providing internal security, and maintaining order on the frontiers. In economic matters the League would assist in encouraging foreign investment and trade, public works, and communications. Abyssinia would be aided in budget preparation, financial supervision, assessment, taxation, and development loans. Assistance would also be extended in the administration of justice, education, and public health.

All this was to be done by foreign specialists with a principal advisor to head each of the four major advisory groups. These principal advisors might be delegates of the League. The delegates and principal advisors would be appointed by the League Council with the agreement of the Emperor; their subordinates would be appointed by the Emperor or nominated by the League delegate. The program was proposed for an initial period of five years.

The Committee further observed that Britain and France had signified their willingness to make territorial concessions enabling Abyssinia to obtain an outlet to the sea. Both governments were willing to recognize a special Italian economic interest in Abyssinia, subject to the protection of their existing treaty rights.[69]

The Committee's proposal lacked the new element that Laval had suggested. But there was a difference from the Paris proposals. Those had envisioned Franco-Italian-British collaboration to supervise the development plan, in essence an extension of the 1906 Treaty and the concept of Abyssinian tutelage to the three powers. The Committee of Five's was a League plan, based upon League advisors and League supervision. Given the grievances that Italy had stated, the Committee's plan was a sensible response to much of the Italian memorandum.

Mussolini's response was more than prompt. Even before he had received the Committee's proposal, he replied in the English press. In a *Daily Mail* interview of September 18, he greeted the proposals with derision:

> The suggestion is apparently made that Italy's need for expansion in East Africa should be met by the cession to her of a couple of deserts—one of salt, the other of stone. They are the deserts of Danakil and Ogaden.... It looks as if the Committee of the League thinks I am a collector of deserts. I got 110,000 square miles of Saharan Desert from the French a little while ago. Do you know how many inhabitants there are in that desolate area? Sixty two.

He had further complaints:

> In the scheme of an international administration and gendarmerie it seems that Italy is not to be represented at all. The suggestion apparently is that all the 200,000 Italian troops in East Africa should be brought home and told that they have been sent out there for an excursion-trip. That certainly will not be done in any case.[70]

There was outrage here and wounded pride. Mussolini had wielded power since 1922 and the more his power grew, the more sensitive he became to affront or what he regarded as such. This is hardly unusual in heads of state.

The report of the Committee of Five had been kept secret from the Italian delegates, Mussolini complained to Chambrun in Rome on September 21. They had learned of its terms from reports in the British press. Had the matter been kept secret, Mussolini said, he would not have rejected it. He would have asked for clarifications. But with the terms made public, Mussolini saw them as a kind of ultimatum. To accept them would have entailed a loss of face.

"They've tried to put me down," he asserted to Chambrun, with visible emotion, "but as long as I'm at this desk, I am not going down on my knees."[71]

Good negotiators strive to avoid placing the other party in a position from which he cannot back down; they attempt to ease his difficulties in moving toward compromise. Laval paid continuing attention to Mussolini's psychology and the possibilities it offered. The British were more inclined to rely upon moral principles, publicity, and public opinion. This did not take into account Laval's advice that, in the end, they were dealing with one man.

Chambrun urged Mussolini not to reject the report before studying it. Mussolini made no attempt to hide his motivations and his emotions. He was certain that Britain wanted war. What else could justify their sending 800,000 tons of naval forces to the Mediterranean to oppose Italy's 300,000? He was sure they wanted to humiliate him. The Committee had never mentioned Italian grievances or given Italy a role in their plan.

"I will never fire the first cannon shot in Europe," he declared. But he would go on in Abyssinia. It was Britain that was putting the match to the powder. "You will see Germany march on Vienna, the Little Entente brushed aside under a German thrust to the Bosphorus," he predicted.[72]

He begged France to avoid military sanctions. Italy had not broken treaties like Germany or annexed 40 millions like Japan. Without sanctions, peace could be safeguarded.

Chambrun conveyed Laval's message urging Mussolini to accept the Committee's proposals. If he did not, all that had been accomplished at Stresa would be in jeopardy. If the proposals were unsatisfactory, Mussolini was free to question and negotiate. And in that process Laval would help him to obtain satisfactory answers "as far as he could do so consistently with the terms of the Covenant."[72]

Mussolini asked Chambrun to tell Laval how much he appreciated Laval's efforts, knowing the cost to him. To Chambrun's final plea, he replied that Italian rejection would come on the morrow.[73]

The Italian rejection followed in due course on September 22. On the next day Abyssinia signaled its acceptance as a basis, it carefully noted, for negotiation. It welcomed and dwelt with satisfaction upon the principles of respect for territorial integrity. There were conditions attached to Abyssinia's acceptance: that the Emperor should have the right at will to reject any advisor and that the plan as a whole should receive the approval of Abyssinia before any action was taken. As to the observations that Britain and France would convey territories, the Emperor coolly replied that this was inappropriate since the League had no power to propose territorial changes. To the observation that France and Britain would accord special recognition to Italy's economic interests in Abyssinia, the Emperor replied with equal reserve that this solely concerned the three powers and that Abyssinia could only say that it would carry out its international obligations and treaties with all powers.[74]

The Emperor's demands upon the League of Nations were in a sense unlimited. He expected that its members would take all steps necessary to defend Abyssinian independence at any cost and irrespective of their own interests. Conscious of his weakness, he adopted a policy of unyielding firmness, the same policy and for the same reason that Charles de Gaulle felt compelled to adopt in later years. Thus he defended his country; but at the same time, amid the turmoil and rivalries of Abyssinian power, he defended his dynasty and his personal position. For Haile Selassie, any display of weakness would exacerbate the rivalry of the turbulent and power-hungry rases.

While his army assembled, Haile Selassie carried on the stately traditions of his Empire. He celebrated the great annual feast of Maskal which marked the end of the rainy season, carrying special significance this year.

The Emperor, on his bed throne, greeted the Diplomatic Corps in the great *geber* hall, its doors and windows draped in orange silk, its floors strewn with reeds and aromatic mint leaves. The Italian Ambassador kissed the Emperor's hand.

Servants dressed in pale green and armed with red swords ushered in a hundred priests who sang prayers glorifying Haile Selassie. There followed the dance of the priests about the table where the Bible lay. They dipped their silver staves and shook their copper rattles to the rhythm of the drums. With the presentation of bouquets of iris and marigolds to the Emperor and the Diplomatic Corps, the ceremony ended.[75]

There was nothing left for the Committee of Five but to report on September 24 the frustration of its efforts. The League Council met on September 26 under the presidency of Senor Ruiz Guinazu, the Argentinian delegate, and determined its future procedure. The work of the Committee of Five was ended. A new committee of all members of the League Council, save only parties to the dispute, would convene, which became known as the Committee of Thirteen. Under the procedure outlined in Article 15, of the Covenant in the case of a peace-threatening dispute, this Committee would prepare its report and recommendations to the League Council and Assembly.

In supporting the adoption of this procedure, Eden spoke firmly of the continuing need to seek a peaceful settlement. No opportunity, he said, should be missed. Laval equally firmly agreed.[76]

There was a sequel to Chambrun's two meetings with Suvich and reports of them which reached Hoare through Laval and Corbin. Hoare took note of Mussolini's angry statements that Britain wished to humiliate Italy and destroy the Italian fleet. He asked his ambassador in Rome to meet with Mussolini and convey to him that, far from having any wish to humiliate Italy, Britain wanted an Italy strong and stable as it had been for years. He had avoided mention of sanctions and closing the Suez Canal. He had not had anything to do with press leakage of the Committee of Five's report. Hoare emphasized his desire for an honorable settlement and he indicated to Drummond the need to save Mussolini's face. But if the League adopted collective action, Britain would back it as a loyal member.[77]

Drummond delivered these messages on September 23. Mussolini expressed his thanks and made no real issue of press leaks or British naval movements. He stood firm on his case. The Committee of Five had made it clear Abyssinia could not stand alone; it followed that the tasks of guardianship should fall to Italy. Italy should have the non-Amharic parts of Abyssinia and control over the rest. The Emperor could continue, safeguarded against the rases' wrath by Italy.

There was no yielding and Mussolini stated what he clearly saw. Germany was growing stronger daily and waiting to profit from the disarray of the Stresa Front.

Drummond painted a somber portrait of Mussolini at the hour of decision:

> I need only say in conclusion that I found the Head of Government calm, affable and unperturbed. If mad, he is a very singular madman; while for one who has set the whole world by the ears, condemned thousands of young Italians to a painful death and millions of his countrymen to an almost animal level of existence, he seems astonishingly untroubled by the remorse of conscience. The explanation lies probably in his philosophy and creed. He believes in war as the means by which a country can be kept vigorous, young, powerful and progressive. He believes also that Italy is the heritor of the ancient traditions of the Roman Empire. He finds his country lacking space, raw materials and the place in the sun which he holds to be its due. These reasons combined have rendered him oblivious of other considerations such as economic and financial facts and have produced in his mind the impression that he is acting as a predestined instrument. He is said to have once told an American visitor that he is subject to periods of trance at which time he is inspired by influences outside his ordinary self. If true, this story confirms my own constant impression of a man who is the victim, not the master of his destiny.[78]

## The British View

The British Cabinet had not met since August 22, and now had to prepare a response to the Italian action which was expected momentarily. It had also to reply to France's request of September 10 for a statement of British policy on the continent.

The pressure of public opinion, impressive in earlier weeks, heightened. The Labour Party had persistently opposed military budgets and preparations. Its leading element, the Trades Union Congress met at Margate in early September to consider a resolution which, while demanding collective security under the League, pronounced with equal fervor for disarmament and international agreements limiting the manufacture and sale of arms. The resolution was overwhelmingly adopted by 2,962,000 to 177,000.[79]

Sir John Simon could not resist commenting on the irony of it:

> It has always been puzzling that the Labour Opposition, while clamoring for the application of collective security, should have resisted the necessary provision of armaments, without which it would be impossible to make our contributions.[80]

A contemporary wit remarked that there were in Britain three kinds of pacifists: those who wished to fight Italy, those who wished to fight Germany, and those who wished to fight Japan. The only point on which they could agree was to resist all expenditure for armaments.

But there were those who were faithful to their peaceful creed and chief among them was the leader of the Labour Party, George Lansbury. He tried to see the issue from the point of view of the religion his mother had taught him. He could not accept war in any way, shape, or form and he would resign the leadership if the Labour Party thought otherwise.[81] This in fact after a celebrated attack by Ernest Bevin, he did.

Sir Stafford Cripps dissented from the TUC action on more original grounds. The League was only a front for imperialism. He would support arms and military action only in aid of an international socialist order against capitalist aggression. The workers ought to use the crisis, not to support the government, but to dislodge it.[82]

These were minority voices. The Cabinet had little doubt where the public stood. A meeting of ministers held on September 23, 1935 reviewed a draft of the British reply to the French note. There were concerns that the answer might be too broad but Hoare responded "that the

Covenant was shown by the outburst of public opinion to have greater validity in the country that (sic) had been thought." Indeed, in closing the discussion, Hoare made clear the intent of the document: "without extending what he had said at Geneva, to give satisfaction to the French and to opinion at home."[83]

Congratulations to Sir Samuel Hoare were the order of the day when the Cabinet met the next day. But Hoare's recommendations to the Cabinet were at variance with his brave words in Geneva. While it was essential to try out the League process and machinery, he advised only the mildest sanctions. He would himself be on guard against being maneuvered into anything stronger. The last thing he wanted, of course, was a singlehanded war with Italy.

The Cabinet resolved in precisely the sense Hoare proposed: Support for the League but no further than the French were prepared to go, sanctions only which all of the members would support and non-members would not render futile, avoidance of a war with Italy.

A reply to France was approved, and at the same time an inquiry: In the event of an Italian attack on British forces or interests, would the other members of the League in general and France in particular render full cooperation?

Having lingered over its reply, Britain now sought a prompt response from France as to its readiness to protect British interests.[84]

Britain's question to France was sent before Britain's answer. The question was put on September 24. Article 16 of the Covenant enjoined mutual support of members who were enforcing its terms. But suppose, Britain inquired, even before Article 16 had gone into effect, and because Britain had declared its intent to act under it, British naval forces were attacked? Could Britain count upon French support, immediate assistance of the French Navy, and the use of French naval bases and facilities? Hoare asked for an answer without delay.[85]

Corbin astutely observed in forwarding the inquiry to Paris that Britain's concern exactly paralleled that of France under Locarno or an air pact. The League might not be willing to act, its procedures might be too slow and formal to respond adequately to the threat. Corbin specifically suggested the case of the Rhineland. It would be wise, he said to put any reply in a general sense, not limited to the case of Italy.[86]

The British reply to the French request was finally sent on September 26. In it Hoare referred to his speech at Geneva and particularly his assertion that the Covenant and the rule of law "had appealed with growing force to the strain of idealism in the British national character, and that they had indeed become part of the national conscience."

References to British idealism and the national conscience were not the kind of response France had in mind.

Hoare now qualified his remarks about resistance to acts of unprovoked aggression. He made it very clear that failure to fulfill the terms of a treaty was not an act of unprovoked aggression. As to a resort to force there were degrees of aggression and degrees of culpability; circumstances could alter cases.

To France, the ultimate safeguard was Locarno and the Rhineland. France now learned that the unilateral violation of treaties would not necessarily occasion British support and that in cases of unprovoked aggression, Britain retained its freedom of action.

France had been concerned that Sir Samuel's speech represented the policy of that day only, and not a long-term commitment upon which France might rely. To this Hoare responded in the British note:

> I may point out that, while my words at Geneva were spoken on behalf of the present Government of this country, those words were also spoken with the overwhelming support and approval of the people of this country.[87]

Corbin immediately saw that the answer did not in fact contain the formal precision France wished. Nevertheless he thought it wise to make as much as possible of the reply and to present it as covering all the hypotheses France could envisage. There was, he thought, a certain gravity in the reply, confirming Hoare's speech and Hoare had tried to confirm the response with the weight of public opinion. This was, at least, something better than English reticences of the past.

When Vansittart presented the reply to Corbin, he asked for a reply to the British inquiry of two days before. Corbin reminded him that the French inquiry had awaited a reply since September 10 and made his own point: It would be necessary to review the British inquiry in the most general aspect. Vansittart expressed surprise, then conceded that this was legitimate.[88]

Corbin had anticipated the French reaction. As press and public saw it, Britain's reply lacked precision. It did not respond directly and keen French critics saw the latitude it left in British hands. Nevertheless there was satisfaction that Britain had gone as far as it had. It was less than France had hoped, more than France had expected.

## War on the Horizon

On September 27, the Emperor presided over the military parade in the ceremonies of the Maskal. This time he did not appear in ceremonial regalia, but in field khaki. When the Abuna approached the Royal Pavilion, a wild thunderstorm engulfed the scene. The Emperor kissed the Bible and turned to the chief purpose of the proceedings—the traditional boasting.

An Adowa veteran did a war dance, shouting "Death to the Italians." Warriors, on foot and mounted, armed with spears and rifles, shrieked vengeance and pantomimed their martial feats. A huge throng followed the War Minister, Ras Mulugeta. "Better die than live as slaves," they cried. "Fear not the politics of the outer world; God is with us," shouted a chieftain, among wildly careening squadrons of Somali cavalry. As the hysteria peaked, the Royal Chamberlain ritually flogged the soldiers. Their number was estimated at 12,000.[89]

The Emperor had appealed to the League to send observers to Abyssinia, but the League had declined. On September 29, he concluded he could wait no longer. Having rescinded an earlier mobilization order, pressed on him by the rases, he now issued an order for general mobilization, but the troops were to remain 30 kilometers from the frontier to avoid incidents.[90]

On the same day, the Italian Cabinet met and issued its communiqué. Italy would not abandon the League. Italy took note of Hoare's cordial message. It had no immediate or remote aims which would harm British interests. The government solemnly declared it would avoid anything which would extend the Italo-Abyssinian conflict.[91]

Vansittart posed the essential issue to Hoare:

> [I]n unfortunately existing circumstances—i.e. a strong and aggressive Germany and a weak England—it is not to *our* interest either to force this burning question anywhere near a conflagration if it can by any means be avoided.[92]

On the same day, *Petit Journal* published another interview with Mussolini. The old journalist did not stint in making himself available to the press. He said he would not refuse a new three-power conference. He had always, since January 29, tried to keep Britain informed. His war preparations had been open for all to see. Eden's proposals had not accorded with Italy's national honor. He paid tribute to Laval "that great statesman." He denied that he had discussed Abyssinia with Laval in January. Laval had made no promises to him but had mentioned French rights in the Djibuti railway.[93]

The door, Mussolini seemed to say to Britain—there was no need to say it to France—remained open. The price of doing business, however, was escalating.

Meanwhile, on India's Northwest Frontier, the tribesmen who had retreated before the British advance through the Nahakki Pass attacked the British force. Two British officers were killed, four wounded and seventy to eighty other ranks killed or wounded; the lashkars, or tribal forces, also suffered heavy casualties. Some of the tribes now sued for peace but others remained in the field. Had Winston Churchill wished to expand his colorful list of the foes of British arms, he could have added the name of the Fakir of Alingarh in the latest episode of the conquest of the Indian Empire.[94]

The British Cabinet met on October 2. It asked Eden to make a fair statement of the case in his report to the League Council without closing the door to an eventual settlement. It reaffirmed that military sanctions were out of the question "in view of the attitude of the French government." This piece of self-justification ignored Hoare's lead against belligerent sanctions in his agreement with Laval. The Cabinet concluded that the aim should be "the maximum of economic sanctions on which agreement can be secured." This was at least consistent with Hoare's declaration that action had to be the action of all and that Britain would not act alone.[95]

On October 2, Mussolini called out the great rally of the nation announced earlier in the month. Like the Maskal ceremony in Addis Ababa, a violent thunderstorm made a somber background for the mass gathering. In Rome, the bells rang, the shops were closed, the loudspeakers were never silent with their repeated programs of martial music and patriotic speeches. Young Fascists carrying torches led the way to the Piazza Venezia where, underneath the balcony, an enormous banner flying above it, stood Mussolini's guard in their hundreds carrying silver daggers. The crowd roared "Duce, Duce" when Mussolini finally appeared. Trumpet blasts silenced the crowd and Mussolini spoke, at first slowly and then with increasing passion.

Twenty million Italians were gathered in the public squares of Italy, he said, the greatest mass meeting of history. They manifested a single will: "This manifestation is to signify that the identity between Italy and Fascism is perfect, absolute, unchangeable."

Italy would avenge the black injustice of 1915, the 670,000 dead, the 400,000 disabled, the million wounded in the war for which Italy received "only the crumbs from the sumptuous colonial booty of others."

He had words for France and Britain. "I refuse to believe," he said, "that the true people of France can associate themselves with sanctions against Italy." And again: "Until there is proof to the contrary, I refuse to believe that the true people of Great Britain want to spill blood and push Europe on the road to catastrophe."

He thrust out his challenge:

> To sanctions of an economic character, we will reply with our discipline, with our sobriety, with our spirit of sacrifice. To sanctions of a military character we will reply with orders of a military character. To acts of war we will reply with acts of war.

To one thing he called for the closest attention: "We will do everything possible to avoid a colonial conflict assuming the character and bearing of a European conflict."

Party Secretary Starace shouted, "Greet the Duce." To the roar of the large throng, the band played the Fascist anthem "Giovenezza." The Duce was going to war.[96]

On October 3, the Secretary General of the League of Nations received a cable from Abyssinia announcing the bombing of Adowa and Adigrat, the resulting civilian casualties, and the battles in progress. The Italian Foreign Ministry's cable put the matter in a different light. It declared that the warlike and aggressive spirit of Abyssinia had found expression in the Emperor's mobilization order of September 28. Italy had thereby been obliged to take the necessary measures of defense.[97]

Both Mussolini's son and his son-in-law took part in the first flights over Abyssinian territory. On October 4, General de Bono, High Commissioner in Italian East Africa, proclaimed the opening of hostilities, though there had been no declaration of war.[98]

Haile Selassie summoned his troops in the traditional way, by the beating of the negaret, the great drum which had called Menelik's warriors to battle at Adowa. Surrounded by thousands of soldiers clad in their white shammas, the drummer accompanied his first slow single beats with the invocation: "Listen, listen. Open your ears. The symbol of liberty wishes words to be said to you. Long may he live and the enemy within our gates may God destroy."

The decree of mobilization was read. The crowd erupted in a frenzy of emotion, of anger, and of martial ardor. "Death to the Italians," was the cry and to the Emperor. "We thank you for your decree. God give you long life."

Amid this turbulent scene, the Emperor maintained that stance of perfect calm and dignity which had characterized him throughout the long prelude to war. He greeted his soldiers and spoke to them with farseeing wisdom:

> Soldiers, I give you this advice so that we may gain victory over the enemy. Be cunning, be savage, face the enemy one by one, two by two, five by five in the fields and mountains. Do not take white cloths, do not mass as now, hide, strike suddenly; fight the nomad war steal, snipe and murder singly. Today the war has begun, therefore scatter and advance to victory.[99]

"Glory to the Emperor" the crowd shouted. Abyssinia was at war and Europe faced the fundamental re-alignment of its Great Powers.

# 4

# The Double Policy

*"Suicidal his [Mussolini] policy may very well be; immoral and hateful it most certainly is; but the unpleasant fact remains that, if it is to receive a real check in the near future, only military measures will prove effective—and military measures mean a European war."*

—Sir Eric Drummond[1]

## An Incontestable Fact

Italy's immediate objectives in Abyssinia's northern border province of Tigre were Adowa, site of Italy's bitter defeat at the hands of the Emperor Menelik and Aksum, holy city of the Empire. Perhaps heeding Haile Selassie's warning, the Abyssinians offered little organized resistance. On October 6, Italian troops entered the silent city of Adowa from which most of the inhabitants had fled. They carried with them a small marble memorial to the Italian dead of 1896.[2]

In Rome there were torchlight processions in the streets, a demonstration beneath Mussolini's balcony in the Piazza Venezia, solemn communications from the Duce to the King, and telegrams of thanks to General de Bono. The press was lyrical. It spoke of the dash and enthusiasm of the troops; "Not even Napoleon would have dared to undertake this enterprise," one paper headlined.[3]

This was lavish praise for an unopposed advance. More significant, and wholly praiseworthy was the accomplishment of an army of laborers who followed the troops and built fourteen miles of road in three days.

The next act on the northern front had been as carefully prepared as the first. On October 11, 1935, the Governor of Eastern Tigre surrendered to the Italians, bringing with him 12,000 men. The Dedjasmatch Haile Selassie Gugsa was more than a provincial governor. He was the son-in-law of the Emperor. He was, moreover, a descendant of the Imperial Family of Tigre and a party to the fierce rivalries attending the Abyssinian throne to which he had a pretender's claim.[4] That the outlying provinces were restless and rebellious under Amharic oppression was a key Italian thesis. The Italian press reported the keen desire of Ras Gugsa to go to Italy to pay homage to the King and Mussolini "whose name," it was solemnly reported, "is highly popular in all the uplands of the Tigre and is held in great veneration."[5]

There was little resistance, too, in the holy city of Aksum. An ancient church there was said to hold the Ark of the Covenant brought from Jerusalem by the son of King Solomon and the Queen of Sheba. On October 14, 1935, the Nevraid of Aksum, its political and religious chief, in full regalia and accompanied by cross-bearing priests, appeared at the Italian outposts. Conveyed to General de Bono, he made his obeisance and delivered the keys to the city while the priests, according to Italian accounts, sang hymns in honor of Italy.[6]

In another act of submission the same day, Malek Halim Khan of Jarobi, spokesman for the Mohmand tribesmen, led some 400 tribal headmen before Sir Ralph Griffith, Governor of the Northwest Frontier Province, to sue for peace. Sir Ralph's response was delivered in perfect Pushtu, garnished with native proverbs. He left his listeners in no doubt of the British Government's firm determination to build roads and control outlaws. The outlaws were, of course, tribesmen who did not take kindly to British rule and Sir Ralph made the point that the task of regulating them could be delegated to friendlier tribes.[7]

Ras Gugsa's reward was prompt. On October 16, he was named Governor of Tigre Province, "the lofty proof," General de Bono told the populace, "of his fidelity," adding that they would do well to emulate him. It was a smartly military occasion. Italian and Abyssinian troops faced each other in the square of Adigrat while an Abyssinian band especially trained for the occasion played the Royal March and the Fascist anthem, "Giovinezza."[8]

Italy's next move was directed to world opinion and echoed again Italian claims of Abyssinian savagery and degradation. On October 20, de Bono published a proclamation abolishing slavery in the conquered provinces. A second proclamation promised Italian protection, continuity of civil administration, compensation for losses, and justice. Market duties, tolls, customs, and tribute were abolished and the message was sent forth: "Traders, trade. Cultivators, cultivate."[9]

Amid these glowing claims came a sinister report from the south. The first Abyssinian casualties to reach the Swedish Mission at Jijiga included in their number victims of poison gas bombing. This was the other face of the Italian invasion.[10]

Haile Selassie pinned his chief faith on the League of Nations and especially Britain. This was a realistic appraisal of the military balance. But he was the King of Kings, the Emperor of a nation of warriors, and he and they did not shrink from battle. On October 17, he reviewed 80,000 troops and sent his War Minister, Ras Mulugeta, to the front.

The Imperial Guard carried modern arms, but great numbers of provincial warriors had no more than sticks and rifle belts. Wave after wave of them approached the Emperor and begged for arms and ammunition.

The war drums, mounted on mules, were beaten by scarlet- turbanned drummers. Among the most feared of the warriors were the Gofa. They were daubed in ochre and paid little attention to the Emperor, looking only to their own chiefs.

Ras Mulugeta, preceded by his horn blowers, drew his sword and approached the throne. The Emperor rose and saluted; the chief swore fealty unto death.

The Emperor repeated his earlier advice to use guerilla tactics and shun the traditional mass attack. The four-mile long column marched out to their appointed camping place on the road to the northern front. Pains were taken to keep the Gofa at a safe distance from Addis Ababa.[11]

The war was now an incontestable fact of European diplomacy and a practical rather than a theoretical problem for the League of Nations.

## After Stresa

The orange blossoms that had scented the air of Stresa had faded, the glory of the magnolias and the azaleas had passed into a memory of spring, the flags and bunting, intertwining the colors of Britain, France, and Italy had been furled and stored away. Less than six months later, the statesmen who had gathered at Mussolini's call to meet the threat of German rearmament faced the problem they had avoided at Stresa.

For two countries, policy seemed clear. Mussolini had determined to expand Italian holdings and influence in East Africa. He never really thought, or understood, that any British or French interest there was threatened; he took pains to make clear that he had no such intention. If there were a danger to Britain and France, it was, Mussolini thought, in Europe, north of the Brenner, and it both amazed and frustrated him that they should not see things his way.

For France, the issue was equally clear. The German danger was a constant, Italian friendship and prospective military support valuable, and an African adventure was an offstage noise in the theater where the fate of Europe (which was then thought to be the fate of the world) was being played out.

Responding to the world's disapproval, the onset of economic sanctions, and Mussolini's adept stage management, the Italian people rallied impressively to the regime. In France, there was never any real issue between a policy centered on Africa and one gazing fixedly at French security on her European borders.

In England, such clarity gave way to muddle. For England, two courses were possible, and the British government pursued not one, but both, in the months to come, with varying degrees of emphasis, all the time attempting to persuade the British people that the two were compatible.

One course was consistent support, indeed leadership of the League of Nations, in firm opposition to Italian aggression, as far as need be, to vindicate the League and the Covenant. To the British public, it seemed that the League, representing the hope of the future, the antithesis of the failures of the balance of power, had found its natural champion in the Minister for League of Nations Affairs. Youthful, handsome, superbly tailored, one of those gallant men of the trenches to whom from failing hands the torch had been passed, Anthony Eden was Britain's chief representative at Geneva. He played a leading role in rallying the League into action.

The second course of action was based, like the French consensus, upon a clear and cogent view of the German threat and the practical need to rally, not the world against Italy, but Italy against Germany. If this were to be done, it would be necessary to negotiate a settlement with Italy, which, under the circumstances could hardly be wholly satisfactory to the League let alone Haile Selassie, whose borders marched not with the Third Reich, but with Eritrea and Italian Somaliland, and whose vital interests lay not in the Rhineland or the Sudetenland, but in Tigre and the Ogaden.

The champion of this course of action was the Foreign Secretary, Sir Samuel Hoare. The two champions were ill-matched to play to the British public. Hoare was, by contrast to Eden, distinctly elderly, bald, unprepossessing, lacking in dash and sparkle to the very degree that Eden possessed these appealing qualities. Ruefully, Hoare later told Parliament that "while I expressed my views dully and drably and with little emotion, he [Eden] adds brilliance and charm to everything he says."[12]

In appealing to the British public, Hoare suffered from another disadvantage. The proceedings of the League of Nation were to a large extent open and the world watched them with fascination. Eden played his part on center stage. In contrast, the ways of negotiation and diplomacy were necessarily private, as they must be if they were to succeed. The progress of diplomacy was widely reported, but it lacked the vivid color, the appealing characters, and the incomparable spectacle of good confronting evil that featured the drama at Geneva.

The two policies had fundamentally different inspirations. The policy of negotiation and compromise was based upon a calculation of national interests and the perception, as Sir Eric Drummond had pointed out, that sometimes there are only bad choices.

Surely the argument could be made, and well made, and it was, that a League policy was in the long run based upon interests. But to a large mass of British public opinion, the League policy was rooted in principle, not interests. This is precisely what Hoare had said at Geneva in September, and this was what League supporters consistently argued and orated. They were as indignant at the claim that British policy was motivated by British interests as Mussolini was cynical and disbelieving that it could be founded on anything else.

Here was another measure of Lord Cecil's triumph. At a critical and fortuitous juncture of events, he had orchestrated an overwhelming show of support for the League of Nations. He had done so in an exercise grounded purely on principle, eliminating any reference to a practical case which had produced an unwanted result at Ilford. He had obtained ringing declarations of support for the League of Nations as the sheet anchor of British policy from the Prime Minister and an equally ringing declaration from the Foreign Secretary at Geneva. That policy, Hoare had declared at Geneva, had the overwhelming support of the British people. In choosing, therefore, which policy to follow, the British Government was not free to act on its best judgment. In a way that had never happened before, the Foreign Secretary and his Prime Minister could never distance themselves from their base of an aroused, alert, and fascinated public opinion.

This was truer still because the British Government had, at the time of its choosing in the next year, to go to the polls in a General Election. Public views on foreign policy would not simply be hue and cry above which a strong and resolute government might rise, but instead they would shortly be translated into votes disposing Parliamentary seats and power itself.

All this was clear to Baldwin, Hoare, and their colleagues. The scope which Baldwin gave Hoare reflected Baldwin's preoccupation with political and domestic issues rather than foreign policy. Could the two courses of action be reconciled? The answer, as Hoare saw it, was that the League policy must be tried, because the public demanded it, and because it would bring pressure on Italy. This in turn might influence Italy, which had rejected British offers, the Three-Power Conference, and the Committee of Five proposals, into negotiations, where, in the end a settlement might be reached acceptable to Italy (at less than it wished to take), to Abyssinia (at more than it wished to give), and thus, if the two parties agreed, acceptable to the League, which would emerge with the honor and credit of having halted a war and vindicated, however modestly, its authority and existence.

If this policy were to succeed, it would be necessary to manage skillfully the diplomacy itself, public and private, and, what is more, the public opinion which was indispensable to validating the final outcome.

In pursuing this policy, Hoare had the consistent support of Laval, to whom conciliation and compromise were instinctive and abstract principles an embarrassment. Laval's political problems were as pressing as those of the British Government, but not in the arena of foreign policy. On the Left, labor was infuriated by Laval's deflationary economic policies as exemplified in his decree laws. On the Right, the semi-fascist leagues abhorred the democratic structures of the Third Republic, dreamed of an authoritarian state, and noisily took their case to the streets.

Each government, British and French, had to maintain its base of political support at home, formulate a foreign policy which its electorate would support, find common ground, each with the other, and together bring the antagonists and the League of Nations into harmonious agreement. All this must be done while operating the policy of collective security through practical action of one kind or another by the League of Nations for the first time in its history.

## Britain and France—Opening Moves

No sooner had Italian troops moved across the Abyssinian border than Mussolini sent, via Grandi, a personal message to Sir Samuel Hoare. He hoped Britain would understand the necessity under which Italy had acted. He did not wish to leave the League. He was determined to avoid conflict with Britain. He had not closed the door to negotiations. To avoid a confrontation, he suggested a simultaneous and reciprocal demobilization of British and Italian forces in the Mediterranean. Hoare was depressed; it was hard, he said, to entertain a negotiation exactly coinciding with an act of aggression. He thanked Mussolini for his message but in response to Grandi's continued suggestions of negotiation, Hoare replied that the attack on Adowa had banged the door in Britian's face.[13]

On the next day, Suvich conveyed a similar message to Drummond in Rome. Had the Committee of Five left more room for negotiation, he observed, the outcome might have been different. He dropped a hint to Drummond that Italy might wait on the Adigrat-Adowa line when perhaps Abyssinia would be readier to come to terms, thus facilitating a settlement.[14]

On that day, October 3, Eden, accompanied by the British ambassador, met Laval in Paris. Laval was, as always, creative and ready to negotiate. What, he asked, did Eden think of a proposal which gave Italy a mandate over the non-Amharic regions of Abyssinia and a program of League assistance (as recommended by the Committee of Five) over Abyssinia proper—with Italian participation, of course?

Eden's reply blended caution and principle. It was, at this early stage, possibly premature to put forth proposals—especially those which seem to reward the aggressor. The British people, he said, were determined to fill their obligations under the Covenant. Laval asked what form economic sanctions should take. They should, Eden replied, be substantial, and they should be effective. Was his presence indispensable in Geneva, Laval asked? It was, said Eden, and Laval agreed to attend. Eden then pressed Laval for an answer to the British inquiry about French support in the Mediterranean. Laval read to him the answer which, on the morrow, he would submit to the French Cabinet.[15]

The formal French reply, delivered to Hoare on October 5, showed precision of thought and a calculated effort to turn the British request to long-term French advantage.

The British proposal, France indicated, if given a wide application, would in very opportunely fill in a gap in the system of collective security "to which our two governments are firmly attached." The conditions of assistance were precisely spelled out. The obligation must be reciprocal, binding Britain to assist France as clearly as it bound France to aid Britain. Attacks on either might come not only at sea, but on land, or in the air. The mutual undertakings must cover each such case. Nor must assistance be limited under the Covenant to attacks by states members of the League of Nations. This was important because Germany's withdrawal from the League would become effective that month.

There ought to be, the French note went on, a mutual investigation of the circumstances under which assistance was requested and agreement that the actions taken were strictly necessary to carry out the League Council's ultimate recommendation.

All this was what France had sought, without success, since 1919, and French assistance was offered upon British agreement to all of these points.[16]

Hoare reviewed Laval's Abyssinian proposals and thought they went too far. He continued to think that territorial adjustments (like the Zeila offer) would be simpler, easier and might add a necessary new element to the Committee of Five proposals. He did not think the Emperor would ever accept a mandate over the Amharic core of Abyssinia.[17]

The door, had, perhaps, been banged in Hoare's face, but he was quickly contemplating ways to open it. From Geneva Eden advised against delegating negotiating responsibility to Laval, which might arouse suspicion as to the integrity of British policy. In so stating, Eden passed opinions on Laval that would characterize subsequent British dealings with him. Laval would, Eden thought, jump at the chance to contact Mussolini—and thereby delay the functioning of the League machinery:

> If we had someone less zigzag than Monsieur Laval to deal with and if the suggestion were likely to bridge the gap between the two parties the foregoing objections would not apply so strongly but I have little hope that the suggestion could possibly provide material for a settlement and I think it very likely that Monsieur Laval has already offered more than this to Baron Aloisi in his interpretation of the Committee of Five's report.[18]

While diplomats pondered problems and possibilities in the relative seclusion of their foreign offices, their chanceries, and consulates, Baldwin went public. He used the Conservative conference at Bournemouth to make a declaration of Britain's stand on the evening of October 4. A great nation and a great Empire, he said, had a great role to play. It could not, he said, in a pointed reference, like the Pilgrim fathers, simply go away. Britain would stand by its pledge to the Covenant and to the Kellogg-Briand Pact. Baldwin's reading of the Covenant would please Lord Cecil. There was no issue between Britain and Italy:

> That we should urge our fellow members of the Council to oppose Italy through selfish or mean motives of our own would not only be repugnant to our national self-respect but an abuse of the whole spirit and intention of the Covenant to which his Majesty's Government would lend no countenance.

Here was a ringing endorsement of Hoare's September declaration before the League Assembly that Britain would enforce the Covenant any time, any place, and without reference to the British interests involved. Baldwin "indignantly" rejected the aspersions cast on Britain's fidelity to the Covenant.

If Baldwin ratified Hoare's declaration, he also amplified the caveats attached to it, warning that Britain had no intention of taking isolated action. All members of the League, he declared, must share its responsibilities as well as its benefits. Baldwin appealed to Italy and lauded the work of Eden in Geneva. But he had another and even more serious message that evening.

Air power and German rearmament had radically changed Britain's position and the whole perspective on the Continent. Disarmament was no longer possible. It had resulted in deficiencies in Britain's defenses which it was the Government's responsibility and obligation to repair.

Baldwin reaffirmed an earlier pledge:

> In no conceivable circumstance, as I have said in the House of Commons, must we feel that we are inferior in the air to any nation within striking distance of this country—and in no conceivable circumstances should it be impossible for our people, whatever may happen, to be secured [sic] in the supplies of their food from overseas.

What the conference really wanted to hear was the Prime Minister's election plan. The auspices were propitious. His party was united, he said, and having elicited interest and anticipation, he said no more.[19]

The unity of the Conservative party followed the passage, under Hoare's guidance, of the Government of India Act. Its greatest foes, Churchill at their head, were now reconciled to the Government and it was Churchill who signaled this in paying tribute, at the Conference, to Baldwin. "In the Prime Minister," he said, "we have a statesman who has gathered to himself a greater volume of confidence and good will than any public man I recollect in my long career." The cheers that greeted Churchill were the best evidence of a united party.[20]

## The League Acts

Ever since Wal Wal, the League of Nations had postponed, it had adjourned, it had conciliated, it had recommended, it had hoped against hope for a solution short of war. Now the Committee of Thirteen, appointed to study the issue after the failure of the proposals of the Committee of Five, had to report on October 5 the stark fact that hostilities had broken out between Ethiopia and Italy.[21]

It was now the duty of the League Council, the report stated, to make the appropriate recommendations under Article 15 of the Covenant, and of the League members to do their duty. The Committee's own sole recommendation was that any violations of the Covenant should immediately be brought to an end.[22]

From Geneva, Anthony Eden gauged the issue. In a letter to his constituents in England he wrote:

> The issues of the dispute are such as must profoundly interest every one of us. It is not purely a question of a colonial adventure of no real importance, as has been urged in some quarters. It is not a question of the imperialist demand of one Power or another Power in the territory of Abyssinia or elsewhere. It is not even just a question of peace or war in an outlying part of the world. The real issue is whether or not the League of Nations can prove itself an effective instrument in the dispute, and whether its members are prepared to respect and uphold the Covenant.... The present dispute is a test case.[23]

The League, which proliferated committees, now appointed a Committee of Six to report to the Council not later than October 7. Its conclusion was clear that the Italian Government has resorted to war in disregard of Article 12 of the Covenant of the League of Nations.[24] When the Council met on October 7, 1935 the report was unanimously adopted.

Here was a response at once prompt and clear, far different from the League's uncertain response in Manchuria. The Council of the League of Nations had declared a member state, and a Great Power at that, to be in violation of the Covenant, indeed an "aggressor." The consequences of this finding were spelled out in Article 16 of the Covenant: The Covenant breaker was deemed to have committed an act of war against all members of the League who undertook immediately to sever all trade and financial relations, indeed all intercourse between their nationals and those of the Covenant breaking state.

It was further the duty of the Council, under Article 16, to recommend what military, naval, or air force the members should contribute to the armed forces to be used to protect the Covenant. Recognizing that burdens might fall unequally, Article 16 further provided that member states would mutually support each other to minimize the losses caused by enforcement. Finally, the Covenant breaker could be shorn of League membership by unanimous vote of the Council.[25]

All this was stern stuff, but there was a loophole. The Covenant left it to each member to decide if its obligations under Article 16 had been invoked. Italy stood ready, with its client states, Austria, Hungary, and Albania, to frustrate a unanimous vote when the Assembly met on October 9.

Eduard Benes, Foreign Minister of Czechoslovakia was among the League's most ardent champions and, as President of the Assembly, he devised a procedure which would avoid precisely this procedural obstacle. The action of the Council of October 7, he declared, had been communicated to all member states. They would now have the opportunity to be heard in the Assembly. Each member was invited to express an opinion. Members could assent, vote against the report, or abstain but there would be no recorded vote. As to enforcement, Benes clearly signaled that such issues could be left to a Coordinating Committee to be set up for that purpose.[26]

If Mussolini had looked to France for support this day, it was in vain. Laval spoke for France.

> I have only a short statement to make.
>
> France will meet her obligations. I said this in the Council and I have repeated it in the Assembly. The Covenant is our international law and we can neither infringe it nor allow it to be weakened.
>
> At this moment, when each of us has to take up his responsibility, it is, as you know, with deep feeling that I assume my duty.

> My country will observe the Covenant. Friendship also lays a duty on me. We are not repudiating our faith in the authority of the highest international institution if, simultaneous with the application of its law, we continue to seek a solution by conciliation.
>
> The French Government will devote itself heart and soul to this work of peace, in which, I am sure, no cooperation will be found lacking in this Assembly.[27]

Eden was firm in his declaration that the foreign policy of Britain was based upon its membership in the League of Nations. His eloquence outshone Laval's:

> The maintenance of peace is the first objective of British foreign policy and the constant ideal of the British people. War is a callous anachronism and mankind will never taste of lasting happiness until it has finally renounced its delusive appeal.

The sincerity of the man who had survived the trenches and lost cherished brothers in the war added poignancy to eloquence.

It was the task of the League, Eden said, first to prevent, and then to stop war. The League must declare the steps to be taken to stop war and Britain would faithfully play its full part. Action must be prompt—a war was in progress.

But Eden's conclusion echoed Laval's:

> We must therefore persist in the action which our obligations under the Covenant command us to assume. But, in so doing, we abate not by one jot our desire for an early and peaceful settlement of this dispute in accordance with the principles of the Covenant. In that task we are at all times prepared wholly to cooperate.[28]

When the responses were tallied, for it was not a formal vote, three states had voted against the reports; Italy's clients, Austria, Hungary, and Albania. Switzerland abstained on the grounds of historic neutrality. But the striking and significant fact was that fifty nations had endorsed the reports and the action of the League Council and stood ready to cooperate in enforcing the Covenant.

It remained to translate readiness into action. Over Italian objection, a Coordinating Committee was formed of all those who had accepted the Committee reports. Its members assembled on October 11 and promptly took action which bore the League hallmark—they appointed another smaller committee, henceforth known as the Committee of Eighteen which became, in effect the steering committee of sanctions. Its most conspicuous member was Anthony Eden.

Eden broadcast a progress report from Geneva to the British people. He recounted League accomplishments to date. There had been no dallying. A beginning had been made and "I can give you this assurance, that as we have begun, so shall we go on."[29]

It was Eden who proposed as the first step a lifting of the arms embargo against Abyssinia and the prohibition of the shipment of arms to Italy. The list of arms was precisely the list proclaimed by the United States in its neutrality legislation. "If this committee is to have authority and satisfy public opinion," one delegate said, "it must do something definite and do it today."[30] The Committee promptly adopted the resolution which was ratified by the Coordinating Committee the same afternoon.[31]

Eden again took the lead in the Committee of Eighteen on October 12 with his proposal to embargo all imports from Italy, thereby cutting some 70 percent of Italian export trade.

While these matters were under consideration, the Committee of Eighteen forged ahead with Proposal No. 2, subjecting Italy to financial restrictions. These prohibited loans, bank accommodation, or other credits, public or private, to the Italian government or nationals or financial participation in any Italian enterprise, all aimed squarely at crippling Italian financial capacity to wage war. Both the Committee of Eighteen and the Coordinating Committee approved this resolution on October 14.[32]

Eden's suggestion became Proposal No. 3 adopted by the Committee of Eighteen and the Coordinating Committee on October 19. Goods grown, produced, or manufactured in Italy were barred to import by League members, including goods some part of the processing or manufacture of which had taken place in Italy.[33]

On the same day, the Committee adopted Proposal No. 4, which had been proposed by France and which would lie at the heart of controversies to come. It barred member states from exporting transport animals, rubber, aluminum ores and products and a long list of metals, including iron ore and scrap iron, to Italy.[34]

The Committee recognized that these measures would have uneven effects. Italy's largest trading partners would suffer disproportionately; others would remain largely unaffected. They therefore completed the first phase of their work on October 19 by adopting Proposal No. 5

providing mutual assistance whereby members would open their doors to imports that might have gone to Italy and otherwise help offset the losses of loyal members through direct aid and international marketing arrangements.[35]

Having thus promptly acted, the Coordinating Committee sent its resolutions to all member states inviting their response, especially including notification of any action they proposed to take. The resolution also went to nonmember states including Germany and the United States.

Everyone agreed that the League's achievements had been substantial. If not comprehensive, the measures had cast a wide net; the implications for Italy were serious. When he came to write his annual review for the Royal Institute of International Affairs the next year, Professor Toynbee attributed this success to two factors. The first was a fear of what failure would mean for the League and the Covenant. The second, as he saw it, was the action and personality of Anthony Eden. It was not only his age:

> [I]n Mr. Eden's case, this fortuitous advantage of belonging to the generation which had borne the brunt of the War of 1914–18 was reinforced by his personal energy, his resourcefulness and his belief in the policy which he was endeavouring to put into effect.[36]

A careful review of Proposal No. 4 will indicate why it was the subject of controversy. It restricted the sale to Italy of some, but not all of the vital materials of war. The measure relating to transport animals was not a piece of antiquity; in roadless Abyssinia it was severely practical. So were prohibitions on rubber, which would affect wheeled transport, and on the ores from which the implements of war are made.

Conspicuous by their absence were steel, coal, and oil. Italy was poor in all three which were equally vital to success over more than the short run. These were not omitted by way of oversight. The Spanish delegate had called attention to these omissions on October 19. But the Coordinating Committee was determined to make sanctions effective. It recognized that there were states outside the League which could supply coal, oil and steel in large quantities, and that among these states were Germany and the United States. Proposal No. 4 was designed to cover those items which the League members essentially controlled while the League sought to work out measures of coordination with non-League members to draw its net tighter around Italy.

There was another reason. In all this the League was breaking new ground; what the impact of sanctions would be was not easy to foretell.

It was thought that sanctions should be applied gradually. The first might produce the desired effect without expanding the war or provoking untoward responses; if they failed, more biting sanctions could be applied. All this was against the background of a delay in the forward movement of Italian troops after the initial advance into Abyssinia.[37] The Times could not know of Mussolini's order to de Bono to consolidate and to "await events on the international plane." But it was generally thought that the campaign would be long and difficult, and the longer it was, the more time there would be for sanctions to tell.

The Coordinating Committee now adjourned to await the replies of the member states. When it met on November 2, the question of adding coal, steel and oil to the forbidden list promptly resurfaced.

## Anglo-Saxon Attitudes

To the meteor drama at Geneva, the British people responded with their usual variety of opinions, their accustomed quirkiness, but often with unaccustomed passion. There were those, always few in number, who genuinely believed in Italy's civilizing mission or drew parallels between imperial policies, British and Italian.[38] Those whose focus was Britain's own Empire argued eloquently that Britain had no business to suppress war wherever it broke out excepting and only excepting the defense of vital British interests.[39] The great majority took another view.

The Archbishop of Canterbury traversed hallowed ground:

> However much the League may try to vindicate the law of reason and justice, there is plainly need in the world of some force that is stronger even than these bonds and covenants. It must be a spiritual force. Mere material force, which pray God we may not be obliged to use, can of itself never establish peace...until men and nations guide themselves by the principles of Christ there will be no foundation and therefore no security for peace.[40]

In the Britain of 1935 this was still a powerful message.

Arthur Greenwood spoke for Labour in deploring Mussolini and Italian aggression. It was the League's plain duty to restrain the lawbreaker. If moral means failed, then financial and economic sanctions would succeed. Like all Labour men, who voted in principle against the defense budgets year after year, he had to face the issue of the use of force. The Abyssinian brawl would have to be ended by the international policemen, the League of Nations.

Yet he was curiously optimistic:

> I cannot logically, much as I hate the use of force, resist the conclusion that if neither moral nor material pressure, nor the threat of war succeeds, then the criminal must be arrested. But, in my opinion, by the time that point is reached, Mussolini will have given himself up to the police.[41]

As was to be expected, George Lansbury stood his ground, and this was why he had been superseded as leader of the Labour party. At the Church Congress on October 10 he called upon the churches to demand of the British Government that it give up its imperial conquests, rule only by the consent of the governed, disarm and invite the world to follow the British example—that is to say, to obey the rule of love and service and not of force.[42]

Dick Sheppard heartily agreed. War and Christianity were, he said, totally incompatible and he could find no distinction between a righteous war and a wicked war.[43]

That veteran churchman, Lord Cecil, brought to the same platform a more measured view. He spoke for collective security, admitting its imperfections. Like Arthur Greenwood, Lord Cecil was hopeful and his prognosis paralleled the division between questions 5a and 5b of the Peace Ballot.

Nobody proposed, he said, to land forces in Italy or engage Italy in Eritrea. It was only proposed to cut communications, and even in the last resort, some sort of blockade:

> No doubt this would be exceedingly disagreeable to the Italians, but it need not lead to any serious fighting unless they should finally decide to go to war with those who were enforcing these measures.[44]

Clement Attlee, the new leader of the Labour party, agreed that if the members of the League "will honestly and whole-heartedly apply economic and financial sanctions, this war can be brought to an end."

Yet he was grimly political. The whole crisis resulted from the Government's mishandling of affairs; and he warned of an election call:

> There may well be an attempt to rush the nation into agreeing to a huge expenditure on armaments. We in the Labour movement do not believe that peace can be secured by piling up great armaments.[45]

To this Attlee added a few days later:

> I hope that the unemployed will remember that their plight is only to be

> seen to after the armaments makers have gotten their full share of the nation's money.[46]

Bernard Shaw found the controversy irresistible. Italy was, he said, building roads through uncivilized country and the Abyssinians were trying to kill the road builders. In a dispute between the road builders and the killers, he was clearly on the side of the former. A vote for sanctions, he said, was a vote for a combined attack by Britain and France on Italy. He offered a "far more sensible and humane" alternative, and this was "to drop the Geneva Council down the crater of Vesuvius."[47]

Mr. Shaw ill reckoned the mettle of the *Times'* correspondents. Mr. D.W. Scott-Moncrieff replied:

> Poor Mussolini by such cares perplexed,
> Banned by the League, with all its sanctions vexed,
> Must now endure the last, the heaviest straw,
> The patronage of Mr. Bernard Shaw.[48]

The majority opinion was not in doubt. Conditioned by the Peace Ballot, buoyed by the declarations of the Prime Minister in response to it, and by the forthright statements of Sir Samuel Hoare at Geneva, there was a swelling tide of support for the League. The League of Nations Union led the way. In its skillful manner, it announced a national demonstration of support for the League to be held at the Albert Hall on October 31. The Archbishop of Canterbury would be in the chair and the speakers would cover the British political spectrum including as they did Sir Austen Chamberlain, Lady Violet Bonham Carter, Herbert Morrison, and of course, its guiding spirit, Lord Cecil.[49]

It was not only Bernard Shaw who moved the *Times'* readers to poetry. Whatever may be said from the literary point of view, there can be little doubt that Mr. J.G. Frazer spoke for a vast majority of British people when he wrote in the *Times* of October 17, 1935:

> Well done, Eden and Hoare! Through you the
> voice
> Of England spoke in trumpet tones that rang
> To the world's end, not in blast of war,
> But in a nobler cause, the cause of peace and
> brotherhood of man.
> The nations heard and answered to the call.
> They did not quail.

Before the Italian tyrant's brandished sword
Now dripping gouts of blood. The Scripture
says
Blest are the peacemakers; surely we say
Blest is England, blest the nations met
In solemn conclave by Geneva's shore.[50]

Mr. Frazer's biblical references echoed Lord Cecil's deeply held belief that the Covenant and the League were "in the direct line of Christian progress." The connection between international law and morality was always clear in his mind. No more picturesque and compelling case could arise for the application of moral judgment to an international crisis than the spectacle of a Christian emperor of Biblical antecedents and his barefoot troops, armed with spears and ancient muskets, defending their homeland and justice against the most modern and sinister engines of death commanded by the Fascist dictator in the service of aggression.

To this was added a stirring sight. In majestic force, the Royal Navy was moving on its lawful occasions through the Mediterranean which the Duce had the temerity to call Mare Nostrum. It was manned by the bulldog breed, the British tar, of whom, referring to the crew of HMS Pinafore, W.S. Gilbert had written: "His energetic fist should be ready to resist a dictatorial word."

Indeed, when Professor Toynbee, a professional historian of encyclopedic scope and long experience, wrote a special volume dedicated to Italy and Abyssinia, his opening lines were:

> The tragic episode of international history which is recorded in this volume is a tale of sin and nemesis.[51]

The use of poison gas by Italy was, he recorded, "a sin in the sight of God in which other states besides Italy were implicated"—both those who possessed and those who sold the oil which fueled the bombers.[52] Toynbee continued:

> In this light, the criminal act of military aggression against a primitive African community, which was being executed by Italian hands, presents itself, on a larger view, as the common crime of Western Christendom.[53]

The more widely such views were held, and the more deeply they were felt, the more they would affect the considerations and actions of those British statesmen charged with determining where the ultimate perils lay and how to meet them. Of this they were keenly aware. Hoare had written to Clerk, the Ambassador in Paris that:

> The League of Nations was, in fact, regarded by all right-minded people in this country in the light of a principle of international conduct, almost perhaps in the light of new half-religion.[54]

And shortly thereafter, the British Minister in Paris told Flandin that, "there seemed to be no appreciation in France of the intense, almost religious, feeling which inspired England's support of the League of Nations at the present moment."[55] Such feelings could only limit the scope within which the British government must steer its course.

## The Other Course

As the move to sanctions gathered momentum, and Italy responded angrily, the British Government continually feared some incident between British and Italian forces in the Mediterranean the ultimate results of which would be incalculable. Its members remembered 1914 and the train of events that had fired tragic and unintended consequences.

They were equally concerned to have at all times the effective support of French naval and military forces and facilities, both to avert the danger and, should it occur, master it.

Hoare had told Laval in September that his chief preoccupation was German rearmament, his chief fear pushing Italy into Germany's welcoming arms. It was this concern that motivated, beneath the surface of the solemn conclave by Geneva's shore, the steady thrust of British policy toward a settlement of the whole grievous issue that would somehow satisfy all of the parties.

As to the first concern, Grandi had already suggested to Hoare on October 4 some kind of a mutual demobilization or détente in the Mediterranean. Hoare had not replied, but Mussolini took up the same theme in an interview with *Paris Soir* on October 6. He would consider a reduction of Italian forces in Libya if Britain would reduce her Mediterranean fleet. A conflict between Britain and Italy was, he said, "absolutely inconceivable." Italy wished to injure no British interest and threatened no British territory: "I am ready at any moment to prove what I say by giving unexceptionable guarantees of the peacefulness and even cordiality of our attitude."[56]

The British Cabinet, meeting on October 9, received this gesture coldly. Britain would not reduce her naval forces but might cancel reinforcements to Egypt. As to Italian settlement overtures, the Cabinet advised the Foreign Secretary to treat them coolly and then only on the basis of detailed proposals.[57]

Throughout October and November diplomatic exchanges on the subject of mutual reduction of forces waxed and waned and in the end produced no concrete result.

With its French ally, Britain had better success, but not without painful difficulties. The French public did not share the moral fervor that swept over Britain and, as usual, continued to believe firmly that the menace was Germany against whom Italy, far from being a threat, was a valuable ally. These attitudes were colorfully expressed in the French press and there were those who were sure that the veteran journalist, Mussolini, and his ample funds lay behind the most scurrilous attacks on Britain. To moral certainty therefore, there was added in British minds, wounded pride. Clerk presented this forcibly to Laval on October 12. Laval, he said, had worked loyally with Eden. Such attacks could have drastic impacts on Franco-British friendship.

Laval liked direct methods and he liked the telephone. In Clerk's presence, he phoned the editor or chief editorialists of five papers, the great men of the Paris press. To all of them, Clerk reported, Laval vehemently said that they were leading France to war and losing British friendship and he extracted assurances from them that they would mend their ways.[58]

The British message was carried to France on October 15 in an interview which Austen Chamberlain gave to *Paris Soir*. Not selfish interests, but the principles of the League of Nations were at stake, he said. What Britain contributed to repel Italian aggression against Abyssinia she would one day also contribute if Germany attacked France. But he warned,

> If today you allow your policy to be dictated by your friendship with Italy, if you do not go to the end with us in the application of sanctions, do not count too much upon us if you find yourselves in conflict with Germany.[59]

Meanwhile, the British Cabinet worried about the message it had received from France on October 5. Like all French documents, the French reply had been drafted with precision. The aid which France would give, after consultation, would be proportional to measures taken by a state in fulfillment of its obligations under the Covenant **or** Locarno. Britain's concern was the support of its fleet in the Mediterranean. Yet it did not escape French attention that the fleet had been strongly reinforced without any notice to France; nor had the League of Nations ever taken any official action to invite the British reinforcement or indeed to ratify it.

There were those in France who said loudly exactly what Mussolini believed: that the fleet was there to protect purely British interests.

The French had asked for specific assurances in September. Hoare had responded with vague generalities. Now Hoare wanted precision. He directed Clerk to press the matter with Laval.[60]

When Clerk saw Laval on October 15, Laval affirmed the principle of mutual support under the Covenant. But he made the reservation Clerk had anticipated. The attack which brought the Covenant in play had to arise from the application of Article 16[61] (rather, say, than from the voluntary presence of the Royal Navy in the Mediterranean).

This was not pleasant news to the British Cabinet when it met on October 16. The French reservation was, it thought unjustified, and left a deplorable impression. Hoare was directed to press Laval for explicit assurances to be followed immediately by talks between British and French naval staffs. Significantly, the Cabinet judged it wise to apply caution in the exercise of sanctions till unequivocal French support was assured.[62]

Hoare once more directed Clerk to resolve the matter with Laval. There was a carrot: Britain would, with unqualified French support, enter into an agreement with Italy for mutual reduction of forces in the Mediterranean. There was a stick: if France persisted in qualifying her obligations under the Covenant, then Britain might find contingencies under Locarno rendering the Treaty ineffective—and Locarno was to France what it had always been, the best available replacement for the failed obligations of Britain and the United States under the aborted Treaty of Mutual Assistance.[63]

Clerk delivered the message forcibly, and reported that "Laval took his head-washing extraordinarily well." It was, Laval said, only a lawyer's question. The British thought, he said, that if it were made clear at Geneva that Britain and France contemplated no military sanctions, no blockade, no closure of Suez, Mussolini would snap his fingers at them. Quite the contrary, Laval thought that, the sword of Damocles removed, Mussolini would be less likely to go to extremes, more likely to listen to reason.

Laval now suggested that if he could announce to the country what he had agreed with Hoare in September—no military sanctions—France would calm down and loyally support the League in financial and economic sanctions.

In any event, he said, the important issue of the British request must be reviewed by his Cabinet colleagues before he could reply, hopefully in an affirmative sense.[64]

In this exchange, Laval was less than straightforward. With respect to military sanctions, he had let this particular cat out of the bag the week before. In a radio broadcast at Clermont-Ferrand he assured his listeners:

> To those who fear military sanctions, I wish to say that in my conversations with the British Ministers there has never been any question of them.

To this he added that any British-French action must be collective within the framework of the League and that Eden and he had the same concern, indeed "the same will to find a friendly settlement of the conflict in conformity with the Covenant."[65]

The French reply which came on October 18, pledged unlimited solidarity of action by France under Article 16.

The note went on to review the Hoare-Laval conversations and understandings of September 9 and 10 and particularly the agreement to exclude military sanctions, blockade, or the closure of the Suez Canal. The French Government would be glad to make these arranagements public which would dispel French and Italian fears, but could detect no similar desire on Britain's part. It approved British suggestions to reduce its fleet in a joint action with Italy and spoke of a desire for the closest collaboration with Britain.[66]

Vansittart thought that the French reply was as satisfactory as could be expected, indeed "quite satisfactory," adding:

> We have had to get it out of the French with forceps and biceps; and if we hadn't the latter we shouldn't have got it at all. But we got it, and we mustn't wonder—or mind—if the client burbles a bit.[67]

Hoare more succinctly told the Cabinet on October 23 that he was clear that the answer was satisfactory.[68] So it happened again, as it had and would again, that under British pressure France responded to Britain's demands and Britain's needs. On October 30, Admiral

Chatfield, Chief of the British Naval Staff met French Admiral Decoux in London. They agreed that in case of war France would make its naval ports and facilities on both sides of the Mediterranean available to the Royal Navy and that in principle France would be responsible for the Western, and Britain for the Eastern Mediterranean. But the French forces, naval and military, were in the low state of readiness, and France would have to postpone any declaration of war until these forces had been brought up to operational levels, which would be a matter of weeks.

Once more the British concluded that such arrangements were as good as could be expected, given the difficult political situation in France.[69]

## Mussolini Makes an Offer

Laval had not been the first to call attention to the possibilities of settlement. There had been Latin American proposals which faded as promptly as they were launched. More serious, as early as October 8, the Pope called the French Ambassador to the Holy See, Charles-Roux, and told him that his own envoy had asked Mussolini for his terms. They were, as related directly by the Pope:

1. Cession of border territories to Italy, taking geography into account.
2. An Italian mandate over non-Amharic territory.
3. An international mandate over the rest of Abyssinia, with Italian predominance.
4. Disarmament of Abyssinian forces.

The Pope recognized that the terms were stiff, but they could always be improved at the negotiating table. He conveyed a gloomy report of his emissary's talks with Mussolini. Mussolini feared war between Italy and Britain. In that case it would spread rapidly in Europe and Germany would celebrate Christmas in Vienna and swell itself with the three million Germans in Czechoslovakia. "Tell M. Pierre Laval," Charles-Roux reported the Pope as saying, "that after Providence, my only hopes are with him."[70]

Laval thanked the Pope, observing at the same time that it was easier to prevent a war than to stop one; the same terms would have been more useful in August or September. He was pessimistic that such terms would appeal today.[71]

But Laval persisted. He told Clerk on October 15 that before deciding the French response to sanctions, he wished to exhaust every possibility of settlement. He had therefore asked the Italian Ambassador to ask Mussolini urgently to state his terms; a proper compromise, he was convinced, would be a decisive success for the League.[72]

The promptness of the Italian response showed how serious Mussolini was. The next day, October 16, the Vatican conveyed to Charles-Roux terms which represented meaningful improvements over the earlier offer.[73]

On the same day, Mussolini received Chambrun and made his offer personally. He referred to it, not as proposals, but as a solution. Such speed indicated that the Italian offer had been considered and prepared well before Laval's message of the day before.

Mussolini offered international assistance for Abyssinia as the Committee of Five had proposed, including Italian participation under the Treaties of 1906 and 1925. The assistance in the non-Amharic territories annexed by Abyssinia in the past fifty years would be in the form of a mandate, but would expressly forbid the raising by Italy of native armies (which Britain and France might fear). Those territories which Italy had newly conquered without fighting would remain under direct Italian control in accordance with the will of the people. The borders of Somaliland would be delimited. If Abyssinia, which had indirect access to the sea through the French port of Djibuti and the British port of Zeila, so desired, Italy would offer the use of its port at Assab.

The sovereignty of the Emperor and the integrity of his Empire would, with the exception of Adowa, in this manner be safeguarded. The question of Abyssinian armament could be reexamined at Geneva. Mussolini told Chambrun,

> You can at this price avoid a war to which the automatic progression of sanctions will fatally lead and of which the consequences will be a British fleet without counterbalance in the seas of Europe and a Reich of 85 million inhabitants.

He painted a chilling picture. Austria trembled, Mussolini went on, and the Little Entente could not resist the attraction of Germany, whose power would soon extend to the Bosphorus.

The terms, Chambrun observed, were all the more interesting in that they contained ameliorations at a time of Italian military success, when important Abyssinian chiefs had given their allegiance to Italy, and the Italian nation, under foreign threat, had rallied to its leader. To refuse might be to plunge Italy into the policy of desperation and despair.[74]

This was a thoughtful proposal containing much of substance. It built on the work of the Committee of Five in calling for international assistance. In the non-Amharic provinces, this would take the form of an Italian mandate. But the mandatory authority flowed from the Covenant and from the League itself, to which the mandatory power was responsible. These arrangements, then, meant an extension of the power and authority of the League. There were safeguards aimed directly at Britain and France. Italy would not raise native troops in territory under its control which might threaten British or French interests in Africa or elsewhere.

Territory passing under direct Italian control would be the minimum gained at this earliest stage of the war. The limitation of Abyssinian arms would be a matter of further discussion. Borders, which had caused perennial problems, would be defined. The offer of an Abyssinian outlet to the sea was both real and responsive to Britain's Zeila offer.

One could be cynical about Mussolini's claim that the Emperor's sovereignty would be preserved together with a large degree of territorial integrity. That could be better calculated in the settlement negotiations.

This was, above all, a basis for negotiation, enhanced by movement forward from previous positions. Mussolini understood and as eloquently pleaded the German danger as he had at Stresa and before.

To avert the possibilities of a clash, to preserve the Stresa front and the authority of the League, it was neither underhanded nor cynical for Hoare and Laval to weigh and pursue this interesting proposal. Mussolini had not thrown down the gauntlet, he had not presented nonnegotiable demands. Indeed, officials at the Italian Foreign Office thought he should have raised his demands to improve his bargaining position.[75] All this seemed to Vansittart a distinct step forward which ought to be encouraged.[76]

Prudent men, therefore, might well ask, starting from this point, what real possibility of an honorable settlement lay within this proposal.

Even before responding to this offer, Hoare tried to ameliorate relations with Italy. He had instructed Drummond to call on Mussolini and to emphasize the total absence of any British hostility. Britain would take no action not required by its League obligations or beyond what was agreed by the League and the idea of a war between the two nations was absurdly untrue.[77]

When Drummond called on Mussolini on October 18, they did not discuss Mussolini's proposal to Chambrun of the day before. But

Drummond forcefully delivered Hoare's message and received Mussolini's thanks.

Mussolini was frank. He had expected moral and financial sanctions. Economic sanctions, limited imports from and exports to Italy, were a serious matter, never before applied, and, in the Duce's opinion, scarcely merited. They could result in a blockade which would mean war. Drummond hastened to say what Laval had said at Clermont-Ferrand—"no one had spoken of blockade or military sanctions." Mussolini told Drummond that sanctions would make a settlement more difficult; no nation could negotiate under such pressure.

They discussed mutual demobilization. Drummond reminded Mussolini of the critical importance of British public opinion. The conversation, Drummond reported, had been friendly but when Mussolini discussed a state of siege and negotiating under duress "his eyes then popped, and his mouth opened wide like a goldfish."[78]

Two days later, Drummond met Aloisi at a private tea party, unknown to the Italian Foreign Ministry. They discussed Mussolini's offer, a Chilean-Argentinean peace proposal, and mutual reduction of forces in the Mediterranean.

Aloisi urged the Italian terms as highly conciliatory, based upon the work of the Committee of Five, and an appropriate basis of discussion. What did the Assab proposal mean, Drummond asked? Aloisi answered that with an overall agreement in principle, a solution would be found.

Would the Emperor accept, Drummond asked? He would, Aloisi observed, remain sovereign over most of his territories if he accepted; he would lose his throne if he did not. If Britain and France recommended the plan, Aloisi estimated a 90 percent chance of acceptance which Drummond thought optimistic.[79]

But it seemed worth trying. Accordingly, on October 23, Hoare and Vansittart decided to send Maurice Peterson, the Foreign Office expert on Abyssinia, to Paris the same day to assist Clerk in discussing the Italian proposals with the French. There was attached a warning from Hoare to the French: first, the sanctions process would not be held up pending these discussions and, second, if matters did not proceed quickly, further hostilities would complicate matters immeasurably.[80]

Whether Laval had induced Mussolini's offer, whether the initiative lay with Mussolini, and the Vatican offer had been its deliberate forerunner, it is clear that Laval saw in the negotiation the only constructive way out of an incredibly dangerous and complicated situation and did everything in his power to further the process. Hoare saw negotiation as wholly consistent with his declarations of support of the Covenant and of the League and the public pronouncements by which he continued to inform his Government, Parliament, and the British public.

He made this clear at a Cabinet meeting on October 23. The questions of military détente with Italy and a possible settlement before sanctions came into effect were closely related. Detente would advance the prospects of settlement. But he warned that it was important to make clear from the start that any settlement must be within the framework of the League of Nations. The Cabinet, informed of Peterson's mission, agreed.[81]

## An Appeal to the Nation

In the midst of this international crisis, the Prime Minister decided to call a General Election. Baldwin had proclaimed to Lord Cecil, in response to the Peace Ballot, that the League of Nations was the sheet anchor of British foreign policy. In the current crisis there was an outpouring of support for the League and the Covenant. Baldwin had told the nation it must rearm, it must not be inferior to any air power in striking distance. He now added that arms were vital to enforce the Covenant.

To his Labour and Liberal opposition, to whom the League was an article of faith, Baldwin thus presented a Government in power confidently executing the policy to which the Opposition could only give lip service. Moreover, he could charge that the Opposition had denied the arms that would make the policy effective. This was a circle which the Opposition could find no way to square.

Baldwin depicted for his Worcestershire constituents, on October 19, the horrors of war, and elaborated on the unfortunate failure of the League of Nations to become universal. But the duty to prevent war, and to put the League to the test remained. If sanctions were required under the Covenant, Britain would play its part, but never in any isolated action. This was no British-Italian conflict; it was no British object to overthrow Fascism, or to interfere in the internal affairs of others. War was the last thing in the Government's mind, Baldwin said, making this clear:

> We are always ready to avail ourselves of any opportunity that may present itself for conciliation.[82]

As was the British custom, the campaign would be brief and the election was set for November 14, 1935. The Government's election program led off with an unconditional statement of its foreign policy stand.

> The League of Nations will remain, as heretofore, the keystone of British foreign policy.

In the specific case of Abyssinia:

> We shall take no action in isolation, but we shall be prepared faithfully to take our part in any collective action decided upon by the League and its members. We shall endeavour to further any discussions which may offer the hope of a justice and fair settlement, provided that it is within the framework of the League and acceptable to the three parties to the dispute—Italy, Abyssinia, and the League itself.

As to arms:

> A Commonwealth which holds the position in the world occupied by the United Kingdom and its partners in the British Empire must always take an influential part in League discussions. But our influence can be fully exerted only if we are recognized to be strong enough to fulfill any obligations which, jointly with others, we may undertake.
>
> The fact is that the actual condition of our defense forces is not satisfactory."

There was, however, this limitation:

> The defense programme will be strictly confined to what is required to make the country and the Empire safe and to fulfil our obligations towards the League.[83]

The message which the National Government conveyed to the electorate was more graphic, more succinct, and eerily reminiscent of the Peace Ballot, its posters read:

> GRIP THE KEY TO PEACE

The key was formed by the words LEAGUE OF NATIONS.[84]

The astuteness of Baldwin's policy was revealed in the opening words of the Liberal manifesto:

> A General Election is being held at a moment of acute international crisis. After long delay the Government have lately been taking definite action at Geneva. All parties support that action. An election is therefore unnecessary.

What need was there, then, to replace the Government? The Government manifesto had made an obligatory reference to disarmament. The Liberal document declared in sterner tones:

> Armaments, on however vast a scale, will not bring security or stop war. The national defense must be kept efficient, and large enough for the needs of the times, but a colossal panic expenditure upon arms is not the road to peace.

Insisting upon strict control of the manufacture of arms and the elimination of the profit motive, the manifesto concluded:

> Through strengthening the League of Nations, and through international disarmament, and there alone, the true path to security lies.[85]

The drafters of the manifesto had, perhaps, failed to notice that three days before its publication, on October 21, 1935, the German withdrawal from the League of Nations had become final. How the League could effectively restrain Germany, no longer a member, or indeed how Germany could be induced to disarm, were questions upon which the Liberal manifesto was singularly unhelpful.

The Labour manifesto led off with domestic issues—unemployment, housing, taxes. There was a bitterness which contrasted with Liberal idealism. Charging the Government with the collapse of the Disarmament Conference and failing to stop the Japanese in Manchuria and Mussolini in Africa, it called the Government "a danger to the peace of the world and to the security of the country."

Labour offered a sweeping program to nationalize not only banking, coal, transport, electricity, iron, steel, and cotton, but also the land itself. In foreign policy it called for speedy League action to halt the war in Africa, to be followed immediately by negotiations for all-round disarmament. Labour would maintain "such defense forces as are necessary and consistent with our membership of the League." The defense of Britain or its interests was not mentioned. Labour abhorrence of arms required the immediately following clause:

> [T]he best defense is not huge competitive national armaments, but the organization of collective security against any aggressor, and the agreed reduction of national armament everywhere.

To this end, Labour proposed complete abolition of air forces, international control of civil aviation, an international air police force, all-round reduction in arms, and the abolition of the private manufacture and trade in arms. Here were reverberations of the questions of the Peace Ballot.[86]

Perhaps the best tribute to Baldwin's political acumen was paid by Lloyd George. It was, he said, "a shabby election." The country stood behind the Government in upholding the League. More than that, Labour had risked a split and had lost a cherished leader. Abyssinia would not be saved, but the Government might. "It is the meanest electoral trick," he said, "ever played by an Administration."[87]

Sir Samuel Hoare was sufficiently recovered from the illness which had weakened him through the summer and fall to lead the last debate of the Parliamentary session.

He laid out his policy which had not changed. He spoke of his "double intention to carry out the Covenant on the one hand, and, on the other, to explore every permissible line of settlement and conciliation."

This was, he thought not only the policy of the party, he said, but of the House and the "policy also of a great majority of men and women in this country as a whole." He was sensitive to the charge that Britain had lulled Italy into believing that Britain would acquiesce in Italian plans. The Italian approach of January had required the serious study given to it; at Stresa, the whole focus had rightly been on German rearmament and treaty revocation, while the Abyssinian issue was under conciliation.

Hoare had stated his problem explicitly. His Government depended on public opinion, beyond which neither he nor the League could go. The British public had been thoroughly instructed in a complex of issues revolving around the League, the Covenant, armaments, and the use of economic and military sanctions in a great, colorful national experience. The Peace Ballot had presented issues of principle which its proponents did not hesitate to cloak in moral grandeur. To national interest, which was deliberately omitted, attached the odium of selfishness, cynicism, the balance of power, and the holocaust of 1914–1918.

But Hoare said no thought of Imperial interest had entered into his calculations. Only by denying direct interest could Hoare now rally the British people to the support of the Covenant. They heard, they remembered, and they agreed.

Having responded to the charge of having done too little, Hoare now replied to those who thought Britain had done too much. He paid tribute to the effectiveness and the appeal of Anthony Eden who had placed

Britain in the spotlight. But it was not true that only Britain had acted and that the whole responsibility for the League's action so far lay with it. He again turned to a keynote theme.

The League had accomplished a great deal, the agreement of fifty nations on a principle and a course of action. What was notable was not how little, but how much had been accomplished. With those who said economic pressure would be ineffective and would lead to war, he disagreed. They could work, but the risks and losses must be borne by all. He paid tribute to the French response to the request for mutual support. It was "completely satisfactory."

He met the issue of military sanctions head on:

> [F]rom the beginning of the present deliberations at Geneva until now there has been no discussion of military sanctions, and no such measures, therefore, have formed any part of our policy.

The precondition of military sanctions—collective agreement at Geneva—simply did not exist; and it was only a collective action in which Britain would participate.

> I emphasize the word "collective" as it is the essence and the soul of the League. Only by this essence can the League live—not by ringing bells or blowing whistles for policemen from the outside. We are not prepared, and do not intend to act alone.

The League, then, might not blow its whistle and as a spectator watched with rapt attention while the Royal Navy barred the Duce's path to empire.

Hoare called specific attention to Laval's speech at Clermont-Ferrand and emphasized once more that "we have never even proposed to the French government the consideration of any military measures." This was met with cheers.

The League must press forward under the Covenant. But at the same time,

> not a day or week shall pass without the members of the League showing their readiness to find an honourable settlement of this unhappy controversy. I take this opportunity of emphasizing this need to search for some means of settlement within the framework of the League.

This theme he repeated, not twice, but thrice, in closing his address.[88]

Attlee echoed Labour's manifesto. The Government had failed to deter Japan and Italy. What the occasion called for were great steps towards disarmament, not rearmament, and he gathered that the campaign was to be about the piling up of armaments. He denied Labour were unilateral disarmers, but they were hardly persuaded that the way to safety lay in the piling up of armaments. Indeed, "in these days, there was no such thing as a national defense."

That sanctions should not succeed would be intolerable, Sir Herbert Samuel said. Was he prepared, Admiral Taylor asked, to use force of arms to enforce them? Samuel's answer was only a hope they would not be needed. Clarity came from Lansbury, who disagreed profoundly with all sanctions.[89]

When Baldwin spoke the next day, he emphatically endorsed both Hoare's policy at Geneva and the search for a settlement fair to Italy, Abyssinia and the League. His own theme was rearmament, not directed, to be sure, against a particular country but "a strengthening of our defensive Services within the framework of the League for the sake of international peace, not for selfish ends."

There were risks for peace. He would pursue peace, adding,

> I will not be responsible for the conduct of any Government in this country at the present time if I am not given power to remedy the deficiencies which have occurred in our defensive Services since the war. I will leave it to those who think the risks are worth taking and who must remember that the Government are responsible for the safety of every man, woman, and child.[90]

The spotlight now turned on Eden. He gave a clear account of the origins and development of the crisis. He painted Britain's loyal participation in the action of the League in glowing terms. It was, after all, "a vital test of the efficiency of the League."

> For the first time, I believe, in the history of the world an attempt is being made to operate an international system based not merely upon power, but upon certain fixed principles of equity. This is an adventure in which we may all be proud to play our part [Loud and prolonged cheers].

To which he added:

> For the first time in my lifetime, England has taken a lead in a great moral cause.

He made two other points. Britain must be adequately armed to play its role. And the Government would always be ready to cooperate in a peaceful settlement subject to these two indispensable conditions—the consent of three parties, Abyssinia, Italy and the League, under terms consistent with the Covenant.[91]

Perhaps these points made less impression, gained less attention, than the clarion call to the adventure of a great moral cause. They were not, in any event, greeted with loud and prolonged cheers.

The Government had put its two courses of action clearly before Parliament and before the nation. It had, at the same time, appealed to a moral standard, an ethical basis of policy which found a welcoming public, but which might not garner equal support for both courses of action.

In the continuing debate on October 24, Churchill put the issue in proportion. He emphasized the danger of German rearmament, "the dominant factor which dwarfed all others" compared to which the war in Abyssinia was a small matter. For years Britain had urged France to make friends with Italy; it was a difficult thing to ask her now to choose between Italy and the League.

Of course he backed the Covenant. How far would he go in support of it? The response was Churchillian: "All the way, with the whole lot."[92]

In the House of Lords, Lord Cecil led support for the League. He was grateful for Hoare's stand. He thought that Hoare's speech had been greeted everywhere as "a new departure...showing that Britain was again taking her rightful place in the leadership of the world."[93]

Lord Cecil did not confine himself to speeches in the House of Lords. The League of Nations Union was founded on his belief in the ultimate authority of public opinion and for fifteen years he had honed and polished its skills in lobbying, publicity, and persuasion. Here was the ultimate appeal to the nation and the LNU stood eagerly ready to influence the outcome.

It suggested a set of questions to be propounded to each Parliamentary candidate, with the answers to be printed in the local papers. Leading the list was this inquiry:

> Will you support the use of the whole collective force of the League to put an end to the Italian aggression in Abyssinia?

The questions that followed were echoes of the Peace Ballot: Did the candidate favor an all-round reduction of armaments by international agreement, the abolition of national air forces, the elimination of private profit, and the removal of the "evil effects" of the private manufacture and sale of arms?[94]

The LNU and the Peace Ballot had generated immense support for the League and the Covenant. The LNU's energetic and practical lobbyists now exerted their enthusiasm, skill, and persistence in lobbying the prospective members of the new Parliament, fully understanding the power of public exposure. Here was a heaven-sent opportunity to convert the propositions of the Peace Ballot into action when the newly elected members should meet at Westminster.

Meanwhile, members of the LNU did not let up on their accustomed activities. "Mayfair is taking an interest in the League of Nations," *Headway* reported in November. "This is partly due to the energy of the Chairman of the Westminster Branch, the Dowager Hon. Lady Barlow and partly due to the international situation."

Lord Listowel spoke on October 9 at an evening reception at the Lyceum Club where Lady Barlow conducted a lively discussion of sanctions. And on October 11, Dr. Margaret Grant gave an evening party at St. James Court so successful that there were not enough chairs for her League study group.[95]

Laval, too, was heavily engaged in political battles. He continued to rule by decree. He judged the situation so precarious that in the October election for the Senate, he ran for two seats, one in Paris and one in the country. The Popular Front was coalescing, a union among not only the Communists and the Socialists, but also the Radical Socialists, led by Herriot, who constituted an integral part of Laval's governing bloc. It was the danger of losing his Paris seat to the Front Populaire that led Laval to campaign for two seats, each of which he won.

The Radical Socialists, like many on the Left, were split on the key issues. They supported the Government against the Fascist leagues; they deplored its deflationary financial and economic policy. Before the new Parliament met on October 27 they issued a serious challenge to Laval. Unless he took steps to dissolve the Leagues before presenting the budget, they would abandon the Government and force a crisis.

Laval stiffly maintained his economic program, with a further set of decrees promulgated by the Cabinet the following day. His political judgment was that neither Herriot nor his party were ready to force the issues lest they be left to face them without a better solution. With Herriot's support, Laval was, for the time being, proved right.

## Negotiations

In Paris on October 24 Laval plainly told Clerk that he had taken the initiative in securing the Italian offer. He would not, however, be an intermediary between Britain and Italy. These two must agree on a suitable counter-proposal. Laval did not consider Mussolini's terms acceptable and had so told the Italian Ambassador. But he was sure that Mussolini expected bargaining, would make concessions, and wanted settlement.[96]

Laval did not suggest postponing sanctions. He did point out that it would be easier to deal before they took effect. Time, then, was of the essence. Mr. Petersen should therefore set to work with his French opposite, M. St. Quentin to propose the technical basis for the counteroffer.[97]

They did this while Italy anxiously watched. Cerutti kept Mussolini informed. Laval told Cerutti France would adhere loyally to sanctions, but impressed on Clerk the opportunity to settle before sanctions became effective, to transfer, as he put it the dispute from the field of battle to the green table.[98]

The response proposed by Petersen and St. Quentin was sent to London on October 26, 1935. It opened with a firm statement that the British and French participation in conciliation and settlement must be exercised within the framework of the League. The Italian proposal had to be modified in order to obtain Abyssinian approval. A mandate might be a sensible solution for the non-Amharic periphery, as Italy suggested, but this would be unacceptable to the Emperor. The same objectives could be achieved through reforms made under an administration like that proposed by the Committee of Five in areas defined as south of the 8th parallel, but excluding Harar, the personal fiefdom of the Emperor. They would remain under Abyssinian sovereignty but with administrative and financial autonomy and a foreign, exclusively Italian administration under a principal Counselor responsible to the Abyssinian Government.

The presence of Italian troops in this area would create difficult problems; hence the suggestion, if necessary, for a Foreign Legion, with Italy to play the role of France in its own Legion.

It was improbable that the Emperor would accept the conquest of Tigre. But border rectifications were not impossible. Rectification of the Eritrean and Somaliland borders would raise no real objections.

The control and limitation of arms in Abyssinia would proceed as in the Committee of Five report. The use of the Italian port at Assab would not suffice to balance the territorial sacrifices by the Emperor. It was therefore essential to grant Abyssinia a corridor to the sea, in Italian territory, since Italy had rejected such a solution at Zeila or in French Somaliland.

The essence of the proposed settlement remained League assistance in Central Abyssinia, and Italian administration in the non-Amharic provinces, with limited border rectifications and a corridor to the sea.[99]

While the proposal was under consideration, Hoare made another offer to Mussolini: the withdrawal of two British battle cruisers from the Mediterranean if Italy would withdraw two divisions from Libya.[100]

Hoare then told Laval that he would sound out the Emperor as to possibilities of settlement, but that it would be vital to make some report to the Coordinating Committee when it met on November 2 to assure them that there would be no negotiation without express authorization of the League.[101]

As Cerutti had done in Paris, in London Grandi pressed Vansittart for a response to the Italian proposal. He asked point blank if a settlement would be possible before the British election. Vansittart told Grandi of the Petersen-St. Quentin discussions, and about Hoare's proposed mutual withdrawals. But he adopted an attitude of measured pessimism. It was a complicated matter and haste might be counterproductive. He would himself be delighted if the whole matter could be settled by Christmas.[102]

Drummond delivered Hoare's message on October 30 to a Mussolini whom he found bitter and depressed. He wanted to make an end of it. He wanted no piecemeal approach—a battle cruiser here, a division there. He wanted a general settlement, and he would not withdraw a single man from Libya until then.

He told Drummond that his proposals had been fair and in the spirit of the League. He pointedly added that he did not doubt that he could reach acceptable terms in direct negotiation with the Emperor, if only Britain and the League did not advise him to reject negotiation. Drummond could only respond that Mussolini's offer was under review.

A gloomy Mussolini said he thought the two nations were heading to war. He was prepared to accept moral and financial sanctions. Economic sanctions wouldn't work. Stopping and searching vessels would lead to military sanctions. Such sanctions, Drummond told him were "absolutely excluded."

But Mussolini was solemn and gave a specific warning. If Italy must yield or go to war "she would definitely choose war even if it meant that the whole of Europe went up in a blaze." He could not give up the conquered territory.[103] Was this firm determination or the stellar performance of an accomplished actor who wished to push a hesitant negotiating partner to closing?

Laval's goal was clear, his attitude positive, but his path was strewn with new obstacles. To what Petersen and St. Leger had agreed, Sir Samuel Hoare on October 30 now disagreed. To put the non-Amharic territories under Italian administration was too much to ask of the Emperor. At war he was more dependent than ever on the rases; to accept might mean his downfall.

The simple solution, Hoare persisted, would be an exchange of territories—say the conveyance of some of the Bale and Borana country, not infertile and unsuitable for settlement, for an Abyssinian passage to the sea.

Hoare wanted no part of a Foreign Legion; he could not accept stationing Italian troops in Abyssinia even on a temporary basis. It would be accepted neither in Geneva nor Addis Ababa.[104]

This rebuff was enough to depress the usually buoyant Laval. He told Clerk Hoare's proposal offered an insufficient basis of negotiation. Clerk wondered if the problem were not that Laval had already conveyed the Petersen-St. Quentin proposals to the Italians.[105]

The Emperor's response was not promising either. He could not enter into negotiations until Italian troops were withdrawn and then he would consider any reasonable terms proposed by the League—not Italy.[106]

In this less than promising conjunction of events, Hoare, Eden, Laval, Massigli, and St. Quentin met in Geneva on November 1, 1935 to frame a position for the meeting the next day of the Coordinating Committee. Earlier in the morning, Hoare had met with Aloisi who made clear his desire to find a settlement. What Italy wanted was not oil or minerals but lands in the southwest suitable for colonization. The Emperor's concessions, he agreed, must be compensated with an outlet to the sea.[107] It is not surprising, then, that Hoare championed his view: an exchange of territories including an Aybssinian corridor to the sea.

Laval said he was wedded to no particular formula so long as it was approved by Abyssinia, Italy, and the League. He calculated that the Italians were eager to settle and that Mussolini's terms could be improved. Abyssinian approval was essential. The settlement could not appear to reward the aggressor. It should be done before Mussolini discovered that sanctions were ineffective. Laval was a practical politician; he could see matters hanging fire till after the British elections, but they must then move swiftly. If Britain and France agreed, he thought that there would be little trouble at the League.

What would they do the next day? Hoare suggested that perhaps Laval could tell the Coordinating Committee that discussions were pending but that any proposal would be referred to the League. This would reassure the League that they were not going behind its back. To all this, Laval readily agreed.[108]

The course of the negotiations was far from secret. That Mussolini had made proposals, that Petersen and St. Quentin had reviewed them to produce a basis for settlement, and that Hoare and Laval would search for a settlement in Geneva were all reported in the *Times* on October 30. This same issue described Laval's appearance before the Foreign Affairs Committee of the Senate and the two considerations he had put forth there: loyalty to the Covenant and the hope of an early settlement within the framework of the League.[109]

Hoare gave similar assurances to his Chelsea constituents on October 30. It was an election speech, and he backed the Government's rearmament program. Spiteful people had said Eden was more go-ahead than he was; but they had always been in complete agreement.

He talked about peace negotiations:

> I wanted to take the opportunity that is always offered by these important meetings of the League to have a talk with Monsieur Laval, the French Prime Minister, and some of the other prominent Ministers of the member states. What could be more natural and simple than these facts? Yet our opponents are trying to make ignorant people believe that there is some disreputable intrigue behind this visit and that it means some sinister change of policy. As to the change of policy, let them once and for all get it out of their heads that there has ever been a change of policy in the British attitude towards the Abyssinian controversy or that there will be a change of policy. Our policy has always been perfectly simple—namely, loyalty to the League and readiness to help with any honourable settlement of the dispute that is acceptable to the three parties concerned—the League, Italy and Abyssinia. That has always been our policy. It always will be our policy, and it is the policy that I shall support at Geneva. In the meanwhile, let us pay no attention to these whispers and innuendoes. Let us take them at their real worth. They are electioneering, pure and simple, and nothing more.... I have spoken in Chelsea about the ridiculous air of mystery that some of these critics are creating about the peace talks. Of course, what they wish is that the electors should be induced to believe that we are trying to sidetrack the League and do a disreputable deal with Italy behind its back. I

have already said that there is no foundation whatever for this malicious suspicion. There is nothing to conceal about what has been happening, nor is there anything suspicious about it. It is common property that several Governments have recently been considering the possibilities of a peaceful settlement, and that the British and the French Governments in particular have been exchanging their views as to what might form the basis of a future negotiation. In order that we should fully understand each other's views, the head of the Abyssinian Department at the Foreign Office has been in Paris discussing a number of complicated details with the officials of the French Foreign Office. For the time being we are engaged in this exchange of views. Nothing has yet emerged, and if anything definite does emerge we shall, of course, take the earliest opportunity to report to the League. If eventually a settlement is proved to be possible, that settlement would, as I have already stated over and over again, be within the framework of the League and would have to be satisfactory to the three parties concerned—the League, Italy and Abyssinia. That is the whole story.

## The Double Policy—The League

By October 31, 1935, the Coordinating Committee could report that fifty nations had agreed to Proposal No. 1, the arms embargo on Italy. Forty-nine had taken action on Proposal No. 2, financial sanctions. Forty-eight indicated readiness to proceed, subject to the necessary internal legislation, on Proposals No. 3 and No. 4 relating to imports and exports. There were thirty nine replies to Proposal No. 5, mutual support. This was prompt and widespread voluntary compliance.

The Coordinating Committee, on November 2, asked the participating governments to put Proposals No. 3 and No. 4 into effect by November 18. It ruled on technical matters—preexisting contracts, and goods in transit.

Much more important, the Canadian delegate proposed that sanctions be expanded to include coal, steel, and oil as soon as such sanctions were widely enough accepted to be effective. The British delegation supported Canada. Here was the crux of sanctions.

Laval now played the role presaged the day before. France was loyally applying the Covenant, he told the Committee. But France had another duty, a duty dictated by the spirit of the Covenant:

> We have all—and I should like to emphasize this point on the very day on which we are taking an important decision—another duty to fulfil, one that is dictated by the spirit of the Covenant. We must endeavour to seek, as speedily as possible, for an amicable settlement of the dispute. The French

> Government and the United Kingdom Government are agreed that their cooperation shall be exerted also in this sphere.

He told them what they all knew; that discussions were underway. He added a promise. He was acting,

> without the slightest intention of putting the results into final shape outside the League. It is only within the framework of the League that proposals can be examined and decisions reached.

Hoare talked, too, of enforcing the Covenant and at the same time seeking settlement:

> It is common talk that, during the last few days, there have been conversations taking place between Rome, Paris, and London on the possibilities of such a settlement. There is nothing mysterious or sinister about these discussions. It is the duty of us all to explore the road to peace. This is what we have been doing and this is what we shall continue to do.

Nothing concrete had emerged; there was nothing to report. When there was, it would be reported to the Council. Hoare added to Laval's assurances,

> Nothing is further from our minds than to make an agreement that is not acceptable to all three parties in the controversy. For let us not forget there are three parties to the controversy—the League, Ethiopia, and Italy.

He was sure, Hoare concluded, that everyone in the room would approve of these actions and wish well to the pursuit of an honorable peace.[111]

This was not the immediate reaction. There was confusion and discomfort among Committee members. Was it testimony to Laval's skills at stage management when the Belgian representative spoke for the negotiators?

> In the circumstances, does it not seem right that efforts towards conciliation should, from this moment, be placed under the auspices and within the framework of the League itself? Since the responsible leaders of two great countries have already devoted a large part of their time and their talents to this task, why should the League not entrust to them the mission of seeking, under its auspices and control and in the spirit of the Covenant, the elements of a solution which the three parties at issue—the League, Italy, and Ethiopia—might find it possible to accept? If this suggestion were to meet with the approval of the members of this Assembly, I think that the

> moral position of the League would be still further strengthened and that the chances of peace would be increased.[112]

There was no formal action, no vote. Equally important, no one said nay. It was recorded in its minutes that "the Committee took note of the desire expressed by the Belgian delegate."

This was widely reported in the press as the "moral mandate" given to Britain and France to negotiate settlement. It was not a legal mandate, for the Committee had no authority to grant one. What Laval and Hoare had done was to make their record, to publicize their attempts to find a solution, thereby conferring a mantle of legitimacy upon such proposals as they might one day bring before the Council. They were clearing the way so that on that day no one could say that they had acted without the knowledge or the approval of their peers.

Time was short. The first sanctions would soon be in effect; the issue of the oil sanction loomed inescapably ahead. The embattled Laval had to hold his coalition in place against the radicals of the Right and of the Left. And the British Government had to face the voters on November 14 and win their support before it could effectively proceed with its double policy and especially the negotiations for which it could now claim a moral mandate.

## The Triumph of the Peace Ballot—2

In a country making an incomplete recovery from the economic crisis of the early thirties, pocketbook issues dominated the thinking of many electors. Yet there had seldom been an election held amid such widespread and passionate concern for foreign policy. The British public had recently undergone an extensive education in just those issues—the League, the Covenant, arms and disarmament—that now presented themselves. That education had been the Peace Ballot, in which more than eleven million votes had been cast, and it was hardly a coincidence that all parties tended to shape their appeals to voter responses that were already known. It is the challenge of political leaders to educate their followers and having educated, lead them. The British electorate, having been powerfully educated by Lord Cecil, the urge was powerful as it was perennial for political leaders to follow their followers rather than to lead them.

Baldwin and Hoare led the Government campaign. Their themes were loyalty to the League and the arms needed both to make the League effective and to protect Britain. The Opposition contrasted its long standing fervor for the League to the Government's which, it implied, was wholly insincere besides being too little and too late. The Opposition paid lip service to the need for defense, at the same time loudly proclaiming that the Government wanted far too many arms in the first place, and was unfit to be trusted with them into the bargain. This loud and persistent charge the Government could not wholly ignore.

Baldwin addressed these themes in an interview published on October 31, 1935:

> Above all, we desire to go on working to maintain world peace and strengthen the League of Nations. But it is clear from recent events that both our own influence in the world and that of the League itself will be weakened unless we fill up the gaps in our defenses. I will never stand for a policy of great armaments and I give you my word—and I think you can trust me by now—that our defense programme will be no more than is sufficient to make our country safe and enable us to fulfill our obligations. That much we must have.[113]

To the Peace Society he spoke eloquently of the shadow of the last war and castigated isolation as selfish. The British Empire was "bound over to make the peace." But it could not make peace alone: "We meant nothing by the League unless we were, after careful consideration, prepared to enforce its judgment."[114]

While the Prime Minister spoke of enforcing the Covenant, the Foreign Secretary indignantly rejected the charges that the Government policy was dishonest:

> The Government are fighting this Election on a policy of peace and loyalty to the League" say these critics, "yet they are letting down the League now, and they intend to let it down more in the future and they are going to build up great armaments for war instead of peace.

All this, Hoare said, was "electioneering claptrap." The League was acting swiftly and "our straightforward and simple policy of loyalty to the League and readiness to look for an honourable settlement is the policy of the League as a whole."[115]

Hoare stood in for Baldwin at the Lord Mayor's Banquet on November 10. Britain had given its word in the Covenant and was bound to keep it. This, he said, "was and is, the opinion of a great majority of my fellow countrymen."

Speaking for them, he said that they would keep their word to Europe and the world, at the same time determined to join honorable attempts to bring the war to an end. For all this, adequate arms were needed for "if we are to defend the cause of peace, we must be able to defend ourselves."[116]

Herbert Morrison, for Labour, charged the Government with being inconsistent and insincere:

> It is trying to persuade progressive peace loving people that it is a friend of the League of Nations; while at the same time it retains the loyalty of fire-eaters like Mr. Chamberlain, Mr. Churchill, and Mr. Amery by declaring for a policy of competitive, swollen armaments.

If you vote for the Government, Morrison warned, you vote for a policy that leads to war spurred on by the militarism of the Chamberlains, Churchills, and Amerys, who were beyond the power of Baldwin to subdue.[117]

Sir Walter Citrine said the Government was asking for a blank check without ever showing that the armed forces were inadequate.[118] Attlee took a grander position. The Government, of course, were not to be trusted; they were using the international situation for partisan advantage. Another war meant quite simply the end of civilization. Modern weapons were too dangerous to be left in the hands of national governments. The only answer then was disarmament and collective security. This was not a clean-cut course of action in the face either of Italian aggression or German rearmament.[119]

If the Conservative election posters showed the League as the Key to Peace, Labour offered more compelling graphics. Posters showing rows of crosses in war cemeteries and babies wearing gas masks evoked the horrors of past wars and of wars to come.[120] In a country where thirty-two leading Anglican clergymen declared military sanctions tantamount to war and impermissible to Christians, such messages spoke to a large and receptive audience.[121]

Churchill said that the British people might hope for peace and pray for peace; but these noble sentiments bore little relation to the "realities of the terrible world growing up around this island." German factories were working three shifts to prepare for war and London was "a great fat cow" soon to be at the mercy of the nearest dictator.[122]

The election results on November 14 confirmed Baldwin's sagacity. Labour had won 154 seats, a gain of 59 over its showing in the abnormal conditions of 1931, and the Liberals lost seats. But the Government, winning 432 seats, was returned with a solid majority.

Tom Jones's appraisal of the results was apt. Baldwin had "reconciled the [Conservative] Party to the League by supporting rearmament, and reconciled the pacifists to rearmament by supporting the Covenant."[123]

Laval still had his political battles to fight. The British Government, firmly in place, could now turn its attention again to the international crisis.

## The Double Policy—November

Meanwhile, the stakes were rising and the pace quickening. On November 6, the Coordinating Committee promulgated its Proposal 4A extending the embargo to coal, iron, steel, and oil and sent the proposal to both League members and nonmembers. If the responses warranted, the Committee would suggest a date for putting the proposal into effect.[124] This was the sanction oil-poor Italy feared the most, the sanction affecting every ship, plane, truck, or tank moving to, over, or across Abyssinia.

On November 4, Marshal Badoglio had asked the French military attache in Rome to ask General Gamelin what value he attached to the "accords" signed in Rome between the Italian and French staffs. From his point of view, these accords remained in full vigor.[125] Italian friendship had its value as well as its price.

Drummond told Mussolini on November 5 that Britain still ardently desired a Mediterranean détente. Mussolini still preferred to deal with all the issues. He did not want war, but it could result from economic sanctions. Once more Drummond clearly stated that his Government did not contemplate military sanctions.

If, Mussolini suggested, it were made clear to the Emperor that the League would not employ military sanctions and Italy would not yield to economic sanctions, he would be ready to negotiate.

Drummond protested British loyalty to the League. Mussolini put his finger on the critical issue: Britain would make economic sacrifices for the League. Would it sacrifice blood?

Mussolini was, Drummond thought, in better spirits. He knew he had hard negotiations ahead but, if certain general principles could be agreed, Drummond was hopeful of success.[126]

Laval had elicited Mussolini's offer and the Italians seemed eager to pursue it. Hoare had raised fundamental issues in response to the Peterson-

St. Quentin drafts. Laval was amenable to any basis of settlement, so long as it was promptly pursued. The British approach was more leisurely. Vansittart had spoken of an agreement by Christmas. Hoare wanted Drummond to pursue a reduction of forces in the Mediterranean; a general agreement, he thought, must come much more slowly.[127]

At the same time, Laval restated for his ambassador in Rome the familiar bases of French policy. The accords of Rome never envisioned a threat to the independence and integrity of Abyssinia. France had always made clear to Italy that it would respect its obligations under the Covenant. It had acted to moderate the crisis, as Mussolini recognized, to the extreme limit of both its treaty obligations and its collaboration with Britain and its other allies and had risked weakening the basic and permanent guarantees of French security in Europe. France had never threatened military sanctions, blockade, or closure of the Suez Canal. It had tried in every way to seek conciliation within the framework of the League between the two antagonists in Abyssinia. He asked Chambrun to appeal to Mussolini to dampen Italian press and public attacks which France might find unacceptable and which would inhibit his own search for a peaceful solution.[128]

Drummond saw Mussolini again on November 12. The exchange was familiar, Drummond seeking mutual military withdrawals, Mussolini interested only in a wider agreement.[129]

There was, it appeared, a reason for the British phlegm. On November 11 Hoare had indicated that as soon as the election of November 14 was over, another approach should be made to Laval to seek his views on settlement.[130] Clerk on November 14 found Laval dreading the November 18 onset of sanctions. He thought the Italian military was doing well; he feared sanctions might not succeed because of the temptation of profits. Could not, Laval asked, some revision be made of the Peterson-St. Quentin plan? Clerk offered scant hope. The British public, so long as the Emperor was in the field and undefeated, would not support a British Government that sought to compel him to accept Italian demands. Only if the opening move came from the Emperor was success possible.[131]

It was in this vein that Hoare impressed on Sir Sidney Barton, Britain's Ambassador in Addis Ababa some unpleasant realities:

> Public opinion in Great Britain is strongly behind the Government up to the point of collective economic sanctions, but it will not go an inch further than this point. It is strongly opposed to action that will involve us in the risk of an isolated war with Italy.

Here was plain recognition by Hoare of the limits within which he was working. Did the Emperor realize this—and that he must dismiss from his mind the idea of collective military or financial assistance? "There is a point," Hoare warned, "beyond which I cannot go."[132]

Meanwhile, the threat of sanctions, far from cowing the Italian people, stiffened their attitude and raised support for the regime. They were united around Mussolini, Grandi told Corbin, ready for any sacrifice; if they had to sell Cellini's *Perseus* and all of their art treasures to the Americans, they wouldn't hesitate.[133]

Mussolini again made the point that economic sanctions would create a situation where they could not be shut off at will, nor the repercussions limited. He appreciated Laval's conciliatory attitude, but what France really was asking was that he declare himself satisfied with being beaten by a stick rather than threatened with a gun. He doubted economic sanctions would ever work against Germany. They took too long to become effective.[134]

This pointed to a critical element. How would America and Germany respond to the League's invitation to comment on sanctions; more important what would America do? Its attitude and action could seriously affect the outcome.

Meanwhile the Italians continued their slow and methodical advance. On November 7 their forces entered Makale in the North and Gorahi in the South. The first reports of sharp action came from the South where both sides agreed that on November 11, Abyssinian defenders had attacked an Italian motorized column. As to the results, they disagreed, each side claiming to have put the other to flight. This evidenced an appreciation by the Abyssinians that they must begin to resist lest the impression spread of overwhelming Italian influence.[135]

With the election returns in hand, Hoare was ready to move. On November 15 he instructed Clerk in Paris to approach Laval. Had Laval had further contacts with Italy? Did he have new suggestions to offer? If not, perhaps it would be useful to bring the League more into the picture.[136] Laval did not demur to this so long as Britain and France concerted a position beforehand. He was happy to hear that Peterson was standing by to go to Paris to pursue settlement proposals.[137] By November 20, Laval still had no new suggestions and still awaited Peterson's early visit,[138] for which, in fact, Vansittart, Eden, and Peterson were preparing that same day.[139]

The Chairman of the Coordinating Committee ratcheted the pressure another notch on November 22 when he called for a meeting of the Committee on November 29 to consider Proposal 4A. He was keenly aware of what others had done. President Roosevelt had warned that Americans trading with the belligerents in goods other than arms, ammunition, and implements of war prohibited by the Neutrality Act did so at their own risk. On October 30 he had appealed to Americans not to be tempted by added opportunities for profit which might prolong the war, adding that the Government would maintain surveillance of all shipments to the belligerents.[140] Another such warning came from Secretary of State Cordell Hull on November 15.[141]

Meanwhile, Germany maintained calculated neutrality, and on November 12 passed a decree by which most goods covered by Proposals 4 and 4C could be exported only by special government license.[142]

Italy had bitterly protested the actions of the Council and the Coordinating Committee as being both unwarranted and beyond the power of the League. The British and French replies had been carefully concerted. They both protested friendship for Italy, the imperative need to fulfill their obligations under the Covenant, and the absence of any hostile intent. The French noted that the Covenant "morally imposes" the duty of seeking a peaceful settlement as soon as possible, while the British could "not conceal their anxiety to facilitate, so far as lies within their power…and at the earliest possible moment, a settlement of the regrettable conflict now in progress."[143]

On November 23, Suvich eagerly inquired of Drummond whether Peterson and St. Quentin had met.[144] That day Laval told Clerk he would ask for a postponement of the November 29 meeting of the Coordinating Committee and asked for British support.[145]

Laval had good reasons. A vote of censure was threatened in Parliament by the Left which wanted the Government to take action on the Leagues before addressing the budget. On this issue his Government would stand or fall. By the 29th, Laval told Clerk, he would be out of office, or confirmed and really able to speak for France, or worst of all, limited by a caretaker's mandate.

Clerk thought Laval justified; at the same time he was glad to have another chance to arrive at a basis for settlement before an oil embargo was applied.[146]

Britain supported Laval. On November 25, the secretariat of the League issued a statement that, at Laval's request, the November 29 meeting would be postponed until an early date. Meanwhile, the Committee of Experts would meet on November 27 and conclude their deliberations before the meeting of the Committee of Eighteen.[147]

Laval hardly needed persuasion to follow his fixed course of negotiations before circumstances became so difficult as to make negotiation impossible. Pleas, nevertheless, came to him from the most influential quarters in Italy. On November 26, Aloisi came to Chambrun with Mussolini's personal message to Laval to avert the oil sanction. "Why," Aloisi asked, "do you wish to inflict so grave an aggravation of sanctions on an Italy disposed to study every proposition tending toward an honorable settlement of the Abyssinian affair? Why not abide the results of negotiations?"[148] And in the Vatican, Cardinal Pacelli, Secretary of State, specifically referring to the oil sanction, advised Charles-Roux that it would be wise to leave sufficient time to see if a peaceful solution were not possible.[149]

Laval's political problems were very real. He scheduled the vote of confidence on his program for November 28. On November 27 he went to the nation by radio. He defended his fiscal policies of deflation and the defense of the franc; it was on the little man, the humblest, that the burden of devaluation would fall. The demonstrations and incidents provoked by the Leagues were intolerable: "They cannot occur without endangering our very liberty...I condemn violence from wherever it comes."

He spoke plainly of the international crisis. Once more he made it clear that, seeking to localize and end the conflict, in collaboration with Britain:

> From the beginning we were in agreement over the avoidance of military sanctions as well as any measures likely to lead to a naval blockade. The closing of the Suez Canal has never been considered.
>
> I have a difficult part to play. I had to maintain intact a friendly collaboration with Great Britain and to demonstrate the fidelity of France to the Covenant and the League of Nations without weakening the bonds of friendship with Italy that I myself sealed in Rome on January 7 last. In acting as I have done, I have the feeling of having served at once the interests of my country and those of peace.

He would seek settlement "as rapidly as possible, a just and honorable solution which will conciliate the principles of the Covenant with the interests of Italy."

There was a longer view, a wider arena than Abyssinia. Mussolini, Laval said, wished to work for peace in Europe. Once a settlement in

Abyssinia had been reached, "we can take up the work which was begun at Stresa with such rich hopes."

He had spoken to the League and to Italy. He now spoke to Germany. The Franco-Soviet pact offered Germany no threat. Pursuing European peace, he sought the help of all and especially good relations with Germany.[150]

It was, in the final analysis, Germany that weighed most heavily on the minds and spirits of French statesmen of every party.

Laval's appeal succeeded. On the vote of confidence on November 28, he won a majority of 120. The Radical Socialists did not wish to defeat Laval and then assume responsibility for a fiscal policy on which they largely agreed with him.[151] On November 29, Laval won another vote, this time by a margin of 77. The subject had been fiscal policy. The real test would come the next week when the issue would be the Leagues.[152]

Meanwhile, Peterson and St. Quentin had been at work. On November 23 France proposed the cession of Tigre, including recently conquered Makale as an autonomous principality under Italian suzerainty. The Ogaden and Danakil frontiers would be rectified. A special zone would be created in the south, bounded on the north by 8° N latitude and on the west by the 37th meridian. If this zone remained under Abyssinian sovereignty, nevertheless Italy would have full economic and colonial settlement rights. Italy would renounce participation in any scheme of administration of central Abyssinia. Italy would cede a port and a corridor to the sea in Eritrea; the French were reconciled to a rival port to Djibuti.

Laval's opinion was that an agreement should first be worked out with Italy for practical reasons; the League itself was unlikely to produce a plan, but might approve an arrangement likely to lead to settlement.

Peterson promised the French a response, but commented to London that the sovereignty of the Emperor over the special economic zone would be a transparent fiction.[153] He laid out what he thought was possible and this was a reversion to Hoare's exchange of territories.

Abyssinia would cede Adowa, Adigrat, Danakil, and most of Ogaden against a port and a corridor. Britain would subscribe to a formula by which Britain would use its influence, if possible, to secure facilities for Italian settlement and economic development in Southern Abyssinia linked up to the plan of assistance formulated by the Committee of Five. There would be special conditions: that Abyssinian sovereignty should be left intact and that the League should arbitrate cases in dispute.

The French preferred, Peterson reported, to consult Rome first, but did not object to consulting the Abyssinian Government. They emphasized the unpopularity of sanctions in France and public concern over tension with Italy.[154]

To all this Vansittart commented that he was entirely in favor of Peterson's proposals as the best available; he would be happy if Italy accepted. Eden agreed, too, subject to approval of the three parties and thought it would be acceptable to Abyssinia only if the special areas had some form of non-Italian League control.

The British resolved their position, and on November 28 Hoare sent instructions to Peterson. He authorized Peterson to proceed on the basis of Peterson's proposals of November 23, omitting only the limitation "if possible" on Britain's efforts to secure special privileges for Italy in the south. The limits of the special area, Hoare said, would clearly have to be a matter of bargaining.

Hoare hoped the French could accept this basis and was prepared for Laval to take it to Rome before Geneva. Consultations with Abyssinia should, he thought, take place simultaneously with or just after the submission to Rome.[155]

When Peterson again met St. Quentin on November 29, he made clear to the French that the exchange of territories could not be unbalanced to the point of being derisory. The economic rights in the south could not be tantamount to annexation but under a League plan of assistance. The maintenance of Abyssinian sovereignty had to be, not merely theoretical, but practical.[156]

Léger observed that the Italians would claim these were no more than their treaty rights which Abyssinia had never been disposed to make effective.

By the next day, Saturday, November 30, the French were in substantial agreement. The special economic zone would indeed be included in the League plan of assistance as formulated by the Committee of Five. Peterson hoped that Laval could review the matter and respond the following week.[157]

While the Peterson-St. Quentin conversations took place, Vansittart was visited by General Garibaldi who restated Rome's settlement proposals. They were Mussolini's old terms, but Garibaldi said they were subject to any reasonable modification.[158] Mussolini himself lofted settlement proposals in an interview published in the *Morning Post* on November 25.[159]

To settlement discussions Hoare wished to add a stiffer note.[160] He asked Clerk to invite Laval to issue a stern warning to Mussolini. It had been reported from Rome that Mussolini, conscious of the impact of an oil embargo, was capable of an act of suicidal folly. He must know, Hoare said, that any attack on Britain was an attack on the whole League, and, finally, an attack on France. Here was a plain request for Laval to bind France to Britain and convey the message to Mussolini.[161] Laval did not hesitate. He promptly told Cerutti that France's friendship with Italy notwithstanding, France would loyally carry out sanctions, and that an attack on Britain would find France at her side to meet it.[162] To this Laval added that the postponement of the Coordinating Committee's meeting on the oil sanctions was wholly due to the French political crisis. Italy had better then, come to reasonable terms before further sanctions were applied.[163]

In this posture of events, Hoare summed up his position on November 29:

> "[T]here is an accumulation of evidence that Signor Mussolini is beginning to realize the full difficulties of his position and the advisability of making terms. Whilst I am not over optimistic and I do not underrate the difficulties, I feel that it is essential that we should test the reality of these reports. I am also inclined to think that, in view of Signor Mussolini's disposition, the actual imposition of an oil embargo would under present circumstances make him more rather than less intransigent. On this account I should welcome a breathing space for these negotiations.... With the embargo hanging over his head he is, I believe, more likely to be reasonable than with the embargo actually imposed. Be this as it may, we intend to use the next weeks for a serious attempt to bring about a settlement.[164]

How this might proceed had already been foreshadowed the day before. Léger, in telling Clerk of Laval's warning interview with Cerutti, also reported Laval's anxious hope that he could meet Hoare, providing, as Hoare said, he survived his Parliamentary difficulties. If Laval went to London he might be accused of being unduly influenced by Britain. It would be, on the other hand, quite natural if the two met in Geneva where the Committee of Eighteen would convene.[165] Here was the genesis of the meeting that actually took place in Paris on December 7 and 8, 1935.

## Complications

The threat of an oil sanction was useful both in inducing negotiations and in enforcing the Covenant. But it was clearly understood that an increase in American supplies could frustrate a League embargo, and American shipments had indeed increased sharply in the third quarter of 1935. Hoare used the oil sanction both ways. He said on November 25 that he would resign if there were to be no oil sanctions,[166] but he also advised that it would be wise to defer the oil sanction until it was known how his talks with Laval would go.[167]

British military and naval readiness were a perennial problem. A subcommittee of the Committee of Imperial Defense had on November 28 reported on serious deficiencies in anti-aircraft ammunition, particularly threatening in view of the exposure of the Royal Navy to Italian air power. To Vansittart it was "unpardonable that we should be so handicapped," particularly since, unlike 1914, the crisis had been long in developing, as a matter of fact "plain as a pikestaff" since August.[168]

What could be done? To Vansittart, the answer was clear. People who don't rearm force themselves by their own logic into negotiations. The British public was not logical, only irritable. As usual it overlooked Germany.

Nor was Hoare uninformed or unaware. A lengthy report from Phipps in Berlin on November 13 reviewed German rearmament and concluded the question was not *whether* but *where* Germany would expand. Phipps grimly concluded that "the present Ethiopian imbroglio is a mere child's play compared to the problem that will in some not very distant future confront His Majesty's Government."[169]

The moment was, then, ripe to bring Germany back into the European system, if not to Geneva. This could only be done, François Poncet, the French Ambassador in Berlin, told his colleague Phipps, on the basis of the closest possible Anglo-French cooperation. If there were a rift between the two, François-Poncet solemnly warned, Hitler would probably proceed quickly to overrun and fortify the demilitarized zone and this, to a Frenchman, was the most horrifying prospect of all.[170]

Phipps again warned on November 27 that "Abyssinia is not the only pebble on the beach." Hitler was watching, waiting, rearming. Britain must rearm quickly:

> [F]or after all the burglars are arming, and the butler of the commodious, not to say luxurious, English country house must clearly provide himself and his staff with proper blunderbusses.[171]

Laval had not overlooked Germany. Beyond his pact with Italy, beyond the Stresa front, beyond the Soviet pact and the Eastern alliances, Laval had never concealed his desire for a rapprochement with Germany. It was much talked about in November, and there were rumors of a visit to Paris by Ribbentrop who had spearheaded the naval treaty in London.[172]

If Britain harbored doubts about Laval, whether of style or substance, Laval speculated darkly on aspects of British character which complicated his task. Gamelin recorded Laval's observations to a meeting, on November 21, of the Haute Comité Militaire:

> I told the English: You will always be the same. Tomorrow you will accept the fait accompli and you will cede to the Italians much more than you could give them today.[173]

"It would be best," he added, "to conclude as quickly as possible."

# 5

# Hoare-Laval

*"Momentarily our Left and Right were at one about something which annoyed them"*[1]
—Vansittart

## Facing the Crisis—Britain

One way or another, December would be a critical month for Italy, Abyssinia, the League and the world. Disappointed by the slow progress of his armies, Mussolini replaced de Bono with his senior commander, Marshal Pietro Badoglio. Having declined Britain's Zeila offer and both the Tripartite and Committee of Five Proposals, the Duce spoke sternly of his unshakeable determination and Italian glory, but in fact his own offer had been on the table since October 16 and he impatiently awaited a reply.

Pierre Laval, in the midst of a long-running political crisis was, in the words of the *New York Times* correspondent, trying to save the franc, the Republic, and Mussolini.[2] Protesting loyalty to the League and his British ally, he had nevertheless made clear his distaste for any measure likely to lead to war and his ardent quest for a negotiated settlement.

The British Government, on the other hand, had been overwhelmingly returned to office. Under Eden's guidance, it had led the League in imposing the sanctions then in effect, an impressive demonstration of international unity. On December 12, 1935, the critical oil sanction would come up for review.

It was under these circumstances that the British cabinet met on December 2, the day before the opening session of the newly elected Parliament. The discussion of the international crisis quickly centered on the oil sanction and the danger of a mad dog attack. Britain must not be seen, Hoare advised, to refuse to participate in collective action, including the oil sanction. Having adopted those positions, and what is more, having fought the election on them, any other course of action would be "disastrous and indefensible."

Hoare reported that French aid was assured; Laval's response had been a "categorical affirmative." Britain ought, he thought, to adopt Laval's suggestions of talks among the Navy, Army, and Air staffs at the same time sounding out Greece, Turkey, and Yugoslavia on the use of their naval and military facilities.

Hoare also reported what readers of that day's *Times* and other newspapers well knew—that Peterson was in Paris continuing settlement discussions. To press these talks Hoare informed the Cabinet, he would himself go to Paris en route to a Swiss holiday to see Laval in search of a settlement.

It was a sticky wicket. They must avoid giving any impression of weakening in support of sanctions. He wondered if the oil sanction (to which, he pointed out, Laval had agreed in principle) would aid or hinder the negotiations. In the end he recommended the oil sanction in principle, proceeding, nevertheless, with peace talks and, if progress were satisfactory, leaving open the date for the operation of the oil sanction.

In the general discussion which the Prime Minister invited, the military equation remained changeless. No one doubted that Britain would maintain command of the Mediterranean; all realized that it might sustain losses serious in themselves and all the more so in the light of weakness elsewhere. Military conversations with France would likely have to wait so long as the French Government was preoccupied with its political crisis.

Eden backed Hoare in urging postponement of the oil sanction to give negotiations a chance. Baldwin agreed that if hostilities should break out, the Government would find itself criticized if it had not taken all steps to avoid war. Should hostilities flare up in dealing with Mussolini, no one would want to tackle Hitler. In any event, he observed, in Mussolini they were not dealing with a "normal kind of intellect." This was unsettling to Baldwin who was, like Warren G. Harding, dedicated to normalcy.

There was no disagreement on the conclusions the Cabinet adopted. They would continue the policy of October 9, that is, to approve an oil sanction provided the other oil-producing and member states joined in it. But the policy should be applied so as to give time for negotiation of a peaceful settlement, which the Foreign Secretary should press by every useful means, at the same time continuing military conversations with the French and mutual support talks with other Mediterranean powers.

If the Hoare-Laval talks indeed showed reasonable prospects of success, the Committee of Eighteen should be asked to defer action for the time being. If the talks did not go well, or if the military talks did not lead to effective cooperation, the Foreign Secretary was instructed to bring the matter back to the Cabinet for further consideration.[3]

All this seemed wholly appropriate to the *Times* which the next day editorialized that the Cabinet had not departed from its fixed and twofold policy. The first part was to end the war by collective action and there was no ground for doubting that Britain would play its full part in an oil sanction. The second part was to discover the terms on which peace could be justly reestablished. This was a policy that had the support of all of the parties and had "been ratified in the plainest way by the election itself."[4]

This was Baldwin's message to Parliament on December 3. Speaking in the place of the Foreign Secretary who was ill, Baldwin said he would lose no chance of making peace instead of war on terms acceptable to the League and the parties. If that was dualism, he was a dualist.[5]

Graver matters still occupied the Cabinet when it met on December 4. The Foreign Secretary had circulated three notes from the Ambassador in Berlin detailing German rearmament and expansion aims. Britain must be strong now, he warned, to avoid an explosion in the future. Even if Germany were itself not ready, Hoare warned, it might be tempted into adventures against countries even less prepared. At the same time, he reminded the Cabinet of a paradox: the more the public were asked to sacrifice for defense preparedness, the more they would demand disarmament. But the Germans were not likely to want to discuss an air pact while the Italo-Abyssinian dispute continued. Here was a somber background to the December crisis.[6]

Hoare clearly explained to the House of Commons on December 5 the policy adopted by the Cabinet on December 2. Britain, he again emphasized, would take no isolated action. The basis of the League was that all members should share the risks and the responsibilities.

He responded, as Baldwin had, to Attlee's charge of dualism:

> [W]e have consistently and steadily followed the double line that has time

> after time been approved by the League and by this House. On the one hand we have taken our full part in collective action under the Covenant, and on the other hand we have continued our efforts for a peaceful settlement.

Led by Eden, he said, the members of the League had shown themselves ready for collective action, even though it meant loss to many. These same members had given their support to the Franco-British effort to seek a peaceful settlement. This was surely open and above board, not going behind the back of the League. The proposals that emerged must be acceptable to the parties: Italy, Abyssinia, and the League.

Hoare spoke bluntly of the oil sanction. The League and Britain had approved it in principle. Whether it would be effective would depend on the action of nonmember states. When the Committee of Eighteen made its recommendation—the postponement of its meeting had been due to the urgent political crisis in France—Britain would be prepared to take its share in whatever collective action was determined. Meanwhile, the postponement would afford a further opportunity to seek a peaceful settlement.

Hoare appealed to Mussolini to cooperate. Britain had no desire to drive a wedge between Italy and France or to interfere with the internal affairs of Italy. The world, he said, needed a strong Italy. There were enough problems in the world without the Abyssinian war and too much inflammable material lying about Europe and the East—the image was 1914—for fresh powder to be added.

To all this Eden, closing the debate for the Government, gave his full assent. There had never been, he said, been the faintest shadow of difference between himself and the Foreign Secretary and his policy at Geneva and that of the Government were in complete accord. More than that, there was general agreement on the Government's policy; he described the feeling of the House as clearly in support of the policy the Government was pursuing.[7]

The same newspapers that reported the Parliamentary debate on December 6 also reported that Sir Samuel Hoare, accompanied by Sir Robert Vansittart, would proceed by air to Paris to meet Laval and to discuss the results of the talks between Peterson and the French experts as to a possible basis for settlement of the Abyssinian dispute. Thereafter, Hoare would go to Switzerland for a holiday necessitated by his health. In his absence, Eden would be in charge of the Foreign Office.[8]

## Facing the Crisis—France

Laval had survived votes of confidence on economic and fiscal policy. The demands of the Left to deal sternly with the right-wing leagues had been the price of their support for Laval's economic policy and payment was now due. How would Laval handle the leagues?

That question was dramatically answered in the Chamber of Deputies on December 6 when Yves Ybarnagaray, Deputy of the Right, spokesman of the Croix de Feu, and intimate associate of its leader, Colonel de la Roque, rose to speak.

The Government might, he said, decree the dissolution of the leagues, but this would be useless if they retained their arms. If, however, all political associations were disarmed, the problem of the leagues would disappear. While denying that the Croix de Feu was armed, Ybarnagaray clearly suggested that it was ready to disarm. Leon Blum leapt at the opportunity. Speaking for the Socialists, he challenged Ybarnagaray: "What we have we are ready to dissolve. Are you ready to do likewise?" The same challenge was put by Maurice Thorez, the Communist.

The Chamber awaited the reply of the Right. It was prompt and it was affirmative. Laval now hurried to the tribune to offer three bills: establishing penalties for carrying a weapon at a public meeting or demonstration; making illegal and dissolving associations that sponsored military training or engaged in armed demonstrations; and adding incitement to murder to the offenses punishable under the press laws.

With a typical concern for the results rather than the technicalities of the issues, Laval arranged for the report of the Legislative Committee on the three bills to be ready at 5:00 PM that afternoon so that the bills might be adopted that night. He would, therefore, ask for a simple vote of confidence.

This was a dazzling performance and no one appreciated it more than the *Times'* experienced correspondent. Laval, he reported, had mastered a problem of extraordinary delicacy which a week before had threatened his administration with collapse:

> The surrender of the Leagues was perfectly stage-managed to secure the maximum psychological effect. It had all the experience of a spontaneous explosion of patriotic emotion sweeping away in a rash of fraternal feelings the divisions, the suspicions and the bitterness of the past two years. Actually it was the fruit of patient negotiation and skilful management by M. Laval, who has once more shown himself a consummate Parliamentary tactician.[9]

Laval addressed himself briefly to the vote of confidence. The Government, he said, had not talked, it had acted. Difficult domestic issues had been resolved. He now turned to international affairs:

> Tomorrow I will resume the diplomatic negotiations which have been suspended. Your vote will increase the authority of the Government. The Government are responsible for protecting Republican institutions; they alone have charge of public order and the security of citizens. They cannot allow factions, whatever their origin, to substitute their authority for their own. You considered certain laws inadequate; I bring you others. When they are voted we shall apply them. I love my country. I am passionately attached to peace, and in defending it I shall be the bearer of your confidence.[10]

The vote carried by the large majority of 132. The passage by the Chamber of the three bills that night was a foregone conclusion.

Having masterfully emerged from two weeks of sustained Parliamentary crisis in which it had seemed certain that he must be overwhelmed, having reconciled, for the moment, the bitter enmities that divided Frenchmen of the Left and the Right, having defended the franc and the Republic, Pierre Laval was entitled to form a creditable opinion of his powers of conciliation and negotiation, not to mention stage management.

It was in a cheerful mood that he said to a group of colleagues after the vote of confidence had been passed on December 6: "Let's go out and eat a dozen oysters. Tomorrow I have to work for peace. I am meeting Sir Samuel Hoare."[11]

## Setting the Stage

It would take all of Laval's skills and the concurrence of widely divergent elements to produce an agreed solution to the Abyssinian crisis. Meeting on December 5, the General Council of the League of Nations Union called for stern measures. If economic pressures did not succeed, it urged the cutting of Italian communications to Africa under League authority. Moreover, the supply of oil to Italy should be stopped immediately (it did not say by whom).[12] Lord Cecil liked to combine idealism and practicality. "Never," he had once advised, "fire over the heads of rioters."[13] But he thought the resolution "extremely moderate," adding that people quite naturally and rightfully were anxious to avoid being plunged into war. Corbin, always an astute observer of the English scene, commented on the amendment of the LNU resolution from "England is ready" to join in cutting communications to "England would be ready," thus, he remarked "avoiding the delicate question whether the British people are disposed to apply military sanctions." The LNU's debate he characterized as "toutes pickwickiennes."[14]

A companion resolution was in the direct line of LNU inspiration and philosphy. It called for the Government not to proceed with rearmament except as part of a policy of increasing collective security and limiting national armaments by international agreement.[15]

Hoare had appealed to Mussolini for cooperation. Mussolini responded on December 7 in a speech to his Chamber of Deputies. He revealed that he had sent settlement proposals to France in October. He warned against an oil sanction. He acknowledged Hoare's call for a strong Italy and admitted the situation had slightly improved. But, speaking without drama, and in measured tones, he warned against premature optimism. If he was not optimistic, observers concluded, he had not slammed the door in the face of further negotiations. Indeed his reference to his own offer conveyed to Laval on October 16 might signal his opinion that it was timely for any new proposals to come forward from Britain and France.[16]

Meanwhile, Peterson had continued his well-publicized stay in Paris and his discussions with Leger which were commonly understood to have as their goal a basis for settlement.[17]

The French proposals of the month before for an Italian mandate over non-Amharic and a League mandate over Amharic Abysinnia had yielded to Hoare's objections and his clear preference for an exchange of territories. In late November, the British position called for an exchange of Adowa and Adigrat (conquered by Italy) and Danakil, plus a large chunk of Ogaden in the south against a Red Sea port and a corridor leading to it. All this would be subject to this formula:

> His Majesty's Government undertake to use their influence to secure for Italy the fullest possible facilities of economic development and settlement in such areas in Southern Abyssinia as may be suitable for these purposes and as may hereafter be determined. In whatever way this development may be linked up with the plan of assistance formulated by the Committee of Five it is understood (A) that the Ethiopian sovereignty over the regions affected will be maintained intact (B) that the League of Nations shall be accepted by both Italy and Abyssinia as arbitrator in all cases of dispute.[18]

Peterson had made it clear to the French that the proposed transaction must be constructed not as a conquest, but as an exchange of territories which must not be so unequal as to appear derisory. A corridor at Assab would be preferable; if not accepted, Zeila could always be proposed again. In the zone of economic development in the south, Peterson had also been clear—this must not be synonomous with annexation. Abyssinian sovereignty should remain intact, not only in theory but in practice.[19]

After a good deal of discussion between Peterson and Léger,[20] the latter agreed to submit the British proposals to Laval, specifically agreeing that the Italian zone of economic development in the south should be a part of the plan of assistance formulated by the Committee of Five.[21]

Peterson now marked time while Laval fought his political battles. Peterson hinted darkly on December 3 that Laval had already sounded out Italy on the terms he and Léger had discussed.[22] On December 5, Léger made personal comments on the British plan, at the same time intimating that Laval found it insufficient as a basis for negotiation. Léger thought it would be difficult to obtain any cooperation from Addis Ababa. He opined that the Italians would insist on more of Tigre than Britain proposed, would not be content with mere economic as opposed to political rights in the southern zone, and, as always, that France looked with little favor on creating a port competitive to Djibuti.[23]

Whatever the French reaction might be, the proposed plan was widely reported. The *Times* on December 4 described British proposals for an exchange of territories including an Abyssinian outlet to the sea.[24] By December 6, with Hoare en route to meet Laval, the *Times* gave more details. Italy would receive territory in Tigre, including Adowa, but not Aksum, and there would be border rectifications in the North and the South. Abyssinia would receive a corridor to the sea, Italy special economic advantages in the south where, possibly some arrangement for League intervention would be made.[25]

The *New York Times* on December 5 correctly reported that the French had accepted the British view against a mandate and in favor of a clean-cut exchange of territories. Italy would receive in Tigre the line Adigrat-Makalle. Abyssinia would obtain the corridor to the sea at Assab and the right to build a railroad or highway to Addis Ababa. Italy would receive important concessions in the south, virtually the whole of the Ogaden, but Abyssinia would remain independent with control and assistance by the League of Nations to aid in reform and administration.[26]

Similar reports appeared in the *Daily Telegraph*, the *Morning Post* and the *Manchester Guardian*. These were, therefore, remarkably public diplomatic discussions and those who cared to read the press would be little surprised at the proposals as they finally emerged.

Meanwhile, in London, Vansittart was trying his own hand at compromise. He met with Grandi, the Italian Ambassador, on December 3, 4, and 5. This was unusual and highly personal diplomacy. While British diplomats criticized Laval on suspicion of passing Britain's proposals to Mussolini, Vansittart was doing the very deed. He urged the advantages of such a settlement on Grandi.

Grandi's diplomacy was equally personal. His goal, he said frankly, was to obtain more favorable terms. He was not, therefore, enthusiastic about the British proposal. He asked flatly for the cession to Italy of all territories south of 8° N. This refused, he proposed that Italy should obtain, in addition to Adowa-Adigrat and Danakil, the Bale territory, and a part of Harar, the Emperor's personal province, thus linking the two Italian colonies east of Addis Ababa. This meant a railway competing with France.

Prospects were dim. Perhaps with cessions in Bale, Ogaden, Adowa, Adigrat, a corridor only in Danakil and Harar, and an economic monopoly in the south as against an Abyssinian access to the sea, a deal could be done. But the difficulties, including French objections, seemed to Vansittart insuperable.[27]

## Hoare-Laval

Hoare, as was the custom, asked the King's permission to leave the country, accompanied by Vansittart. "If, as I hope, M. Laval and I agree upon a basis for a peace negotiation, Vansittart will stop on in Paris for a day or two in order to clinch the details."[28]

Hoare did not lack for advice. Vansittart was surely the only British diplomat ever to have put a play on the Paris stage. "Don't forget," Eden warned Hoare, "that in Paris Van can be more French than the French."[29]

Vansittart asked Hoare: Do you intend to fight? Certainly not, was Hoare's reply. Then, Vansittart said, you have to compromise. It may be unpopular but there is no third way.[30]

Perhaps the advice that counted most came from the Prime Minister. Italy had taken a hard line on the oil sanction, declaring that it would be "an unfriendly act,"[31] and Baldwin had noted to the Cabinet on December 2 the risks of dealing with an adversary who did not possess a normal kind of intellect. His advice to Hoare was simple, straightforward, and repeated: keep us out of war for which we aren't ready.[32]

Hoare's mission was to find with Laval a basis for negotiating a settlement of the Abyssinian war, as he had recommended to the Cabinet, as the Cabinet had unanimously directed him to do, and as he had told Parliament. He knew Laval's aversion to military measures and his dedication to a negotiated settlement. Laval's style of negotiation was to keep his lines of communication open but to stake out a firm position from which to negotiate. Thus, he reminded his ambassadors at London and Rome, on the eve of his meeting with Hoare, of the warnings he had given Suvich on November 28: that Italy ought not to misjudge France's efforts at conciliation; that there should be no doubt as to France's loyalty to the League and the Covenant; that any attack on Great Britain would evoke the solid and effective response of France. Indeed, France had consented to the postponement of the meeting of the Committee of Eighteen only because of genuine political necessity. He reported to them Hoare's urgent plea for new proposals from Mussolini.[33]

On the day Hoare and Laval were to meet, their ambassadors in Rome called jointly upon Mussolini. They directed his attention to the Paris discussions and indicated that they would welcome his sympathetic response to and readiness to carry on these same discussions.[34] The stage was now set.

After welcoming Hoare, Laval reported on his ambassador's visit with Mussolini. Mussolini, Laval said, was ready to negotiate. At the outset, it was natural for him to stand on his October offer.

They discussed the oil embargo. It would be effective, Laval said, and could lead to dramatic and unforeseen consequences. He had himself wished to conciliate before applying sanctions, but had followed the British lead. Now it would be better to negotiate, applying the oil sanction only if negotiation failed. It was not a question of abandoning the oil embargo; and in any case, he pointed out the United States could take no effective action before Congress convened in January.

Laval recounted both his assurances to Britain and his warning to Italy: France would stand by her engagements.

Hoare needed reassurance. He again asked Laval if Britain could count on France. Sanctions were unpopular, Laval replied; and for that reason he wanted to exhaust all possibilities so that in the worst case the French public would back the government. But to reply directly, France would honor its engagements.

Hoare agreed that they must first press on with negotiation so long as it seemed that Mussolini was seriously disposed to negotiate. If such negotiations were fruitful, everyone would understand the wisdom of a delay in the oil sanction. But if Mussolini were intransigent, the sanction could no longer be delayed.

They now turned to the real issue—a settlement acceptable to the parties and the League. Laval saw a gap which had to be bridged between Italian pretensions and British reservations. Italy had to have at least that part of Tigre she had conquered, but not Aksum. What Italy needed was land to colonize and this was surely not the Ogaden desert. Laval insisted on Italian influence in the territory south of 8°N, not as a mandate, but under terms enabling Italy to protect her nationals settled there. Laval wanted to uphold the Covenant; the key element of solution would be giving Abyssinian access to the sea.

Hoare warned of the danger of weakening the League and rewarding aggression. The solution was to rest on the proposals of the Committee of Five with League control, Italian economic advantages, and Abyssinian access to the sea—excluding once more all thought of a mandate. Laval again agreed. As Hoare summed it up: "The arrangement must be a judicious mixture of an exchange of territory and the conferring of economic concessions."

Laval kept his lines open to Mussolini and, conscious of their shared beginnings—Latin, meridional, modest, and ambitious—pondered Mussolini's psyche. The limits of the transaction for Laval were what he could sell Mussolini. The limits for Hoare were what the British public would accept.

Nevertheless, the situation looked promising. The parties were moving forward to a joint understanding. Hoare agreed to defer his holiday by a day and stay on for further discussions on the 8th.[35]

They issued a communiqué affirming their commitment to close collaboration, and reporting continuing discussions the next day to determine bases which might be proposed for the friendly settlement of the Italo-Abyssinian dispute.[36]

The following day they reached agreement. Laval fought for a corridor to Assab, not Zeila, which might prejudice the Djibuti railway. Hoare emphasized that the influence of Italy in the southern zone must be economic, not political; the administration must remain Abyssinian under League surveillance to protect Italian nationals. The British public would never accept direct Italian control. Laval was concerned not to humiliate Italy; why not, he suggested, instead of League supervision, an annual report to the League?

Hoare emphasized, as he had so often, the need to base the plan on the Committee of Five proposals. He could never consent to Italian sovereignty in fact. Only the League could carry off the plan.

From all this emerged the proposed plan, hastily typed the same day while further discussions on procedure took place. The provisions are worth noting carefully.

France and Britain would recommend to the Emperor his consent to the following territorial adjustments:

1. Cession to Italy of eastern Tigre, excluding Aksum.
2. Rectification of the Danakil frontier and the grant to Abyssinia of an access to the sea to be defined.
3. Rectification of the Ogaden frontier, safeguarding the pasturage rights of the British Somaliland tribes.
4. The access to the sea would comprise Assab and a corridor abutting French Somaliland. In case of insuperable objections, the Zeila corridor and port could be substituted. France and Britain would attempt to obtain from Abyssinia guarantees against slavery and arms trade in the acquired territories and an undertaking not to build a railroad competing with the Djibuti railroad.

In addition, Britain and France would press both the Emperor and the League to establish a zone south of 8°N and east of 35°E for Italian economic expansion. In this zone, an integral part of Abyssinia, Italy would enjoy exclusive economic rights, which could be administered by a chartered company which, while preserving acquired rights would contribute to the economic development and social welfare of the indigenous population. The administration of this zone would be exercised under the sovereignty of the Emperor and a League plan of assistance in which Italy would have a predominant, but not an exclusive part. In these services, the principal advisor would be the delegate of the League reporting to the Emperor but neither Italian, French, nor British.

A duty of this administration would be to protect Italian nationals and the development of their enterprises under a detailed League of Nations program.[37]

All this Hoare summarized for the British Cabinet:

(1) An outlet to the sea for Abyssinia.
(2) in exchange for the outlet the cession of some of the occupied territory in Tigre to Italy and a frontier rectification in the east and South-east.

(3) a large zone in the south and South-west in which Italy acting under the League will have the monopoly of economic development.[38]

Hoare recognized that as important as the substance of the proposed basis for negotiation was the procedure by which it was to be presented to the parties. Here Laval prevailed. He was confident he could persuade Mussolini and he had the Rome accords of January as evidence. It was always his plan to induce Mussolini to enter negotiations, thereby casting the onus of refusal on the Emperor. To the contrary, he had neither contact nor rapport with the Negus, who, the oil sanction imminent, had every reason to hold back and let the League do his work. If Mussolini said yes and the Emperor said no, then France's position was enormously simplified. It could claim to stand for the League and the Covenant, not to mention the Italian alliance in the face of Abyssinia intransigence. Under such circumstances, France could in principle decline to participate in an oil sanction.

They agreed that the British Government must approve what Hoare and Laval proposed. Immediately upon such approval, the French and British Ambassadors in Rome would communicate to Mussolini, in identical terms and "*strictly confidentially*" an outline of the Hoare-Laval proposals. In what detail? "All they should do," Hoare reported to the Cabinet, "is to give him [Mussolini] the heads of the discussion upon which we are prepared to embark."[39]

Mussolini would then be asked if he would accept in principle this basis of negotiation, without prejudice to the result of the discussions which, it was proposed, could take place in the Committee of Five. Hoare wanted the matter in League hands, not his, and had been relieved when Laval agreed. He told the Cabinet that he and Laval agreed that there could be no bargain with Mussolini on the oil sanction. But they both clearly saw that the action of the Committee of Five would supersede the Committee of Eighteen, thereby in practice deferring discussion of the oil sanction.

On the next day, the British and French ministers in Addis Ababa would inform Haile Selassie that their governments were seeking a solution by conciliation based on the proposals of the Committee of Five (which the Emperor had accepted), and asking him to send a representative to the Committee of Five.

Upon receipt of favorable word from Mussolini, the President of the

Council would be asked to summon the Committee of Five to meet on December 12.[40]

All this done, Laval was both confident and optimistic. "Now we are finished with Italy," he said.[41] Presumably he could now, as every French premier should, fix his attention on the main issue—Germany. Hoare went off to skate in the Engadine, in a frame of mind as positive as Laval's.

They issued a communiqué stating that, animated by close Franco-British friendship, they had in long discussions sought a formula which might be the basis of a friendly settlement of the Abyssinian dispute:

> There could be no question at present of publishing these formulae. The British Government has not yet been informed of them and once its agreement has been received it will be necessary to submit them to the consideration of the interested Governments and to discussion by the League of Nations.
>
> We have worked together with the same anxiety to reach as rapidly as possible a peaceful and honourable solution.
>
> We are both satisfied with the result which we have reached.[42]

## What Did It Mean?

Of critical importance in assessing the Hoare-Laval proposals is to understand what they were intended—and not intended—to be. Certainly they were not a fixed and final plan to be imposed upon recalcitrant parties. Instead the aim was to draw the parties into settlement discussions by presenting a basis on which those discussions might begin.

This aim was precisely articulated in a Foreign Office memorandum of December 2, 1935, before Hoare and Laval met, which stated the goal:

> to overcome the dangerous crisis, not to solve the Abyssinian question, which is going to be with us for years. But if we can stop the war, passions will cool and there will be more chance than at present of reducing all these rather general and perhaps slightly theoretical proposals to practical shape.[43]

The communiqué made it clear that the proposals were preliminary and that the British Government had not seen them. Hoare had proposed; he had not disposed.

His own view was that he had secured important modifications of earlier Peterson-Léger proposals in Abyssinia's favor. He had, he wrote the Cabinet hastily on the afternoon of December 8, greatly reduced the territorial cessions. There would be no cession to Italy of fertile lands in the south but only frontier rectification in Danakil and Ogaden and cession of the already occupied territory in Eastern Tigre in exchange for a corridor and a port. The presence of strong Italian forces in the occupied territory was simply a fact which raised this practical question: did there exist a superior force available to eject them and, more important, the will to use it?

The reduction in territorial cessions, Hoare thought, would justify the expansion of the proposed zone of Italian economic monopoly—so long, Hoare was careful to point out—as it was not another name for a transfer of sovereignty or a mandate. Hoare's positions here were specific: there must be Abyssinian sovereignty and League supervision over the zone—non-Amharic territory he pointed out—such as the Emperor had already accepted for his country as a whole under the Committee of Five plan.[44]

When the proposals were in fact sent to Mussolini and the Emperor, two important terms were omitted. There was no reference to the Zeila alternative, nor to any limitation on Abyssinia's right to build a railway. This was consistent with the preliminary nature of the proposals, deferring these questions till they should rise, if they did, once hostilities had ceased and discussions begun.

The procedure was clearly designed to achieve the same end—not instant agreement, but negotiations. To Mussolini there was offered the inducement, but not commitment to defer the oil sanction; to the Emperor a reduced opportunity to abort the negotiation.

A useful test is to compare the proposals to what had gone on before. In June, to Eden Mussolini had demanded annexation of the non-Amharic territories and political control over the Amharic core of Abyssinia.

The Committee of Five had proposed a League plan of reform, assistance and administration, under League appointed advisors aided by foreign specialists for the whole of Abyssinia. At the same time, Britain and France offered territorial adjustments looking to Abyssinian access to the sea, and suggested a special Italian interest in the economic development of the country. All this was predicated upon the preservation of the sovereignty, independence, and territorial integrity of Abyssinia.

Mussolini's October offer accepted the League assistance program for Amharic Abyssinia, adding to it an Italian mandate over non-Amharic

Abyssinia, frontier rectifications, and Abyssinian access to the sea. By these means, Mussolini said, the Emperor's sovereignty and the country's independence would be protected.

The Hoare-Laval proposals neither accepted an Italian mandate over all non-Amharic Abyssinia nor proposed a League plan of assistance and control over the whole country. Instead they offered in the south the special zone of Italian economic influence under a League plan of assistance, but under Abyssinian sovereignty. There would be border rectifications and the proposed exchange of territories which recognized the fact of Italian military occupation (but excluding conquered Aksum) and offered in return for the territorial cessions a corridor and a port.

This was substantially less than Mussolini's offer. The Committee of Five proposals had never defined the proposed border rectifications, exchanges of territory, or Italian economic interests. Nevertheless, the Hoare-Laval proposals could claim the Committee of Five proposals as legitimate ancestors in these essential components: League assistance under Abyssinian sovereignty over, not all of Abyssinia, but a special zone where Italian economic interests would predominate, and an exchange of territories which recognized a change of facts—the Italian conquests.

The difficulties of the problem, both African and European were manifest. To Laval and Hoare these proposals were reasonably addressed to the problem, reasonably related to what had gone on before and, above all, a reasonable basis for continuing discussions which might defuse the crisis and lead to solutions that could be accepted if not embraced. It was, in fact, an exercise in the art of the possible.

It was all very urgent and Peterson was dispatched to London with the French typescript of the proposals and Hoare's request that they be considered by the Cabinet the next day.

While Peterson travelled by boat and train to London, the presses rolled in Paris. Thus it happened that when Peterson delivered the proposals to Eden on the morning of Monday, December 9, there appeared in *L'Oeuvre* and *L'Echo de Paris* outlines of the proposals under the pens of Mme. Genevieve Tabouis and Pertinax. Laval was thought by many, then and later, to be the source of the leak.

Laval valued above all the confidence of Mussolini and studied his psyche. He knew that leaks had doomed both the Zeila and Committee of Five proposals and that at any time, more especially now, to publish anything Mussolini might view as an ultimatum would be disastrous.

Mussolini would never, he had told the Italian Chamber on December 7, negotiate under duress. To the contrary, Laval's consistent aim was to deal with Mussolini privately and personally. Mme. Tabouis, on the other hand, proclaimed that her fixed intent had been, by publicizing the proposals, to destroy them, thereby enhancing the authority of the League.[45]

## The British Cabinet Considers

Years later, Eden wrote in his memoirs that he was astonished to read the Hoare-Laval proposals, that he advised Baldwin that neither the Emperor nor the League would accept them; and that he wished to have nothing to do with them and to resign.[46]

Such afterthoughts hardly jibe with Eden's performance at the Cabinet meeting on the evening of December 9. It was Eden who, in Hoare's absence, presented and explained the proposals and what is more supported them, although, he told the Cabinet, he felt bound to point out that "some features of the proposals were likely to prove very distateful to some states members of the League of Nations including states represented on the Committee of Five."[47]

Eden reported Laval's assurances that France would honor her obligations to the League, then promptly cast doubt on those assurances, especially if France accepted and the Emperor rejected further negotiations.

That the proposals were a basis for discussion was clear to the Cabinet. It discussed how the proposals compared to the Committee of Five report and Mussolini's demands. Eden was firm that the proposals must be sent to Italy and Abyssinia at the same time, all the more so now that they had been leaked.

The Cabinet agreed with both Hoare and Eden. They decided, first and foremost: "To support the policy of the Secretary of State for Foreign Affairs as set forth in his Memorandum."

This was subject to the modification, as proposed by Eden "with the object of securing the support of the League of Nations to the basis for discussion as soon as possible" that Britain and France should ask the Committee of Eighteen on December 12 to refer the matter to the Committee of Five, assuming, meanwhile, postponement of the oil sanction.

Eden was authorized to send the proposals to Italy and Abyssinia simultaneously and instructed to obtain French approval of this procedure. The British Minister in Addis Ababa was asked "to do his best to induce the Emperor to accept, or at least not to reject it out of hand."

The Cabinet had backed Hoare without dissent and without serious differences of opinion. Its members knew and respected the Foreign Secretary who, in the hierarchy of British politics stood second only to the Prime Minister. They had special sympathy for the state of his health. It was as natural that they, having commissioned Hoare to engage in discussions, should back their colleague as it would be unnatural to disown him except on the most serious grounds and most serious consideration. That the situation was difficult all knew; how serious it was began to be apparent the next day when the proposals were tested in Parliament.

## The Morning After

On December 10, the *Times* published a brief outline of the proposals. It was accurate in stating that Italy would receive Danakil and Eastern Tigre including Adowa and Makale but not Aksum and that Abyssinia would receive a corridor and a port at Assab. It was highly inaccurate in reporting that Italy would receive outright all of the territory south of 8°N and east of 35°E; this was the proposed special zone of League assistance and Italian economic advantage. It reported instead Abyssinian sovereignty and a program of League assistance for the rest of Abyssinia, doubly confusing the issue.[48] The *Times* reported that France welcomed the British Cabinet's assent and that Mussolini took a guarded approach.[49]

These stories aroused intense curiosity, and in many quarters incipient anger and a sense of betrayal. In Parliament when Baldwin was asked outright to detail the proposals, he declined on the ground that they had not yet been finalized and submitted to the parties and that, even then, they were only a basis for discussion. Moreover, he cautioned, there appeared to be substantial inaccuracies of the press reports. He would inform the House as soon as he could.

Attlee raised the critical issues:

> It is a matter which has been subject of a General Election. We understand that the proposals overthrow the whole position of the existing League system in order to settle this question.[50]

Labour Member Lees-Smith vigorously seconded Attlee. If half the newspaper reports were true, he said, then the proposals were "in contradiction of the Covenant of the League of Nations and an abandonment of the policy on which the Government fought the General Election."

Eden argued the Government's position. He called to mind the moral mandate, the repeated statements of Laval and Hoare of their dual policy and their efforts to seek a settlement acceptable to all the parties. Everyone knew and approved this, "and I am bound to say that to me that seems an eminently wise and reasonable course."

There were indeed important inaccuracies in the press reports and the procedure for forwarding the proposals had yet to be agreed with France. "It would be unprecedented," Eden said, "at this stage to make public the proposals which we hope will make a basis upon which people will talk before the principals have even had a chance to read them." He added,

> We have never said that either party must accept the proposals, we are not seeking to impose terms on anybody—we have no authority to do it—but we are trying to find out by communication with the parties whether we can find a basis upon which peace negotiations should be possible, and I make no apology for that.[51]

It had been suggested that the proposals were contrary to the League. That, Eden replied, was for the League to say and if it did, Britain would accept it.

That was all he would say to the House as he departed for Geneva to hear the views of others and to pursue with them the same two objectives—restoring peace and maintaining the authority of the League.

The basic issues had surfaced early in the day. To the suggestion of one speaker that the proposals would reward aggression, Mr. McGovern, an Independent Labour Member asked: "Are you in favor of military action?" The speaker sidestepped: "This is not the time to discuss that point."[52] It was, nevertheless, a point that had been inherent in the Peace Ballot and in the issue of economic versus military sanctions, the will and the ability to enforce them.

After further angry questions, Baldwin closed the debate, as gingerly as he had opened it. In a celebrated passage he said,

> I have seldom spoken with greater regret for my lips are not yet unsealed. Were these troubles over I would make a case—and I would guarantee that not a man would go into the lobby against us.

He reiterated that Eden could only propose to the League and the parties; he could not enforce. He recounted one member's observation: "He said that a large number of voters at the General Election would support sanctions but did not wish war." "I do not believe," Baldwin added, "that there is anyone in this country who wants it [war]." [53]

The riddle remained: sanctions and war and how far one could exist without engendering the other. Baldwin promised to follow the dual policy. The House approved, 281 to 139, a majority of 142.

But the barometer was falling. The storm clouds were gathering, suspicions waxing, doubts growing. For this there were many reasons. Despite repeated statements of the dual policy, there were many whose gaze had been fastened on Geneva and sanctions, rather than Paris and Rome. The proposals were endowed by some with a fiat and a finality that Hoare and certainly Laval had never intended. The inaccurate press reports hinted at huge rewards to Italian aggression quite contrary to Hoare's intent and what he believed the proposals to mean.

These factors were, in turn, molded by political positions and passions which would in the end determine policy. Labour had decisively lost an election, an election in which it had sacrificed a beloved leader to back the government's League policy. Had it all been a trick?

A.L. Rowse was an ardent Labourite on his way to becoming a distinguished historian:

> After the trickery of the Red Letter scare in 1924, after the trickery of 1931 repeated in 1935, no decent Labour man would accept anything from these men, even when they were right—as, too little and too late, over armaments.[54]

Never mind that the question—are you willing to fight?—was unanswered and that Labour had attacked the Government's rearmament policy the week before; there burned in many a Labour heart a fierce determination to defeat both Italy and the Government, and to uphold principle over compromise and expediency.

All this was to be expected from the Opposition and the Government had, as it showed on December 10, a strong majority in the House. A new and important factor was the rising tide of doubt and dissatisfaction among members of the Government party, newly elected to office, and upon whose support the Government depended.

## Vansittart and Laval

At its meeting on December 9, the Cabinet had directed Eden to obtain French agreement to the simultaneous transmission of the proposals to Rome and Addis Ababa. Vansittart, who had stayed on in Paris, took on the task. It was two AM when he met Laval who conducted the business clad in a soiled nightgown, edged in pink, thereby offending Vansittart's patrician instincts.

Laval had not wanted to send the proposal to Italy and Abyssinia at the same time, believing Abyssinian refusal likely, precisely to bring about the oil sanction. But he agreed, on the understanding that, if Italy accepted and Abyssinia refused, there would be no oil sanction. Otherwise, he said, he could never get public support for the proposals. Vansittart did not object; he wired Eden that failing agreement on this point there would be an impasse.

Vansittart had seen the Italian Ambassador in Paris the same day who was sure Mussolini would negotiate. This was added reason for France and Britain not to fall out.[55]

Nothing could be done before this issue was resolved. The Cabinet met on December 10 to consider Vansittart's report. Peterson answered questions about the proposals which, he thought, filled out the Committee of Five proposals in Italy's favor. But he judged the exchange of territories reasonable and the economic zone justifiable. It was not very salubrious, unsuitable for Northern Europeans though, Peterson offered, "the Italians might find it less unsuitable."

How, Peterson was asked, would the proposed settlement affect a prospective aggressor? Laval had made the point, Peterson replied, that the settlement would mean better conditions in Europe by putting Franco-British relations on a firm footing and by bringing the Italians back to the Stresa front.

Before framing instructions to Vansittart, the Cabinet discussed the political difficulty that would arise if Abyssinia refused the proposals. It concluded that the proposals must be sent to Italy and Abyssinia at the same time. Otherwise there was little chance that the proceedings at Geneva could be adjourned.

Moreover, Britain could not agree to Laval's request that, if Abyssinia refused, there should be no oil sanction. There were too many imponderables. The question was one for the League. The parties might not answer with a simple yes or no. The prospect of oil supplies from nonmember countries would have to be negotiated; an oil sanction seemed to the Cabinet highly unlikely in the near future except if Italy rejected the proposals. All these were reasons not to give the undertaking.

Britain did give this assurance: were Italy to accept and Abyssinia reject, it would neither propose nor support further sanctions until it was clear that there was no chance of an agreed settlement. But it could not pledge itself to oppose sanctions for all time under conditions which could not be foreseen.[56]

Vansittart met Laval that evening to convey the Cabinet's reply. Laval was clearly disappointed: "But I told him," Vansittart wired the Cabinet, "his only real assurance in any case would always be the good sense and good faith of His Majesty's Government and that on these characteristics he could surely always count."[57]

For Laval, it must have been a wearily familiar exchange: the French search for precise assurances, British protestations of good faith. It was quite the same as Eden's reply to Laval's September question—would Britain enforce the Covenant as enthusiastically in Europe as in Africa?

Laval nevertheless accepted the British response. He wanted, above all, to move the proposals forward and discussed how he would put pressure on Mussolini. He was aware, Vansittart said, of the British Government's difficulties and did not want to add to them. "Once he was persuaded to meet us in return, he did so handsomely."[58]

The plan was promptly dispatched to Rome and to Addis Ababa where Ambassador Barton was asked to use his "utmost influence to induce the Emperor to give careful and favorable consideration to these proposals and on no account lightly to reject them."[59]

Laval presented his case to the Emperor with far greater diplomacy. He asked his Ambassador in Addis Ababa to emphasize that the proposals had been developed in response to the invitation of the League Council, derived from the principles of the Covenant, respected Abyssinian sovereignty, and would be developed by the Committee of Five.[60]

In directing Drummond jointly with Chambrun to present the proposals to Mussolini, Eden asked him to urge on Mussolini Britain's desire to take account of Italian aspirations "so far as these can be made compatible with the principles of the Covenant of the League of Nations and respect for Abyssinian sovereignty." It should be made clear to him that this was "a basis of negotiation in principle without prejudice to the discussions which would subsequently take place before the Committee." Eden added two delicate points. Were Italy to reject the Assab corridor, Drummond could state the willingness of Britain and France to provide a port and corridor as they had to the Committee of Five. For his information, Britain and France had agreed to obtain, at some future date, an undertaking from Abyssinia not to construct a railway in competition with the French. Laval's instructions to Chambrun included only the first of these two points, neither of which had been included in the proposals to be delivered to Mussolini and to the Emperor.[61]

Late on December 10, therefore, the proposals were on their way to the parties under the authority of the British Government, and the French Cabinet which had given its prompt approval the same day. Herriot predicted neither Mussolini nor the Emperor would accept, but the proposals were solidly backed, not only by the French Government, but by the press and by the French public.[62]

An official statement from Rome announced that the Head of State "appreciates the effort at collaboration" made in Paris and "reserves for himself an examination of the proposals which had been presented to him." There was not, as there had been in the past, an immediate rejection. Reports from Rome persisted in stating that Mussolini was ready to accept the proposals as a basis for discussion and to negotiate on them. Cerutti had in fact called on Laval to convey this assurance.[63]

It took longer for the proposals to reach Addis Ababa and for the ambassadors to concert their action. Even before the proposals could be presented to the Emperor, who was at the Northern Front, the Ethiopian Minister in Paris issued an uncompromising statement.

Abyssinia, it said, had been the victim of an act of aggression solemnly condemned in Geneva. It would firmly decline any proposal which rewarded aggression and disregarded the Covenant.[64]

## The Rising Storm

If the initial Abyssinian response was predictable, the Italian open, and the French generally approving, there was elsewhere the same kind of discomfort, frustration, and anger which had surfaced in the House of Commons.

In Geneva there were many, especially representatives of the smaller countries, who had taken risks to uphold the Covenant and who asked, if the aggressor were to be rewarded, what security the Covenant might offer them.[65]

Opinion in America was generally adverse. In a nation determinedly neutral, there was talk in the press of both rewarding the aggressor and betraying the Covenant—to which, of course, the United States had never adhered.[66] American opinion was important because of America's ability decisively to influence the effectiveness of the oil sanction.

Opinion in the Dominions and in the Empire was generally critical at a time when their role in British policy was growing.

But it was in Britain where the proposals ignited the fiercest controversies and the deepest passions. Lord Cecil had always maintained that ultimate power lay in public opinion. He had waged a mighty campaign to educate the public about the League of Nations and in the Peace Ballot the public had approved the League by a 97 percent vote. He had brought this power sharply to the attention of the Government. As no British government had ever done before, that Government now instinctively looked over its shoulder to see if the public was following.

Important segments of the press attacked the plan. The *Herald* appealed to Baldwin for the sake of peace, the League, and the honor of the country, to reach a plan consistent with the principles of the Covenant. The proposals, said the *News Chronicle* would sacrifice the whole collective system on the eve of success. To the *Star*, the proposals were "horrifying men with a sense of justice" in Britain and elsewhere. The *Yorkshire Post* called on Britain to maintain the postwar principles of international morality. In a like tone, the *Nottingham Guardian* called for a "moral victory." Both the *Liverpool Post* and the *Birmingham Post* expressed the view that public opinion would not support the proposals, that most people were shocked and would view the plan as a surrender to Italy. To the *Manchester Guardian*, the proposals were utterly remote from anything the country had been led to expect—or should approve.

Opinion was not unanimous. The *Morning Telegraph* and the *Evening Standard* noted that Italy held substantial territory won by force of arms and that there were no forces standing ready to eject her. There were those who took a practical view of the need for peace through compromise.

On the isolationist Right, the *Daily Mail* thought the British public weary of the whole Mediterranean business. The *Evening News*, in a coinage of which Spiro Agnew would have been proud, castigated "the mad mullahs of meddlesome pacifism" and their "ridiculous doctrine that the League is Boss."[67]

Politics in Britain usually proceeded more calmly than in France, with less tumult and shouting, perhaps more underlying humor and, in Parliament, a greater sense of fellowship. But, from time to time, issues arose which engaged the emotions and dominated the consciousness of the British people. The Peace Ballot, Hoare's September declaration at Geneva, and the November election had placed the League in the vanguard of British thought. War exerted its timeless fascination, accented by the exotic locale and colorful dramatis personae. The Hoare-Laval proposals united these elements and presented an issue that would deeply move the British people and bring on a political crisis which, for its intensity and breadth, had few equals in Britain's long history.

All this became clear when, on December 12, a Liberal Member of Parliament tabled this resolution:

> That this House condemns any settlement of the Italo-Abyssinia dispute which violates the territorial integrity or the political and economic independence of Abyssinia in favor of the declared aggressor and would regard any settlement on these lines as a betrayal of the League of Nations and as an act of national dishonor.[68]

The resolution was in itself to be anticipated. What was unanticipated was the inclusion, in the list of sponsors, of prominent Conservative members whose numbers grew on succeeding days.

The motion filed in the House of Lords was in the same vein:

> That this House will not assent to any settlement of the Italo-Ethiopian dispute which ignores our international obligations under the Covenant of the League of Nations by granting the aggressor State greater concessions after its unprovoked aggression than would have been obtained by peaceful negotiations.[69]

On December 11, the Cabinet met for the third consecutive day. It was informed that Laval had agreed to the Cabinet's conditions and that the proposals had been sent to Rome and Addis Ababa. They now discussed what position Eden should take at the meeting of the Committee of Eighteen, to be held the next day.

Eden had backed the proposals in Cabinet and Parliament. He now hoped "he would not be expected to champion the proposals made to Italy and Abyssinia in detail at Geneva." They would likely not succeed, he said, because the representatives would have made up their minds. He wanted to resist any proposal by Laval to bend the terms in Italy's favor, and to tell Laval of the reaction of Parliament and the public. For practical purposes, he added, the oil sanction would likely be held up pending replies to the proposals.

It was the sense of the Cabinet that Eden,

> would have to use his discretion, according to the circumstances he en-

> countered at Geneva, as to how far it was necessary for him to champion them [the proposals], especially in detail.

He ought, it was suggested, to take his position on those three propositions which were indeed Hoare's own summary: exchange of territories with advantage to both sides, League assistance to Abyssinia including social, economic, and administrative development, and special facilities for Italian economic development.

Eden was to indicate no change in Britain's backing of the oil sanction, but that, pending replies to the proposals, no date would likely be fixed. Indeed "the important thing for him to secure was that during the coming week there should be no date fixed for oil sanctions."[70]

In all this, the Cabinet was deeply impressed by a new factor—the initial public reaction to the proposals and an ongoing factor—the fear of pushing Italy into war. There were signs of a softening of position which contrasted to the backing the proposals had received on each of the two preceding days. The authority given Eden had the potential to convert advocacy into damnation by faint praise.

## At Geneva

At its formal meeting on December 12, 1935, Eden and Laval assured apprehensive members of the Committee of Eighteen that their proposals were intended to be considered by the League. Laval recounted to the Committee the efforts at conciliation, with League knowledge and approval. There was "nothing sinister or mysterious about those discussions and no thought that final decisions would be reached outside the League's framework."

Eden was deeply affected by those Committee members who feared a Mussolini triumph over the League[71] or who leveled what was to him the most damaging criticism of all—that Britain wasn't playing fair.[72] He, too, referred to League approval. After conceding that there had been no legal mandate for the conciliation efforts, he proceeded to use the discretion that the Cabinet had conferred upon him:

> The proposals now put forward are neither definitive nor sacrosanct. They are suggestions which it is hoped may make possible the beginning of negotiations. If the League does not agree with these suggestions we shall make no complaint.

To emphasize the point, he closed by saying,

> I emphasize that so far as the British Government are concerned we will not only readily accept the judgment of our colleagues but we will continue to use our best efforts to further the two objectives which have been constantly before us in this dispute—the restoration of peace and the maintenance of the authority of the League.[73]

In London Eden was the loyal supporter of the Government and of the Foreign Secretary. In Geneva he was the champion of the League and in this mode he presented the proposals as an unwelcome and unpleasant task. Herriot thought his presentation seemed "to be asking for a disavowal."[74]

The issue had not been debated in Parliament. The British Government still stood behind the proposals. Neither Italy nor Abyssinia had responded to them when Eden issued an open invitation for their rejection or at the very least made clear that Britain would not contest the decision of an agitated and discomfitted League. This was hardly the procedure Laval has envisioned or likely to lead to his goals: compromise, an end to war and threats of war, and the restoration of the Stresa Front.

The Committee of Eighteen prudently indicated that the task was one for the Council, to which, on December 13, Eden and Laval addressed the proposals for their further consideration.[75]

## The Rising Storm—2

On Sunday, December 8, Hoare had departed Paris for Switzerland, pleased with the results of his diplomacy, lauded by his staff, both for his efforts and the outcome. Only five days later, the proposals were in deep difficulties and the Government in crisis. The proposals had not yet been published; but the initial adverse reaction gained volume and force daily. The rising tide of public anger and dismay was matched in Parliament. Serious technical difficulties arose to perplex the Cabinet. The final complication had occurred on Swiss ice on Tuesday, when Sir Samuel Hoare suffered an ominous fall, shattering his nose in two places. He was confined to his bed, unable to travel at a moment when he most needed the support of his Cabinet colleagues and they most needed his explanation and enlightenment.

The Government's staunch supporter, the *Times*, on Friday, December 13, spoke of "the experience of this week, and in particular…the determined manifestation of public opinion which will long make it memorable."

The "depth and strength of the feeling roused even by the general tenor of the Paris proposals" was reflected throughout the country:

> It reaches the newspaper offices by letter and telegraph; it is heard in the lobbies of Parliament, in the constituencies, in the City, and indeed, wherever men meet.

The *Times* accepted the mediating mission and was inclined to believe that the prime responsibility lay with Laval and France. Its conclusion was blunt: the proposals failed to satisfy the Government's own pledges:

> Neither good sense nor good faith requires that the Government should stand upon terms which should never had been put forward, were bound to be tentative, and are now bound to fail.[76]

In succeeding days, the *Times*' letter writers exhibited their accustomed learning and furnished apt quotations from the Bible, Shakespeare, Samuel Johnson, and *Alice in Wonderland*. There were, at the outset, a few defenders of the proposals; these were soon overwhelmed by the tide of adverse reaction. Writers spoke of their "bitter sense of humiliation"[77] and of the millions who had voted for the Government expecting a firm League policy. A staunch Tory labeled the proposals "one of the most discreditable documents ever issued in the name of the British people"[78] and a future Conservative Prime Minister, calling the proposals "cynical and shameful," observed,

> I have never attended the funeral of a murdered man; but I take it that at such a ceremony, some distinction is made between the mourners and the assassins.[79]

All this affected members of the Government where they were most sensitive and most vulnerable. Neville Chamberlain noted on December 15,

> Nothing could be worse than our position. Our whole prestige in foreign affairs at home and abroad has tumbled to pieces like a house of cards. If we had to fight the election over again, we should probably be beaten.[80]

The proposals were finally published on Saturday, December 14. Surely more dramatic than the legalese of the terms and profoundly greater in their impact were the accompanying maps revealing large shaded or cross-hatched areas of Abyssinia which were the proposed territorial cessions or special zone. The *Times* editorialized that the impression given by the proposals had confirmed the forecasts: "that it was proposed to hand over to Italy the effective ownership and control of a good half of Abyssinian territory," adding that both the future of the League and the principle of collective security were at stake.[81]

Questions were put down to be asked in Parliament about the plan and about oil sanctions; and a deputation from the League of Nations Union headed by Lord Cecil called on the Prime Minister with a resolution "urging the Government to support no settlement of the dispute which failed to make it clear that aggression does not pay."[82]

Italy maintained its reserve; its spokesman said the proposals must be the subject of careful study, exploration and possible bargaining.[83] Abyssinia made eloquent objection, grounded on principle and asked for an immediate meeting of the League Assembly to consider the issue.[84]

Fuel was added to the fire on Monday, December 16, when, in response to the rising demand for the facts, the British Government published a White Paper. In addition to the plan itself, it contained the instructions to the British Ambassador in Rome, indicating that if Italy were unwilling to cede Assab, Britain and France would stand ready with the Zeila alternative. This raised the issue whether Italy would make any sacrifice at all; at the same time there appeared the telegram to the British Minister in Addis Ababa asking him to use his "utmost influence" to secure the Emperor's favorable reception of the proposals.

Worse yet, for the proponents of the plan, the *Times* published with the proposals the report from Paris that, at a convenient moment, when he was too committed to withdraw, the Emperor would be informed that he could not build a railway to the newly acquired port. This was accompanied by the day's leading editorial, which took its title from the eloquent statement that the corridor "was apparently to remain a strip of scrub, restricted to the sort of traffic which has entered Ethiopia from the days of KING SOLOMON, a corridor for camels."

The Thunderer went on to thunder:

> The Paris proposals, with or without reservations and undertakings, were dead for all practical purposes from the moment that their general tenor was known.[85]

The proposals, the *Times* said, were repugnant to nearly every section of British opinion, and Britain, which could not negotiate an unjust peace, ought not to press the proposals in Geneva.

These views found a response across the nation as concerned and angry citizens wrote their newly elected members of Parliament. J.H. Thomas remarked in a Cabinet meeting that, after twenty-five years in Parliament, he "was receiving most terrible letters from the best people in his constituency."[86]

A learned study has since concluded that the volume of letters was less than the avalanche popularly reported at the time.[87] What emerges is that there was an unusually high volume of comment, almost wholly adverse, and the perception that it represented a large, determined, and vocal majority. In a political democracy, such voices are heard.

## Policymaking

Amid the turmoil, Hoare returned from Switzerland on December 16 and promptly took to his bed. In Parliament, Eden bore the brunt, in Hoare's absence, of searching questions about the plan to his great discomfort. The Government had to face three excruciating problems: what position to take before the League Council on Wednesday, December 18, in Parliament the day after, and finally and most personally anguishing to his colleagues, what to do about Sir Samuel Hoare.

A council of ministers met on December 16 to draw up a statement which Eden would deliver in Geneva. Their proposals were to be reviewed by the full Cabinet the next day.

While the ministers met, interesting indications came from Italy. It was announced that the Fascist Grand Council would consider the proposals on Wednesday, December 18, and that no reply could be given until then. On the same day, Grandi called on Vansittart to ask questions which might be assumed to be bargaining points. He raised the issues of the exclusion of Aksum from the ceded territory, boundary issues in Tigre, Danakil, and Ogaden, and wanted to know how the rights of Italian settlers in the special zone would be safeguarded. He wanted to discuss sovereignty of the Abyssinian outlet to the sea. To all this Vansittart replied that filling in the proposals was now the League's task.[88]

The Italian Ambassador in Rome raised the same issues the same day.[89] The matter appeared to be under consideration.

Meanwhile Vansittart busied himself with cleaning up the tangled issue of the railway. The problem, he wrote to Clerk in Paris, was that the limitation didn't apply to Assab, only to Zeila because this was an undertaking of the 1906 Treaty. Were Assab chosen, there was no issue;

but it was expected that Italy would reject Assab, again raising the issue. The practical business answer, Vansittart thought, was for Abyssinia to build a railway connecting Zeila and Djibuti, serving all interests. The whole thing had happened because of rough and ready drafting without legal experts.[90]

Hoare was sufficiently recovered the next day to try to put the issue in the most favorable light. The Paris proposals, he wrote Clerk, were based on the Assab cession which carried no limitation on building a railroad. Only, Hoare argued, if Abyssinia asked for Zeila instead would the issue arise, and was, in his opinion, purely hypothetical.[91]

The issue was not quite so simple to the Cabinet on December 17 and they saw clearly the political issue if the Zeila alternative were taken. They were also embarrassed that the issue had not been raised when they first approved the plan. They cautiously decided to check the record to see what had been and hence what could be said, and prudently determined that the matter could not be usefully discussed in Hoare's absence. The Prime Minister was deputed to see Hoare, "clear up the position," and decide how to handle the issue in Parliament.

The ministers now discussed Hoare's proposed stance in the debate—that sanctions could not succeed unless the whole League and not only Britain were prepared to back them. The defects were quickly pointed out: that it was far from clear that such support did not exist, and, in any case, the defeat of sanctions did not warrant a bad plan. It would be better, Chamberlain offered, to defend the basic principles on which the proposals were based, if not, at this point, the proposals themselves.

In the end, they agreed on the statement that Eden would deliver at the League Council meeting on December 18. Its critical passages read:

> It must be emphasized that the Paris proposals which were put forward last week were not advanced as proposals to be insisted upon in any event. They were advanced in order to ascertain what the views of the two parties and of the League might be upon them, and His Majesty's Government recommended them only for this purpose. If, therefore, it transpires that these proposals which are now before you do not satisfy the essential condition of agreement by the two parties and by the League, His Majesty's Government could not continue to support or recommend them. In its view, this particular attempt at conciliation could not then be regarded as having achieved its object, and His Majesty's Government for its part would not wish to pursue it farther.[92]

Baldwin, Chamberlain, and Eden then went to call on Hoare, who had already seen and approved the statement. Baldwin asked Hoare, "How do you feel?" to which Hoare replied, "I wish I were dead." Eden thanked Hoare for approving the statement which meant the end of his plan, then left for Geneva. "Thank you so much for all your loyal help," Hoare said to the departing Eden.[93]

Baldwin and Chamberlain stayed with Hoare. "We all stand together," Baldwin told him.[94] The proposals were dead; the Foreign Secretary still lived.

In Paris, the perennially embattled Laval ably defended the proposals in Parliament. He recounted his views on the rhythm of sanctions and conciliation, his agreements with Hoare not to use military force or a naval blockade, his attempts at conciliation, his yielding to British views because of the paramount importance of British collaboration and France's loyalty to the Covenant and the sanctions already imposed.

He ended with a plea for European reconstruction and peace. His majority this day was reduced to 52, but Pierre Laval, too, survived.

Aristocratic and sometimes supercilious, British diplomats had criticized Laval's character, his haberdashery, and his table manners. Pleased with his victory in the Chamber, Laval thought of the agony of Sir Samuel Hoare, and in an exquisite example of courtesy and kindness gave Clerk a personal message to him:

> "[H]e desires to offer you his personal regret for the worries and attacks to which you have been exposed as a result of the Paris conversations. These worries and attacks had made him even more grateful, if that were possible, for your collaboration in Paris and he would have expressed himself in this sense far more fully than he actually did in his speech in the Chamber today if he had not been afraid of saying something which might prove an embarrassment to you when you speak on Thursday.[95]

Laval now met Eden who showed him the statement approved by the Cabinet, which to Laval meant the frustration, not only of his settlement efforts, but of his whole policy. Laval tried vainly to persuade Eden to change it, pointing out that neither party had as yet said the terms would not be accepted. But Eden had no authority; he told Laval world opinion had given the answer. Laval remarked bluntly that he never had much luck negotiating with the English.[96]

In Geneva, on December 18, events ran their course. Eden made his statement. It had been right to attempt settlement and to ascertain the views of the parties: "If therefore, it transpires that these proposals which are now before you do not satisfy the essential condition of agreement by the two parties to the dispute, His Majesty's Government could not continue to recommend or support them."

Laval was brief. It would not be useful to explain again the mediating mission or the proposals. The parties had yet to be heard from. He ended on a note of subdued hope:

> In any case, I think it my duty to state forthwith that, if this effort does not secure the consent of all the interested parties, the Council will not be relieved of its duty to explore every avenue and to allow no opportunity to escape with a view to bringing about an honourable and just solution of the present conflict, such as is required both by the interests of peace and by the spirit of the League of Nations.[97]

Abyssinian displeasure had long since been made known. The Emperor had on December 16 castigated the proposals as a "negation and an abandonment" of the League's principles which would place a premium on aggression. Yet in the end, it was not international law on which he took his stand: "The vital interests of Ethiopia are in question, and for us this takes precedence over every other consideration."[98]

This was followed by a lengthy declaration on December 18 eloquently arguing Abyssinia's case.[99] But after Eden and Hoare spoke, Wolde Mariam again stated that Abyssinia did not wish to reply to the proposals until they had been fully reviewed and discussed by the League[100] and that his own forceful comments did not constitute a reply. In this posture, the Council, observing that replies had not been received from Abyssinia or Italy, adjourned.

The Cabinet met on December 18[101] for its final session before the Parliamentary debate the day following, knowing that in Geneva that day, Eden was pronouncing the death-knell of the Hoare-Laval plan. Hoare remained ill at home. The minutes of this meeting were marked "Most Secret" and so they remained for decades. What was at stake was not the proposals but the political fate of the Baldwin government.

Baldwin opened the Cabinet discussion saying Hoare must be allowed to present his case in his own way. Neville Chamberlain agreed that Hoare probably felt on trial "though, of course, the Cabinet were with him." Chamberlain emphasized that Hoare would say that he still considered the plan right even if, because of public opinion, the Government could no longer support it.

Hoare would defend the peace terms as more favorable than Mussolini had demanded, the best he could get from France, with a reasonable chance of Mussolini's acceptance. But he accepted that the proposals were dead. Britain had done what it could alone. The future lay in the hands of the League.

Chamberlain had said the Cabinet were with Hoare. The first round of comments dispelled that notion. Sir Kingsley Wood, Minister of Health, disliked the speech Chamberlain outlined. Oliver Stanley, President of the Board of Education was blunter. The speech would be "disastrous." He put his finger on the problem:

> The criticism would be made that the public had been let in for this issue at the Election without being told what the real position was.

Ministers began to take cover. Lord Swinton, the Air Minister, declared that the Cabinet would not have approved the terms if they had been presented before Hoare left for Paris. What the Cabinet knew of the long continuing negotiation and what authority or limitations they had approved he did not say.

With the hint that the Cabinet might absolve itself, J.H. Thomas, Colonial Minister, proceeded to the fatal conclusion, couched in language of admiration for Hoare, that he ought to resign. "Members would be going back to their constituencies to celebrate their victory and would find themselves faced with disintegration." But, if Hoare resigned, the whole thing would be dead.

Other ministers indicated their difficulties in supporting Hoare. Only Lord Zetland, Secretary of State for India, stood firmly on the proposals and said flatly that the Government ought to accept its responsibility.

Opposition to Hoare mounted. To Lord Eustace Percy, the political situation was "tragic." William Ormsby-Gore, Commissioner of Works, sketched his personal dilemma:

> He recalled his own answers during the election to the first of the questions put by the League of Nations Union, as to whether he was prepared to resist the triumph of force, to which he had given an affirmative reply.

The only way out, then, was to admit a mistake had been made. Ormsby-Gore was far from alone. Of the members of the new Parliament, 90 percent are known to have returned the LNU questionnaires. Of these, 97 percent had answered the same question in the affirmative. This was clearly a substantial majority.[102] The LNU had taken pains to make these results public in the constituencies and these new members, as Ormsby-Gore so plainly said, had become, like Baldwin himself, captive to Lord Cecil's bow and spear.

Sir John Simon, now Home Secretary, attacked his successor for his unwillingness to admit the proposals were wrong, at the same time affirming that he had been right in Manchuria. As to the Opposition's resolution, in his opinion: "This was very nearly what the Cabinet felt."

Baldwin said he had not yet arrived at judgment: "All he could say was that though he was not rattled, it was a worse situation in the House of Commons than he had ever known."

It was Halifax who administered the final blow. It was not so much his opinion that Hoare should resign that told but his reasons:

> [M]uch more was at stake, namely, the whole moral position of the Government before the world. If the Prime Minister were to lose his personal position, one of our national sheet anchors would have dragged.

Whether he settled his mind in response to this plea, or after he had closed the meeting, Baldwin thereafter called on Hoare; the support of the day before was reversed, and Hoare agreed to resign.

## The Duce Embattled

Italian progress had been slow and largely unopposed when, in mid-December, four large Abyssinian armies closed with the enemy on the Northern front. The northernmost army, under Ras Imru, crossed the Takazze River on December 15, while the armies of Ras Seyum, Ras Kassa, and Ras Mulugeta maintained their pressure to the south. In bloody fighting that lasted till December 17, the Italians admitted large casualties. Warriors attacked the Italian tanks with bare hands, putting them out of action and beheading their crews. The victory was important in terms of both material and morale. Ras Imru's men captured not only fifty sorely needed machine guns and quantities of ammunition, but had the immense satisfaction of putting the enemy to flight.[103]

This was the beginning of Italy's "black period." Mussolini had followed a double policy, too. Behind the strident, aggressive public posture, there was the realist who kept his options open. The public Duce struck characteristic poses on December 18, at Pontina, where he had gone to celebrate completion of another phase of the draining of the Pontine Marshes.

He would not send the flower of Italian youth to distant and barbarous lands except for victory. It was a war of civilization and liberation backed by the Italian people who would not be throttled or tricked with impunity. "The regime," he declared, "will go straight ahead."[104]

The Italian people responded. In a great national rite on the same day, several million Italian women gave up their most cherished, and to many their most valuable possession, their gold wedding rings in a symbolic exchange for rings of steel. It was a profound gesture which bound the people to the regime.

The diplomatic Duce pursued the other leg of the double policy. That he would take less than all he had made clear to Eden in June and he had made his own offer after the war had begun. The campaign ahead was uncertain, economic sanctions were in place, and yet substantial inducements lay ready to hand.

Mussolini had, therefore, prepared a communiqué to be issued after the meeting of the Fascist Grand Council on the evening of December 18. The communiqué expressed appreciation for the mediating efforts of France and Britain. More important, it announced the Council's decision to "consider the proposals as possible bases for discussion, leaving the Government the necessary reservations to safeguard the rights of the nation."[105] The Government, of course, was Mussolini.

There was in fact a majority of the Grand Council in favor of accepting negotiations; in this they had the agreement of the professionals of the Italian Foreign Office, who had attempted to elucidate the proposals and who thought they offered a good way out of a bad situation. In Rome, where the influence of the Holy See was significant, the Pope, through his diplomats, made it clear he believed the proposals should be accepted—and quickly.[106]

Thus it came about that while Hoare was resigning, Italy was preparing to agree to the first and most important part of the Hoare-Laval plan—the beginning of negotiations, for which the plan was the basis, without prejudice to the rights of any party or the solutions which might evolve.

The dramatic news of Hoare's resignation reached the Grand Council just before it convened. In the utter confusion and puzzlement that attended the news, the Council resolved to adjourn, and to meet again on December 20 when the situation might be clearer.[107]

## Hoare vs. Baldwin

The decision had been made. Hoare had resigned, the proposals were dead. But something more was required, a public manifestation combining of the qualities of an accounting and a ceremony, akin to the last act of a tragedy in which the characters measure their actions and intentions against an inexorable fate.

In the House of Lords, Lord Cecil regretted the proposals and championed the Covenant. He accepted Halifax's explanation that there had been no instructions to or communications with Hoare, which was central to Halifax's thesis that the Cabinet, in accepting the proposals, had supported a highly regarded and trusted colleague and thus been led to a tragic error.

If political pressures dominated the Commons debate, there were those lords whose seats being hereditary, could say what was unpopular. There had been no betrayal, Lord Newton said:

> The only people who could claim to have been betrayed were the clients of Lord Cecil—the 11,000,000 people who signed his peace manifesto and who might find themselves called out to fight for a principle they did not understand.[108]

Lord Phillimore interpreted the election results:

> The recent General Election was a vote for peace, and if the Government thought they were to lead the country into war for the Covenant of the League they were making the mistake of their lives.

To this, the Earl of Mansfield added:

> The people of the Country were not prepared to go to war in defence of the Covenant of the League of Nations...Sir Samuel Hoare had been sacrificed to make not a Roman holiday but a League of Nations Union holiday.[109]

Hoare did not recant that day or ever after. He came to the House from his sickbed and faced the storm. His urgent goals as Foreign Secretary had been to prevent a European conflagration or an isolated war with Italy which, to the cheers of the House, he said he had no doubt Britain would win. He reminded the House what Halifax had forgotten—his publicly proclaimed, continuing search for a peaceful settlement. He had not gone off to Paris on a frolic and a detour; he had been pressed hard to go by his colleagues. What he and Laval proposed was a basis for discussions; its purpose was to start a negotiation even though he himself disliked some features of the plan. There had been no intent to impose a solution on the belligerents.

He put the best face on the proposals in outlining their bases: international supervision, exchange of territory and a special zone for Italian economic development and related them to the Committee of Five proposals. He firmly announced that Abyssinia's Assab corridor would be with full sovereignty including the right to build a railway. Abyssinia would remain sovereign in the special zone under League supervision. All this was far less than Mussolini had demanded.

He now uttered a prophetic concern:

> I have been terrified with the thought—I speak very frankly to the House—that we might lead Abyssinia on to think that the League could do more for them then it can do, that in the end we should find a terrible moment of disillusionment in which it may be that Abyssinia would be destroyed as an independent State. I have been terrified at that position, and I could not help thinking of the past, in which more than once in our history we have given, and rightly given, all our sympathies to some threatened or downtrodden race, but because we had been unable to implement and give effect to those sympathies, all that we had done was to encourage them, with the result that in the end their fate was worse than it would have been without our sympathy.

So it was, when the time came in 1939, that Britain was not then, nor has it ever since been, been able effectively to redeem the pledge upon which the Polish nation staked so much.

Peace could come, Hoare said, by negotiation or surrender. He preferred negotiation. For the moment, his negotiation had failed. He acknowledged that the plan was dead.

There were problems of collective security. He did not recriminate. But he recalled that only Britain had brought force to bear. "Not a ship, not a machine, not a gun has been moved by any other member state."

He closed with conviction. His conscience was clear:

> I say to this House that I cannot honestly recant—and I sincerely believe that the course that I took was the only course that was possible under the circumstances.[110]

As he sat down, he suffered a paroxysm of pain and put his hand to his nose. There were those who said he had cried, a charge he ever after rejected as vigorously as he refused to say that he had erred.[111]

Attlee now strongly attacked the Government. If it was proper for Hoare to resign, it was proper for the Government to resign. The proposals betrayed the electors in the General Election, Abyssinia, and the League; and Conservatives had said this as vehemently as Liberals and Labour. He thought the Government was quite cognizant of the plan, which it had now abandoned at Geneva. He twitted the Prime Minister whose lips had been sealed. What would he say today?

All this was within the practice and manners of the House. Attlee now went one step further. It was more than a question of policy. There were questions, he said, of the honor of the country and of the honor of the Prime Minister.[112]

In the excited condition of the House, this very personal attack on Baldwin gained him a sympathetic hearing. Baldwin commenced his abandonment of Hoare by paying tribute to him. He spoke of an absence of liaison with Hoare and of the Cabinet's dislike of the proposals. But they had not wished to retract their support from an ill and absent colleague.

Hoare had maintained he was right. Baldwin confessed error, an error of judgment, the Cabinet's and chiefly his. Never, he said, had he and his colleagues thought that they were not being true to every election pledge they had given.

> But I was not expecting that deeper feeling which was manifested by many of my hon. friends in many parts of the country on what I may call the ground of conscience and of honour. The moment I am confronted with that I know that something has happened that has appealed to the very deepest feelings of our countrymen, that some note has been struck that brings back, from them, a response from the depths.[113]

It had become obvious, he said, that there did not exist "that volume of popular opinion which it is necessary to have in a democracy behind the Government in a matter so important as this."

The proposals were dead, the Government would make no attempt to revive them. The storm had shown him he had done something unwise.

He pleaded devotion to the League, which brought laughter, and loyalty to election pledges, which raised cynical cries. He muddled through. He wanted no unilateral war; the League must be strong to render help; he invoked peace.[114]

This was Baldwin's weakest performance both in manner and substance. He had always prided himself on his intuitive understanding of the people and of the House. Now, he had to confess that not only had he misread the people but that they indeed had administered a lesson to him in conscience and honor.

Attlee's attack misfired. Austen Chamberlain, who could have rallied many party loyalists against Baldwin, now said: "The past is past" and that Attlee's imputation "made it certain that no supporter of the Government would abstain."[115]

Earl Winterton's motion supported the Government in settling disputes on terms the League could accept, and in pursuing the foreign policy outlined in the Government's electon manifesto and approved by the country. The real issue, he said, was Germany. The present storm had shown, he said in a lapidary phrase, the strength, but not necessarily the wisdom of democracy.[116] Now there was heard support for the plan, from Harold Nicholson who thought the terms not unreasonable,[117] while Neville Chamberlain plainly said the Cabinet knew of the Paris discussions and had specifically asked for settlement proposals. The Opposition cried "Get on with sanctions whatever they cost," but, Chamberlain replied, "At the same time they also cried 'above all do not let us have any armaments.'"[118]

Hoare gained sympathy and respect. Baldwin gained the votes. A member of Parliament with a taste for paradox summed it up: Hoare said I have done nothing wrong, therefore I resign. Baldwin said, I have done everything wrong; therefore I do not resign. Confession went over better than conviction; morality had proved sound—or at least adequate—politics. The Government prevailed on Winterton's motion by a solid majority of 225 votes.[119]

This stunning reversal had left Mussolini perplexed. On the day of the debate in Parliament, the Italian Foreign Office announced that the Pontina speech was not a reply to the Hoare-Laval proposals and Mussolini himself said that they were still under consideration.[120]

But the next day, there was nothing left to consider. The League Council adopted a resolution thanking France and Britain for their suggestions, announcing that, under the circumstances, it did not feel called upon to express an opinion and passed the matter on to the Committee of Thirteen. This was a formal funeral rite. Laval was appropriately glum: "Gentlemen," he said, "you have observed your minute of silence."[121] Eden then pronounced the funeral oration—there should be no let-up in the policy of sanctions.[122]

The Fascist Grand Council met on December 20. It referred to the proposals which it had reviewed two days earlier, but said no more about them. Instead, it discharged effusions of Fascist rhetoric lauding the Duce, the black-shirts, the soldiers, the nation, the civilizing mission and Italy's destiny as "marked out by the Duce." An official statement the next day said that there had been no further mention of the proposals because their sponsors had declared them dead. But Italy was always ready to listen to anyone who made offers and maintained them.[123]

Shortly after these climactic events, Mussolini reflected on it all in an interview which appeared in the London *Observer*:

> Yes, I had already drafted a cautious formal acceptance as a basis for negotiation and the Council of Ministers was sitting when the news came and you gentlemen in London, who praised Sir Samuel Hoare so highly in September, had dismissed him with ignominy on 19th December.[124]

Sir Austen Chamberlain had hoped to crown his career by once more becoming Foreign Secretary, a hope perhaps not entirely absent from his mind when he came to Baldwin's rescue. Instead, after several days of delay and some confusion, Baldwin appointed Eden Foreign Secretary on December 23, the youngest in British history. It was, Vansittart observed, a lovely Christmas present.[125]

## Dernier Cri

The last scene of the drama was played in Paris where it was freely predicted that Laval and his government must fall. Indeed it was speculated that he would voluntarily hand in his resignation. Instead, he prepared to fight.

First, he put his record in order. He wrote to Mussolini on December 22. Friendship, he said, required frankness. In the Rome accords of January 7, France had sacrificed important interests. At the same time "rich future perspectives" were opened to Italy. But the advantages conferred on Italy were to be developed peacefully. France had worked hard for a peaceful but honorable settlement which would have benefitted Italy. He regretted Italy had not accepted the December proposals; he did not regret having made them. And he had again reminded the League Council that the way of conciliation ought to remain open.

Mussolini had written him in October that the European and perhaps world situation rested in the hands of France. Today, Laval wrote, the peace of Europe lay in Mussolini's hands. He closed with an eloquent plea to Mussolini not to rebuff new efforts for a peaceful solution.[126]

Mussolini responded on Christmas Day. He sincerely appreciated Laval's efforts at conciliation on a basis favorable to Italy, and, if he could not agree with all Laval had written, that did not retract from the full recognition of Laval's efforts and good will.

He could not wholly agree that Italy's action in Abyssinia should proceed only by peaceful means. There had been much talk in Rome of a free hand, which had never been clearly defined, save to preserve French rights under existing treaties. Simple economic rights did not suffice without political control. But this he conceded: "Naturally, I do not mean to say that you gave your consent to the war which circumstances made inevitable."

He reviewed the history of events since Wal Wal, explaining why he had deemed each proposal insufficient and the League's action inappropriate. He then gave a remarkable survey of the Hoare-Laval proposals and Italy's response.

The proposals had shown "remarkable progress." If he could not say he would have accepted the proposals, he could not say that they did not represent a basis for negotiation. Mussolini clearly had second thoughts about his delay in responding for he commented at length on the need for measured reflection on so complicated a matter, especially after he had made serious inquiries in London and Paris. Such reflection was further required by Eden's discouraging presentation to the League Council.

He came to the point; he had indeed intended not to refuse the proposals. In the Grand Council on December 18, the response would not have been unfavorable. But then the news had arrived of Hoare's resignation; it appeared that the proposals were definitely dead.

He was, this all proved, not intransigent, not hostile to negotiations. He needed no urging. He confirmed his readiness to negotiate on any serious basis which furthered Italian needs for security and expansion, but only if such negotiations could proceed "with a calm and absolute discretion without which diplomatic negotiations are destined to fail."

Laval had said that European peace was in the hands of Italy. Mussolini assured Laval "in the clearest and most formal fashion" that he would do nothing to create an irreparable breach, the actions of Great Britain and the Mediterranean mutual assistance program notwithstanding, that he would continue his support of Laval's efforts in the spirit of Franco-Italian friendship.[127]

What was important, Laval wrote Mussolini, closing the correspondence on January 23, 1936, was not to debate the meaning of "a free hand" since Mussolini had conceded the point essential to Laval—that he had given no consent to the war.[128]

When Laval defended his policy in the Chamber on December 27, he first set the standard by which he wished to be judged:

> The essential question before you is to know whether the policy I have pursued is in conformity, or not, with the interests of my country. That is the only question which has to be examined by the French chamber.[129]

He had no regrets. He had respected the Covenant, and his understandings with and undertakings to Britain. There had been a risk of war inherent in the oil sanction. He thought the proposals reasonable. But they were dead. What to do?

> My determination is not weakened because my action has not succeeded. Other attempts will have to be made which may have no more success. I must not be discouraged. I shall persevere, whatever happens, in fervent and tireless effort in favor of peace.[130]

There followed attacks which confirmed the eloquence and passion of which the French Chamber is capable. The primary safeguard to France, Leon Blum said, was not Italy, but the unlimited aid of the Soviet Union. He ended with a slashing personal denunciation:

> You have proceeded in the great affairs of the world as we have seen you proceed here, every day in petty affairs and petty dealings. You tried to give and at the same time to take. You have tried to play both ends against the middle.... What is deplorable and unhappy for our country is this: insensitive to the nobility and power of great and disinterested things, you have reduced them to the scale of your petty means.
>
> And that is how, with your petty mistakes, you have succeeded in accumulating a great disaster.[131]

M. Taittinger injected a lighter note:

> The English have a touch of the friar mendicant about them. Whatever party they belong to, they consider they have a mission to instruct the World. One must not make fun of them for their League of Nations mysticism.[132]

Paul Reynaud, was a supporter of the Government but he now joined the Opposition. He had attended the debate in Parliament on December 19. He told the story of the Peace Ballot to show that Britain's interest was not selfish; indeed the British people had placed a moral idea ahead of all else. The rebuff to the Hoare-Laval plan was a victory, he said, for France, which had always looked to the Covenant for her defense. Faced with the German threat, France, more than ever, needed collective security and British support. The Chamber had an obligation, he challenged its members, to choose between Italy, which was the breaker of the Covenant, and England, its champion.[133]

Had a vote been taken then, observers were sure that Laval must have fallen. Laval faced the challenge the next day. He had always been a humdrum speaker, preferring to exercise his powers of persuasion on a more personal basis, in corridors and committee rooms. This day, the *Times*' correspondent noted: "He revealed himself for the first time as a great speaker—great not in rhetoric, but in lucidity, in coolness and in courage, with an undeniable mastery of emotional effect, sparingly used."[134]

Again he reviewed France's commitment to the League, to its Treaties, including Locarno, the Little Entente, the Rome agreements, and the Franco-Soviet Pact and pleaded loyalty to them all. Once more he told of his agreement with Hoare not to employ blockade or military sanctions, the search for a settlement, for conciliation, for a basis for negotiation. The oil sanction he adroitly turned to his own use. It was an issue so vital that he would put it to the Chamber: "You are sovereign, you are the mandatories of the nation."

France had tendered to Britain all the support she had been asked and more than that had proceeded with technical arrangements—alone of fifty-four nations—to make her support real.

He denied having given Mussolini license to make war. He had wanted only to secure cooperation with Italy to advance collective security in Europe. He had moreover continually warned Italy of the danger of war and that France would honor her engagements.

He now turned to the most fateful issue—Germany. Without an effective rapprochement with Germany, peace was at risk in Europe. But such rapprochement could exist only in the framework of European collective security. He had taken care that the Franco-Soviet treaty would be precisely in conformity with the Treaty of Locarno, which was the basis of French security. This showed his attention firmly focused on the most grievous threat to France—German reoccupation of the Rhineland:

> I have finished. The vote you are going to give is serious. It is not only the fate of the Government which is at stake. I have been at the Quai d'Orsay for 15 months. I have been Prime Minister since June. You have given me heavy tasks. With the help of my colleagues—yes, of all my colleagues—we have defended the franc, and, if this vote of the Chamber allows it, the Budget will be passed two days from now.... You have supported the Government, your manifesto will be the acts you have accomplished, the spirit of self-denial and sacrifice which you have shown in defending the vital interests of the country. The whole orientation of French policy is at stake. You are the representatives of the country and its responsible mandatories. Choose![135]

Laval had not relied on oratory alone. His tactics, his organization and the shrewdness by which he threw the budget in the face of a chamber reluctant to accept responsibility for it all contributed to his victory, by only 20 votes, to be sure, but the judgment of France on his policy.

Earlier that week, *Osservatore Romano* had reflected that this had been "the saddest Christmas since the war" and argued that the Hoare-Laval proposals were not dead either for the League or France.[136] But Mussolini told the Cabinet on December 30 that the proposals had been aborted before the Grand Council could consider them, adding, after the fact, that they did not satisfy Italy's minimum aspirations. There would be, he said, as in every colonial war, an "indispensable pause."[137] That day, Abyssinia urgently protested to the League of Nations against Italy's use of poison gas against its troops on the Takazze.[138]

## A Watcher on the Rhine

A shrewd and interested observer of this crisis was Adolf Hitler. When he met with Sir Edward Phipps, the British Ambassador, on December 13, he was convinced that Mussolini would accept the Hoare-Laval proposals. He opined that Mussolini had acted foolishly; he should have first come to an agreement with Britain.

Phipps had come to press for progress on an air pact. Hitler objected that the Franco-Soviet Pact had raised serious questions. If the French wanted a bilateral air pact, von Neurath suggested, then logic called for abolishing the demilitarized zone of the Rhineland. Hitler promptly added that he could have reoccupied it without a fuss on March 16, but he had been content with Locarno.

Hitler was out of sorts, fervently denouncing the Soviets and slyly suggesting a confidential German-British exchange of secret information about their air forces.[139] Phipps thereafter speculated that the likelihood of a settlement of the Abyssinian affair had been the cause of Hitler's ill-temper since he feared above all else a resurrection of the Stresa Front.

Phipps issued a stern warning to London. Germany would probably proceed to remilitarize the Rhineland at the earliest favorable opportunity. Germany would rearm "at her own sweet will and to the limit of her capacity." He concluded: "To rearm, is I firmly believe, our most urgent task" accompanied by no signs of weakness towards a regime that admires only force and finds generosity despicable.[140]

François-Poncet spelled out German apprehensions on December 19. What Germany feared most, he reported to Paris, was that the peace plan would terminate the war in Africa and bring Britain, France and Italy together again, to concentrate their attention on the problems of Europe. Hitler put it succinctly to François-Poncet on New Years Day, 1936. Mussolini was, he said, "a mad adventurer": "I do not understand Mussolini's attitude," he said. "He should have accepted these proposals immediately. For him, here was an unhoped for chance."[141]

But he had not. The question remained not whether Hitler would try to turn the collapse of the Hoare-Laval proposals to his own advantage, but how and when.

## Post-Mortem

When Vansittart was about to leave with Hoare for Paris, he asked Rex Leeper of the press department how long it would take to prepare public opinion for the Paris proposals. Leeper replied three weeks to which Vansittart responded, "We only have three days."[142]

At the height of the crisis, Vansittart urged Baldwin to call in the press, to state the case for the proposals. But instead Baldwin talked only to the *Times,*[143] and when the case was finally made, it was not made by Baldwin, but by Hoare in his resignation speech.

There was no doubt about it. It had been, as Toynbee wrote the following year "a sensational demonstration of the prevailing public opinion."[144]

His contemporaries agreed. Lord Tweedsmuir, Governor General of Canada ruminated:

> I don't profess to understand exactly what happened...but what seems plain is that public opinion suddenly took a hand in directing the *game* which is a most interesting phenomenon and proves that after all we are a genuine democracy.[145]

The British Government had been caught short. It had not rallied public opinion to its policy and in the end dramatically reversed its course—and sacrificed its Foreign Secretary in yielding to public opinion.

Lord Cecil had not been caught short. He had been both forehanded and opportunistic. With 500,000 workers and 11 million votes he had educated the British public on the issues as he saw them and had elicited the responses he had desired. In June, when the Peace Ballots had been counted, he asked "What shall we make of it."[146] He now proceeded brilliantly to answer his own question.

He had not foreseen the Abyssinian crisis, but he had made the League of Nations the most visible element of British foreign policy. As the crisis developed, he was there, at the Prime Minister's side, leveraging his massive vote into a public declaration that the League was indeed the sheet-anchor of British policy.

Hoare had confirmed at Geneva in September that his declaration that the League was the basis of British policy was a direct response to public opinion, by which he plainly meant the Peace Ballot.

When the election came, in which the Peace Ballot inspired the platform of all of the parties, but most especially the Government's, Lord Cecil did not rest or relax. Not enough for him were the ringing endorsements of party manifestos, the appealing slogans of posters and pamphlets. His LNU went directly to the candidates and extracted from them very specific and very public commitments to the League which, in Parliament and in Cabinet, they felt bound to observe. Whether it was the public or the members of Parliament who played the key role has been debated. Lord Cecil had prepared them all to do their part. His goals remained clear—collective security through the League of Nations and disarmament—and in the matter of the League he had brilliantly succeeded.

The public and its representatives had been deeply influenced by the Peace Ballot. The question remained—what did it mean? Support for the League, certainly. For economic sanctions, certainly. But what about war, war for the League, a British war for the League? It was evident that many had believed economic sanctions would succeed without war, and that the negative votes and abstentions to the military sanction were large indeed. Were the British people prepared to go to war for the Covenant? This was the central question. Neither Baldwin, nor Hoare, nor the Cabinet believed they were, and this had been the true basis of the Hoare-Laval proposals. The proposals were dead. How far the British people would go in support of the League and the Covenant remained to be seen.

Contemporaries then and historians since have attached a label of peculiar infamy to the Hoare-Laval proposals. Beneath the label is a tangle of myths and legends, the substance of which is that the wily and devious Laval seduced the naive and trusting Hoare into repudiating the policy of strength and virtue with which Great Britain was in the process of vindicating the League and the Covenant. This was the view dramatically expounded by Professor Toynbee in the *Survey of International Affairs for 1935*. This view has naturally proved popular in Britain, and in France Laval's subsequent career has lent it an appeal and support which are far from justified. Keenly aware of the German threat and, conversely, the price of a falling out or worse still a war with Italy, the British Government from the start pursued a mediatory role and sought an agreed settlement. This was true at the League as the crisis developed, when the Zeila offer was made, at the Tripartite conference, and in the League Council and Committees both before and after the war began. The double policy which the Prime Minister, the Foreign Secretary, and the League of Nations Minister never ceased to proclaim was therefore more than a statement of policy; it was an active program of which the search for settlement was a vital and highly visible component.

The British Cabinet followed the issue closely and was well informed of the progress of settlement proposals and negotiations including the Peterson-Léger conversations which continued over weeks and months. Far from being a casual drop-in visit by Hoare to Laval, or a busman's holiday as Vansittart would later say, the mission was carefully prepared in response to the state of negotiations and the pressures of the League's progress on sanctions.

The Cabinet had every opportunity to instruct or to limit Hoare and clearly expected him to bring back settlement proposals for the Cabinet's further review. Far from supinely yielding to French policy, Hoare had exacted from France precisely those commitments of political and military support to protect a British fleet unilaterally placed in harm's way on France's doorstep, at the same time maintaining traditional British reluctance to undertake reciprocal obligations on the European continent.

The Hoare-Laval proposals basically reflected Hoare's concept, not Laval's, and Laval continuously adjusted to changes in British policies and desires. Hoare had clear notions of the essentials of an agreement, of which Abyssinian sovereignty, beneficial development under League auspices, together with a meaningful exchange of territories, were essential parts.

As he saw it, these elements were successfully incorporated in the proposals, which were to remain secret, which were to be reviewed by the British government—as Hoare had promised—and which were, in any case, to serve as a basis for a discussion from which it was hoped would emerge a plan upon which Abyssinia, Italy, and the League could all stand.

An effective champion of sanctions at Geneva, Eden was a loyal aide to Hoare in pursuing a negotiated settlement. He represented Hoare in presenting the Paris proposals to the Cabinet and the House of Commons and backed them until the tenor of public opinion became unmistakable.

Through it all, Laval's goals were as clear as they were clearly stated. If he sought a rapprochement with Germany, it was from a position of strength, the elements of which were the Stresa Front, the Rome accords, the Soviet Pact, the Little Entente, and above all a close association with Britain which he supported at every critical point. He wanted to make public what Britain wished to conceal. His policy was marked by honesty verging on bluntness. His methods of conciliation and negotiation were those which in his view and based upon his experience would best serve to bring about the result he so publicly pursued. Certainly he had planned to get Mussolini's adherence first on the premise that it was, unlike the Emperor's, more nearly within his control. With that in hand, there were practical chances of success. To give the Emperor, on the other hand, a veto would doom the plan as the case proved.

Mussolini had good reasons to settle and there is ample evidence he might have done so. He had gauged the German threat and sought to contain it at Stresa. He preferred France and Britain to Germany as partners and threatened no British or French interests. That he would take less than all was clear, and his plan of campaign, after the initial conquests that avenged Adowa, was to halt and await a political solution. His diplomats affirmed what the Duce stated: that he might well have considered the Paris proposals as a basis for negotiation and he was shocked when they were no longer available.

He now had no choice but to continue his campaign, not only to justify his rhetoric, but to preserve his regime in its newfound popularity. He must therefore face the existing sanctions and such others as might be added and Britain and France must continue to be his adversaries. He did not hesitate. He carried on, his attention riveted on Africa, open to new friendships and a new policy in Europe.

The choice had been Baldwin's. He had, even under the most difficult circumstances, a strong majority in the House of Commons. He could, had he determined to stay the course, to stand by the policy for which he was ultimately responsible, and to make the case for the Government which Hoare made for himself, have ridden out the storm.

Baldwin's precipitate retreat enhanced neither his reputation for shrewdness nor integrity. He later explained it to his friend Tom Jones: "They knocked me endways. For two days I did not know where I stood."[147]

It was a personal, emotional, and moral crisis which cost Baldwin dearly and from which he slipped into a state of depression that deeply affected his grasp and his performance in the critical months to come.

Haile Selassie had made it clear that in the ultimate analysis, the interests of his country must come first. The only question, Laval told the Chamber of Deputies, that they ought to consider was whether his policy had served the interests of France.

But Baldwin had abandoned his policy and his Foreign Secretary on grounds, he said, of honor and conscience. This appeal to honor and conscience, it should be noted, saved his political career. He did not put the case in terms of British interests. He played, instead, to the mood of the British people. Certainly that mood reflected the Peace Ballot's emphasis on principles detached from cases. That had been deliberate. This was a moment when, to a nation in pursuit of a grander vision, the national interest not only smelled of the sordid, the parochial, the petty, not to mention the immoral, but was seen as leading inevitably backwards, down the dark path to the balance of power and its inevitable concomitant—war, war which would destroy civilization.

All this Lord Cecil deeply believed, and had successfully conveyed to the British people. The problem remained whether the mood of the British people and the moral principles that inspired them would be an adequate basis for a policy to meet the inevitable challenges of the immediate future. Morality had been vindicated, but at what price remained to be seen.

# 6

# Hitler Bides His Time

*"That the Government of the Third Reich would seek to remilitarize the Rhineland was an unarguable factor in European diplomatic equations by 1936."*

—Thomas Emmerson[1]

## A New Year

The year turned. The tumult and the shouting of the Hoare- Laval proposals began to die and before the month was out, captains and kings had departed. Hoare had already been replaced by Eden; during January Herriot left the Laval cabinet withdrawing his party's support, and, without awaiting a vote of confidence, Laval handed in his government's resignation.

On January 20, King George V died. Of the crowned heads of the Great Powers of 1914, only he and his throne had survived. His Hohenzollern and Romanov cousins were dead or in exile; the Hapsburgs were forbidden to return to the remnant of Austria. The British dynasty had emerged stronger and the British Empire larger than ever before. The attention of the British people was concentrated on the King's last illness, and upon the elaborate ceremonies and rituals attending his death, which evoked, in a world of depression and dictatorship, the spacious grandeur of an era that had irrevocably passed less than a quarter of a century ago.

The League Council had adjourned until January 20. That day, the Committee of Thirteen concluded and reported to the Council that no useful prospect of conciliation existed.[2]

Negotiations having collapsed, Mussolini, after moving great forces to Africa with great panoply, had no alternative but to carry on his war. Hitler's astute ambassador in Rome, Ulrich von Hassell reported on January 2 that the Italian Foreign Office was convinced Italy had made a mistake in not promptly pursuing negotiations. He added his own conclusion that a Mussolini driven to desperation by sanctions might go to war with Britain, even at the risk of his own destruction and that of the Fascist regime. "That such a development is not in any way in our interest," Hassell concluded, "is obvious."[3]

Mussolini appeared tired but resolute when Hassell saw him on January 6. He confirmed that he might have accepted the proposals as a basis of negotiation if his inquiries had been answered and if the proposals had not been rejected by the storm of public protest. In the event of an oil embargo, he would, he said, withdraw from the League of Nations.

With a war in progress, economic sanctions in force and more threatened, Mussolini was isolated, open to support. He appreciated, he told Hassell, Germany's benevolent neutrality. He quickly went to the point. It should be possible to improve relations between Germany and Italy by disposing of their only dispute—the Austrian problem. Since Germany had declared that it did not wish to infringe upon Austrian independence, Mussolini suggested that Germany and Austria enter into a treaty of friendship and a nonaggression pact which would "in practice bring Austria into Germany's wake" leaving her no other foreign policy to pursue but one parallel to Germany's: "If Austria, as a formally quite independent state, were thus in practice to become a German satellite, he would have no objection." Indeed, he saw advantages for both Italy and Germany. German-Italian mistrust would be eliminated and a Danubian Pact frustrated, as well as any inclination of Austria to side with Czechoslovakia and France.

Hassell wanted to be very sure of what he had just heard. To his paraphrase of Mussolini's proposal, Mussolini gave express confirmation.

Hassell probed the current status of the Stresa concept and Franco-Italian air and military talks. Mussolini replied that these could only have meaning in the context of a political agreement which did not exist. To the contrary, Mussolini said, Stresa was "dead and buried, once for all."

They discussed possibilities of a widened war. Hassell advised that the world would bow to accomplished facts and that military victories in Abyssinia were of critical importance. Mussolini agreed. He expected decisive victories soon.[4]

The fortunes of war and the threat of sanctions had wrought a fundamental change. Mussolini had not only championed Austrian independence in 1934, but had sent his troops to the border. He had composed his differences with France; he had presided over the Stresa conference with the express object of containing Germany; he had urged a common front against the unilateral revocation of the postwar treaties. He had vividly warned of the threat of Hitler. What was important to him now was not Austria but Abyssinia as he clearly signaled his willingness to let Austria slip into the German orbit.

Indicating that no Foreign Ministry had a monopoly either of wisdom or blindness, a German official who reviewed Mussolini's proposal concluded that it should "be rejected in the politest possible manner."[5]

## Under the Volcano

Still Prime Minister, Laval read the signs clearly. The discrete, conciliatory attitude during the past year shown by Germany toward Austria, he warned his ambassadors in Vienna, Prague, Bucharest, and Belgrade on January 11, 1936, ought not to delude anyone. Germany was determined to swallow Austria. The whole project for a Central European Pact, which had been a subject of the Rome conversations of January, 1935, of the London conference, and of Stresa, had to be adjourned for an indeterminate period during which Italy, indifferent to its continental interests, pursued its African policy. Under the circumstances, and for a long time, Italy would be in no position to renew the show of force which had braked German enterprises in Austria.[6]

To Corbin in London Laval gave another warning. Recent information indicated increasing German military planning for the demilitarized zone of the Rhineland. It was possible that Germany would reoccupy the zone either totally or partially, on January 30, the anniversary of Hitler's taking power.[7]

The two issues, Austria and the Rhineland, were intimately related. At Locarno, Germany had voluntarily confirmed the Rhineland provisions of Versailles. Britain and Italy were the guarantors of Locarno. Italy had been Austria's defender. A rift among the Locarno parties, and especially between Britain and Italy, offered Hitler inviting possibilities.

The year opened with a consensus of informed opinion that Hitler would move into the Rhineland; the only issue was when. Phipps had sent his plain-spoken warning to London on December 13.[8] François-Poncet, in a New Year's Day interview with Hitler, expressed his concern that Germany might renounce Locarno. This Hitler denied.[9] Far from convinced, François-Poncet raised the subject at a diplomatic reception on January 10. Franco-British military talks, he assured von Bulow, State Secretary for Foreign Affairs, related only to the Mediterranean and not to Germany. Repeated references in the German press to the Franco-Soviet treaty and Franco-British conversations seemed to him to show a Germany searching for a pretext one fine day to reoccupy the Rhineland. von Bulow cited Hitler's repeated denials and added his own.[10]

From London, Corbin repeated the same warning to Laval.[11] The French Ambassador in Brussels signaled to Laval Belgian fears of a German move into the Rhineland.[12] On January 14, the French Government carefully reviewed the juridical position and the known facts about German activity in the zone. As to fortifications, studies had been made, but not executed. But the Rhineland police, whose counterparts elsewhere in Germany had already been incorporated into the army, simply constituted camouflaged divisions. Perhaps this alone might not justify action and sanctions, but certainly a German proclamation that it no longer recognized the restrictions of Versailles and Locarno would. It would be prudent, then, to warn London, and to let Berlin know that such action would be immediately brought to Geneva and might well be followed by military measures.[13]

Warnings of German intent now came from the French military attache in Berlin—"only the date is uncertain"—and from the highly observant French consul at Cologne, Jean Dobler.[14]

The General Staff of the Army analyzed the growth of German military power and carefully considered France's position before and under the pact of Rome and since the outbreak of the Abyssinian war. Its report called special attention to German armor. Unlike the cavalry of the past, it was pointed out, German armor was designed to bring to bear a massive shock, great penetrating power, and great strategic and tactical mobility capable of achieving profound results. This was an accurate appraisal. Recent information, it added, suggested in the near future the reoccupation of the demilitarized zone, or at least the east bank of the Rhine.[15]

At the January 18 meeting of the Haut Comité Militaire, Maurin, Minister of War, reported the results of the breach with Italy. One fifth of all French forces, which had been moved to the German border, must now be returned to the Alps and the Mediterranean. German superiority in manpower was incontestable; they were on the verge of passing France in material. General Gamelin added that Britain could only supply land forces inferior to those of 1914.

Gamelin succinctly described the German threat. Following a reoccupation of the Rhineland, Germany could attack France's allies of the Little Entente with impunity. Real help could come only from Poland and the Soviets. But the Soviet Union could not intervene without entering Poland and this Poland was unlikely to accept.[16] The theoretical problem Gamelin stated in 1936 became the reality of 1939.

The day the Haut Comité Militaire met, Herriot announced that he and three other Radical ministers would resign from the Cabinet upon Laval's return from Geneva where with Eden he was attending the meetings of the League Council and committees. The Committee of Thirteen arrived at an unremarkable conclusion on January 22—that the war was still in progress. Its other findings were negative; it could find no way to respond to Abyssinia's request for financial assistance or to examine into the conduct of the war and it saw no chance for settlement.[17] Its resolution to watch the situation carefully gave scant comfort to Abyssinia

The Committee of Eighteen, which was the sanctions committee, decided, as Laval and Eden had agreed[18] on January 22 to convene a committee of technical experts to advise on the effectiveness of an oil embargo. The inquiry was not whether to apply the sanction—that decision had been made—but only when and how.[19]

Eden now had his last conversation with Laval as Prime Minister. Laval impressed on Eden that Germany would soon reoccupy the Rhineland. Germany was making enormous strides in preparing for war. It would be ready in eighteen months.

It was not idle conversation. "More than once," Eden later wrote, "the turn of the conversation showed clearly that they would have liked some definite assurance from me that his Majesty's Government would stand by them were a challenge ever made. I did not feel called upon to respond."[20]

But Laval warned, the question would soon be put. In his last act as Prime Minister, Laval continued to seek the will o' the wisp that he and his predecessors had never been able to grasp—a clear statement, indeed a British commitment to France in the event of the threat that most directly affected her—the reoccupation of the Rhineland.

In Paris the same day, Herriot and his colleagues officially resigned. Laval did not hesitate. He went to the Elysee Palace to give the President the collective resignation of the Cabinet. He declined the invitation to form a new ministry. He then summed up his tenure:

> The franc, which I was appointed to defend, is intact. The Budget, diminished by one-fifth, has been passed. The measures taken in every direction are beginning to bear fruit, and the first signs of a recovery of industrial and agricultural activity are apparent.

Naturally, Laval saw the foreign policy record in terms of his own goals:

> During the last few months, in the foreign field grave difficulties appeared. Peace was maintained; our obligations to the League were carried out; our friendships and alliances were kept intact; the independence of our foreign policy was assured and reinforced. That is our record.[21]

Since national elections would be held in April and May, the new government would be an interim government. It was headed by Albert Sarraut, who had been Minister of Colonies and Prime Minister in 1933. His Foreign Minister was Flandin, who had been Laval's predecessor as Prime Minister.

## Under the Volcano—Britain

To the public, Eden appeared the champion of sanctions as Hoare had appeared the champion of conciliation. Eden owed his elevation, as Hoare owed his dismissal to the power of public opinion, a power which Eden, in his tenure as Foreign Secretary was bound to respect. He had before him, of course, the problems of Germany and Italy. He replied to Phipps's suggestion of the month before that Germany and Britain should secretly exchange air information.

It was a "constructive proposal" Eden told Phipps on January 8, but impossible because it was linked to no publicly disclosed agreement, such as the Naval Treaty. He added virtuously that it would be impossible to conceal the information from Parliament and unwise to conceal it from France.[22]

Vansittart thought the same. On January 9 he wrote Phipps:

> In all the circumstances, we do not think it is necessary to tell the French anything about the secret proposal. It would not do them much good to

> know it; and it would get back to the Germans that we had told them. In the circumstances, we would prefer to do nothing.[23]

A week later Eden thought differently. The Germans generally and Hitler personally might be offended and think all their constructive proposals rebuffed. There was, perhaps, another way to skin the cat. A new German air attaché had been posted to London; the Air Ministry could, Eden suggested, take him into their confidence and through mutual exchanges develop mutual confidence and perhaps in the future fuller disclosures of German air policy. In all this, Eden observed, "there is of course no question of publishing or communicating to other Governments technical details which raise no question of principle or major policy."[24] By other governments he meant France.

On January 10, Grandi called on Eden. Would Britain or France, Grandi inquired, have any proposals for conciliation to offer? Eden was confident that they did not. Grandi asked the British attitude on the oil sanction. Equally unforthcoming, Eden said this was a question for the League and not Britain alone, on whose behalf, in any case, he could give no answer.[25]

The next day, Grandi persisted. Again he asked Eden if there were further prospects of conciliation; again Eden thought not, nor would he be drawn out on the subject of the oil embargo. Grandi was pensive. The more deeply Italy was engaged in Africa, he said, the less she could do in Europe. Europe meant Austria; Italy's preoccupation was Germany's gain. And Italy was receiving persistent indications of German support. What Grandi wanted now, he said, was to see the African war settled so that Italy could once more play her part in Europe.[26] There was no response. Mussolini's suggestions to Hassell received from him and would receive from Hitler a far more sympathetic hearing.

The exchange of air information was a small matter. The Foreign Office prepared the Cabinet for a discussion of the German problem in its full magnitude; and this occupied various hands in the second half of January.

The French had taken care to keep Ralph Wigram, head of the Foreign Office's Central Department, the principal subject of which was Germany, informed of the anticipated threat to the Rhineland. Would it not be possible, Wigram asked in a Foreign Office memorandum, to use the proposed air pact as a way out of the demilitarized zone; that is to say, first anti-aircraft defenses could be permitted in the zone, then recruiting, and so on.

The problem remained unchanged. Britain's peril was in the air, France's on the Rhine. It was logical, then, to Wigram, to trade the demilitarized zone for an air pact. The French would not, he suggested, fight for the zone, but they would protest violently:

> But I regard its maintenance over anything but a very restricted future as quite impracticable; and therefore it seems to me that what all of us had best be thinking about now is the means of securing its peaceful disappearance. It was established against a weak and disarmed Germany. We have allowed Germany to become strong and to rearm; and in the face of such a Germany the zone is not likely to survive.
>
> If we could get some little benefit from its disappearance, I would believe we would be wise to take it. The state of French public opinion is likely to make it very difficult to get such a benefit.[27]

This was not a new idea. A year before, on January 14, 1935, the British Cabinet had determined that the Rhineland was not a vital British interest.[28]

Wigram was consistent. In November he had written a major paper with Orme Sargent that clearly recognized Germany's aims in the Rhineland, Austria, the Sudetenland, and Eastern Europe. Of three alternatives: drift, an anti-German front (which the authors labeled encirclement), and coming to terms with Germany, the authors firmly declared for the third. Perhaps colonies would have to be given to Germany. In any event, such an agreement might favorably affect Germany's future course of action.[29]

These opinions did not pass unchallenged. L.R. Collier, agreed on the German aims but disagreed that Germany could be satisfied. Germany's aims, taken one by one, were essentially nonnegotiable. He thought that the British people in the recent election had given a mandate for rearmament and those arms should be used to continue the policy of restraining Germany.[30]

Vansittart for once took the middle position. One ought not, he said, call "a policy of encirclement anything that puts us in a stronger bargaining position." Yes, Germany would raise the issue of the Rhineland. How could you say what German aims were logical and reasonable and how could you modify German ambitions in the East?

But, Germany would expand, Vansittart thought, and better in Africa than in Europe. He did not rule out colonial concessions. The time was not ripe, in any case; better enter into discussions when there was greater strength to back them.[31]

So the issues had been well briefed when the new Foreign Secretary distributed to his Cabinet colleagues a collection of papers on the German threat covering 1933–35. As others had before, he starkly stated German aims: destruction of the peace settlement, internally to militarize Germany, externally to absorb all Germans and to acquire new markets, new sources of raw materials and European hegemony.

From all this Eden drew two conclusions. First it was vital to complete British rearmament. The second conclusion had been foreshadowed by Wigram:

> [I]t will be well to consider whether it is still possible to come to some modus vivendi—to put it no higher—with Hitler's Germany, which would be both honourable and safe for this country and which would, at the same time, lessen the increasing tension in Europe caused by the growth of Germany's strength and ambition.[32]

In further preparation for the Cabinet meeting of January 29, reports were prepared on the military significance of the demilitarized zone. The Air Staff concluded that the speed and range of modern aircraft made its defensive value negligible.[33]

The Army saw it differently. It had already prepared a current analysis of the strength and rate of expansion of the German Army.[34] It now concluded that the zone denied Germany a protected base from which to launch an attack and that it weakened Germany from the defensive point of view.[35]

King George V had died on January 20. To his funeral came not only his fellow monarchs, but the foreign policy establishment of Europe, the foreign ministers, the ambassadors and their naval and military advisors and aides. It was a prime opportunity to practice the diplomacy of the old order. So it came about, on January 27, that Eden toured the diplomatic horizon with Baron Constantin Von Neurath, the German Foreign Minister. They discussed Italy and Abyssinia, then the Rhineland. With the Saar dispute behind, Neurath repeated Hitler's declaration that there were no issues between France and Germany. Germany fully intended to respect Locarno, he told Eden, adding that Germany expected others to observe it in spirit as well as in letter.[36]

Flandin followed Neurath. His conversation with Eden was his first as Foreign Minister and he opened with a principle, followed by an issue. The principle was this—he would always consult Eden before taking any action and he hoped Eden would do the same. The issue was the Rhineland where France feared impending German action. Whether the action were immediate or deferred, he was sure that the Rhineland was Germany's ultimate aim. If Germany moved, what response did Eden advise France to make? Eden's reply had been long prepared. What value, he asked Flandin, did France attach to the zone? Would they maintain it at any cost? Or would they prefer to bargain with Germany while the zone still had value?

These were questions, Flandin replied, which the two governments must carefully consider and on which they must consult. When Flandin asked Eden's views on the Franco-Soviet Pact, Eden again sidestepped; this too was an issue for France to decide.[37]

To Maxim Litvinov, Eden was equally reserved. In answer to the question what Britain would do if Germany reoccupied the Rhineland, he replied, first that he didn't think it imminent, and second that he hoped the issue would arise later rather than sooner since, in its present state of armaments, Britain was in no position to take effective action.[38]

The Royal funeral was also a family occasion. Among the visitors was the Duke of Coburg. He was a German cousin to the new King, who had been born Saxe-Coburg-Gotha and had become Windsor only in the heat of the World War. He saw Edward three times.

An alliance with Germany, the as yet uncrowned Edward VIII said, was an urgent necessity, a guiding principle of British policy—not against France, but including her.

Would a visit between Baldwin and Hitler be useful, the Duke asked? The new King had not yet acquired his father's grasp of constitutional practice. "Who is King here," he demanded, "Baldwin or I? I myself will talk to Hitler and will do so here or in Germany. Tell him that, please."[39]

Against this background, the Cabinet met on January 29 to discuss Eden's report on Germany. He renewed his recommendations,

> that it is vital to hasten and complete our own rearmament, and secondly, that (whilst pursuing our rearmament), it will be well to consider whether it is still possible to come to some modus vivendi with Germany.[40]

What advice the Foreign Office would give is indicated in a memo prepared by William Strang the day after the Cabinet meeting. Britain should try to ease relations with Germany, recognizing her predominant position in Central and Southeastern Europe. There ought to be no more declarations about the independence and integrity of Austria. With chilling indifference Eden said,

> It is to be hoped that the absorption of Austria by Germany, which is probably inevitable in the long run, can be arranged peacefully.

And, Strang advised that British should "Dispose of the demilitarized zone, in due season, for what it will fetch, e.g. an Air Pact."

Of this Vansittart wrote that "I would certainly dispose of the demilitarized zone in Germany's favor. And I would restore her colonies to Germany." But this was subject to the caveat that nothing must be given away save in an overall deal that was both possible and permanent.[41]

Far from the Cabinet rooms, the chanceries and foreign offices of Europe, and equally far from Geneva, the war in Abyssinia carried on and indeed, in both southern deserts and northern mountains, gained momentum. The first real Italian victory came in the south. The Abyssinians, 40,000 strong under Ras Desta, advanced in early January on Graziani's base at Dolo, but the desert and the Italian air force decimated their columns.

Graziani's offensive on January 12 was heralded by a gas attack. The battle was quickly decided; bombing and superior weaponry on the ground slaughtered the starved and waterless Abyssinians. On January 20, Graziani entered Negelli, the provincial capital of Galla Borana where resistance had ceased.[42]

On the northern front, in order to forestall the expected offensive, Badoglio attacked the armies of Ras Seyoum and Ras Kassa. The defenders not only resisted stoutly, but counterattacked and forced the Italians to retreat to the Warieu pass where they were besieged. Ras Kassa sought reinforcements to turn the siege into victory. His failure reflected two fatal defects of the Abyssinian defense. Ras Mulugeta, perhaps harboring personal resentment that Ras Kassa had been promoted over him, procrastinated. And there was no radio in the camp of Ras Imru's fresh armies to the northwest. Runners needed fourteen days to complete the circuit between the two armies and the issue was decided long before then.

The picture was one from a century of colonial wars: the beleaguered Italian garrison exhausting its last supplies of water, the timely arrival on January 23 of the relief column under General Vaccari. To Badoglio it was the crossfire of the uniting Italian forces that forced the Abyssinian withdrawal. Ras Kassa attributed his defeat to incessant gas attacks.

The Abyssinians had suffered heavily, 8,000 casualties, and spent most of their ammunition. The Italians were bloodied too, but the Abyssinian offensives had been blunted.[43]

Contrary to the gloomy prognostication of many experts, the Italians had fended off Aybssinian thrusts, won a crushing victory in the south and stood on the offensive in the north. Despite these victories, Grandi remained hopeful of a negotiated settlement. But Eden told him firmly on January 31 that Britain would take no initiative and Flandin concurred.[44] The oil experts were about to convene and the fate of his predecessor's peace talks had surely made a lasting impression on the new Foreign Secretary.

## Hitler Decides

Having returned to Rome from Berlin, Hassell found Mussolini on January 28 both physically fresher and more optimistic about the situation in Abyssinia. He again carefully retraced the meeting of January 16, recalling Mussolini's statements about Austria and his disinterest in returning to Stresa.

Hassell had understood correctly, Mussolini said. He was little interested in Austria; facing a military bloc led by Britain, he could not engage himself there. If he had as yet taken no steps to change his Austrian policy, he would. He understood how closely Austria and Germany were linked by language and political thought. There could be no impenetrable barrier. Again Mussolini affirmed, Stresa was dead.

The only way out of the Abyssinian situation now was victory. Nevertheless, if the Emperor made reasonable proposals, he would not reject them.[45]

Mussolini conveyed the reorientation of Italian policy to Vienna. The German ambassador there reported to the watchful Führer on February 6 the Italian minister Franz von Papen recent declarations to the Austrian government. Though Italy still backed the sovereignty and independence of Austria, it was striving for an agreement with Germany on questions of international, particularly Central European policy. The Stresa front was a thing of the past. From all this von Papen concluded that Mussolini "has really modified his attitude to the Austrian question" even though the Austrians were trying to conceal it.[46]

From Rome, Hassell kept Berlin's attention fastened on Italy. Italian policy in 1934–35, he wrote on February 6, had been dictated by the German-Austrian conflict. Weakness had changed Mussolini. His approach to Germany might simply be a ruse tempting Germany to embroil herself in Austria, distracting attention from Abyssinia. But Hassell thought Germany wise enough to avoid that. It was a risk, he said, to look on Italy as a trustworthy ally, but this was by far preferable to a Stresa combination against Germany.[47]

Aloisi now led into Hassell's hand. He asked on February 12 what action Germany would adopt, as a party to Locarno, if the Soviet Pact with France were ratified. Hassell diplomatically responded that Germany had come to no conclusion. Again he heard from Aloisi what he had heard from Mussolini—Stresa was dead.[48]

That reoccupation of the Rhineland would cause fierce opposition in France was sure. The critical question was what attitude Britain would take. A valuable signal was given by Eden on February 12. He was asked the precise question in the House of Commons, phrased in neutral terms: would the provisions of Locarno requiring Britain to come immediately to the aid of France and Germany in the event of a flagrant violation of Articles 42 and 43 of Versailles be rigidly adhered to?

Eden's answer was carefully scrutinized in Berlin:

> The obligations of his Majesty's Government are specified in the Treaty of Locarno itself. His Majesty's Government stand by the obligations and, as has been previously stated in this House intend, should the need arise, faithfully to fulfull them.[49]

Hitler had an instinct for such things. The answer was read in Berlin as dry, pro forma, and legalistic, lacking profundity or conviction. On February 14, Hitler summoned Hassell to Munich. He had clearly paid close attention to Hassell's reports.

He was considering, he told Hassell, "an extremely far reaching question." He had only discussed it with Neurath, Ribbentrop, Goering, and the soldiers Blomberg and Fritsch. Should he seize upon French ratification of the Soviet Pact to denounce Locarno and station troops in the demilitarized zone? It was, he told Hassell, from the military point of view an absolute necessity.

He had always planned the move for 1937. Perhaps, though, the psychological moment had arrived now. Britain was weak, France divided.

He anticipated no military sanctions, and even economic sanctions were by now thoroughly unpopular.

Ought he not, then, approach Mussolini and suggest that the Duce use the Soviet Pact to denounce Locarno? Hassell replied that Germany's low profile had been a success, that Italy was searching for a way out of the terrible mess of Abyssinia. He was confident he could use the opening already created to discuss the matter with Mussolini. But on one point they must be clear. Would Germany denounce the treaty in any case, whether Mussolini agreed or not?

It was typical of Hitler that he reflected only briefly and answered decisively: Tell Mussolini, he said, that Germany would act in any case, but point out the advantage to Italy of acting first. Hassell expressed readiness to take on the mission, but sagely warned Hitler that success could not be assured.[50]

If his diplomatic and military advisors had been hesitant, Hitler had overcome their doubts.[51] He had good reasons to advance the date of the reoccupation. Italy was heavily engaged in Abyssinia. World attention was focused on Geneva and Italy would be far less likely to react than she might a year later, as victor. Italy was subject to League sanctions and Hitler thought it unlikely the League could simultaneously sustain sanctions against two major powers. Britain was rearming; perhaps in a year she would have made up some of the deficiencies that restrained her policy. For the present Britain was weak and her naval strength overextended by the Mediterranean deployment.

Opportunistically, the Franco-Soviet Pact to which he had taken repeated and public objection offered Hitler, a superb opportunist, a juridical basis for reoccupation, a case he could argue against charges of lawlessness.

There was another factor. Hitler had reason to believe that Britain would prefer an understanding with Germany to backing France. That had always been his ideal. The Anglo-German Naval Pact and British hesitancy concerning Locarno were good signs. At the moment when Hitler was making his decision for reoccupation, there came to him extraordinary evidence that seemed to confirm that this was indeed the new orientation of British policy.

On January 29 the British Cabinet had taken under consideration Eden's recommendation to pursue both rearmament and an understanding with Germany. On February 3, 1936 Hoesch, the German Ambassador in London, carefully sounded out Wigram on British attitudes toward Germany. He was concerned about conversations during King George's funeral among French statesmen and others about an understanding between Britain and the Soviets. Wigram denied any rapprochement with the Soviets, which he hinted would be contrary to practical measures to secure the peace of Europe. "He added," Hoesch noted,

> the further remark that the Cabinet were at present considering how practical work could be done towards stabilizing conditions in Europe. No definite decisions had, however, as yet been taken.

In Berlin, a notation was added to Hoesch's report in an unidentified hand: "Very interesting."[52]

More specific indications soon followed. On February 12, Prince Otto von Bismarck, Counsellor of the German Embassy in London, called on Wigram and again quizzed British attitudes toward Germany. Wigram promised to speak frankly, "giving me information which, as he said himself, he had no authority to do," and extracting a most solemn oath of secrecy.

Wigram told Bismarck that on the very same day the Foreign Office, under Cabinet instructions, was drawing up a "working agreement" among Britain, Germany, and France. What was most important was that absolutely nothing of this should become prematurely known to France. The whole point was to find common ground between Britain and Germany; France could then be brought along.

Intriguing details were supplied. The agreement need not contain written understandings except the air pact (which had been so steady a goal of British policy). More was to come: "Wigram made a somewhat obscure allusion to its being possible to render an air pact still more interesting by omitting from it things contained in the Locarno Treaty." This could only be the Rhineland and ample reason not to tell the French. To sharpen this suggestion, Wigram cited very specific fears that Germany would, at a suitable moment, send more military forces into the Rhineland.

The British goal was modest enough: "for Germany to state that she subscribe to the general British view in foreign policy" and, critically, that change in existing relationships should be made not by force but by mutual agreement. Britain did not want to encircle Germany; to the contrary she wanted an understanding. British cards were turned face up on the table with increasing rapidity. Britain had, Wigram assured Bismarck, no interest involved in the Franco-Soviet Treaty, which was purely a question of Franco-Soviet relations. To this he added, under strictest secrecy, that the Cabinet was preparing a White Paper on rearmament, but would not repeat the mistake of 1935. It would be based on increases in arms in all countries, and not simply Germany.

Bismarck solemnly swore secrecy. It would not be possible, he told Berlin, to assess the Working Agreement till more was known, but it certainly confirmed Wigram's hints to Hoesch on February 3.

Wigram's opposite number, Dieckhoff, marked Bismarck's dispatch "Urgent" in forwarding it to Neurath.[53]

Wigram had remarked to Bismark that it would be useful to have someone at a higher level than himself confirm his approaches. Eden being unavailable, he invited Bismarck to call on Lord Cranborne, Parliamentary Undersecretary of State and Lord Cecil's nephew. Cranborne on February 15 conveyed Eden's message that Britain sought friendly relations with Germany. Bismark reported what Wigram had told him. Cranborne responded that cultivating friendly relations with Germany was for Eden "one of the guiding principles of his policy."[54]

When Hassell arrived in Berlin on February 19, Hitler was better informed than he had been at the earlier meeting. Hassell first saw Neurath. Neurath was again hesitant; perhaps speeding up the time table wasn't worth the risk. He mentioned the British desire for a Working Agreement, to be kept secret from France, even though she would later be a partner. Hassell summarized his views. Italy would not denounce Locarno before Germany or even with Germany. But if France and Britain took any action, Italy would not cooperate with them and thus, de facto, violate her own Locarno obligations.

Hassell repeated his views to Hitler and Ribbentrop. He agreed with Neurath that there was no need for haste since other opportunities for abolishing the demilitarized zone would come to hand.

Hitler was firm. He gave his reasons. The longer it lasted, the more inviolable the zone would become. Further Italian military successes would stiffen British attitudes. As a victor in Africa, Mussolini would be harder to deal with. No, passivity was no policy. Attack was the better way, Hitler said, using the Soviet Pact as a pretext.

Occupying the Rhineland would destroy the remaining restraint of Versailles, would shatter Locarno which Hitler had pledged to observe, would deal France a staggering blow and totally upset the military, political and strategic balance of Europe. These were all goals Hitler relished. To overcome opposition and insure success, he reverted to tactics which had succeeded before.

He would, of course, assure the world that he planned no aggression. This would appeal to those who would believe him because they wanted to believe him. He would strike on a Saturday while the English were off for the weekend; and, by the way, France had a caretaker government. Most important, he would accompany his thrust with a peace plan. That had gone down well the year before when he had reinaugurated the German army and air force.

Hitler would offer the world a new demilitarized zone—but on both sides of the French and Belgian frontiers, plus a three-power pact with Holland and Belgium promising to defend their independence. So much for the smaller powers. For Britain there was the promise of a limited air pact; for France a long-term nonaggression pact; for Italy a return to Mussolini's cherished Four-Power Pact concept, but limited to the West.

The violation of Locarno, Hitler slyly suggested, could now be packaged as a restoration of Locarno, but with the unilateral demilitarized zone abolished.

Hassell and Neurath saw Hitler later the same evening. Hitler relayed a report from Paris: Cerutti had told Flandin Italy held fast to Locarno and Stresa. Hassell cast doubt on the report but acknowledged care was needed in his talks with Mussolini. Neurath submerged his doubts and accepted the Rhineland decision. The question was now not whether but when to march. Hitler wanted to strike when the French Chamber of Deputies ratified the Soviet Treaty. Neurath wanted firmer ground—ratification by the French Senate, too.[55]

Hassell carried out his mission expeditiously and cannily. He told Mussolini, on February 22, of his meeting with Hitler and the need for secrecy. Britain, he said, was standing shoulder to shoulder with the Soviets and pressing sanctions, which could well be intensified. This meant Europe was open to Soviet influence and penetration. He was, therefore, puzzled, he told Mussolini, to hear Cerutti's reference to Locarno and Stresa.

He had struck a sympathetic chord. Cerutti had spoken out of turn, Mussolini assured Hassell. Stresa was dead and Locarno would disappear when Italy left the League of Nations. True, the Franco-Soviet Pact did not affect Italy directly, but it was harmful and dangerous. France was sliding into the hands of the Left. Leon Blum was the uncrowned king of France. The more Italy succeeded in Abyssinia, the more likely Britain would take stronger steps against Italy.

Even now, Mussolini said, Haile Selassie might talk peace on an acceptable basis. But the League defended him and Britain would not allow him to give way. Further sanctions would raise the question whether there would be a war in Europe or whether Italy would have her way in Abyssinia—which he added, even now need not be *all* of Abyssinia.

Hassell plainly told Mussolini that Germany would react if Locarno was violated by the Franco-Soviet Pact. He carefully abstained from stating how. The Fuhrer had not decided, he said; in any case, he would decide alone and then only in the final thirty six hours.

If Hassell had understood correctly, he now insinuated to Mussolini, Italy "saw no occasion to do anything in the event of the Pact's being ratified."

Yes, Mussolini replied, Italy disapproved the Pact, which did not concern it.

Hassell persisted. Would Italy stand aside, do nothing "in the event of any German reaction whatever to the ratification"? Would Italy decline to cooperate with Britain and France if they claimed Italy was obliged to act?

Twice Mussolini answered yes, affirming the words that Hassell had so deftly placed in his mouth. Hassell now steered the conversation to Central Europe. Mussolini promised everything in regard to Austria that they had previously discussed, and reported that he had appropriately instructed the Italian Minister in Vienna.[56]

This was all very gratifying to Hassell, but with German thoroughness, he wanted to nail down this vital understanding. He had his chance on February 26 when Suvich showed him a memorandum of Hassell's conversation with Mussolini. Hassell was precise in offering amendments. In the first place, Suvich had not been present; the reference to him was stricken. Hassell then clarified Mussolini's statement that after Italy left the League, Locarno would lose all meaning.

In summarizing the talk about a German reaction to the Franco-Soviet Pact, Suvich had written that Mussolini would take no position on any German reaction "if confined within legitimate bounds." Nothing of the sort had been said, Hassell pointed out. Suvich admitted to having been hurriedly briefed by Mussolini and obligingly struck out the limiting phrase.

All was now as Hassell would have wished. He asked the purpose of the memo. Internal use, Suvich replied. He would amend it, resubmit it to Mussolini and send Hassell a copy of the amended document.[57]

On March 3, 1936, Hassell saw the amended report indicating Mussolini's approval. The main points were precise. It said that Hitler had not decided his reaction to ratification of the Franco-Soviet Pact. Italy "would not participate in any counter reaction which might be called forth by a German reaction to the ratification."[58] Hitler was ready. Discord among the Locarno partners was his best guarantee of success.

## France Plans

France's new Foreign Minister, Flandin, said: "I had one preoccupation: the Rhineland."[59] The stream of warnings continued[60] and the issue was thoroughly studied in the Foreign Ministry.[61]

On February 6, his staff sketched for Flandin three scenarios in the Rhineland. In the first case, France could claim that action already taken or in process constituted a breach of Articles 42 and 43 of Versailles. France could take the issue to the League Council, but it would be prudent first to sound out Belgium and Italy where the situation would be delicate indeed.

In the second case, German denunciation of the treaties, France could follow the same procedure. But it ought to explain any military precautions on the border to Belgium, Britain and Italy to avoid a possible German initiative which Germany might claim justified by the French move. The third case was the critical one: the entry of German military forces into the Rhineland, with or without a formal denunciation of the treaties. This would be a hostile act. In addition to informing the League Council, France would be free to take such military measures as appeared necessary. The other guarantors would also be free to intervene without awaiting the Council's decision.

The memo concluded with a serious qualification. Though nothing in the treaties compelled France to subordinate its own initiative to the views of London or Rome, excepting only the case of a direct attack, France ought not to take military action save with the advance understanding that its decision was understood, at least in London.[62]

The note neatly comprehended French problems and concerns. France wished at all costs to avoid the charge of being the aggressor. The need for support was deeply felt. France could act alone, if necessary; London and Rome lacked veto power. The position of Italy was special; there was not much hope there. But it would be rash to proceed without the prior approval of Britain. Obtaining that approval became one of

Flandin's priority tasks. The other was to obtain a military program from his own armed forces that would enable him to move swiftly and effectively to counter a German move.

On February 8, Flandin met with the Ministers of War, Navy, and Air. The discussion shifted from the Naval Conference then in progress in London to an air pact, and especially how to link the naval pact, which Britain and Germany signed but France did not, to an air pact to French advantage.

Flandin again warned that Germany would seek a pretext to modify the Rhineland limitations when she was ready. France had to think clearly of how Germany would act, the bases of protest and the counter measures to take in different cases. There had to be understandings with Britain to avoid confusion. It was understood that, in deference to British public opinion, the matter had to be sent to Geneva and that France must not be seen as the aggressor.

The Ministers speculated on German air power and possible help from Locarno guarantors and allies. Gamelin pointed to the gloomest hypotheses of all—a German-Italian conjunction.[63]

But bringing the matter to the League did not necessarily bar all independent action. On the same day, the French Council of Ministers decided that "the demilitarized zone could not be subordinated to any condition" and that the French Government "has decided to assume the responsibility for any decisions it might make."[64] Flandin made these resolutions public on February 12. Like Laval, he wanted to make France's position clear. There was an added reason; on February 11, the Chamber of Deputies had begun its debate on the ratification of the Franco-Soviet Treaty.

The Rhineland was a vital interest. To Flandin at this juncture, France must stand firm and be seen as firm. How Germany would act and when could not be known. The League must be an integral part of the French reaction. Nonetheless, that France might have to take its own counsel and act upon it was at this point accepted, clear, and made public.

On February 12, General Joseph Maurin, estimating Germany might move from the Spring of 1936 to early 1937, informed Flandin of the proposed military responses. They would be restrained to avoid provoking a conflict: manning the border fortresses, moving troops into the border zone, and guarding lines of communication. Any further moves would await political decisions of the Government.[65]

This was discouraging to Flandin who replied that it was not enough to await further political decisions; the military response must be prepared now. It was not enough simply to respond to a German thrust, but instead, if possible, to discourage Germany.[66] He pressed Maurin for a more illuminating response. Nor could Flandin be encouraged by Corbin's latest report from London: The Rhineland was simply not viewed as a major British interest; it was seen as useful but not essential to the security of France and Belgium. In fact, Britain would be more disposed to give satisfaction to Germany in the Rhineland than to make any colonial concessions.[67]

Flandin had considered the possibility of calling the League's attention to German activities in the Rhineland, the police force there, the air fields, the preparations so carefully reported by Dobler, perhaps using them to seek a new understanding which, if it did not totally forbid German forces in the demilitarized zone, limited their number, arms and fortifications. But even such a plan required British support. Flandin asked Maurin's opinion on this point.

Maurin's reply was as uninformative as it was unenthusiastic. He opined that it was not in France's best interest to use its right to occupy the demilitarized zone. But he also advised against entering into discussions with Germany; once concessions were offered, there would be no end to it.[68]

On February 18, the General Staff envisaged two kinds of German reoccupation: partial and progressive, building on existing violations or total. British aid would be sought, in the form of air defense, British squadrons and troops in France and British naval demonstrations on the German coast. But all this would be a mere show; so far as the General Staff was concerned, the principal action would be in the political sphere.

There was method in the General Staff's passivity. Faced with a fait accompli in the Rhineland and the common enemy across the French border, Britain might enter into a new Franco-Belgian-British alliance backed up by military accords. This would be far better than Locarno; this massive new combination would easily compensate for the loss of the Rhenish "no man's land." But if France failed to strike while the iron was hot, the result could be a new Locarno—nothing more than the old pact with the Rhineland zone subtracted.[69]

The military responses, however varied and imaginative, had a common characteristic. None envisaged, in response to a German thrust, that France would march. On February 19 Gamelin told the French Chiefs of Staff that it would be well to maintain the demilitarized zone at least till 1942 when the low birth rate years of the World War would have ended. It would be well, too, to have foreign, for instance, British troops on the frontier, on the trip wire theory that German action would involve Britain as well as France. But his conclusion was dark: Germany could not permanently be barred from doing what she wished inside her own frontiers.[70]

Chambrun in Rome followed closely and accurately reported to Paris Hassell's journeys to Munich and Rome. On February 22 he met Suvich who candidly told him the subject of these discussions: Italy's position on the ratification of the Franco-Soviet Pact and the repercussions on Locarno, Italy's progress in Abyssinia, and Italian attitudes toward eventual Austro-German negotiations.[71]

The Foreign Ministry was disgusted as ever, on February 24, by Maurin's "clarification." Maurin, it was acidly commented, seemed to view German reoccupation of the Rhineland as a chance to obtain new government credits for the military. There had been no consideration of a riposte. That was the question bound to arise, the question Maurin had not considered: how to intimidate the enemy and how, when he had entered the zone, to make him withdraw.[72]

While Flandin pondered the Rhineland, he was subjected to renewed pressure over Abyssinia. On February 12, the Committee of Experts filed its report. Italy, it concluded, had supplies of fuel and lubricants which would last for two and one-half to three months. Supplies in transit represented another half month. Were an embargo to be declared, and applied by all League members, it would take three to three and one-half months to become effective. The oil embargo would be effective only if the United States limited its shipments to the normal level prior to 1935. The fact was that in the last quarter of 1935 such shipments had increased to 17.8 percent of Italian oil supplies compared to 6.3 percent in the prior nine months, and 1.4 percent in the full year before.[73]

Mussolini's military prospects in Abyssinia were improving with major victories. He opposed the oil sanction as violently as ever. On February 25 Suvich spoke plainly to Chambrun. Why would France back an oil sanction of doubtful efficacity at the expense of a veritable military alliance with Italy? The Italian government would deplore having once more to send troops to the French border. He conveyed a message direct from his chief: If the oil sanction were applied, Italy would leave the League. Suvich had always been the partisan of rapprochement with France. Chambrun read the position thus: Mussolini would prefer to adhere, if possible, to the French line. But that depended strictly on France's decision on the oil sanction, which could readily occasion a radical change of Italian policy.[74]

This was the stick. On February 27, Mussolini himself exhibited the carrot. He, too, could say what his auditors wanted to hear. He was as revolted as any Italian by sanctions. But he had been faithful to Stresa. News of German-Italian talks had raised suspicions in France, Chambrun told him. "I can assure you," Mussolini replied, "that today there is nothing, absolutely nothing in the diplomatic realm between Germany and me. My sentiments about Germany are exactly as they were last April."

But, he warned, he must look to Italy's interests. He would not let Britain and France push him further. It could mean war; further measures would only enhance Italian enmity.

Once more he spoke directly about the meeting of the Committee of Eighteen scheduled for March 2:

> I tell you without ambiguity, that if the meeting of March 2 results in the aggravation of sanctions already in effect, Italy will react, and will respond by refusing to sign a naval agreement, by walking out of the League of Nations and by denouncing the dispositions arrived at between General Gamelin and Marshal Badoglio, and between General Denain and General Valle.

The warning was followed by another invitation. What would Italy do, Chambrun asked, if the discussions at Geneva came closer to meeting Italian desires. Mussolini did not hesitate. He wanted a settlement with Abyssinia which would give Italy sufficient protection. "But it need not be a diktat imposed on the Negus." "Everything is possible," Mussolini said, "so long as new sanctions aren't put into effect."[75]

The French Council of Ministers met February 27 and determined its Rhineland policy. It was the policy that reflected the thinking of February 8 and France's need for support without giving up the right to act as French interests might require. Each part of the formulation was important:

> a) The French government will not take any isolated action. It will only act in accord with the co-signators of Locarno.
>
> b) In case of a violent and incontestable breach of Article 42 and 43, the

> French government will report it immediately to the English, Belgian, and Italian governments with a view to concerting a common action pursuant to the Covenant of the League of Nations and the Locarno agreements.
>
> c) In awaiting the advice of the guaranteeing powers, the French government reserves the right to take all preparatory measures, including measures of a military character, in view of the collective action which could be decided by the Council of the League of Nations and by the Locarno guarantors.[76]

This was communicated the same day to the Belgian Foreign Minister. Flandin undertook to convey these resolutions to Eden when he saw him in Geneva on March 2. The French policy could be broad. It could be firm. It could be flexible. It could respond to the varied circumstances under which Germany might raise the vital issue. Its strength would be in the wisdom and firmness of the government in applying it. Its weakness was in the will and the means of the French armed forces to lend effective support to the policies that the government might decide on. On the day the Council of Ministers affirmed its policy, the test drew a step closer. The French Chamber ratified the Soviet Treaty.[77]

France did not ride roughshod over Hitler's objections to the Treaty. Flandin took care, during the debate, to declare that the French Government stood ready to submit to the Permanent Court of International Justice at the Hague the issue whether the Franco-Soviet Pact was compatible with Locarno. France would abide by the court's decision.[78]

Meanwhile, Hitler was preparing his coup of which a vital element was surprise. On February 28, *Paris Midi* published an interview Hitler had granted Bertrand de Jouvenal the week before:

> I wish to prove to my people that the idea of a hereditary enmity between France and Germany is an absurdity. The German people has understood this. I have been successful in a far more difficult task of reconciliation—the reconciliation of Germany and Poland.

Why, then, de Jouvenal asked, did Hitler not now revise the hostile paragraphs of *Mein Kampf* that declared France an eternal enemy? The Chancellor replied graciously:

> If I succeed in bringing about the Franco-German rapprochement, that will be a correction that will be worthy to be made. I enter my corrections in the great book of History.

France, Hitler said, could put an end forever to the "German peril", concluding grandly: "Let us be friends."[79]

## Britain Chooses Between Germany and France

Hitler had decided to march into the Rhineland. France's greatest fear, since the collapse of the American and British guarantees, would be realized. France, certain of the move, uncertain when, prepared its response. It would not act alone. Laval's efforts to secure Italian backing had been frustrated by events in Abyssinia. Once more France looked to Britain and what had proved so elusive in the more distant as in the recent past—a commitment of British support.

But Britain did not look to France. Instead, and precisely to avoid that commitment, Britain turned to Germany. Hitler's shrewd assessment of Britain, and Britain's own actions in reaching out its hand to Germany were surely elements in Hitler's decision to strike.

On January 29, Eden had recommended to the Cabinet a twofold policy: rearmament and an understanding with Germany. On February 3, he met Vansittart, Wigram, Sargent, Collier, and Malkin at the Foreign Office; they discussed concessions to Germany. Was it always necessary to advise the French in advance, the question was raised, as the negotiations proceded? The minutes of the meeting do not record an answer.[80]

Eden prepared the Cabinet to study the issue. He circulated Vansittart's memo on February 11, which he characterized as "the outcome of prolonged and anxious study" of German rearmament and policy. That program, Eden estimated, had impoverished Germany. Economic failure could inspire foreign adventures, à la Mussolini, leading to war:

> Our purpose being to avoid war, it should follow that we should be wise to do everything in our power to assist Germany's economic recovery, thereby easing the strain upon the German rulers, and making an attack less likely.

Yet he admitted the risk that an economic recovery could enhance German preparations for war. Britain was rearming, too. Eden had learned something about public opinion. Would it continue to support rearmament unless an effort had been made to come to terms with Germany?

Such an effort was bound to raise suspicions in France and the Soviet Union. And the attempt could fail:

> On balance, however, I am in favor of making some attempt to come to terms with Germany, but upon one indispensable condition: that we offer no sops to Germany. There must be no concession merely to keep Germany quiet, for that process only stimulates the appetite it is intended to satisfy.

> We should be prepared to make concessions to Germany and they will have to be concessions of value to her if they are to achieve this object, but these concessions must only be offered as part of a final settlement which includes some further arms limitation and Germany's return to the League.[81]

The final settlement was to prove elusive. But the considerations to be offered were at hand. Would Britain offer colonies? The demilitarized zone? Economic incentives? A committee should be appointed, Eden advised, to consider the matter. Baldwin appointed the committee on February 14. It included himself, MacDonald, Eden, Chamberlain, Halifax, Simon, Thomas, and Runciman.

Wigram had met with Bismarck on February 12 and hinted at the Working Agreement, which would omit certain matters contained in the Locarno Treaty; and this had been followed, at Eden's suggestion, by Bismark's meeting with Cranborne on February 15.

Eden now gave a practical answer to the inquiry that had been raised concerning the French. Things were moving at a lively pace. He instructed Clerk in Paris that he would deprecate for the present any discussions with France about what attitude the two countries should adopt "in the hypothetical case of a violation of the Demilitarized Zone." It was, he said, "highly delicate and complicated." He would not wish to commit himself regarding either British policy or British treaty interpretation.

He was sure Flandin would inquire and Clerk "should not give him any encouragement to hope that his Majesty's Government would be prepared to discuss the matter on the basis of a statement of the British attitude."

What, Eden inquired, had Flandin meant, by the way, when he said German infraction of the zone would be treated by France as casus foederis? Did it mean referring the matter to the League? Or did it mean France would take military action and invite Britain to do likewise. The matter was not clear, but Eden did not wish to pursue it. He preferred to let this sleeping dog slumber undisturbed.[82]

Eden followed this up with another memo for the newly formed Committee on Germany. A German reoccupation of the Rhineland could not be discounted, even if not necessarily imminent. He repeated his distaste for discussion with the French when he thought they were themselves uncertain. Perhaps they would use the British attitude as an excuse for inaction. He did not think France would attack Germany to maintain the demilitarized zone.

But Britain ought to be clear in its own mind as to the value of the zone. He referred to the reports of military and air staffs. He recognized the profound effects of a reoccupation:

> [T]he disappearance of the Demilitarized Zone will not merely change local military values, but it is likely to lead to far-reaching repercussions of a kind which will further weaken France's influence in Eastern and Central Europe, leaving a gap which may eventually be filled either by Germany or by Russia.

Notwithstanding this devastating effect upon France, Eden concluded:

> But taking one thing with another, it seems undesirable to adopt an attitude where we could either have to fight for the Zone or abandon it in the face of a German reoccupation. It would be preferable for Great Britain and France to enter betimes into negotiations with the German Government for the surrender on conditions of our rights in the Zone while such surrender still has got a bargaining value.[83]

This was precisely the argument Simon had made the year before to legalize German rearmament. But Hitler had acted too swiftly. He always preferred action to negotiation.

The German Committee was to meet on February 17. The Foreign Office prepared still another memo on February 15 elucidating the proposed negotiation. In Western Europe, the key elements would be the substitution of an air pact for the demilitarized zone. In Eastern Europe, Britain and France would recognize Germany's "special interests" so long as Germany did not exploit those interests in a manner inconsistent with British principles and the Covenant of the League This could be seen as a direct invitation to Germany to use economic duress and internal subversion to accomplish her ends rather than force of arms.

While inviting Germany to exploit interests in the small nations of Central and Eastern Europe, Britain extended no offer of her own possessions. Let Germany raise the issue of colonies. Britain would not.

To launch a program like this, it would be necessary to have due regard for German sensibility. For instance, Britain ought to disassociate itself from the policy of the Franco-Soviet Pact. And, as always, there was the question of informing France. It was, to be sure, natural, but raised problems. Perhaps, then, "a more effective procedure" would be to try to ascertain as soon as possible, "and *privately and quietly*, perhaps through the German Embassy here, whether the outline of the proposed arrangement is one respecting which Herr Hitler considers he could negotiate."[84]

When the special committee met on February 17, there was no debate on the desirability of following Eden's recommendations. The only issue was how to proceed. Eden made it clear that British public opinion would not accept a new arms program unless at the same time an attempt was made to reach a political settlement in Europe. MacDonald and Simon heartily agreed.

One way to open the negotiation with Germany would be to discuss raw materials and colonial territories. This was always a sensitive issue. MacDonald preferred to use an air pact as the opening move. But he injected a note of realism. So long as German doctrine was that German sovereignty must follow German blood, negotiations would be impossible. The Committee was not deterred. They came to no conclusion; but they had dismissed no possibility.[85] Britain would carefully distance herself from France and with equal deliberation move toward Germany.

British feelers to Germany were not rebuffed, reflecting directly as they did, on the policy Germany was in the process of executing. On February 25, Neurath directed Hoesch, in his next conversation with Eden, to sound him out as to what progress had been made and whether Britain had developed a more concrete idea of the Working Agreement.[86]

## Arms and Abyssinia

The other major preoccupation of the British Government at this time was its rearmament program and particularly how it should be coordinated. There was a great public debate on the need for a Ministry of Defense to coordinate the War, Admiralty, and Air offices. Any substantial arms program raised issues of priorities of manpower and materials among the three services and equally issues of the same allocations as between the civil and defense sectors. Britain was enjoying an economic recovery which the diversion of resources to arms could stunt. It was a classic dilemma.

One thing was clear: the need for increased arms. The issues were discussed by the Cabinet on February 17, when there was little support for a Ministry of Defense.[87] Instead, Baldwin suggested a minister to coordinate the service departments rather than a new ministry to supersede them. A Committee on the Coordination of Defense was established with Baldwin as Chairman.[88]

The Cabinet met again on February 24, and after some debate adopted Baldwin's suggestion. He would, as Prime Minister, remain Chairman of the Committee of Imperial Defense and the Defense Policy and Requirements Committee, but a new minister would relieve him of much of the burden and day-to-day detail and would coordinate the defense process.

This system was the basis of the new arms program, the White Paper of 1936 which was scheduled for completion and release at the month's end.

Who would the new Minister be? Churchill had his claims and a vivid interest. Here again, public opinion was considered decisive. Churchill's appointment would offend Liberals and would promptly tar the Cabinet with the brush of militarism. Baldwin was prescient. Better to save Churchill, he said, against the day when he would be needed as the war leader.[89] Churchill, bitter at the time, later looked back and ascribed his exclusion to Fate: "Over me beat the invisible wings."[90]

On Abyssinia's northern front, Badoglio prepared to follow up his victory over Ras Kassa and Ras Seyoum. He told the assembled correspondents:

> You will have the privilege of witnessing a tremendous, indeed a stupendous spectacle, gentlemen. We shall win the war with a campaign of utmost brilliance, a campaign unequalled since the days of Napoleon. In less than two months, beneath the weight of our assault, you will see the Ethiopian empire crumble to dust.[91]

He had reasons to be confident. He commanded 70,000 men, backed by ample artillery, air power, and supplies including 70,000 lemons to refresh his troops. The Abyssinian army, ill-armed, defenseless from the air, occupied a strong position on Amba Aradam, a precipitous mountain that barred the way to the south. Badoglio executed an encircling movement. Predictably it brought forth a furious Abyssinian attack on February 12 which, Badoglio later commented "though carried out with the greatest determination, gave no sign of any homogeneous plan or any efficient exercise of command."[92]

Italian aviation and artillery maintained pressure until February 15 when Badoglio launched his final assault on Amba Aradam, led by the Alpini. Violent Abyssinian attacks could not halt the advance; the threat of encirclement compelled retreat. The retreat became a bloody rout. Italian airmen hunted down the Abyssinians. A more horrible fate pursued the fugitives on the ground. The Azebu Galla, inspired by hatred of their Amharic overlords and Italian pay, mounted on horses, their traditional scarlet cloaks flying in the wind, charged, ran down, and massacred the remnants of Ras Mulugeta's army, taking special care to concentrate at the fords of the rivers and the mountain passes. They killed Ras Mulugeta's son, then ritually mutilated his body. The old warrior turned in his flight to avenge his son, was spotted by an Italian pilot and was mortally wounded. The fate of his family was the fate, too, of Ras Mulugeta's army.[93]

From Dessie, where he commanded, via Sir Sidney Barton, the Emperor sent a pathetic plea for help to London. He had refused the Hoare-Laval proposals, because they were unjust, and because the British Government had refused to accept them. Mussolini had offered to negotiate directly for peace. He asked Britain to name a place for the negotiation, in the meantime an armistice being called.

His final plea was more far reaching. He proposed to place Abyssinia under a British protectorate or mandate to help achieve a higher civilization.[94]

In forwarding the message, Barton acknowledged that the Emperor's proposal was unlikely to be practical, but, he urged, Britain must accept some degree of responsibility for a negotiated settlement.[95]

When the Cabinet met on February 24 to discuss defense coordination, it had before it Haile Selassie's plea, which it declined, to assume a British mandate or protectorate over Abyssinia. Instead, Eden offered the unhelpful suggestion that Abyssinia again apply to the League for conciliation on the basis of the report of the Committee of Five.[96]

Britain, of course, wanted no war with Italy, nor to furnish any proof of what Mussolini had always claimed—that she was motivated not by idealism, not by principle, but by the same self-interest that had built an empire.

Eden did, indeed, on February 24 reaffirm to the House of Commons Britain's desire for the "speediest and most satisfactory settlement of this dispute," specifically referring to the good offices of the Committee of Five. Against Opposition attack, Eden defended the speed and effect of the sanctions already in place. Moreover, he declared that the Government had not departed from its decision in principle to use the oil sanction nor from its resolve to play a full part with others in the collective action that the League might determine. Since the League would meet on March 2, precisely to discuss the oil sanction, this was a stern message to Mussolini. For Hitler, Eden had gentler words. Britain must rearm:

> It is essential, however, in reaffirming our attachment to collective security, that we should distinguish clearly between that policy and encirclement. His Majesty's Government would take their full share in collective security; they will have neither lot nor part in encirclement. The distinction is surely clear.[97]

Eden was mollifying German sensibilities and traversing the oft made charge of encirclement, preparing the ground for his approach to Germany. The pressure being exerted on Italy had a curiously parallel effect on Mussolini who was in the process of turning to Germany at the same time.

The Commons debate of February 24 brilliantly illustrates the cross-currents of thought and emotion that moved members. Sir Archibald Sinclair said that the issue was not victory or defeat, but world peace or destruction. Colonel Wedgewood declared that the Abyssinian issue must be settled on the basis, not of expediency, but of right and wrong. Leopold Amery offered a distinctly contrasting view that looked back to the turbulent days of December: "If the Government had the courage of their own convictions and stuck to the Hoare-Laval proposals, they would have carried them."[98]

The Cabinet held a full-dress review of the oil sanction on February 26. It was argued that it would not work because nonmembers would ship oil to Italy, that the economic effect of sanctions on the British coal trade was disastrous, the Fleet in the Mediterranean was strained, and Mussolini might be encouraged into alliance with Hitler. Contrary arguments were heard including some remarkably short-lived prognostications: "That there was no danger of an Abyssinian collapse"; that the risk of a German-Italian alliance was small "owing to the contempt in which Herr Hitler is believed to hold Italy."

What all agreed was that "there was absolutely no question of a blockade."

The positive reasons for the oil sanction included the negative impact on the future of the League if it was not employed, and the negative effect, too, on the trade unions and Labour who had strongly backed sanctions. Indeed, the oil sanction could help secure Labour support for the rearmament program. But the discussion ultimately focused on the Cabinet's critical concern:

> To repudiate an oil sanction after the statements that had been made in the Debate in the Hoare-Laval peace proposals would be particularly disastrous.

Baldwin now signaled his agreement with the oil sanction. He agreed, too, that the refusal to impose an oil sanction "would have a disastrous effect both now and at the next General Election."[99]

The approval the Cabinet gave Eden was tempered with caution. He was authorized to tell the Committee of Eighteen that Britain would back the oil sanction and try to secure an early date for its application. But, on the other hand, he should avoid taking the lead at Geneva and, as a matter of fact, "carry out the policy of the Government with as little publicity to himself as possible."[100]

Since Mussolini had made it clear that an oil embargo would precipitate an Italian reaction including withdrawal from the League and the denunciation of military agreements with France, when Eden arrived in Geneva on March 2 to play his self-effacing role, he would be met by an anxious Flandin, desperately situated between Mussolini and Hitler. This is indeed what Corbin told Eden on February 26. Flandin would ask to speak to Eden at Geneva about the demilitarized zone. He added that Flandin wished to take up a firm attitude on the issue.[101]

Eden wrote an analysis on February 27 of the use of an air pact as an appropriate procedure for the British approach to Germany.[102] He also saw Hoesch who wondered, since his talk with Cranborne on February 15, whether Eden had any particular steps in mind. Eden vigorously denied any intent to encircle Germany, quoting his recent statements in Parliament. He coldly disclaimed an interest in the Franco-Soviet Pact. His warmth was reserved for an air pact, which he was anxious to pursue. Hoesch cited the difficulty caused by the Abyssinian war. It was not enough, Eden replied, to register the difficulties without attempting to overcome them. He would see Flandin in Geneva the next week and on his return inform Hoesch fully. Thus, Eden kept active his approach to Germany.[103]

From Berlin, Phipps, who had been kept informed of these plans, reported to Eden on February 29 the Italian Embassy's denial of any new political link with Germany. It was essential, he advised, to reform the Stresa Front. Based on strength, a settlement with Germany would be a "probability instead of a dim possibility." The formation of the Stresa Front would be worth almost any price, and that price might be light compared to what would be paid without it.[104]

The armies of Ras Kassa and Ras Seyoum had been defeated in the first Battle of Tembien but not destroyed. Badgolio proceeded to destroy them in a two-day battle that started February 27. A daring assault by Alpini rock climbers on the mountain citadel of Amba Worcq, which anchored the left of the Abyssinian line, started the Abyssinian defeat. Once more there were desperate Abyssinian assaults with reckless courage and antique arms, once more Italian artillery and aviation were merciless. When the retreating generals finally reached the Emperor's headquarters, they were almost alone.

The forlorn Emperor wrote to Ras Imru, who commanded the last remaining army on the Northern front:

> Our army, famous throughout Europe for its valor, has lost its name; brought to ruin by a few traitors, to this pass it is reduced...Ras Kassa and Ras Seyoum are with us but have not a single armed man with them.[105]

Ras Imru's day of battle would soon come. Meanwhile the Italian troops, victorious at Amba Aradem, had continued southward and taken Amba Alagi. This was historic, the site were Italian troops had advanced farthest into Abyssinia in 1896 before being annihilated.

Abyssinian prospects dimmed further on February 29 when the American Congress extended its Neutrality Act until May 1, 1937. Earlier drafts of the law had covered not only arms, ammunition and implements of war, but other articles (of which oil would be one) in excess of normal exports to belligerents. That limitation did not appear in the new law. Instead of such limitations, the nation received an exhortation from its President based, as he said, on "high moral duty," so to conduct its trade with belligerents as not to seek new opportunities for profit or prolong war.[106]

It was widely held that America had been prepared to do more, indeed to support League sanctions without admitting it, and that the shock and indignation occasioned by the Hoare-Laval proposals had killed that chance. This much is true: at the end of February, the debate on the oil sanction had become academic as Italy stood on the verge of a victory which would become final in two more months.

## On the Eve

Blomberg issued his marching orders for the reoccupation on March 2. François-Poncet found Hitler that day not violent or disagreeable, but nervous, downcast, reticent, impatient, and much less keen on argument than usual. These were apt observations; Hitler was entering a period of maximum strain and suspense. Hitler railed against the Soviets; François-Poncet in turn noted Hitler's protestation of desire for friendship with France in his interview with de Jouvenal. He asked if the Führer had any concrete proposals to offer.

Hitler indicated that despite the vote on the Soviet Treaty, he was working on and would send some precise propositions to France.[107] François-Ponçet conveyed skepticism to Flandin. In 1935 Hitler had restored an army and air force. 1936 would be the year of the abolition, or attenuation of the demilitarized zone and "it would be completely vain to have, in this regard, the least illusion."[108]

On March 3, Hitler received final confirmation of Mussolini's benevolent attitude. Hassell had received Suvich's revised memorandum which clearly stated the two vital points: Italy would not participate in any counter-reaction to the German response to ratification of the Franco-Soviet Pact; and Italy desired a normalization of relations between Germany and Austria.[109] The way was now clear.

On March 5 Hitler informed his ambassadors to the Locarno powers that he would reoccupy the Rhineland on Saturday, March 7. The shrewdness with which Hitler endowed his coup was commensurate with the shock it would register. The entry would be made by small army, air force, and anti-aircraft contingents, obviously incapable of moving against or threatening France. It would be, for the moment, as Hitler thereafter loudly proclaimed, a symbolic occupation. This addressed directly the issue whether the reoccupation was a flagrant breach of Article 42 and 43 which would justify a military response, a point, specifically to be made by the ambassadors.

The memorandum which was to be delivered to the Foreign Ministers ably argued Germany's case that the Franco-Soviet Pact "would nullify the fundamental assumptions and conditions of Locarno." But Hitler did not intend to rely on argument. To illustrate what he characterized as the "purely defensive character" of his move and Germany's "eternal and abiding longing for a real pacification of Europe," he accompanied, just as he had done in March, 1935, his stroke with offers of peace.

As he had previously planned, the proposals included a new demilitarized zone on both sides of the German-Belgian-French borders "on the condition of full parity," and a twenty-five-year nonaggression pact among the three nations, which Britain and Italy would be invited to sign as guarantors. The Netherlands, if it wished, could enter this system. The proposals were not limited to the West; Germany would enter nonaggression pacts, like its Polish Pact, with Germany's Eastern neighbors.

Responding to British hopes and importunings, Hitler indicated his readiness to enter an air pact. The final stroke would delight lovers of peace and champions of collective security everywhere. Germany, now fully sovereign in its own territory (and the statement was in itself a message to all who had burned with the resentment of injustice to Germany) would be prepared to return to the League of Nations. This would not even, it was generously stated, require as a condition equality in colonial rights, in the confidence that that issue would be clarified through friendly negotiations at a reasonable time.[110]

## The Historian Meets History

Amid these momentous developments, Professor Arnold Toynbee arrived in Berlin at the end of February to address the Nazi Law Society. He was surprised to learn that he was to meet the Führer himself.

This had come to pass because there had been called to Hitler's attention a passage which the chronicler of civilizations and current history had written in the newly published *Survey of International Affairs for 1934* describing the Blood Purge. It had been a shocking spectacle, Toynbee had written, to see a head of state "shooting down his own former henchmen in the style of an American gangster." Hitler complained,

> That isn't fair. The American gangsters do it for money, and I did not do it for money. Arrange for me to see the Englishman when he arrives.[111]

So it happened that Toynbee met Hitler in the presence of Ribbentrop, Neurath, and Dieckhoff, Permanent Under Secretary of State. Now the self-educated Führer, who had left the Linz high school without a diploma at seventeen, who had gone hungry to buy books, lectured the world-famous historian for two and a quarter hours on Germany's role in history. Far from being bored or put off, Toynbee listened in rapt attention as Hitler carried on "with masterly coherence and lucidity." "I cannot think," he later reported, "of any academic lecturer to whom I have ever listened who could have spoken continuously for that length of time without ever losing the thread of his argument."[112]

In all the Führer's long discourse, he never once mentioned Italy. But Dieckhoff, an old acquaintance, did when he met Toynbee later. The British people, he observed, had vented their indignation at Italy when they compelled the Government to dismiss Hoare and reject the Hoare-Laval plan:

> Now that they have found their scapegoat in Hoare, I think we shall find they will take no further action. Ethiopia's fate is going to be something far worse than the Hoare-Laval proposals that raised such a storm in Britain. If those proposals had been submitted to Mussolini and accepted by him, Ethiopia would have got off with the loss of some slices of her territory. This loss would have been painful, since the severed slices would have been large; but at this price the rump of Ethiopia would have survived as a nominally independent state. As things are now, I think we are going to witness the total conquest and annexation of Ethiopia by Mussolini, and I predict that this is not going to arouse the British people to take any further action. You have found a whipping boy for Mussolini in Hoare. Now that you have relieved your feelings at Hoare's expense, you will not feel any impulse to save Ethiopia by having a showdown with Mussolini."[113]

Dieckhoff's point, that the British public was moved by emotional considerations rather than by competent analysis of the national interest, would be as well indicated by the events to follow in the Rhineland as in Abyssinia. That understanding of British psychology, wholly shared by Hitler, was a moving consideration in his decision.

## Flandin and Eden

At Geneva on March 2 for the meeting of the Committee of Eighteen, Eden bluntly told Flandin that the British Cabinet had decided in favor of the oil sanction.[114] Flandin told of Mussolini's threats, in such event, to leave the League, not sign a naval agreement and denounce military agreements with France.

Clearly, they were coming from different viewpoints. Eden's was that to withhold the oil sanction in the face of Mussolini's threats would permit the aggressor to choose his own sanctions. Flandin's was that the oil sanction would be neither practical nor effective. Flandin proposed instead a new appeal to the belligerents. When Joseph Paul-Boncour suggested the risk of an Italian-German rapprochement, Eden observed that he did not think Germany eager for an Italian connection.

Flandin and Eden finally agreed that, before the discussion of the oil sanction in the Committee of Eighteen, Flandin would propose a further peace appeal. If no satisfactory replies were received within a short period, say forty-eight hours, the Committee would reconvene. At the meeting, Eden supported Flandin's proposal, but made it clear that his government favored an oil embargo. All this was duly accepted by the

Committee which in turn forwarded the matter to the Committee of Thirteen for its action the next day.[115]

That Committee in fact issued its appeal on March 3 to Italy and Abyssinia for immediate negotiations. It would meet, not in forty-eight hours, but on March 10 to consider the replies, despite Eden's preference for an earlier date.[116]

Flandin had graver concerns than Abyssinia. Meeting with Eden before the session of the Committee of Thirteen, he precisely outlined his fears that the oil sanction could lead Italy to leave the League, withdraw from Locarno, and denounce military agreements with France. All this raised the possibility of a German-Italian rapprochement and German action in the Rhineland. Nothing could be more perilous for France. He gave Eden the statement which the Council of Ministers had adopted on February 27: no isolated action, but action only with Locarno co-signers; in case of flagrant violation, France would inform the League and Belgium, France, and Italy in order to concert common action. France would reserve the right to any measures, including military measures, in anticipation of collective action by the Council and the guarantors. He followed this with a special inquiry. It formally stated the concerns Flandin had voiced and added significantly:

> But there is a grave risk; and Germany may be tempted to profit by the situation in the demilitarized zone.

Italy might then disinterest itself in Locarno. Now came the precise point: France counted on Britain to support France, even in the absence of the other guarantors, even alone.

Before taking so critical a step as the oil sanction, the French asked Britain's reassurance on this point.[117]

This was the latest in the long line of French appeals for British support on France's German frontier. This, Eden said, was a matter on which he must consult his Cabinet colleagues. He promised to do this promptly.[118]

On March 4, the Foreign Affairs Commission of the French Senate voted for ratification of the Soviet Pact.[119] Phipps wired the Foreign Office of impending German action in the Rhineland should Mussolini decline the appeal of the Committee of Thirteen and leave the League and Locarno.[120] In Britain, the Government published its 1936 White Paper on Rearmament. It called for four new infantry battalions, two battleships, increasing the number of cruisers to seventy, an aircraft carrier and steady expansion of the destroyer and submarine fleets. The bulk of the program was devoted to the air force. The 1935 goal of 1,500 front-line air-craft in Britain was increased to 1,750. There would be a coordinated system of air defense, utilizing the results of the latest scientific research and experiment. Special provisions for the utilization of industry, the mobilization of manpower, and the organization of supply would back the fighting forces.[121]

A debate in Parliament was set for March 9, 1936. The Opposition motion is eloquent of the state of mind of many Britons as Hitler prepared his masterstroke:

> As the safety of this country and the peace of the world cannot be secured by reliance on armaments but only by the resolute pursuit of a policy of international understanding, adherence to the Covenant of the League of Nations, general disarmament, the progressive improvement of international labour standards, and economic co-operation so as to remove the causes of war, this House cannot agree to a policy which in fact seeks security in national armaments alone and intensifies the ruinous arms race between the nations, inevitably leading to war; views with alarm proposals for the reorganization of industry on a war basis which will enormously extend the vested interests in arms manufacture and create a serious menace to organized labour and to trade union standards; and has no confidence in His Majesty's Ministers whose unworthy and ambiguous foreign policy has largely contributed to the present state of world unrest.[122]

On March 5, there were indications of response to the appeal of the Committee of Thirteen. The Emperor would agree to the opening of negotiations subject to the provisions of the Covenant being respected, which apparently meant Italy could claim no occupied territory.[123] Mussolini told the French Ambassador that his forces were winning a major battle in Shire against Ras Imru's army; that there were no important obstacles before his armies. An oil sanction had been threatened. He would not negotiate under threat. No nation worthy of consideration, he said, would.[124]

This was the situation when the British Cabinet met on March 5. The political atmosphere was incisively described in Corbin's dispatch of the following day:

> Since the denouement of the Hoare-Laval proposals it [the Cabinet] expected at every instant a revolt of public opinion against those initiatives which seem most likely to put an end to the Abyssinian war. Is not Stanley Baldwin haunted by the memory of the agitation of his supporters during

> the days of December 18 and 19 which forced their chief to make an amend honorable. Can he forget that after having forced his Foreign Secretary to resign, he paid homage to the same arguments that had served him? And Eden, who expressed reasonable and moderate views some days ago, is he not the prisoner of his past declarations and of all the hopes placed in him by an electoral mass blindly loyal to principles of which it is not ready to accept all of the consequences?[125]

Eden reported to the Cabinet on proceedings in Geneva, explaining why he had thought fit to announce British support of the oil sanction. He outlined Flandin's apprehensions that the oil sanction would lead to Mussolini's rapprochement with Germany and Germany's taking action in the Rhineland. He laid on the table Flandin's requested assurance as well as the French position as adopted on February 27.

The Cabinet speculated whether Germany would commit a flagrant breach of Articles 42 and 43 and what procedures the League was likely to adopt. But what was the status of the Treaty of Locarno, if one of the guarantors, Italy, opted out? What did Locarno really mean in saying that the parties would come to the assistance of the complaining power? These were complex issues; the inevitable result was to refer them to a committee.

Eden, at least, stated his views. If Italy opted out of Locarno, Britain would not be discharged from her obligations. MacDonald urged that the issue be handled politically so the question would never have to be answered. To this Baldwin, Chamberlain, and others added that the reality of the situation was that neither France nor Britain was in any position to take effective military action against Germany.

France had appealed to Britain for help. Eden offered the Cabinet a solution that was in the spirit of his earlier proposals and the work of the Committee on Germany. Britain, he suggested, should turn to Germany. He would ask authority from the Cabinet, unknown to the French, to approach Germany on an air pact. The hoped for result would be Germany's raising the issue of the demilitarized zone, which could then be settled. Settled, to Eden, of course, meant negotiated away. Thus the Cabinet agreed that Eden should approach Germany to offer her precisely what France sought British aid to defend.

There was, as always, intense suspicion of France. Flandin should be asked, it was suggested, just what France was prepared to do. Several members opined that France had put the question, not because France sought British cooperation, but to give France an excuse before French public opinion not to back the oil sanction.

Eden reminded the Cabinet that Flandin's question was pending. He could only hold off Flandin for a few days. The Lord Chancellor knew equity when he saw it. France had a good case to raise the question, he said.

Chamberlain was not so clear; he suggested that if one party to Locarno withdrew, the other parties should confer. This was not a rapierlike riposte to a German thrust.

Baldwin, as so often, settled the case. He backed Eden's proposal. The legal issues were referred to a committee. Thus it came about that Eden, upright and moral, supercilious to the point of scorn of the deviousness of French statesmen and policy, now went forth to meet in secret with Germany to aid in the perpetuation of the Nazi regime and the bartering away of French security.[126]

Eden did not dally. He met Hoesch on March 6. He could, he told Hoesch, now reply to Hoesch's inquiry of February 27 about concrete proposals. He stated Britain's wish for relations of confidence with Germany and Germany's return to the League. He again denied any intent to encircle Germany. He proposed an air pact, and indicated the points it might cover. He would be happy to elucidate any point for Hitler. Hoesch listened in silence. He had earlier said that he had an important communication from Berlin which he would deliver on the morrow, March 7.[127]

At nine o'clock that evening Hitler met with his assembled ministers, the whole command of the Third Reich.

He told them of his decision to occupy the Rhineland. German troops were already on the march. On the morrow, Saturday, in the Reichstag he would make an announcement to the world. He now added to his peace proposals another potent appeal to public support and world approval. He would dissolve the Reichstag, hold elections on March 28, and submit his action to the vote of the electorate. Thus Hitler prepared to bind the German people to his program and demonstrate his legitimacy to the world. Needless to say, the Führer's proposals were unanimously approved. Hitler would now launch the strike from which the British Empire and the Third Republic would never recover.[128]

# 7

# Hitler Strikes

*"Statesmen and generals can hardly plan as much as a sensible policy unless the voice of the nation speaks clearly to them."*

—L.B. Namier[1]

## Die Wacht am Rhein

Military aircraft overhead, even while Hitler was addressing the Reichstag, told the Rhinelanders that the reoccupation had begun. Infantry, cavalry, and artillery followed. Physically fit, Prussian-smart, the troops were met by crowds, whose numbers and enthusiasm swelled as the day wore on. Flags and flowers were everywhere, and when in the Domplatz of Cologne, the troops, goose-stepping precisely, marched past General Kluge, who took the salute, the populace were frantic with the joy of a dream come true.

The next day was Heroes' Day. Hitler laid a wreath at the national war memorial. At the State Opera House, General Fritz von Blomberg spoke for the armed forces. His backdrop was a huge black iron cross and thirty-six immobile soldiers and three sailors holding aloft the battle flags of the lost war. Blomberg pledged allegiance:

> To the creator of the Third Reich, who is our supreme commander, the defense force renders thanks from an overflowing heart for the most honorable task assigned to a German soldier—that of rearing a new defense force, anchored in the people through a universal obligation to service.[2]

Sixty million German hearts beat faster. German troops once more manned the watch on the Rhine.

Hitler's shrewdly crafted speech launched its multiple appeals to all those in whose hearts and minds hope transcended analysis and faith defied experience. A demilitarized zone on both sides of the border would be, Hitler proclaimed, a new Locarno shorn of inequality. (But how could France give up her Maginot Line?) He offered twenty-five year nonaggression pacts among France, Germany, and Belgium, to be guaranteed by Britain and Italy, inviting the Netherlands to join the system. The proffered air pact was bound to please and for all those who feared détente in the West and aggression in the East, there was the offer of nonaggression pacts, like the Polish Treaty, with Germany's neighbors to the East. (Austria was a conspicuous omission.) Nor was this all. Hitler's masterstroke was Germany's proposed return to the League of Nations.

Hitler's peace plan was accompanied by solemn oaths: Germany had no territorial demands. Freed from the servitudes of inequality, Germany would work unceasingly for European understanding. Hitler used all the right words—"European collective collaboration" and "obligations not only regarding our own nation but also concerning the other European states."[3] This was Adolf Hitler, the Good European, at his zenith.

## First Response—Britain

When Hoesch gave the German memorandum to Eden on March 7, Eden expressed his deep regrets at the German action. In Berlin, Phipps said it would create a lamentable impression upon His Majesty's Government. Both pointed out that Germany had voluntarily entered and freely affirmed Locarno, and that the issue of the Soviet Treaty could have been impartially adjudicated at the Hague.[4]

All this Berlin would have expected. Of greater significance were Eden's statements to Hoesch that while he must study the document and consult his colleagues, clearly the return of Germany to the League of Nations was the most important element. Hoesch reminded Eden that the offer of an air pact was responsive to their discussion of the day before.[5] He reported to Berlin that Eden, in closing, asked him to hold himself in readiness for further discussions in the next few days.[6] He must have left Eden fairly confident that Britain would take no immediate action.

Even before he talked with Baldwin, Eden saw Corbin, the French Ambassador. The German action was, of course, deplorable. Nevertheless, he told Corbin, even a hasty reading of the memorandum disclosed important points: a new pact among France, Belgium, and Germany, and Germany's return to the League of Nations. He would have to consult the Cabinet on Monday and then could talk freely and frankly with France.

"I felt sure," Eden told Corbin, "that until consultation had taken place, the French Government would not do anything to render the situation more difficult."[7]

Corbin heard this request in a firmer phrase: that, prior to consultation, there should be no action "tending irremediably to engage the future."[8]

It was not only, Eden said, that a calm and steady examination of the situation was a procedural requirement. Germany had created a fait accompli:

> Nonetheless we must not close our eyes to the fact that a 'contre partie' was offered and that would undoubtedly have a very considerable effect on public opinion. We could not leave this side of the situation unconsidered.[9]

Indeed the discussions at which Eden hinted were just those that he had himself attempted to launch only the day before.

Here, then, was another of those dazzling reversals of position which had characterized relations between Britain and France during the past year. Only a week before, at Geneva, Eden had disclosed to the shocked and pained Flandin Britain's intention to apply the oil sanction against Italy as soon as possible. To do otherwise, Eden had argued, would be to allow the aggressor to choose his own sanctions and make the League look ridiculous.

Now, in the face of an incontestable fait accompli, the breach of treaty upon which the principal security of France depended and of which Britain was the guarantor, Eden saw value in Hitler's proposals and merit, not in the enforcement of existing treaties, but in the negotiation of new arrangements, which, he trusted, would lead to a more secure future.

If, Corbin shrewdly observed, Eden had formally disapproved of the denunciation of Locarno, he had done so without emotion: "His attitude was that of a man who asks himself what advantage can be derived from a new situation rather than what barriers can be opposed to an adverse menace."[10]

## First Responses—France

François-Poncet responded to the German memorandum far less politely, more sharply than his British colleague. The fait accompli, he remarked to Neurath, was a method which rendered it singularly difficult to enter into future arrangements and most unlikely to inaugurate a reign of peace in Europe. What use did Germany intend to make of the reoccupation, he asked? These were small units, purely symbolic, Neurath replied, and there was no intent to establish strong garrisons. Only that day, he insinuated, he had received from his Ambassador in London Eden's suggestion for an air pact.[11]

François-Poncet warned Paris that France must react vigorously. Hitler should know that France would not negotiate under the pressure of military measures in the Rhineland, even if they were only symbolic.[12]

This was precisely the message Flandin conveyed to Clerk. There had been, Flandin said, not only a unilateral, but a flagrant violation of Locarno. France would, as planned, present the issue to the League Council. He wanted a meeting of Locarno powers as soon as possible. He understood the meaning of the German offers and did not definitely oppose all negotiation. The critical issue was this: "France could not negotiate under threat of denunciation of Locarno and under the menace of a remilitarized zone and loss of French security."[13]

His meeting with Clerk left Flandin concerned. He promptly wired to Corbin in London his opinion that the British Government had not recognized the gravity of the situation. Clerk had referred to the appeal of Hitler's proposals to Britain. Flandin had replied that France would not negotiate on the basis of the practical abandonment of the demilitarized zone. He urged Corbin to do all in his power to alert the British Government to the dangers ahead.[14]

When the French Council of Ministers met on March 8, it was characteristic that Georges Mandel, Clemenceau's protege and spiritual descendant, demanded prompt military action to force a German withdrawal. In this he was joined by Sarraut, Paul-Boncour and one or two other ministers.[15]

Such a response was, in hard fact, not feasible. There existed neither the appropriate military force, the plan, nor the will to make such a countermove. The German generals had looked forward and seen the blitzkrieg. The French generals looked back and saw the motionless stalemate of the trenches of the Western Front where the awful power of defense had decimated a generation. France had no mobile strike force; its military posture was purely defensive, epitomized by the majestic and complex works of the Maginot Line. This had been a deliberate choice as reflected in the debate of 1935 when Parliament had rejected the plea of Reynaud and de Gaulle for just such a combination of men, machines, and methods as could now lend force to French policy.

At a meeting of military and naval leaders that day, Gamelin related how he had advised the Government that in a war on the German-French border, saturation would soon occur and the fronts would become frozen. Only aircraft then would be capable of offensive action.

He had been asked if the army was ready to push the Germans out of the demilitarized zone. His reply: the entry of French troops into the zone would mean war and war meant general mobilization. France would need the help of the Locarno guarantors, English and Italian troops. What measures had Gamelin taken? Manning the border fortifications and cancellation of home leaves in the East.

But, Admiral Durand-Veil objected, nothing could be expected from the British so long as the Abyssinian affair carried on. There was scant hope of concerted action by Britain and Italy, locked as they were in a state of mutual hostility.[16]

The Council of Ministers concluded that there would be no immediate countermove. Instead the appropriate notifications would be sent to the League of Nations that day, demanding its immediate action[17] just as the ministers had determined on February 27. The French position was clearly defined. France did not accept the fait accompli and France would not negotiate on that basis.

Flandin wished to avoid positioning France as an aggressor or as the instigator of a war no one wanted. The 1923 occupation of the Ruhr had poisoned relations among France, Britain, and Germany for over a decade. But he needed and desperately wanted maximum support for French policy from Belgium, from Italy, and above all from Britain.

Flandin's policy was not simply to enforce the status quo. There would have to be negotiations with Germany and such negotiations could materially alter the status of the Rhineland. But he thought such negotiations, to be effective, had to be based on good faith and international law; a new treaty would have little legitimacy and less hope of success if it were based solely on a fait accompli.

Flandin's objective was to achieve a clear adjudication that Germany had violated her treaty obligations, and by meaningful and effective pressure to secure a German retreat to some form of status quo ante. This was the program which Flandin would present to the Locarno powers. It would, if it succeeded, represent a very real victory for France, her allies and Locarno co-signers, and a genuine setback for Hitler which might be pregnant with fruitful consequences for Europe's future. It would be an outcome far more conducive to French security than a discussion of Germany's terms backed by German forces in the Rhineland.

When Prime Minister Albert Sarraut broadcast to the French people on the evening of March 8, he did not talk of negotiation. Germany, he declared, had violated Locarno, without seeking just that adjudication by which France was prepared to abide. Far from welcoming Hitler's proposals, he decried their worth, based as they were on unilateral repudiation of treaties and contempt for international law:

> There can be no peace in Europe, no more international relations, if these methods become general. In opposing them we are serving the cause of the European community. The French Government, for their part, are firmly resolved not to negotiate under threats. The very fact that, in contempt of solemn engagements, German soldiers are now stationed on the Rhine, forbids all negotiation for the moment.
>
> Having conscientiously examined the situation, I declare in the name of the French Government that we intend to see maintained that essential guarantee of French and Belgian security, countersigned by the British and Italian Governments, which is the Treaty of Locarno. We are not disposed to allow Strasbourg to come under the fire of German guns.[18]

Flandin now set about his task. He had notified Eden that France would take no isolated action but wanted a meeting of the Locarno powers followed by a meeting of the League Council at which a resolution condemning Germany could be passed, like the resolution of May 17, 1935, which had condemned German rearmament. He had, with Belgian cooperation, notified the League of the German violation and clearly defined his position: No negotiation under the menace of a remilitarized zone and the loss of French security.[19]

## Britain Shows Her Hand

After his discussion with Corbin on March 7, and conversations with the Belgian chargé d'affaires and the Italian Ambassador, Eden drove to Chequers to report to the Prime Minister. Baldwin was guarded but said he was clear that there would be no British support for any French military action. Eden agreed. A Cabinet meeting was set for Monday, March 9, after which Eden would make a statement to Parliament. The meeting of the Locarno powers in Paris was set for the following Tuesday, March 10.[20]

Blickling was a stately home indeed, a Jacobean mansion set in a 4,500-acre park, the childhood home of Anne Boleyn. The grandeur of the state rooms was eclipsed by the 127-foot Long Gallery. Its master was Phillip Kerr, 11th Marquess of Lothian. He had been private secretary to Lloyd George at the Peace Conference, and the longtime Secretary of the Rhodes Trust. He would in 1939–40 become Britain's highly respected Ambassador to Washington.

Like their host, the guests assembled that weekend represented exalted levels of standing and influence in the affairs both of society and the state, which had only recently begun to diverge. Lord and Lady Astor were there; their estate at Cliveden rivalled Blickling as a political gathering place. Astor was owner of the *Observer*; Lady Astor had been the first and remained the most celebrated woman member of Parliament. Sir Thomas Inskip was a well-known barrister whom Baldwin would shortly name his Deputy Minister for the Coordination of Defense. Sir Walter Layton was the veteran editor of the *Economist*. Vincent Massey, heir to a Canadian industrial fortune, was presently serving as Canada's High Commissioner in London.

Transatlantic influence was also represented by the American Norman Davis, a banker who had served on the Reparations Commissions, and represented his country at the 1935 Naval Conference.

Arnold Toynbee was there, fresh from his visit with Hitler the week before. While other guests golfed, Toynbee walked with Tom Jones and reported that Hitler sincerely desired peace and friendship with England. Better than that, he said, any English response to Hitler's overtures would "produce an enormous counter response to us from Hitler." These views Jones recorded and sent posthaste to Eden.[21]

Jones, educator, retired civil servant, deputy secretary of the Cabinet from 1916 to 1930 and intimate friend and confidante of the Prime Minister also carefully recorded the weekend discussions.

There was an absent guest. Anthony Eden had planned to spend the weekend at Blickling, but his plans had been preempted by affairs of state, his trip to Chequers to consult Baldwin, and his preparations for the Cabinet meeting Monday.

The news of the reoccupation reached Blickling via radio. Jones convened the guests into a Shadow Cabinet, and put to them the task of writing a draft of the Prime Minister's response to the German move. They agreed on these key points: that the Germans would not withdraw from the zone, French insistence notwithstanding, and that the British public, quickly attracted to Hitler's proposals, would not back France.

These were not detached observers engaging in an amusing charade. They were men and women of influence who meant to use it. Their conclusions were promptly telegraphed to Baldwin. The first of these was: "Welcome Hitler's declaration whole-heartedly."

The entry of German troops into the zone was to be condemned but treated as the last and least of German violations of Versailles. It should, the assembled pundits resolved, be treated as "relatively *de minimis*," especially in view of the accompanying peace proposals: "Versailles is now a corpse and should be buried."

The reoccupation should be treated as an assertion of equality and not an act of aggression. There were limits, however, to optimism. Britain must stand by France were there an act of aggression and Britain must continue to rearm. Above all, the company advised, accept Hitler's declaration in good faith and put that good faith to the test of negotiations via a new international conference.

There was an urgency to all this. "This is the last 'bus' and all turns on S.B. catching it tomorrow," Jones wrote. These were men and women Baldwin knew and trusted. Jones' object was clear:

> What I am trying to secure is that S.B. should have his mind made up on the major issue of accepting Hitler at his face value and trying him out fairly now that the last trace of humiliation has been removed. One wants S.B.'s mind firmly made up *before* he enters the Cabinet.[22]

At the Foreign Office, preparing a memorandum for the Cabinet's guidance, Anthony Eden arrived at remarkably similar conclusions. Germany had clearly violated Locarno. But the reoccupation of the Rhineland was precisely the topic he had hoped to raise when he had secretly approached Hoesch. It was, therefore, not so much what Germany had done, but the manner of doing it that he deplored. He would, of course, convey to the Cabinet the French position as Flandin had stated it.

Germany, Eden advised, would repudiate any inconvenient treaty, even a freely negotiated treaty. From this unpromising start, the paradoxical conclusion nevertheless followed that Britain should conclude "as far reaching and enduring a settlement as possible whilst Herr Hitler is still in the mood to do so."

Eden knew that something would have to be done for France as the last and most critical limitations of Versailles were dissolved. He understood that in French eyes Hitler's offer of a new Locarno was a gross insult. He also knew the response could take two forms: the first a League resolution condemning Germany; the second economic and financial sanctions. At Stresa France had pressed for sanctions and carefully and forehandedly crafted them into the Stresa resolution the League Council had adopted in April, 1935, condemning Germany's rearmament as unilateral breaches of Versailles.

Eden thought a condemnation inevitable. For economic and financial sanctions, the ardent and popular champion of sanctions against Italy had no appetite whatever.

But above all: "We must discourage any military action by France against Germany." Eden laid before the Cabinet the same basic program that the self-appointed Shadow Cabinet at Blickling had recommended: negotiations to test Hitler's good faith: "The essential thing will be to induce or cajole France to accept this mandate."

To do this, one step was essential. It would be argued that the breach of Locarno by one party released the others from their obligations. Eden thought this neither good international law nor good policy. While accepting negotiation, the outcome of which none could foretell, he was prepared firmly to pronounce that in the event of actual attack on Belgium or France, His Majesty's Government would be honor bound to come to their assistance." To all this, Vansittart added his firm agreement.[23]

The members of the Cabinet, when they assembled at 11:00 A.M. on Monday, had had the opportunity to read the morning papers, chief among them, the *Times*. There had been a breach of treaty, the *Times* said, which "the more sensationally minded" could call an act of aggression. The *Times* made a popular distinction between German troops occupying German territory and "an act which carries fire and sword into a neighbor's territory."

British opinion, the *Times* estimated, would be nearly unanimous in wishing to turn Hitler's coup to advantage and to strengthen the collective system:

> The old structure of European peace, one-sided and unbalanced, is nearly in ruins. It is the moment, not to despair, but to rebuild.[24]

The Cabinet took Eden's advice, approved his statement to Parliament, and authorized Halifax to go with him to Paris the next day. Eden told the House of his meeting with Hoesch, how he had expressed regret at the German action. To a waiting public he also revealed his declaration to Hoesch that Britain must carefully consider the proposals of which Germany's return to the League was the most important.

Once more Eden piously deplored the unilateral breach of treaty, but added a cheering note:

> There is, I am thankful to say, no reason to suppose that the present German action implies a threat of hostilities.

He pronounced his assurance of aid to Belgium and France if attacked. Eden now spoke words that effectively resolved the crisis, no matter how agitated the turmoil, how intense the activities, and how varied the pronouncements of the following weeks. Eden's words signaled Hitler's greatest victory. To the House of Commons Eden said,

> It must be obvious to all that in the existing circumstances the transition from a bad past to a better future will be an arduous and hazardous enterprise. At the same time, we are not merely concerned with the past or the present. We are concerned also with the future. One of the main foundations of the peace of Western Europe has been cut away, and if peace is to be secured there is a manifest duty to rebuild. It is in that spirit that we must approach the new proposals of the German Chancellor. His Majesty's Government will examine them clear-sightedly and objectively, with a view to finding out to what extent they represent a means by which the shaken structure of peace can again be strengthened. In the present grave conditions of international affairs his Majesty's government feel that no opportunity must be missed which offers any hope of amelioration.[25]

Baldwin then spoke to the White Paper on defense. Attlee had little to say about Eden's statement. German troops stood on the Rhine; but Attlee bitterly attacked the White Paper. The safety of the country and the peace of the world were to be found, he said, not in arms, but in disarmament, collective security, the improvement of labour standards and economic cooperation to remove the causes of war.

Only the day before, Sarraut had pronounced a policy very different from Eden's. France would not negotiate under threats; the German action forbade negotiation *for the moment*. This did not rule out all negotiation. But it was a position of strength, leaving it open for France to act as she saw fit, to threaten to act, or to demand conditions before entering into negotiations.

Eden sent a very different message to Hitler who was bound to appreciate, indeed savor each point. Eden had spoken only of Western Europe. He had clearly ruled out any immediate British action; and without setting any price or precondition, he accepted Hitler's invitation to negotiate. This was the weakest position possible. Each day of negotiation would enable Germany to consolidate the Rhineland and increase the military discrepancy between it, Britain, and France. Still graver was the discrepancy between Britain, and France as to the urgency and value they placed upon negotiations and the objects to be obtained.

In the short span of three months, Anthony Eden had effectively disposed of two issues critical to the fate of Europe and the world. At Geneva, on December 12, the Hoare-Laval proposals had not yet been conveyed to Abyssinia and Italy and what response the Duce might make, and the conditions upon which that response might be based, were wholly unknown. That the proposals could, as intended, serve as a basis for negotiation, was a legitimate possibility, and a possibility which Hitler both believed and feared.

Yet, on that day, Eden did not hesitate to damn the proposals with the faintest of endorsements, at the same time indicating with what alacrity he was prepared to abandon them, if what was, in essence, his invitation to abandon them were accepted. Lacking firm British support, Laval's efforts to find a common ground with Italy were doomed, and the temptation was proffered to Hitler to profit from that doom.

Now, before the meeting in Paris, before discussing and concerting with the other Locarno powers, without taking cognizance of, weighing, deliberating upon their interests and concerns and collaborating with them, Eden made it clear that Hitler had little to fear from Britain, and that in the disjointure between the French and the British positions lay his greatest hope of triumph. What were required now of Hitler were patience and the ability to prolong negotiations while pursuing his own ends, and in both of these qualities, he was richly endowed.

## The Reason Why

Anthony Eden had spoken not only for himself and for the Cabinet, but for the British public. Up and down the country the press counseled against action and demanded negotiation "with cool heads,"[26] "without agitation,"[27] and "with calm consideration.[28] There was general agreement that Germany had committed no act of aggression by occupying her own territory[29]; the alternative, said the *Daily Herald*, was to go to war to prevent German troops from garrisoning German towns,[30] adding "surely the problem has only to be stated for the decision to be obvious."

Distaste for offshore commitments persisted. Britain, the *Evening Standard* said, had awakened from a nightmare, concluding prematurely that she had freed herself from Locarno.[31] "Will Britain be involved in war?" the *Daily Express* inquired. There will be no war it concluded—"and if there were, we should not be involved."[32]

Hitler had foreseen these responses—the ready acceptance by the *News Chronicle* of the "symbolic" nature of the reoccupation[33] and "the vista," espied by the *Sussex Daily News*," of established order" on the Continent which it would be "an everlasting disgrace" not to convert into a better world.[34]

*Headway*, the organ of the League of Nations Union, asked if March 1936 might not be a turning point in world history which offered "Hopes of a Brighter Day."[35] Lord Snowden was more emphatic. The people, he said, would not permit *this* peace offer to be ignored.[36] Arthur Greenwood characterized the situation as "pregnant with new and great opportunities for the future of the world."[37]

Jan Christian Smuts, doyen of Empire statesmen, saw a great opportunity for a solid and lasting peace, prosperity, and the disappearance of the legacy of trouble left by the Paris Peace Conference where he had, paradoxically, been an eminent figure.[38] Predictably, the Archbishop of Canterbury, having convened the various churches to consider the situation in Europe, welcomed proposals for an international conference, a "singular opportunity" he deemed it, which would inaugurate a new era of peace based upon international equality and justice.[39]

When, on March 9, Eden journeyed by cab to the Foreign Office, he took counsel with the cab driver, who responded to Eden's inquiry: "I suppose Jerry can do what he likes in his own back garden can't he?"[40] Remarkably similar comments were heard in various quarters. Bernard Shaw, as oracular as any cab driver, said that it was as if the British had occupied Portsmouth. Lothian declared that the Germans had walked into their own back yard.[41] As early as March 7, Eden had asked the Foreign Office's press expert, Rex Leeper, what the press would say tomorrow. Leeper accurately responded: "I think they will say that Germany is on her own territory."[42]

To the man in the street, the man in the third class railway carriage, international correspondent Phillip Gibbs reported, Hitler's seemed like a pretty good offer[43] and he asked rhetorically: Why not believe it? Why not put it to the test?

A critical reason why Hitler had advanced the date of the reoccupation was the Italian adventure in Abyssinia. Not only would it distract attention from Hitler's move, but it would provide a comparison immensely to Germany's advantage. The comparison was promptly taken up; the *Northern Mail* said:

> Sanctions against a nation that has openly attacked another member nation of the League and against a nation that has illegally moved troops within its own borders are two vastly different courses.[44]

Lord Cecil made the same distinction; the reoccupation, he thought, could hardly be called a resort to war. But, he was consistent with his principles, and nearly alone, in favoring sanctions.[45]

*Headway* warned that the public must not be diverted from Italy's crimes by Germany's petit larceny, adding that Italy was making war, people were dying; in the Rhineland, Hitler made no war, none died.[46]

Beyond these practical distinctions, there was a deeply felt moral issue. Reflecting on these events in the following year, Professor Toynbee castigated the French view that,

> the Italian offense of attacking an unoffending neighbor in violation of the Covenant and of all Italy's other treaty engagements and then waging this unjust war by methods of barbarism which Italy pledged itself to eschew, counted for nothing by comparison with the heinousness of the German offense of militarily reoccupying German-owned and German-administered territory in violation of treaties but without the taking of a single life or the dropping of a single explosive or poison gas container. And this obliquity of moral vision was attested, for the information of Posterity, by the proposal—which was officially put forward, in all seriousness, as a result of the consultations between the Locarno Powers other than Germany—that the majesty of an offended law of nations should be vindicated by the posting, during an interim period, of Italian troops, cheek by jowl with British comrades-in-arms, to keep the peace along the Franco-German and Belgo-German border.[47]

Canon Davey of the Liverpool Cathedral was equally indignant. To continue to impose inequality upon German was monstrous, an unnecessary degradation of the soul of a great people; to do it at French behest would "lend aid to malice" and to countenance Italian participation in an international force was the unkindest cut of all. "We cannot," he said in declining to offer a prayer for the Cabinet, "pray a blessing on such proposals."[48]

Professor Toynbee did not base the condemnation, which he commended to Posterity, upon a dispassionate analysis of British interests, or indeed the interests of any nation or group of nations, but upon a moral vision. Canon Davey dealt with the living, but his concern was with their souls and not with their interests.

So it had been with the Hoare-Laval proposals. A torrent of anger and hostility on the part of public and parliamentarians had killed these proposals because they were seen as a betrayal of the pledges of loyalty to the League and collective security that Baldwin had given to the Peace Ballot voters, that Hoare had trumpeted in Geneva, and that the Government and its candidates had repledged to the electors in the General Election. Baldwin had not chosen to ride out the storm on the grounds that the safety, security, and interests of the nation required nothing less. Instead, in his celebrated turnabout, he had frankly acknowledged the moral basis of the country's opposition to the plan.

The British public thought Hoare-Laval was immoral and hence found it unacceptable. The reoccupation of the Rhineland was acknowledged to be illegal, but it was not seen as immoral. Indeed, there was widespread sympathy for Germany in the City, in Parliament, and in the country based to a substantial degree on the perception that morality lay with Germany. On the other hand, none doubted that the bombing and gassing of Abyssinian villages was immoral and the comparison gained added hostility to Italy and sympathy for Germany.

Thus, Dieckhoff's prophecy to Arnold Toynbee, so recent and so apt, came to pass: "Now that they [the British people] have found their scapegoat in Hoare, I think we shall find they will take no further action."

He had referred, of course, to Abyssinia and quite literally no further action was ever taken. But his prophecy applied with equal precision to the reoccupation of the Rhineland. Having achieved catharsis in the Hoare-Laval explosion, having exhausted themselves and their emotions, the British people had little righteous indignation to stir them to action against Italy and virtually none to oppose the movement of German troops into the Rhineland where righteousness was not seen as a material issue.

Lord Cecil had said that the public must have an opinion and that opinion must be right. In two great crises, the voice of the people was heard. Whether it was right may be argued, whether it was effective may not.

Anthony Eden was at the center of all these events. When he looked back years later, he recorded hard facts:

> There was not one man in a thousand in the Country at that time prepared to take physical action against a German reoccupation of the Rhineland. Many went further than this and thought it unreasonable that Germany should not be allowed to do as she wished in her own territory, nearly twenty years after the end of the war.[49]

He ruefully concluded:

> Academically speaking, there is little dispute that Hitler should have been called to order, if need be forcibly at his first breach of an accepted international engagement. But nobody was prepared to do it, in this country literally nobody.[50]

It was against this primal fact that Flandin struggled and lost.

## Flandin's Mission Impossible

The meeting of the Locarno powers at Paris on March 10 was a disconcerting experience for Eden and Halifax. They looked, albeit reluctantly, for a condemnation of Germany to be followed by negotiations, such as Eden had sought independently to inspire on March 6.

Cerutti made it very clear that Italy, a state under sanctions, would participate in no action—political, economic or military; it would watch and listen.

Flandin was equally clear. After asking the League Council to declare Germany in breach of Versailles, France would put all of her resources, military, naval, and air at the disposal of the Council. Worse still, from the British point of view, it would call upon the Locarno powers to render aid under the Council resolution of April 17, 1935, carefully crafted by France, calling for economic and financial sanctions against a Treaty breaker, which MacDonald had so stubbornly fought and tried to obfuscate at Stresa.

Flandin was firmly backed by the Belgian Prime Minister, Van Zeeland. He would negotiate, but only after international law had been vindicated. Everything was at stake. If they did not accept the German challenge now, conditions would deteriorate. If there were one chance in ten that war would follow, Van Zeeland was prepared to take that chance; otherwise war would be certain.

Eden subjected the Franco-Belgian position to cross examination and doubts. He pleaded the British public's fear of missing an opportunity to reach an agreement with Germany and his own statement to Parliament of the paramount task of reconstruction. When all this failed, he asked the direct question: did Flandin contemplate military action by the Locarno powers independent of the League?

Flandin's answer was as simple and straightforward as Laval's reply to a similar British inquiry at Stresa: "Yes."[51]

All this was far beyond Eden's instructions from the Cabinet. Instead of proceeding to Geneva and the League Council, it was agreed that the Locarno powers would meet in London, two days later, on Thursday, March 12, and the League Council would meet in London on Monday, March 16. Eden could then be in continuous contact with his colleagues and the proceedings could, in his words, be kept "as closely as possible under British influence."[52]

Flandin came to London to secure adoption of the French position, clearly laid down in Paris: negotiations only after the evacuation of the Rhineland, to secure which there should be used in succession, as required, financial, economic, and finally military sanctions.

Returning forthwith to London, Eden told the Cabinet on March 11, that the British proposal of condemnation and negotiation had no chance of success. He outlined Flandin's program, culminating in military measures which Britain would be asked to join.

The ministers considered unpleasant facts. It might be necessary to tell the French how ill-prepared Britain was to fulfill its Locarno obligations, an admission fraught with grave consequences for the future of the League and collective security. And, as always, there was an active and aroused public opinion strongly opposed to military action. In fact,

> many people, perhaps most people, were saying openly that they did not see why the Germans should not reoccupy the Rhineland.

Baldwin fretted that the French plan could mean war, the upshot of which would be a Bolshevik Germany. He had, a week before, approved without French knowledge an approach to Germany hoping to open negotiations deeply affecting French security. When France took its security vigorously into its own hands, the Prime Minister complained that "it seemed very unfriendly of them to put us in the present dilemma."

What to do? Eden's proposal was consistent with his action of the week before. He turned not to France, but once more to Germany. He recommended a plea to the German Ambassador for a German "contribution," a reduction of the occupation troops to a "symbolic" level, and an undertaking not to build fortifications, following which Britain, whose anxiety for a peaceful settlement Eden would emphasize, would lead the way in negotiations for a new series of pacts on which the peace of Europe would be based. All this the Cabinet approved with the express instructions that Eden should see the German Ambassador "that very evening" and above all make it clear to him that the French had not been informed.[53]

Eden's proposal that evening, so indicative of British weakness and discord with France, received no encouragement from Hoesch.[54] Berlin promptly and firmly rejected the plea and what is more publicized it so that the next day, when Wigram talked to Flandin, he was quite sure that Flandin knew.[55] The measure of German confidence was their declaration that all of Hitler's proposals would be void if any coercive action were undertaken.[56]

Although Flandin received little enough encouragement from his military advisors, for whom a limited military or naval demonstration evoked only doubts and no enthusiasm[57] and although he had every reason to believe Britain was intriguing with Germany,[58] he maintained a firm front in London. He still demanded German withdrawal, a ban on fortifications, and a clear statement of the obligations of the Locarno guarantors. Even a symbolic troop presence, he said, would bless an illegal act and deprive any new settlement of legitimacy. The appreciation his staff had prepared for him on his departure for London had ended thus: "The question of the moment is to know whether Europe will or will not become German."[59]

Van Zeeland undertook, on March 13, to produce a draft proposal that might harmonize all positions.[60] The Van Zeeland draft was discussed the next day, March 14, and found wanting by Flandin. He was fortified by Paul-Boncour, just arrived from Paris. He was staggered, Paul-Boncour said, by the drift away from firmness which the French people could not understand or accept. He again backed a succession of measures, economic, financial, and military. Van Zeeland agreed. In this impasse, the initiative passed to Flandin who agreed to prepare his own proposals.[61]

On this day, the Council of the League met to consider the Franco-Belgian appeal. It agreed to invite Germany, as a Locarno party, to attend the session of the League Council on March 16 in which the appeal would be heard,[62] an invitation which Phipps pressed Hitler to accept,[63] even to the point of assuring him that nothing would be said at the League meeting wounding to German honor.[64] All this was seen in Germany as equivalent to Simon's persistence in visiting Berlin the year before after another breach of treaty. Little was now to be feared. Hitler seeing how his peace proposals had succeeded with the British statesmen and the British public now looked forward with enthusiasm to prolonged negotiations.[65]

His confidence was at a high level. He told a plebiscite rally in Munich on March 14 that "I go with the assurance of a sleepwalker, the way which Providence dictates." His proposals were the greatest gesture for peace that any European statesman had ever made. Only one thing was not negotiable and that was German honor, which, by the way, included Germany's right to decide her own *lebensraum.* Only Germans could fully judge this and that would be decided at the March 29 plebiscite.[66]

There are scenes that will live in history because of the union of their intrinsic significance and their deep human appeal. Such scenes are more often sad than happy. On March 14, and in the days thereafter, Flandin learned the fatal truth that Britain would not and could not come to France's aid.

Wigram and Churchill arranged for Flandin to see Baldwin on March 14. Baldwin had, he told Flandin, no great knowledge of foreign affairs. "In that," Flandin later commented, "he was too modest." But he knew the British people. They only wanted peace. Flandin pleaded that the best way to peace was to stop Hitler now; the chance might never come again.

As Flandin related it, he asked Britain only for a free hand to conduct a police operation which would result in a German withdrawal. That is disputed; certainly the records do not reveal the military will or capacity for such an operation.

What is not in dispute is what Baldwin told Flandin: "You may be right, but if there is *even one chance in a hundred* that war would follow from your police operation, I have no right to commit England because," and he paused, "Britain is not in a state to go to war." He buttressed his case with facts and figures.[67]

The scene was repeated to a succession of audiences. Wigram presented Flandin to politicians and journalists, assembled in his own home in North Street.

"If you do not stop Germany now, all is over," Flandin told them. "France cannot guarantee Czechoslovakia anymore, because it will become geographically impossible.... If you do not stop Germany today, war is inevitable."[68]

When Flandin spoke to a group in the House of Commons, Harold Nicholson described his manner:

> He has got all his thoughts perfectly in order, and he deploys his procession of argument quite gently but firmly, like a nun escorting a crocodile of foundlings to church. The result is overwhelming.

France could have occupied the zone immediately just as Britain had sent her fleet to the Mediterranean, Flandin said. But France had chosen to go to the League which had only to condemn Germany and leave the Locarno guarantors to do the rest. Now he found the British Government wished to break their word. And if Germany succeeded, the world would know that only force counted, that Germany would become master of Europe. France would then leave the League.

Flandin insisted that he would never accept German fortifications in the Rhineland. That would deprive France of any chance to intervene to save Austria. He spoke plainly. Britain had wounded France by carrying on conversations with Hitler behind her back.

If he spoke quietly and placidly, Sir Robert Boothby noted an icy passion which made a deep impression. Yet the response was always the same, chilling and comfortless. Britain, which had exacted France's support in defense of the Covenant in Abyssinia, now turned her back on France when Versailles and Locarno were shattered and France placed in mortal peril in the Rhineland.[69]

Flandin faced reality. Italy was moving toward Germany. France could not afford to lose Britain. He must salvage what he could. There must be new guarantees—the continued recognition by Britain and the automatic functioning of its Locarno obligations, the best limitations that could be put on the German presence in the Rhineland, especially a ban on fortifications, and military preparations with France and Belgium precisely to balance the security which had been lost in the Rhineland and to insure the prompt and agreed operation of the new guarantees.

## A Compromise Satisfactory to None

Hitler's diplomatic and military advisors may have wavered, counseling caution and even retreat, but his own confidence was growing. Germany would attend the League Council meeting, but, he said haughtily, only to discuss the German proposals "forthwith."[70]

This was too much for Flandin. He told journalists on March 15,

> I came to London in order to establish Germany's breach of treaty, and not to negotiate with the Reich. Otherwise I should prefer to return to Paris and if necessary even cease to represent France at the League of Nations.[71]

It is instructive that France and Britain stood firm and Germany yielded. There had been a mistranslation, Berlin said. Not "forthwith," but "in due course" had been intended, and thus the discussion would not be limited exclusively to the German proposals.

With Italy remaining aloof, Flandin sought the best bargain he could get. What Britain offered did not please him: a condemnation of Germany, referral of the Franco-Soviet Pact to the Hague, and, pending and during the negotiations, the following: a reaffirmation of Locarno, an international force on both sides of the border, a recommendation to Germany, France and Belgium to suspend all further troops, material and fortifications in the border zone. All this would be followed by negotiations on the German proposals, the revision of the status of the Rhineland and further, but unspecified compensation to France and Belgium for the diminution of their security.[72]

The stationing of an international force on both sides of the border, limiting France and Belgium equally with Germany, Flandin told Eden, simply lumped France and Belgium with Germany as guilty parties. His mission to London had been a failure. He would leave London on Thursday, March 19, with a heavy heart, Paul-Boncour would carry on. It was apparent to Eden that something had to be done.[73]

The essence of the Belgian proposals had been, not simply a reaffirmation of Locarno, but automatic functioning of the guarantees of any new treaty, backed up by military arrangements to make those guarantees effective.[74] The British Cabinet struggled with these demands on March 18. It had before it gloomy reports from its military advisors on the state of British arms with a special warning that, with its main forces concentrated in the Mediterranean and in Egypt, there was little left to back up a stand in Europe.[75] No doubt the danger was grave, and they were informed that the fortification of the Rhineland might soon commence. But the same difficulty remained:

> The Cabinet was reminded by several members that military conversations on that basis would be very unacceptable to public opinion in this country which was strongly opposed to any forcible action to compel the Germans to evacuate the Demilitarized Zone.

The Cabinet finally concluded that it could accept military conversations strictly limited to defense against German aggression during the period of negotiations. It stood by an international force on both sides of the border, and rejected any of the forms of a letter of guarantee to France and Belgium that had been proposed.

Eden warned the Cabinet that, on this basis, the negotiations were liable to break down that night.[76] He had reasons. In the discussions of the Locarno powers that had preceded the Cabinet meeting, it became clear that Flandin had reached his limit. He had been compelled by circumstances to abandon his basic plan of requiring a German withdrawal before negotiating. He had moved far toward a compromise position which left German troops firmly ensconced in the Rhineland. In this dangerous situation, French security demanded some replacement for what had been lost.

Though there would no military sanction, Flandin was still hopeful of economic sanctions. He had done his utmost to accommodate Britain. But there was a point beyond which he could not go. If Britain could not accept the letter of guaranty, or something like that, agreement would be impossible. He would have no choice but to go back to Paris.[77]

At 2:00 AM on the morning of March 19, agreement was finally reached. It was, in the end, more than Britain wished to give, far less than Belgium and France thought prudent. It was called a Text of Proposals.

Its first order of business, after reciting Germany's unilateral breach of treaty, was to declare that nothing had happened which freed the Locarno powers from their obligations. They would undertake General Staff contacts to arrange the conditions in which the obligations should be carried out in the event of aggression.

Germany was invited to submit its case on the Franco-Soviet Treaty to the Permanent Court of International Justice. The following arrangements were proposed during the pendency of the negotiations: the dispatch by Germany of troops and material into the Demilitarized Zone should be suspended leaving troop strength at agreed levels. No fortifications should be prepared or air fields laid out or equipped. France and Belgium would, in response, not send troops into their border zones.

An international force was proposed for the German side of the border and an international commission to supervise all of these arrangements. Germany was invited to negotiate on her proposals, including revision of the status of the Rhineland and new mutual assistance treaties open to all Locarno signatories.

A draft resolution prepared for adoption by the League Council condemned Germany and further proposals were tendered for agreements enhancing collective security, limiting arms, and improving the international economy.

Finally, there was attached a letter of guaranty to be executed by Britain and Italy in the event of the failure of negotiations. Those governments would then consult on steps to be taken to meet the new situation and immediately come to the assistance of Belgium and France in accordance with Locarno in respect of measures jointly agreed to. Moreover, the guarantors, under reciprocal assurances, would "take…all practical measures available…for the purpose of ensuring the security of your country against unprovoked aggression." To effect this, the military conversations already referred to would take place.[78]

In the end, then, the Germans were to remain in the Rhineland. They had been invited to limit their activities there, but there was no threat, hope, or suggestion of enforcing Versailles or Locarno. The proposals for grandiose conferences on disarmament, collective security, and economic development had long since lost credibility. This was the measure of France's defeat.

Locarno was reaffirmed. The words of the Text and of the Letters of Guaranty might be read by the French as some increment to the British obligations under Locarno, by the British as no such thing. Indeed, this is precisely what happened. The military conversations, which were strictly limited and were to prove feckless, seemed to lend an air of military respectibility to otherwise innocuous proposals.

Flandin left for Paris on March 19, the day the League Council was to meet. Wigram escorted him to Victoria Station. This is another scene which Churchill has contributed to history.

Wigram's understanding had deepened and his views changed since he had so recently championed a Working Agreement with Germany. Wigram's wife wrote to Churchill,

> After the French delegation had left, Ralph came back and sat down in a corner of the room where he had never sat before, and said to me, 'War is now *inevitable* and it will be the most terrible war there has ever been. I don't think I shall see it, but you will. Wait now for bombs on this little house.'[79]

The Text of Proposals was announced the day the League Council met. It heard Ribbentrop state the German case, then promptly adopted the resolution of condemnation, with only Germany dissenting. On grounds that the parties were in negotiation, the Council adjourned to a further day which, in fact, never came.[80]

The interesting feature of the meeting had been Italy's vote. Italy would fulfill its Locarno obligations, Grandi said. But he called attention to the difficulty for a party subject to sanctions to participate in sanctions against another—a plain enough invitation to lift the sanctions against Italy.

Mussolini was twice displeased. He had been angry not so much at Hitler's coup as at his proposal to rejoin the League of Nations. This would nullify Italy's most effective threat against the sanctionist powers—to leave the League. Skillful German diplomacy had mollified the Duce. Now he was angry with Grandi and put it out that Grandi had acted against instructions.[81]

There was a continuing thread here. Often in the discussions of the Stresa Powers in London, Flandin had suggested that Italian backing against Germany could readily be had at the price of lifting sanctions. Returned home, he put the matter in the best light to the French Chamber. He described the new security arrangements, including the military provisions (which he said France had insisted upon) as both "a capital reinforcement of French security" and "a decisive phase in Franco-British relations":

> The peaceful front of Stresa can now be reconstituted, thanks to the opening of negotiations which.... should quickly bring about the simultaneous suspension of hostilities in Abyssinia and of sanctions against Italy.

This was, of course, Laval's policy brought down to date. Flandin was realistic. He painted no unalloyed triumph. Had France insisted on military or economic sanctions, he told the Chamber, she would have lost the support of the Locarno powers. The agreement was the best France could get. The Chamber accepted it in that light.[82]

The reconstruction of the Stresa Front was easier dreamed than achieved. The Committee of Thirteen's appeal to the belligerents in

Abyssinia had been overwhelmed by events in the Rhineland. The Committee finally reassembled in London on March 23. Italy had earlier and promptly signified its agreement in principle to the opening of settlement negotiations.[83]

But, notwithstanding that Ras Imru's army, the last remaining undefeated force on the northern front had been destroyed in the Battle of Shire during the first week of March, the Emperor was obdurate.[84] Italy, he said, had not agreed to negotiate within the framework of the League and in the spirit of the Covenant. He rejected the appeal.[85] Having suffered this rejection, the Committee instructed its Chairman, Salvador de Madariaga, to issue a new appeal to the parties to negotiate a settlement.[86]

Germany promptly indicated that it had little interest in the Text of Proposals, rejecting with a special firmness the reference to the Hague Court and the limitation on fortifications as insulting to German sovereignty.[87] Such firmness evoked the usual British response: a plea to Germany for a "contribution." Eden told Ribbentrop that if the Germans wished to make counterproposals, they would receive a fair hearing.[88]

Halifax was more pliant yet the next day at a public meeting in Bristol. The proposals, he said, had not been intended as an ultimatum; Germany was free to make counterproposals, which would constitute "a solid and substantial German contribution" to European peace. Germany's proposals would receive "the most careful and anxious consideration."[89]

Negotiators ought never to appear anxious. Such talk caused anguish in France which regarded the Text of Proposals as indivisible.[90]

In Berlin, perceptions of British weakness could only encourage Germany to negotiate further while consolidating the reoccupied zone. On March 24, Germany indicated that although rejecting the Text of Proposals, the Führer was drawing up new and positive proposals. These must, however, await the completion, on March 29, of the German plebiscite.[91]

Those who followed Hitler's election campaign had little reason to hope the new proposals would be generous. In Berlin on March 24 Hitler stated his unyielding principles:

> If the rest of the world clings to the letter of treaties, I cling to an eternal morality. If they raise objections about paragraphs, I hold by the vital eternal rights of my people, by the equality of rights and duties. If they try to read avowals of guilt into such letters and paragraphs, then I, as the representative of the German people, must assert the nation's right to live—its honour, freedom, and vital interests.[92]

To this Flandin responded with a series of questions addressed to Berlin, devastating in their logic and clarity, inquiring how, on such a basis, there could be a negotiation on any proposals.[93] Berlin was offended.

Logic, firmness, and wit were hardly characteristic of the British position. The British Cabinet met on March 25 to consider the German rejection and prepare for a debate on the proposals in the House of Commons the next day.

The Letter of Guaranty had not been delivered to the French, but it would be difficult to delay it much longer. The Cabinet hoped that negotiations could be held up till after the French election. Facing the German rejection, the Cabinet arrived at its accustomed conclusion. Eden was directed to ask Ribbentrop for a statement of German approval of the Franco-Belgian-British military conversations and an undertaking not to fortify the Rhineland in the immediate future. Of course, the French were not informed.[94] This pathetic request was promptly rejected by Ribbentrop to whom the notion of such military arrangements was like a red flag to a bull.[95]

Having recounted to the Commons, the history of the crisis and elucidated the Text of Proposals, Anthony Eden made a ringing declaration: "I am not prepared to be the first British Foreign Secretary to go back on a British signature."

The House cheered the right honorable and gallant gentleman, the dashing and handsome survivor of a Lost Generation, the exemplar of British fidelity and straightforwardness. The truth was that from the moment Eden told Hoesch that Britain must seriously consider the German proposals, from the moment he publicly proclaimed the duty to negotiate, the spirit and essence of Locarno, if not its letter, were shattered for ever. Eden now proceeded to qualify his pronouncement. Military conversations, he said, could in no way add to Britain's political obligations; there was no parallel to 1914; the proposals were indeed only proposals to which German counterproposals would be welcome, though they must contain some meaningful contribution.

His threefold objects, Eden said, were to avert war, create the conditions for negotiations, and finally,

> to bring about the success of those negotiations so they may strengthen the collective security, further Germany's return to the League and in a happier atmosphere allow those large negotiations on economic matters and matters of armaments which are indispensable to the appeasement of Europe

> to take place. I assure the House that it is the appeasement of Europe as a whole that we have constantly before us.

Neville Chamberlain underlined that there had been no extension of Britain's Locarno obligations. Labour firmly backed sanctions against Italy, but had no appetite for action against Germany. Hugh Dalton told the House,

> bluntly and frankly that public opinion in this country would not support and the Labour Party certainly would not support the taking of military sanctions, or even economic sanctions against Germany at this time in order to put German troops out of the German Rhineland.

The distinction between the Rhineland and Abyssinia, he said, was not only clear but proper. The proposals for military conversations were wholly unacceptable to Labour.

For the Liberals, Sir Archibald Sinclair demanded that Hitler's offer to negotiate be followed up. Churchill declaimed on the need to rearm, but he did not urge, or even suggest that any action be taken now. He had gone on a painting vacation in Morocco to avoid taking a stand on the Hoare-Laval proposals. Now in the face of the supreme crisis, Nazi Germany's gravest and most perilous challenge, Churchill lapsed into unaccustomed silence. When Boothby took the lonely stand that Hitler was bluffing and that his bluff should be called, there was no support, but only overwhelming approval for the Government's policy.[96]

Hitler sealed his vitory with a massive triumph at the polls and few could doubt that the 99 percent approval of the reoccupation represented the genuine will of the German people. Having cast his vote, each elector received a badge enscribed "Freedom and Bread, March, 1936" as public evidence of the fulfillment of civic duty. The Führer cast his vote in the modest third-class waiting room of a railway station near the Chancery. Crowds gathered there in the evening, calling for the Führer and singing "Deutschland Uber Alles" and the Horst Wessel song.[97]

A pessimistic France had secured what she could: a League condemnation of Germany, a reaffirmation of Locarno with military talks appended, a position against fortifications in the Rhineland. Britain had preserved the peace—peace with as little dishonor as possible, Oliver Stanley said.[98] It now optimistically looked forward to negotiations which might produce the elusive and long-hoped-for General Settlement.

In Germany, there was the confidence that victory was total, that no further action need be feared, that Hitler could proceed with his rearmament and his plans for the Greater Germany that were becoming with every passing day less a dream, more an achievable goal. There had been protests before, there had been condemnations before, and the lesson was pronounced on March 28 by Goering:

> Protests are no good if they are not backed by bayonets.[99]

# 8

# The Triumph of the Dictators

*"This [Abyssinian] dispute was not an isolated event in a world which had no other cause for anxiety."*

—Anthony Eden[1]

## Mai Ceu

From his headquarters in a cave on Mount Aia, Haile Selassie looked across the plain of Lake Ashangi to the Italian positions at Mai Ceu. He had once warned his warriors to avoid open battle and to wage guerilla warfare. He how made a different decision.

> Since our trust is in our Creator and in the hope of His help and as we have decided to advance and enter the fortifications and since God is our only help, confide the decision of ours in secret to the Abuna, to the ministers and to the dignitaries, and offer unto God your fervent prayers.[2]

It would be a frontal assault on the Italian position. The Emperor was supported by his greatest chiefs, Ras Kassa and Ras Seyoum, and the remnant of their forces which had escaped from the carnage at Tembien. He had fresh troops, the army of Ras Getachew Abate from Kaffa and the Imperial Guard, six well-trained infantry battalions and a brigade of artillery. The Schneider 75s, the Oerlikons, and the Brandt mortars were firepower the other Abyssinian armies had never had. There were some 31,000 troops in all, perhaps the best army to carry the Emperor's standard, but utterly lacking in air cover or any protection against gas.

Why had the Emperor decided to put all to the test of a final battle? The reasons lay in history and in his place in it. The frontal assault was the classic Abyssinian tactic, even if it suited the Abyssinians' temperament better than their means. Moreover, the Emperor always had his crown and his dynasty to preserve. An Emperor who did not lead his nobles and his warriors in the climactic battle might no longer expect to retain their loyalty and respect. In guerilla war, the local chieftains would count for more than the distant Emperor. There was always, too, the memory of Adowa, and the hope of a decisive victory that would break the Italians' will.

At war's outset, the Emperor held his great *geber* in Addis Ababa to summon his chiefs and warriors to battle. Now on March 24, the *geber* was held in the cave at Mount Aia. The Emperor sat on an improvised throne and the feast of raw meat was washed down with quantities of tef. He had sent off his Russian advisor, Konovaloff, disguised as a Coptic deacon, to scout the Italian positions. They were, Konovaloff reported, lightly defended. In the same cave the Emperor met with the Azebu Galla, pouring into their hands Maria Theresa dollars, lavishing striped silk shirts, and black satin capes upon them, instructing them to harry the Italian flanks, and receiving in return their protestations of loyalty.[3]

But the attack was delayed. The Italians intercepted the Emperor's radio messages; they outbid the Emperor for the services of the Galla who betrayed his plans. By April 1, St. George's Day, the Italian lines had been fortified and reinforced.

The assaults were as desperate as the defense; the Abyssinian artillery was well handled and deadly, but neither the first nor the second assault wave could dislodge the stubborn defenders. The Imperial Guard led the third wave, and for three hours the battle continued. Finally the attackers were repulsed, but far from defeated.

It was late in the afternoon when the Emperor launched the final attack against the weary and ammunition-short defenders. Now the Galla horsemen, who had watched the day's struggle, moved down on to the field of battle, not to attack the Italian flanks, but to fall upon the Abyssinian rear. These, together with the Italian bombers, forced the Abyssinians to retire to the positions from which the attack had been launched.[4]

On the next day, the exhausted and bloodied Italians, their ammunition almost gone, awaited the Abyssinian attack which never came. Rain was falling, their attack had failed, the Galla were hostile. The chiefs would no longer yield to the Emperor's entreaties to attack again. That night, he ordered the retreat.

The final scenes of the battles of Tembien and Shire were repeated in even greater horror. Once more the unopposed bombers with their cargos of high explosives and mustard gas destroyed the retreating army. Lake Ashangi was poisoned by the gas, and rendered even more terrible the fate of the wounded men and harried animals that sought relief in its waters. What the bombers left, the Galla finished, despoiling, mutilating, and castrating the survivors. The chiefs made as best they could for their own lands. Only a remnant followed the fatal road to Addis Ababa.

For once the Emperor's own composure broke under the responsibility, the horror and the defeat. "I don't know what to do," he told Konovaloff, "my brain no longer works." While his troops struggled south, he left them and made a pilgrimage to the holy city of Lalibela. In the church, hewn from living rock centuries ago by the Zagwe kings, he meditated, prayed, and fasted for two days before he rejoined the defeated army.[5]

## The Balance Sheet

By the end of March, it had become clear that Hitler and Mussolini had won great victories. The German armed forces had reoccupied the Rhineland, which they immediately began to fortify. There had been no riposte, only protests. The League of Nations had pronounced its condemnation, to no practical effect whatever. Hitler had won the massive support of the German people. Now it was to his advantage to spin out negotiations while he proceeded with the military buildup which it was the precise objective of the reoccupation to protect.

Mussolini had crushed the Abyssinian armies. The road to Addis Ababa lay open. Only the direct military intervention of the League powers could halt him. Of this there was no prospect. The Duce remained open to negotiation with the Emperor upon terms, of course, reflecting the military realities. The prospect of a negotiated settlement of the war, and the attitude of the League, and especially of Britain and France, to continuing, or even enhanced sanctions, were for Mussolini a critical consideration as he pondered the direction which Italy would take. There were two choices: a return to Stresa or a very different path that led to Berlin.

## Hitler's Triumph

Hitler's new proposals, which Ribbentrop delivered to Eden on April 1, were not promising, nor did Hitler intend them to be. The heart of the

Text of Proposals had been meaningful limitations on Germany: suspension of further German troops and material in the Rhineland, and, most important of all, a ban on the construction of fortifications and air fields during the period of negotiations. These limitations would be supervised by an international force on the German side of the border and the legal issue referred to the Permanent Court at the Hague.

All this Germany coldly rejected as one-sided discrimination. What Hitler finally offered was not very different from his peace proposals of March 7. Since it was, he said, obvious that Germany had no intention of ever attacking France or Belgium the proposed Locarno staff talks were without reason.

He proposed a three-stage negotiation, the first of four months to set up procedures, the second of actual negotiations, the third to consider the long-term issues of economics and disarmament. In the first period, Germany would agree not to reinforce its troops on the border providing France and Belgium did the same.

There were proposals for twenty-five-year nonaggression pacts among the Locarno powers, to which the Netherlands was invited to adhere, proposals for air pacts, but not air limitations, a stated willingness to enter into communications with Germany's eastern neighbors to discuss nonaggression pacts, and a suggestion for a new international court.

All this was garnished with proposals that were well calculated to arouse sympathy and enthusiasm among certain elements in France and Britain. Hitler proposed to modify education in France and Germany to eliminate whatever might poison the relations between the two. He specifically cited derogatory or contemptuous attitudes which, it appeared, the author of *Mein Kampf* and veteran street-corner rabble rouser, now deplored. There was talk of disarmament, limitations on bombing, tanks and artillery, economic conferences, and Germany's return to the League of Nations.

There was, in short, everything but a meaningful response to the Franco-British-Belgian proposals. Of that which the French desperately needed, which the British so persistently requested—a genuine contribution to the resolution of the crisis—there was none.

Eden clearly understood this and told Ribbentrop as much.[6] Nevertheless, he also told Ribbentrop that the German proposals deserved careful study and he repeated this to the House of Commons on April 3.[7]

He had his reasons. In the first phase of the crisis, the French had firmly maintained that Versailles and Locarno must be vindicated and the Rhineland evacuated. They had yielded to the March 19 Text of Proposals only on the condition that Germany negotiate on its terms. Chief of these was that there should be no fortifications pending negotiations. For this, France had extracted a new British guaranty and military talks.

France was now in a position to claim that conciliation and negotiation had failed. It was also in a position to take action and call for British support to make good on the pledges of March 19. In the state of British opinion, this was what Eden and his government wanted desperately to avoid.

He had finally, Eden told the Commons, delivered the letters of guaranty to France and Belgium. That did not mean, he was careful to tell the House, that in the Government's view conciliation had failed. Nor, he added, did the letter of guaranty imply any new obligation.[8]

All this, of course, made Hitler more intransigent than ever. As the months passed, and Germany coldly and contemptuously rejected British advances, refusing any meaningful discussion, or indeed any discussion at all, Eden maintained the pleasant fiction that conciliation had not failed and that the parties would one day meet to create a new Locarno.

In this he received warm support. The *Times* welcomed the German proposals. "Nothing," it concluded, "in Herr Hitler's tone refuses discussion and everything in his plan invites it."[9] The *Economist* agreed[10], and the *New Statesmen* added that there would be a violent revolt if the proferred talks did not take place.[11]

The facts, which were clearly known to the British and French Governments, did not match the Government's dedication to negotiations or the public's optimism. In the first days of April, Vansittart reported,

> The German Government is determined to take the offensive as soon as rearmament is sufficiently advanced. The Nazi party are bent on conquering Czechoslovakia and Roumania and annexing Austria.... To insure success in these plans, France and Britain must be prevented from interference. The most important immediate task for the Reichswehr is to complete a zone of fortifications along the frontiers facing France, Belgium, Luxembourg, and Holland. These defense works have already begun and now employ tens of thousands of Labour Corps and other workmen. The object is to prevent the advance of French armies into Germany and enable the German Air Force to operate from points as close to the frontiers as possible.[12]

All this was confirmed by copious French reports. Others drew grim conclusions. "If Germany is allowed to fortify the Rhineland," the Czech Foreign Minister observed, "we are lost."[13]

The French did not share British optimism. To them it was crystal clear that conciliation had failed and that Germany's treaty violations entitled France and the other Locarno parties to take action.[14]

Would France call for sanctions, Eden nervously asked Flandin on April 8? Paul-Boncour answered. He had no doubt. "They surely would." Just, he added, as sanctions had been applied against Italy. But, Eden protested, Germany had not invaded France. "M. Paul-Boncour retorted that Germany was doing something much worse than Italy had done; she was preparing the invasion of Europe. Precautions ought therefore to be taken by the most energetic means."[15]

The French had prepared a critique of the German plan. They had also prepared a French plan. The critique was devastating. Recalling Hitler's speech of March 24 in which, in opposition to the letter of treaties he had proclaimed "the vital, eternal rights of my people" and "the nation's right to live—its honor, freedom, and vital interests,"[16] the French memorandum inquired how a Government which proceeded by fait accompli could give effective assurance of the sanctity of treaties; whether the vital rights of a nation authorized unilateral cancellation of inconvenient treaties; and whether Germany would recognize the existing territorial and political arrangements of Europe including, by the way, Austria, Czechoslovakia, and the much disputed and debated status of Danzig and Memel?

The French plan was in legitimate line of descent from earlier French plans. It called for the creation of a European commission, an organ of the League, with a military force at its disposal to enforce a binding commitment to respect for twenty-five years the existing territorial status of Europe. Of real interest was the proposal to divide Europe into a series of eleven regional ententes. Instead, therefore, of an obligation by every League member to take action however remote in geography and interests, here was recognized the essential unity between geography and national interest.[17]

Like its predecessors, the French plan aroused little interest and no response. But the French government, a caretaker Government at that, pending the national election, was reluctant to repeat Louis Barthou's action of two years before in breaking off negotiations with Germany, for which the British had never ceased to blame France.

On April 10, therefore, the four Locarno powers, Italy included, met at Geneva. Aloisi, representing Italy, said that his country had in the Rhineland crisis honored her Locarno signature. Was the presence of

Italy and her collaboration wished in the work of European reconstruction? The issue was clear—sanctions versus the Rhineland. If not, Italy could assume no new risks or responsibilities and would remain on the sidelines.[18]

Italy abstaining, Britain, France, and Belgium reached agreement and a communiqué was issued. Germany, it was noted, had made no contribution. France reserved its rights in the event of any important change in the Rhineland pending negotiations. The staff talks would commence on April 15.

All this was face-saving. What counted was the joint announcement that Great Britain would communicate with Germany to raise those issues which were unclear in the German memorandum. The real issue was how to assure Germany's compliance with its proposed new undertakings.[19]

The British Government and people heaved a collective sigh of relief. France's demand for action had been translated into a British formula for inaction. No action would ever be taken and the rights France had reserved would never be asserted.

France did not think Britain free to draft the inquiry as it saw fit. Concerned that the questionnaire might not fully reflect its own concerns and interests, France thought it should be consulted as to its final form and sent a statement of its concerns to London.[20] This request Britain coldly denied.[21]

The questionnaire transmitted via the British ambassador in Berlin on May 7 raised important questions. Was Germany in a position of equality permitting her to conclude "genuine treaties?" Did it regard the remaining clauses of Versailles as still operative? Would air pacts be accompanied by air limitation agreements? What nonaggression pacts would Germany enter into in Eastern Europe? In view of its proposal for a new international court, how did Germany view the Hague Court and existing provisions for arbitration, conciliation, and judicial review in treaties to which Germany was a party? No mention was made, however, and no word was said, about the issue which concerned France most—the fortification of the Rhineland.[22]

When Phipps saw Hitler on May 14, Hitler suggested he would make no reply till after the French elections. On the issues raised by the questionnaire, he was distinctly unhelpful. He raised the issue of fortifications himself. If anyone dared tell him he should not build fortifications on German soil, he thundered, he would tell them to mind their own business.[23]

Hitler was impressed by the victory Mussolini had won in Abyssinia. Britain, he told Phipps, should have made a deal with Italy to protect British interests. Phipps replied that Britain had not considered her own interests but had joined collective action against aggression. "It was a religion in England," he told the Führer, "that there should be no more aggression."

Hitler's smile was a smile of pity. His comment encapsulated the history of the decade. "With dictators," he replied, "nothing succeeds like success."[24]

Hitler was not about to commit himself to anything binding, Phipps concluded. Wigram and Vansittart in London agreed. Thus, Vansittart wrote,

> I wonder if anyone who really knows his job really expected any other attitude than that, as Sir E. Phipps warns us once more & clearly as usual, Hitler will not bind himself in a fluid Europe—fluid, that is, for an intending aggressor. He will play for time to avoid, on any pretext, giving to us a clear & reassuring answer.... These telegrams strengthen my conviction that the two dictators will tend to be brought together not only by the similarity of their systems but by the similarities of their appetites.[25]

Hitler had his reasons. On May 15, Neurath told William C. Bullitt, the U.S. Ambassador to London, that, until the fortifications were built on the French border, Germany would remain inactive in Austria and Czechoslovakia, adding,

> As soon as our fortifications are constructed and the countries in Central Europe realize that France cannot enter German territory, all these countries will begin to feel very differently about their foreign policy and a new constellation will develop.[26]

The British questionnaire had not been a success. It was viewed in Germany as an insult and in France as a breach of trust. Nevertheless, Eden pressed unsuccessfully for a German response.[27] Hitler was enjoying his success. In June he reflected that he would never have gone into the Rhineland unless Britain and Italy had been quarreling and he repeated the idea that, had the French marched, the Germans would have evacuated the territory.[28]

Belgium suggested a new meeting of the Locarno powers, perhaps under the theory advanced by Vansittart that, though nothing was done, everyone felt better when there was a meeting. This again raised British fears that Britain would be forced to recognize that conciliation was at an end bringing the letter of March 19 into effect and obliging Britain to support France.[29]

There was, however, a new factor. With the election victory of the Popular Front, Leon Blum was now Prime Minister and Yvon Delbos his Foreign Minister. Blum proved more malleable than Laval and Flandin. He favored a meeting[30] agreeing at once that there would be no talk of a breakdown of negotiations, only the attempt to arrive at a new Locarno agreement.[31]

Italy was invited to attend, but declined if Germany were not also invited. Britain, France, and Belgium determined to meet nevertheless. The purpose of the meeting, Eden told the Cabinet[32] on July 16, was not to discuss a new Locarno, but only to issue an invitation to a Five-Power Conference which Germany and Italy would attend. Was that not a shallow and futile agenda, it was asked.

The Cabinet minutes reflect a brutally simple and straightforward answer:

> The answer given to this was that would not in fact be futile because France would be agreeing [if she did agree] for the first time to invite Germany to a Conference, and would be abandoning all the conditions and safeguards she had always insisted on. Moreover public opinion would be pleased at the invitation sent to Germany.[33]

France agreed, eschewing the pointed and persistent questions raised by Laval and Flandin: Would Britain back sanctions in Europe as she had backed sanctions in Abyssinia? The final communiqué of the July 23rd meeting showed the progressive emasculation of the French position.

The French draft of the communiqué had spoken of the *obligations* existing among France, Britain, and Belgium, and stated as the purpose of the meeting to examine the development of the situation since March 19. It stated the agreement of the three powers to abide by the fundamental provisions of the arrangements of March 19.[34]

But the British did not wish to look backward. There was no reference in the final communiqué to Locarno obligations, only to the interests of all European nations in a general settlement. Reference was made in passing to the arrangements of March 19, Hitler's proposals of March 31, and the French plan of April 8, but no more was said of the first of these.

The communiqué said that there should be a new meeting of the Locarno powers, to which Germany and Italy would be invited. No condition was attached, no contribution requested. If the meeting succeeded, the communiqué said, the discussions could be broadened to issues other than the Rhineland.[35]

No wonder Eden was now pleased with the French and declared of Franco-British relations during the second half of 1936 that "it would be difficult to recall a time when they were better."[36]

Italy and Germany promptly accepted the invitation[37] but the proposed meeting was never held.

Hitler's Rhineland triumph was definitive. France had indeed agreed to a general conference on European security without regard to the action of March 7, now clearly a fait accompli, without regard to the obligations of Locarno, and without further conditions.

The three powers, Eden told the House of Commons on July 27, did not look backward; they now looked "definitely to the future," a formula which confessed total defeat.[38]

Austen Chamberlain did not share Eden's self-congratulation. The questionnaire, he said, had been rebuffed with "a studied contempt." The more Britain offered, the higher German demands rose.[39]

Nor did subsequent developments support Eden's hopes. On August 24, Germany announced the extension of the compulsory term of military service from one to two years.[40]

Locarno had been the cornerstone of Belgian foreign policy and Locarno had failed. King Leopold drew the conclusion and on October 14 he declared Belgian neutrality. Belgium would remain armed and would defend herself but would no longer be bound to aid France if France were attacked. This immensely simplified Germany's defensive problem; it could concentrate its defensive preparations on the French border. Conversely, it complicated the French position, depriving France of Belgian space and time and the benefit of a coordinated response to the German attack.[41]

On April 27, 1937, France and Britain formally released Belgium from its Locarno obligations. Hitler's triumph over Locarno was now as complete as his triumph over Versailles.

Vital to this triumph was the view taken by the British public. Britain, Eden told the Soviet ambassador in April,

> could not admit, nor would public opinion in the country endorse, the view

> that Germany's action in the Rhineland was on all-fours with Italy's aggression in Africa. Nobody condoned Germany's action in unilaterally denouncing a treaty she had freely accepted, but Germany had not thereby attacked the territory of a State Member of the League as Italy had done.[42]

Hoesch, Germany's Ambassador in London reported his talk with Lord Lothian, who was convinced the broad masses sympathized with Germany. "The so-called 'man in the street,'" he wrote his Foreign Ministry, "does not care a damn if the Germans occupy their own territory with military forces which is a thing all other States do anyway. He does not have the slightest intention of getting himself involved." This knowledge had a powerful sustaining influence on German policy throughout the crisis.[43]

The gaze of the British people was not fastened upon the Rhineland where, after all, only vital British interests were at stake. Instead, the British public was captivated and transfixed by a drama it found far more colorful and exciting, the tragic final act of an unequal struggle between a hero and a villain, a drama with a moral dimension which compelled their attention, aroused their emotions and fed their indignation, besides which the calculation of vital national interests would seem a Faustian bargain with the Devil.

## Mussolini's Triumph

Abyssinia's situation was desperate after the defeat at Mai Ceu. A special envoy told Eden on April 3 that there was imminent danger of collapse and asked what advice Eden could give his government.[44] Eden's predictable response was to call for a meeting of the League Committee of Thirteen.[45] To strengthen his hand, the Cabinet authorized Eden to state that Britain would join in an extension of sanctions which other nations were prepared jointly to apply.[46]

France took a very different view. French Ministers meeting on April 3 viewed the Rhineland and Abyssinia as aspects of the same problem. If the Rhineland brought about the rebirth of the Stresa Front, it would be a net defeat for Germany; if it united Germany and Italy, France would have suffered a calamity.[47]

The Germans, François-Poncet warned, were simply carrying out the fundamental doctrines of *Mein Kampf*. Corbin expounded the British view. British public opinion, he advised Paris, had a great tendency to illusion and optimism and the wish to believe that everything could be arranged so long as the parties agreed to sit at the same table. You ought not to ask the British, he said, to make a critical analysis of the German plan. They looked at it as a whole and accepted it as a possibility of peace.[48]

Chambrun reported the situation in Rome. Mussolini, he stated accurately, had been surprised by the denunciation of Locarno. He wanted to reestablish Stresa. He had given assurances to Austria. Sanctions were the crux of the matter. Sanctions, Mussolini told Chambrun, gave the Emperor the assurance the world backed him. If the British counseled the Negus to sue for peace, Italy would make peace before her next victory. Sanctions could be lifted and the Stresa Front reformed.[49] This remained the ultimate goal of French policy. The difficulty, Flandin explained, was this: If France demanded the lifting of sanctions, all of British public opinion would rise up in opposition.[50]

The lifting of sanctions was feared in other quarters. In Berlin it was feared that it would lead to a French-British-Italian reconciliation and back to Stresa.[51]

Mussolini had, in fact, offered Abyssinia terms. They included the cession of Tigre, long occupied, excepting the holy city of Aksum, the cession of large parts of the Ogaden and portions of Burana, economic concessions, the appointment of Italian advisors and the cession of a corridor along the frontiers of British and French Somaliland so that Abyssinia's eastern border would be wholly Italian. This was a lot, but it was far less than all, and left the Emperor on his throne, his Amharic realms more or less intact.

But the Emperor's response had been a point-blank refusal[52] and at Geneva on April 8, Flandin reported to Eden that the Emperor still demanded the complete integrity of Abyssinian territory. The only way to achieve that, he commented, was for the members of the League to mobilize against Italy and no government was ready to do that.[53]

On April 12, the Vatican Secretary of State again acted as Mussolini's channel in conveying to Charles-Roux proposed peace terms which maintained, after annexations, the Emperor on his throne under Italian control.[54]

The French outlook was clearly stated in a memo his staff prepared for Flandin on April 9. British public opinion, it noted, was hypnotized by the Abyssinian affair and might even, in the face of grave events in Europe, be passive. To face up to Germany, the African affair had to be liquidated.[55]

The Committee of Thirteen heard charges on April 8 of Italian use of poison gas and appointed a committee of jurists to examine breaches of international conventions. After protracted procedural moves, Italy offered, on April 15, a military armistice to be followed by direct negotiations between the belligerents, of which the Committee of Thirteen would be kept informed. Such negotiations, it added, had to be based upon the military realities after six months of operations.

This, too, Abyssinia rejected, claiming that Italy had not offered to negotiate within the framework of the League or the spirit of the Covenant, which to Abyssinia meant that the League must be a party to the negotiation. That Abyssinia understood the context of the issue was made clear by its statement:

> In demanding that the Ethiopian people should be abandoned to the aggressor the Italian Government was in reality doing nothing less than fixing its price for a deal: Italy would sell her support in a European dispute in return for the raising of sanctions and for the abandonment of the League's concern with Italy's act of aggression.[56]

There was nothing left for Señor Madariaga, who had been charged with the peacemaking mission, but to report failure on April 17 and refer the matter to a further session of the League Council.[57] This took place on April 20 when Italy again proposed direct negotiations which Abyssinia rejected, demanding that the League apply all of the provisions of Article 16 of the Covenant to forestall the next aggressor.

To this, Aloisi replied that a check to conciliation would necessarily postpone Italian collaboration in the pacification of Europe. Eden made it clear, as he had been authorized, that Britain would maintain the economic and financial sanctions then in force and stood ready and willing to consider further economic and financial sanctions.[58] Paul-Boncour made equally clear the concerns that had animated the French ministers:

> We need peace in Ethiopia in order to address ourselves to the dangers with which Europe is threatened. We need a settlement of the position of a great country vis-a-vis the League of Nations in order that this country may take part in the work of European construction; and I note with satisfaction that the representative of Italy has graciously drawn our attention on this point, to the fact that this is also the desire of his own country.[59]

Since no nation was willing to take new action, whether to extend or lift sanctions, they remained in place. In the end the Council issued to

Italy its "supreme appeal" to bring to the settlement of the dispute "that spirit which the League of Nations is entitled to expect from one of its original Members and a permanent member of the Council."[60]

The next day Mussolini reviewed the issues with Chambrun. He was skeptical that Britain would ever stand by the guarantees of March 19. But the Italian guaranty to France of aid against a German attack, the Gamelin-Badoglio accords, remained, he said, in full force.

He would continue to defend Austria, Mussolini said, adding significantly, as long as his forces were not tied down elsewhere. It wasn't a matter of the heart, but of vital interests. The Duce told Chambrun,

> I can assure you that once freed in Africa, I will defend these stipulations (the Covenant) because then I'll be the most conservative of all.

It was important, Chambrun said, to return to Stresa. Mussolini agreed. There was no irremediable breach, he said, between Italy and Britain; as soon as a solution was reached in Africa, he would make direct arrangements to safeguard British honor and would neglect nothing to reach a rapprochement.[61]

While these proceedings were taking place, and Galla tribesmen were clearing the way, the Italian armies of the North advanced, almost unopposed, upon Addis Ababa in what Mussolini dubbed "The March of the Iron Will." The Emperor summoned the male population of Addis Ababa to battle. Every able-bodied man, with food, rifle, and ammunition, was to report for marching orders to his chief. Failure was to be punished by flogging and a fine of £70.[62] Meanwhile, the British Government steadfastly declined to respond to the Emperor's appeals for arms and financial assistance[63] or to the renewed suggestion that Abyssinia become a British mandate.[64] Eden's fervent declarations of support for collective security were not accompanied by tangible support for the Emperor's cause.

The Emperor was reduced to eloquent and ominous warnings that he conveyed to the *Times* correspondent on April 29:

> Do the peoples of the world not yet realize by fighting on until the bitter end I am not only performing my sacred duty to my people, but standing guard in the last citadel of collective security? Are they too blind to see that I have any responsibilities to the whole of Humanity to face? I must still hold on until my tardy allies appear. And if they never come, then I say prophetically and without bitterness: 'The West will perish.'[65]

On May 2, 1936 the Emperor made a fateful decision. He renounced the direction of the affairs of state in favor of a Council of Ministers and prepared to leave Addis Ababa and Abyssinia, to carry on the struggle before the League and the World.[66]

He departed by train for Djibuti the next day. Before leaving, he threw open his palace, from which streams of humanity issued laden with clothing, furniture, bedding, and ammunition, which they proceeded to fire off with immense abandon.

This was followed by rioting and looting, especially of European and Indian stores, and attacks on foreign legations. There was relief, therefore, when on May 5 the Italian army entered Addis Ababa and restored order.

This was Mussolini's supreme moment. The floodlit Piazza Venezia in Rome was packed that evening when the Duce appeared from his balcony. He placed himself in a long perspective. In thirty centuries of history, he proclaimed, Italy had lived memorable hours, but this was one of the most solemn. "Abyssinia is Italian!" he cried, proclaiming not only the right of the sword, but the triumph of civilization over barbarism, justice over arbitrariness, the redemption of slavery.

There was something else:

> At the rally of October 2 I solemnly promised that I would do everything possible in order to prevent an African conflict from developing into a European war. I have maintained that pledge and I am more than ever convinced that to disturb the peace of Europe means to being about the collapse of Europe.

But he would defend his victory. Flags, banners, and streamers floated above the exultant crowds in all of the principal streets of Rome, buildings were illuminated and posters proclaimed the Duce's creed: "From the Alps to the Indian Ocean the arms of Fascism affirm the power of Italy," and "In the name of Mussolini we have conquered and will conquer."[67]

Perhaps the only unhappy Italian was Graziani who, with the Southern Italian armies, stood disconsolate, two days' march from Harar.

The Emperor and his family with a few close advisors sailed from Djibuti on HMS Enterprise for Haifa and thence, on the first stage of his journey, to Jerusalem, Solomon's capital. The Conquering Lion had come home to Judah.[68]

## Anglo-Saxon Attitudes

The war was finished, but there were battles still to be waged, principally where Englishmen gathered and spoke, in homes, in public houses, in the streets and the parks, in newspapers and magazines, in Parliament and in Cabinet. To France, the issue was uncomplicated; settle with Italy and get about the business of defending Europe against Hitler.

France feared for England which might, Flandin told his ambassadors, prolong, if not the war, the crisis and render a return to Stresa impossible.[69] Corbin reported from London Eden's concern that British policy should be inspired by the principles and not by the interests of the country.[70]

Eden had good reasons. He had just received a deputation from the League of Nations Union, headed by Lord Cecil, supported by Gilbert Murray, Lord Lytton, Norman Angell, Arnold Forster, Philip Noel-Baker, Sir Archibald Sinclair, and other fervent League supporters. They had quite naturally urged Eden to press enforcement of the Covenant and support of collective security. Anything else, they said, was an admission of failure, an alternative which could not be contemplated save with grave danger to the moral authority of Great Britain and the risk of war in Europe.[71]

In the House of Commons on May 5, Eden vigorously defended the policy that had failed and in the defense illuminated some reasons for the failure.

Sanctions had been imposed which took time to be effective and time had overtaken them. The only other policy was to close the Suez Canal. Who, Eden asked the House, would have supported that? To any member of the Opposition who said yes, he launched this challenge:

> Yes, he would have closed the Canal, then how utterly illogical is the position of the hon. gentlemen opposite when they vote against all Estimates and when they denounce the budget of my rt. hon. friends as a war Budget. The truth is that while hon. gentlemen opposite protest to support the League with horse, foot and artillery, they really only mean to support it with threats, insults, and perorations....
>
> If hon. gentlemen wish to take military action, then I must warn them that you cannot close the Canal with paper boats.[72]

Mr. Bernays put the point with equal eloquence:

> We thought we could all enjoy the moral fervor of a crusade without any of the dangers and discomforts of a crusading expedition. The logical post-

script to Sir Samuel Hoare's speech was a declaration that behind the speech was a pledge that Great Britain would throw in the whole resources of her Army, Navy, and Air Force against an aggressor. But members all went off to their constituencies and told their constituents that in no circumstances would they support military sanctions.

A dictator who was not afraid of losing his head would always win against politicians who are afraid of losing their seats.[73]

Eden had correctly identified the dichotomy between principle and the interests of the country. Far from damping debate on British policy, the defeat of Abyssinian intensified it.

A longstanding correspondent of the Foreign Ministry observed that the defeat of Abyssinia had exacerbated feelings against both Italy and France:

> [T]here is the feeling (not the less strong because it may be erroneous) that we have somehow let down the Abyssinians. Those who consider last point see France as the country which has thrown the monkey-wrench into the machinery, and this thought awakens the always existent anti-French feeling and provides the basis for that disconcerting pro-Germanism which crops up from time to time. Nowhere is there any questioning of the moral right to impose sanctions; everywhere it is said that existing sanctions must be continued, if only to salve the conscience of the British nation.[74]

In no heart did the flame of conscience burn more brightly than in Professor Toynbee's. We Europeans, he wrote to the *Times* on April 22, had committed a double breach of faith and morality, by waging and condoning aggressive war and not daring to carry out more than a fragment of the Covenant.

Was it not better, like the Abyssinian, to die a painful and honorable death today than to die in dishonor tomorrow? He contributed a Greek verse to illuminate his point.[75]

Canon Sheppard ranged himself firmly on the side of the angels and pointed out to the *Times* readers that the Anglican bishops had, in 1930, passed a resolution that war as a method of solving international disputes was "incompatible with the teaching and example of Lord Jesus Christ."[76]

In a Parliamentary by-election in late April, the Labour candidate, Lewis Silkin, defined his party's position. It stood, he said, for peace by arbitration and collective security, rejecting isolation and military alliances, calling for international agreement to reduce arms to a minimum. Mr. Silkin did not address methods of securing these ends or refer to Eden's questionnaire which Hitler had thus far not deigned to mention in public.[77]

Lord Cecil was not content with deputations to high places. He had written to the *Times* on April 25 recommending closure of the Suez Canal.[78] His faith never wavered that world public opinion, led by Great Britain, could solve the Abyssinian problem.

He called a great public meeting on May 8 at the Albert Hall. "Even now," he challenged the public, "the League can fulfill the high great purpose for which it was created. Even now Abyssinia can be saved."[79]

Ten thousand attended the meeting and enthusiastically adopted Clement Attlee's motion to express indignation at Italian aggression and to urge upon the Government "the maintenance of sanctions against Italy until she is ready to accept terms of peace approved by the Council of the League."[80]

Lord Cecil fought to succeed but he was realist enough to face the prospect of failure. Just because a great experiment had not succeeded in one case, he told the House of Lords on May 13, this was not reason enough to abandon the League.[81] The alternative was to go back to 1913.

But thoughtful men now began to see the matter in another light. Churchill wrote to the *Times* that France would have, if she gave up her pact with Italy, to extend the term of military service to three years:

> I wonder how many of the 11,000,000 [Peace] balloters would be prepared to enforce a similar sacrifice in time of peace upon the British people. I wonder what the British people would say to those who did. Yet this was the kind of thing we asked of the French.[82]

He was amazed, he said, by the lengths to which Laval went in facilitating sanctions and by France's commitment to come to Britain's aid if she were attacked. What the Government had done, Churchill said, out of the highest motives, was, without helping Abyssinia, to put France into grievous trouble. [83]

There was something to be said, veteran journalist J.A. Spender wrote to the *Times* on May 12, 1936, for the old style of diplomacy. It would have kept Mussolini guessing and saved something from the wreck by an honorable compromise. His commentary was trenchant:

> If (1) settlement by compromise is to be vetoed in the name of League principles, and (2) the League is unable to make these principles prevail, our last state will be worse than our first. We shall have lost the advantages of ordinary diplomacy, and gained none of the benefits of the new order.[84]

Edwyn Bevan told the *Times* readers that the root of the dilemma was the fear of war. To enforce the Covenant meant war and governments would not take the risk. "It is unfair," he said, "to blame the governments; they knew the temper of their peoples," adding,

> It is an ironical reflection that the very same fear of war which won so many votes for the League of Nations in what was termed a 'Peace' ballot is the thing that paralyzes the League even in the face of an aggression so brutal and atrocious as the Italian.[85]

Suppose another ballot put the question of war for the Covenant to the British people. Would the ayes prevail? He very much doubted it. The unwillingness of the British and French people to go to war, even a collective war, made collective security nothing more than a great illusion.

Churchill took up the issue again in the *Times* on May 9. He had deliberately absented himself from England in December, preferring painting in Morocco to participating in the Hoare-Laval debates in Parliament. Short time had furnished a long perspective. He expansively wrote,

> Everyone could now see that the Hoare-Laval agreement was a very shrewd, farseeing agreement which could have saved the Negus of Abyssinia from ruin before his army was destroyed.[86]

By month's end, even the Archbishop of Canterbury saw the dilemma. Military sanctions had been ruled out; economic sanctions had failed:

> In the existing temper of the world and with the existing membership of the League, were its members really prepared for the possibility of war with an aggressor...and with an aggressor who might be remote in distance and interest from themselves, in a more automatic fulfilment of the Covenant? He doubted whether their own people, the great majority of whom were in enthusiastic support of the League, had yet thought out what its obligations might involve, what (to put it bluntly) they were in the last resort prepared to fight for.[87]

It had been Lord Cecil's proud boast that the Peace Ballot had taught the British people what membership in the League of Nations meant. By May, 1936, this was far from clear.

## Closing the Books

Abyssinia's supporters had hoped for successful resistance to aggression, they had hoped for rains, and with Italy's military victory, they continued to hope that Mussolini would now somehow defer to the League of Nations in organizing the aftermath of victory. They were again disappointed. On May 9, in another ceremonial rite, Mussolini proclaimed the annexation of Abyssinia of which Italy's grateful King was now proclaimed the hereditary Emperor. Badoglio was made Duke of Addis Ababa and Graziani a Marshal and later Marquis of Neghelli. Mussolini declined to become a prince, but his wife, the humble and retiring Donna Rachele, received a bouquet of roses from the Queen.[88]

The annexation complicated matters at the League of Nations where Italy now declared Abyssinia no longer existed and hence should not be recognized as a member.[89] Haile Selassie appealed eloquently from Jerusalem against recognition of the conquest. He had left the country, he said, to end the most inhuman war of modern times and to avoid the extermination of his people.[90]

On May 12, the League Council decided to seat the Abyssinian delegates. In response, the Italian delegation quit the meeting. The real issue of sanctions was deferred until the June meeting of the Council.[91]

Abyssinia's defeat had not affected Lord Cecil's determination or his vigor. At the end of May he addressed "the most serious and urgent communication" he had ever sent to all of the members of the League of Nations Union. The obligation remained to preserve Abyssinian independence: "The least one should insist upon is that the terms of peace should be approved by the League Council. Until Italy agrees to that, sanctions should be maintained, and, if need be, increased." Members were urged to telegraph and write members of parliament, the Foreign Secretary and the Prime Minister, hold meetings, pass resolutions, and write to the newspapers.

This was accompanied by an appeal for £10,000 to sustain the Union's activities. There was pride in the Union's past accomplishments:

> Its work for the 'Peace Ballot' and for the rejection of the Hoare-Laval Treaty had a profound effect not only on British action, but on the political thought of Europe.

Could not the former glory be restored?

> It is absurd to suppose that a movement which could muster in the Peace Ballot 11,000,000 voters can only supply half a million subscribers to the Union, and less than 12,000 who subscribe as much as £1.[92]

Haile Selassie arrived in London on June 4, accompanied by his family and Ras Kassa. He was greeted not by the Foreign Secretary but one of Eden's private secretaries on the grounds that this was normal practice for a royal visitor who had arrived in Britain incognito. He did not want for a warm welcome. He was met by Lord Allen, Norman Angell, his vigorous Parliamentary champions, Vivyan Adams and Elinor Rathbone, and the great organizer of Abyssinian aid and support, Sylvia Pankhurst, who had found a new cause.

Lord Allen described the occasion in a letter to his daughter:

> He is a very beautiful looking black man with a lovely face. As he got out of the train, lovely flowers were given to him, and then we were introduced to him one by one. Mummy made a lovely curtsey.[93]

The Ethiopian Minister announced a diplomatic reception for the following Saturday afternoon to present the Emperor. Cheering crowds waited outside Waterloo Station and lined the streets to greet him. Beneath an Abyssinian flag at his new residence, Haile Selassie acknowledged London's welcome.

He was gracious when he called on Eden on June 5. He thanked Eden for the courtesies accorded him and generously said that Britain had done all that was in her power.

Haile Selassie was an hereditary emperor who never doubted that he ruled by divine right. He apologized to Eden for having set the reception before he had an audience with the King. It was Eden's turn to apologize. A previous engagement would prevent his presence.[94] The reception was not well attended. The Emperor took Peterson, the Abyssinian expert, aside and much to Peterson's embarrassment asked where Baldwin and the cabinet ministers were.[95]

The British Cabinet reflected the division of public opinion. It had on May 6 basically adopted a waiting attitude, instructing Eden to advocate nothing new before the League.[96] By May 27, the price of maintaining sanctions and the benefits from lifting them began to be discussed. Neville Chamberlain thought that perhaps a deal could be done whereby, in response to raising sanctions, Mussolini would agree to cooperate with Britain and France in Europe. But no decision was reached.[97]

A press interview with Mussolini was arranged. The Duce was conciliatory and expansive. He told the *Daily Telegraph* on May 27 that the end of sanctions would mark the entry of Italy into the ranks of the satisfied powers. He spoke of collaboration for peace and the future of the League and protecting British interests in Africa:

> The end of sanctions will produce a general easing of the situation and will open up a favorable prospect for stabilization and collaboration in Europe.[98]

The next day Grandi called on Eden to deliver personally the Mussolini interview and to reinforce Mussolini's assurances. If only sanctions were lifted, Italy was ready to enter into Mediterranean security arrangements. Indeed, Mussolini wanted a fresh start with Britain letting bygones be bygones. Lord Cecil's talk of closing the Suez Canal had made Italians extremely nervous. What Mussolini wanted, Grandi reported, was a British- French-Italian rapprochement "on a Locarno basis." There was no question, he added, of a rapprochement between Italy and Germany.

Nor was there a threat to British interests in Africa and the Near East. After all, Italy had fifty year's work to do in Abyssinia. Grandi reverted once more to Austria. Italy did not want Austria to become Nazi. Her policy instead was based on Stresa and the Rome protocols.

Grandi and Eden regretted their countries' differences. Each had felt compelled to act as he had. They parted with elaborate courtesies and Grandi's final observation that "it was imperative for the future of Europe that we should work with the French."[99]

All this disposed the Cabinet on May 29 to wait and see, especially to see if Mussolini could be induced to represent to the League what he had said to the *Daily Telegraph* and what Grandi had said to Eden.[100]

As the champion of sanctions, much praised by the League of Nations Union, Eden was in a difficult position. He saw, he told the Cabinet on June 10, the advantages of raising sanctions. But no action was taken. Neville Chamberlain, the most strong-minded member of the Cabinet, thought the time had come to take the matter into his own hands.

Collective security had been tried and failed to prevent war or save Abyssinia, he told a dinner of the 1900 Club at Grosvenor House that night. Yet the League of Nations Union was appealing for a continuance, even an intensification of sanctions, to preserve the independence of Abyssinia. "That seems to me the very midsummer of madness," he said in a famous phrase.

It would only divert practical men from practical solutions. He proceeded inexorably to his conclusion. Sanctions involved, if not war, the risk of war. He asked,

> Is it not apparent from what has happened that in the presence of such a risk, nations cannot be relied upon to proceed to the last extremity of war unless their vital interests are threatened?[101]

On June 17, the Cabinet agreed that Britain, on its own motion, after informing but not consulting France, would take the lead in Geneva in proposing that sanctions be abandoned.

Eden was dignified and candid in his presentation to the House of Commons on June 18. Sanctions had failed. Only war could restore Abyssinia and no one was prepared to go to war. Sanctions no longer had purpose or meaning. All that in no way reversed the October verdict of Italian aggression.

The outrage of the Opposition was unlimited. The General Election, Attlee charged, had been the greatest act of political treachery in the history of the country. Lloyd George harked back to the desperate days of the World War. Never had he expected to hear a Prime Minister say that Britain was beaten and must abandon an enterprise it had taken in hand. He did not mince words. It was "a cowardly surrender," he said, "and there are the cowards."

In the midst of his indignation, Lloyd George committed a non-sequitur. While defending the rights of small nations, and referring to the overwhelming sacrifice Britain had made to vindicate Belgium, he proclaimed that whatever Government was in power, there would never be any question of going to war for an Austrian quarrel. What then was the guiding principle?[102]

With vast relief, the French Government promptly announced that it would follow the British lead.[103]

Baldwin sounded familiar themes in addressing a Conservative mass meeting in the North on June 22. No country had been prepared to go to war for collective security. He reminded his listeners of what he had said in October; he was prepared to support collective security, but only on condition he was given power to remedy the deficiencies in Britain's armed forces. If you want to stop an aggressor, you must be prepared for war. How then could you call for collective action and vote against every ship for the Navy, every plane for the Air Force?

He eloquently stated his underlying fear. He promised,

> whatever people may say and however much they may talk about lost prestige, to keep our people, certainly unless the whole of the League of Nations will come in with us, away from the perils and horrors of modern war in Europe.

> If that fire is ever lighted again on the Continent no man can tell where the heather will stop burning, and it is not a risk that I, for one, am going to take for my country, so long as I have any control of the Government.[104]

Winston Churchill announced his firm support of Baldwin.[105] At the meeting of the General Council of the League of Nations Union in Scarborough, Lord Cecil disagreed. There should be no cringing before Mussolini, he said:

> We must take our courage in both hands and do what is right and what we are bound to do under the Covenant.

On the same day he issued a manifesto on behalf of the International Peace Conference in which he recalled the Peace Ballot and urged a similar manifestation on an international basis.[106]

The LNU Conference on the next day adopted Lord Allen's resolution calling for disarmament by international agreement. Allen made an interesting concession. Baldwin, he said, was probably right to think that the British public would not fight for the League "in first this remote area of Europe and then that."

Arthur Henderson's son moved a resolution calling for full support of collective security, accepting the fullest implications of that support. This raised the pregnant question: Must those who did not accept the full implications, that is to say the pacifists, leave the LNU? It speaks volumes for the confusions of the LNU and of the Peace Ballot that Gilbert Murray assured those who opposed the resolution that they could do so and remain members of the Union. The resolution carried.[107]

On June 23, the Government easily defeated Labour's vote of censure. Sir John Simon was quick to penetrate the opening Lloyd George had furnished. Why would he refuse to fight for Austria and say that it was cowardly not to fight for Abyssinia? The French Parliament was equally decisive in affirming its government's decision to abandon sanctions.[108]

A year before, the League of Nations Union had been at the peak of its popularity and authority as it announced the results of the Peace Ballot. Things now appeared in a different light. The principles on which the Peace Ballot was deliberately grounded had collided with immovable realities. First Lord Queensborough, its treasurer, then Sir Edward Grigg, and Major Hilles, both members of the Executive Committee, then its long-time champion, the Duchess of Atholl, and above all, Austen Chamberlain now resigned.

At Geneva, the Assembly of the League of Nations convened on June 30. The stage was set for the final curtain on the Abyssinian tragedy.

It is a scene from history as poignant as it is immortal. Haile Selassie stands before the Assembly of the League of Nations. A black cloak and his stoic dignity enhance his slight stature. He speaks in his native Amharic. Never before has an Emperor addressed the League of Nations.

He detailed the horrors inflicted on his people, and his unavailing pleas for help. The issue was broader than Italian aggression:

> It is a question of collective security; of the very existence of the League; of the trust placed by States in international treaties; of the value of promises made to small States that their integrity and their independence shall be respected and assured. It is a choice between the principle of the equality of States and the imposition upon small Powers of the bonds of vassalage. In a word, it is international morality that is at stake. Have treaty signatures a value only insofar as the signatory Powers have a personal, direct, and immediate interest involved?

This was indeed the vital issue with which the European statesmen struggled. Haile Selassie had no doubts as he pronounced an historic judgement:

> If a strong government finds that it can, with impunity, destroy a weak people, then the hour has struck for the weak people to appeal to the League of Nations to give its judgment in all freedom. God and history will remember your judgment.[109]

Eden spoke with feeling on July 1. The Emperor's appeal "delivered with a dignity which must have evoked the sympathy of each one of us" had made this a painful occasion. But the reality was that no further economic sanctions, only military action, could change the situation and of this there was literally no possibility. It was "with infinite regret" that he conveyed the decision of the British Government to raise sanctions. He supplied the argument opposite the Emperor's plea. He asked,

> Was failure due to the fact that there are certain risks which nations are not prepared to run save where their own interests are more directly at stake than they were in this case?[110]

In any event, the issue of recognition remained and Britain was not prepared formally to recognize the Italian conquest.

Blum, for France, tied failure in Abyssinia to the unsettled issue of the Rhineland. France did not wish war but thought, above all, of the Europe of tomorrow.[111] The German threat, Litvinov warned, was now made more menacing.[112]

The Emperor filed two appeals with the Assembly on July 3, asking nonrecognition of the Italian annexation and £10 million in financial aid. The Assembly sidestepped these requests. It considered instead a resolution which, in its preamble spoke eloquently of strengthening the authority of the League by applying the lessons of experience, but in the end asked the Coordinating Committee to raise sanctions.[113] The votes in favor of the resolution numbered 44. Four nations abstained. One nation voted against. It was Abyssinia. The Assembly proceeded now to the Abyssinian resolutions. One vote was cast in favor, 23 against, 25 abstaining.[114]

On July 6, the Coordinating Committee resolved to lift sanctions on July 15. There was left only the issue of the credentials of the Abyssinian delegates to attend further proceedings at Geneva. It was a bittersweet victory when on September 23, the Credentials Committee approved the Abyssinian presence, Italy abstaining.[115] The League had not yet inflicted upon Abyssinia the final indignity.

In the bitterness of defeat, there were those who soldiered on. There was no hope of reviving sanctions, the Secretary of the League of Nations Union wrote in the August *Headway* but "It is not in us to accept defeat." "Our Union," he wrote, "is more concerned with far-reaching principles than with immediate policies." The first such principle he enumerated was disarmament.[116]

The same issue printed the declarations earlier adopted at a Manchester conference. They expressed apprehension at the Government's rearmament proposals. If international danger arose from the discontents of others, they should be mitigated and not perpetuated by force. The immense sums the Government sought for rearmament could better be spent on social and economic reconstruction. Finally, there was a call for a new Disarmament Conference.

The Declaration was signed by the League of Nations Union, the Friends Peace Committee, the Anti-War Council, the Women's International League, the Fellowship of Reconciliation, the World Alliance, the Teachers Peace Society, and the Youth Peace Council.[117]

## Mussolini's Choice

The German attitude toward the Abyssinian affairs was cautious and restrained and for good reason. In essence, Germany could not lose so long as she did not commit or embarrass herself.

If Italy were defeated, Germany could proceed with greater assurance in Central and Southeastern Europe to carry out Hitler's program. If Italy won, Germany would be freed from the threat of effective collective action, whether by the League of Nations or by Italy in collaboration with Britain and France.

Observers, especially in France, were quick to note signs of an Italian move toward Germany which the British were not always ready to believe. During this period of watchful waiting, it was always Hitler's fear that the Duce would once again align himself in the Stresa Front.

Mussolini was, indeed, a long time in making his decision. He had tried to keep his options open. He had tried, in January 1935, to clear his program with Britain, which had looked aside. He had joined with France and Britain in a declaration against the unilateral revision of Versailles. He had warned in chilling terms of Hitler's ambitions, and he had convened the Stresa Conference to confront the threat they posed. He had at every opportunity made clear to Britain that he offered no threat to British and imperial interests. He had held the pass, protecting Austria; he deeply feared Germany on his border.

He had advised General de Bono to stand still, after the earliest initial conquests on the Northern border. He had been deprived of an opportunity to pass upon the Hoare-Laval plan by action taken before he could respond. He had, during the Spring, signified his willingness to negotiate with Haile Selassie on terms, let it be said, reflecting the military position.

He was, throughout all this, genuinely baffled by the British response. The British people were acting out of motives which he simply could not understand, and in the end put down to simple hypocrisy, hostility, and the desire of the world's greatest empire to humble and demean, not only Italy, but the Duce himself.

In the hour of victory, Mussolini still hesitated. On April 23, 1936, as the March of the Iron Will approached Addis Ababa, he ordered a cessation of press attacks on Britain.[118] On March 27, Mussolini had multiplied to Chambrun assurances of friendship and offers of collaboration for peace and, very significantly, a Stresa policy to confront the German threat.[119]

On May 28, bearing Mussolini's conciliatory statement to the *Daily Telegraph*, Grandi conveyed to Eden all these earlier messages in explicit terms.[120] Italy was a satisfied power, Mussolini told the French, as well as the British press. "I ask nothing of England," Mussolini told *L'Intransigeant* on May 25, "I am ready to give her all possible reassurances."[121]

It was true, however, that at the same time Mussolini was assuring Germany that these assurances were only tactical.

The choice was, nevertheless, a difficult one. The path from Stresa to Berlin was neither direct nor foreordained. Sanctions continued in effect; in the hour of his greatest triumph, Mussolini's vanity became a stronger component of his decision-making machinery.

When the League lifted sanctions, it was clear that the nations had acted not to appease Italy, but because there was no other practical course of action. They had bowed before the accomplished fact and expressed their true opinion by denying to the Duce and his newly proclaimed King-Emperor recognition of their conquest.

When the fateful choice was made, it centered neither on Addis Ababa, the Rhineland, Paris, or London, but Vienna. In January, Mussolini, seeing no chance for a negotiated peace following the collapse of Hoare-Laval, resigned to campaigning in Africa, had told Hassell that Italian policy ought to parallel Germany and more particularly that Italy would not object to Austria's becoming a German satellite.[122]

The long struggle between the Austrian Government and its Nazi minority, incited and supported by Germany, which had waxed and waned in 1934 and 1935, now entered a new phase. The two nations entered what they called a Gentlemen's Agreement, announced on July 11, 1936.

By its terms, Germany recognized full Austrian sovereignty and promised mutual noninterference in internal affairs. At the same time, Austria agreed "to maintain a policy based always on the principle that Austria acknowledges herself to be a German State."[123]

France quickly perceived the true nature of the agreement. It did not, François-Poncet reported from Berlin, mention the independence of Austria or the integrity of its frontiers. It would lower the barriers between Berlin and Vienna; the immense mass of Germany would exercise a tidal pull on Austria, which would be submissive to directives from Berlin. It was, in short, a Trojan horse which the ingenious Herr von Papen had introduced into the heart of Austria.[124]

The French appraisal was sage. The unpublished agreements contained a provision for the entrance of Nazis into the Austrian Government.[125] Fundamental changes were taking place in the balance of Europe.

Mussolini promptly cabled his approval to Schuschnigg. The agreement would be, he said, a notable step on the way to European reconstruction. He later told Reich Minister Hans Frank on September 23, 1936 that he had seen Schuschnigg on June 5 and told him: "Make peace with Germany. I do not forget that Austria is a German state."[126] In *Popolo d'Italia* he wrote on July 14 that the controversies that had separated Germany and Italy had been surmounted and spoke of a "great central zone comprising Germany, Austria, Hungary, and Italy."[127]

Laval had left the center stage six months ago. Mussolini neither understood nor liked Leon Blum. He had made another fateful decision—to intervene in the recent revolt in Spain. His foreign policy advisors changed. His son-in-law, Ciano, had become Foreign Minister in June; his policy from the start was to bring Italy and Germany together.

Perhaps what Mussolini said when the Anschluss became an accomplished fact sheds light on the state of mind in which he stood aside from Austria and veered decisively toward Germany:

> Once an event is fated, it is better that it should happen with you than in spite of you, or worse still, against you.[128]

Having adopted a new course of action, he pursued it with characteristic enthusiasm. He would back all German colonial ambitions, he told Frank on September 23. He and Hitler were not simply Heads of State but "Leaders of Movements which are today conducting a life and death struggle against almost the whole world." He would be glad to go to Germany to meet the Führer "whom I admire with all my heart."[129]

Ciano pursued his plans to align Italy and Germany. High on the agenda was German recognition of the Italian conquest of Abyssinia.[130] This was duly announced on October 24[131] following the adoption of a German-Italian Protocol settling the issues between the two nations.

On November 1, 1936 Mussolini spoke scathingly of the illusions—and one of them was disarmament—that were "the allies of the great shipwreck of Wilsonian ideology." He announced the Rome-Berlin Axis, "this vertical line between Rome and Berlin," "an axis round which all European States animated by the will to collaboration and peace can also collaborate." Germany, Mussolini said, had not adhered to sanctions. Germany had recognized the Italian Empire. With the Agreement of July 11, the last element of discord between the two nations had disappeared.[132]

For France, Mussolini had only harsh words. After seventeen years of dissension, the January 1935 agreements with Italy had been signed. "These Agreements," Mussolini said, "could and should have opened up a new era of really friendly relations between the two countries. But sanctions intervened."

Friendship froze. Winter passed. Victory came in the spring. Sanctions continued. After two months in Addis Ababa, sanctions still continued. Mussolini went on,

> A classic example of the letter that kills the spirit, of formalism strangling the living, concrete reality of existence.
>
> France still today holds her finger pointing to the age-yellowed archives of Geneva and says "The Empire of the very much former Lion of Judah is still alive."[133]

Meanwhile, on October 23, 1936, the German-Japanese Anti-Comintern Pact was initialed in Berlin by Ribbentrop and the Japanese Ambassador, followed by the signature of the Agreement on November 25.[134] Italy adhered to the Pact on November 6, 1937.[135] On December 11, 1937, Italy finally left the League of Nations.[136]

On December 15, 1936, Ciano told a German journalist:

> My cherished plan of a close association with Germany has come true. I heartily rejoice that it was reserved for me, as Italian Minister for Foreign Affairs, to have the opportunity of laying the coping stone on this momentous change in the political constellation of Europe.[137]

# 9

# Paradoxes Of Peace

*"History is predominantly the story of unlearned lessons."*

—Arnold J. Toynbee[1]

## How it Began

On January 1, 1933, the world, which was a European-centered world, was recognizably the world of the peacemakers of 1919 and Germany was the Germany they had envisioned. That is to say, Germany was disarmed, and however much German ingenuity could do, the German army of 100,000 was without tanks and heavy artillery, the modest navy was denied submarines and no German air force flew the skies. The Rhineland, which had only recently seen the early departure of the Allied armies of occupation, lay open to the victorious French, as it had in 1923.

What the peacemakers had not foreseen and would not have wished was a Germany in economic crisis, with more than five million unemployed, a failed democracy which had given way to government by decree. That government was unable to master a state of virtual civil war between Nazis and Communists who viewed it with equal contempt.

Turning its gaze and its energies inward, the Soviet Union had largely withdrawn from the affairs of Europe which regarded the Soviet state with varying degrees of ignorance and apprehension. The withdrawal of the United States from the European scene was as pronounced, if less mysterious.

The League of Nations, the visible manifestation of the world order, reflected these salient facts. Neither the United States nor the Soviet

Union was a member; and the League was a deliberative body, lacking, by the will of its founders, an effective executive or any power to enforce its judgments.

Where true power rested was clear. Britain and France were each the seat of a great empire. The Royal Navy and the French army were forces widely superior to any foreseeable foes. Besides its army, which aroused charges of militarism that had characterized Prussia in another time, France was completing, at enormous expense, the elaborate defensive works of the Maginot Line.

They were buffeted at varying times and to varying degrees by the economic storms of the thirties and the social dislocations they engendered. But on January 1, 1933, Britons and Frenchmen could feel secure and confident that, however pressing the economic and social problems of the day, they were safe and secure from any threat of external force.

They were, both nations, great, free, and enlightened polities, with representative governments, governments indeed representative of largely educated and literate electorates operating in remarkably open societies. It was neither foolishness nor wishful thinking for Englishmen and Frenchmen to believe that the very real problems facing their nations and the world could be attacked and resolved, or at least treated, with rational and above all peaceful methods.

This was the world which three years and three months later lay totally shattered. In March, 1936, Germany, united behind its Führer, was methodically and efficiently embarked upon an immense economic expansion. The purpose of the economic expansion was clear: to back a fast-growing military power. One by one, Hitler had destroyed the critical limitations of the Versailles settlement. He was building an army, a navy, and an air force, equipped and gunned to his heart's desire, and had not hesitated to place that military force on the French border. The Rhineland was now a prospective jumping off point for the attack which France feared rather than an unprotected and open back door to the industrial heart of Germany.

Hitler was now in position to carry out the program he had enunciated, first on street corners and in beer halls, then in *Mein Kampf*, and in later years with growing confidence and candor. By his reoccupation of the Rhineland, he had denied to France the ability effectively to come to the aid of its allies to Germany's East who stood in the pathway of Hitler's grandiose Eastern plans.

The Third Republic, born in the fires of a German invasion, was by its failure to respond to the reoccupation of the Rhineland, morally and physically moribund, its numbers and its economy unable to compete with Germany, dependent upon British guidance, until it expired in the flames of yet another German invasion in 1940.

An even greater power on the world scene died on March 7, 1936—the British Empire. In a glorious moment in 1940, it stood alone and defended the cause of freedom for all men. But that glory should not obscure the fact that from March, 1936, the collapse of the British Empire was as inexorable as it was, in the perspective of history, swift.

From the peace and security of New Year's Day, 1933, Britain, France, Europe, and the world were, by March 31, 1936 being borne relentlessly toward a cataclysm of which the Holocaust was only a constituent part, six years of death and destruction, physical and spiritual, under conditions of unimaginable horror. The final figure, 45 millions of human lives, cannot begin to measure the cost to civilization.

That these awful events should have come to pass is rendered the more terrible by this fact: it was the fervent devotion to peace of men and women of high ideals, good will, and great courage that was a vital and moving cause of the tragedy they had sought to avoid. This was the paradox of peace.

## The Paradox of the Peace Ballot

Lord Cecil's great aim in promoting the Peace Ballot had been to strengthen the League of Nations. The result was just the opposite. The fatal coincidence of the campaign for the Peace Ballot and Mussolini's campaign in Abyssinia laid bare the internal contradictions inherent in the Ballot and in its results.

The British public gave nearly unanimous support to the League. What they would not effectively give was their support to a war to enforce the League's mandate. But the very measure of their support for the League doomed all efforts at realistic compromise. Deprived of effective enforcement on the one hand and compromise on the other, the League could only deliberate, adjourn, postpone, and in the end fail.

If the immediate aim of the Peace Ballot had been to strengthen the League of Nations, the ultimate goal was peace through collective security. Here again, the Peace Ballot achieved only a perversely opposite result. This massive demonstration of British public opinion must be regarded as a direct and contributory cause of the war that finally came in 1939. Thus were Lord Cecil's goals frustrated and his hopes laid waste, in meaningful part by his own hand.

For the Peace Ballot was a ringing call for disarmament at a time when arms were desperately needed. The clear and present danger lay in Hitler's Germany. The Peace Ballot diverted attention from the German threat and forced Britain to confront an Italy that saw more clearly than Britain herself the German menace. In the end, the Peace Ballot contributed mightily to the complete reversal of Italian policy and drove Italy into Germany's calculating and waiting arms.

At this critical juncture, the Peace Ballot lulled the British public into an unwarranted reliance on economic sanctions as a painless method of resolving international disputes. By the same token, only 58 percent of the balloters gave their support to military sanctions. The public had responded differently in 1914–18. Baldwin read his public and the message he read was: all sanctions short of war. American presidents a generation later learned that democracies do not wage war effectively with only majority consent.

These unhappy results of the Peace Ballot were rooted in its very nature. It was first and foremost an exercise in principle. It never asked where British interests lay or how far Britain's means corresponded to the ends the Peace Ballot dictated. In the hour of the Peace Ballot's triumph, a very real case arose to which the Peace Ballot could give no practical answers. It was never true that Britain could enforce the Covenant at all times, in all cases and places, irrespective of the British interests concerned. Yet it was precisely the expansive nature of the Peace Ballot that led Sir Samuel Hoare to make his uncompromising declaration at Geneva in September. Both immediately before and continuously after that declaration, Hoare keenly recognized the practical problem that had been thrust upon him. The same vivid and unlimited principles of the Peace Ballot barred an effective compromise of the dispute.

Lord Cecil himself had often proclaimed it. There was something more than abstract principle involved in the propositions of the Peace Ballot. It was, he declared, rooted in Christian morality. That same morality did not lend itself to a clear analysis of the case at hand. In every way, the moral analysis distorted the issues and the values involved and led to skewed attitudes and conclusions that led in turn to disaster.

This was a time when there abounded these simple propositions: war is immoral. Hence, arms are immoral. This was playing Hitler's game.

The Treaty of Versailles was immoral. If this were so, Britain was immoral, from which the equally simple conclusion was drawn that morality lay on the side of Germany, even Hitler's Germany.

France possessed arms. Hence, France was immoral. France insisted on Versailles; France was thereby doubly immoral and Germany doubly wronged, even Hitler's Germany. These things mattered in a critical era when a British ambassador to France could look back and observe that, "The real defect of English policy since 1918 has been to mistake the Germans for Englishmen and the French for Germans."[2]

Italy was clearly immoral in invading Abyssinia, and became, in 1935 and early 1936, the focal point of British policy. When Hitler reoccupied the Rhineland in defiance of Versailles and Locarno, the morality of this peaceful, but fatal action was contrasted favorably to the immorality of Italy's war that employed poison gas against defenseless peasants. For all his immense learning, for his clear recognition of the critical nature of the Rhineland and the threat of an Italo-German combination, Arnold Toynbee was content to rest his Rhineland conclusions on moral grounds. The consequences of this conjunction of events ultimately proved fatal to 45 million souls. All this happened because scholars, statesmen, and the man in the street who looked to them for guidance, looked past the hard facts with which they were confronted to principles that did not correspond to the facts. Of course the Italian war in Abyssinia was immoral, in its means as well as its ends. The difficulty is that an absolute standard of morality can often do more harm than good in international affairs. To confess that morality is relative is especially difficult for the churches, which is why they were, as leaders of public opinion, so distinctly unhelpful in this era. The hard truth was perceived by Sir Eric Drummond, Britain's ambassador to Rome, when he speculated that in the end, the choice rarely lay between good and evil, but instead, between two evils.

Here indeed lay another grave problem in basing policy on morality. Opposing interests may be compromised and composed. But if morality is the principal guide, then it is just as difficult to compromise with the lesser as with the greater evil.

## The Arithmetic of Interests

What, then, was the policy dictated by British interests? Quite clearly Germany was the principal threat. Sir Horace Rumbold had early and accurately reported the character and aims of the Nazi state. His successor, Sir Eric Phipps, had never failed to keep London fully informed on the economic and military progress that Germany was making in pursuit of Hitler's aims. The vital role of the Rhineland was never in doubt. That the Low Countries were a vital British interest had been for centuries the cardinal point of British foreign policy.

However Mussolini vaunted Italy's power, however glowingly he spoke of his eight million bayonets and his air force, no one believed that Italy's economy or its armed forces were in any way comparable to Germany's. That Italy could inflict meaningful damage on Britain in the Mediterranean was accepted, but neither the British Government nor its military and naval advisors ever doubted the ultimate victory.

To the contrary, the Maffey Committee had carefully studied the threat posed by an Italian conquest of Abyssinia and had concluded that it was immaterial to British interests whether the Negus or the Duce reigned in Addis Ababa.

The common sense of the situation, then, was to prepare to meet the German threat. To this, Mussolini, who gauged the threat accurately, wholeheartedly agreed, and at Stresa exerted himself to create a front that would restrain Germany. Italian support strengthened Austria and curbed, as it had in 1934, the German thrust into Central and Southeastern Europe.

Since the German threat was direct and lethal, Britain required arms to meet the threat. If she could not meet force with equal or superior force, in whatever combination, then she must yield.

Above all, British interests required steady, strong, and unswerving support of France, Hitler's declared eternal enemy and the fundamental obstacle to the realization of his goals.

An armed and vigilant Britain, closely tied to France, in league with Italy, and enjoying the benefits of the Franco-Soviet arrangements, could face the German threat with greater dignity and confidence than a Britain dubious of France, aloof from the Soviet Union, desperately seeking, from a position of weakness, an accommodation with a Germany to whom Italy was now allied.

When, therefore, the Abyssinian war began, there was every practical reason to seek a compromise solution, a solution which would have offered Britain harmonious and effective relations with France and the adherence of Italy to the anti-German front. Such a compromise might also preserve for the Emperor his throne and the central part of his

Empire, when in fact, at grievous cost, he lost it all. A compromise solution accepted by Abyssinia, by Italy, and by the third indispensable party, the League of Nations, could have enhanced the role and prestige of the League as a peacemaker and as an appropriate forum for the resolution of international disputes. Spared the costs and losses of the campaign that followed, Italy could, to her great advantage, have pursued a very different path from that which led to ruin.

Long condemned as a shady and immoral transaction, the Hoare-Laval proposals were a practical and realistic effort to resolve the Italo-Abyssinian dispute, not only as an independent issue, but in the context of the threat of war which loomed over and later engulfed Europe.

The Hoare-Laval terms were less by far than Mussolini had demanded and in the end took. They recognized a military conquest, then at its earliest stage, which no party was willing to reverse by force of arms. The frontier rectifications in the north and east were meaningful but the corridor to the sea could significantly enhance Abyssinia's economy and independence. The Emperor would remain sovereign over all but the ceded territory, sovereign, too, in the larger zone in the South reserved for Italian economic expansion. There the League of Nations would play a significant role in administration, a buffer between Abyssinia and Italy, a guide to development and progress. Beyond a vital part in the peacemaking process, this role, too, would have lent the League of Nations new authority and new opportunities to work for peace and progress.

These prospects, and the hopes of Franco-British-Italian-Soviet collaboration to restrain Hitler were swept away in the storm of moral indignation that greeted the Hoare-Laval proposals in Britain. In France, the proposals had been welcomed and understood. A leading editorial writer in *Figaro* summed it up in January, 1936:

> If one considers...the Laval policy, one perceives, despite errors of detail, which are above all, errors of international psychology, that it corresponded to three essential ideas, all perfectly just: 1° to prevent the African conflict from degenerating...into a European conflagration; 2° to maintain Franco-Italian amity which remains a necessity for the future of Central Europe; 3° to find a settlement for the conflict, which, as equitable as possible within the framework of the League, still takes account of the realities.[3]

This matched Churchill's conclusion that the Hoare-Laval proposals were a "very shrewd, very farseeing agreement which would have saved the Negus of Abyssinia from ruin before his army collapsed."[4]

They would have saved much more. All this became clear to the strident pacifist, Beverly Nichols, whose 1933 work, *Cry Havoc*, had counseled the utter folly of any war and fueled opposition to rearmament. In *News of England*, published in 1938, he carefully acknowledged authorship of *Cry Havoc*. He had learned since then, he said, that there were things worth fighting for:

> It is possible that by the time these words are printed, the British Government may have sulkily accepted the inevitable and recognized the Italian conquest. But by then it will be too late. The harm has been done. Italy has been driven into the arms of Germany, a Fascist bloc has been formed, and the world has been split into two hostile camps.
>
> You will search in vain through English history to find any period of our foreign policy which can offer even a faint parallel to the ineptitude and criminal negligence which has characterized the conduct of our affairs in this matter.[5]

The deficiencies of British statesmanship in this period are lamentable and clear, but they proceeded neither from ignorance, blindness, nor lack of devotion to duty. Behind British statesmen where those millions of British men and women of goodwill and high ideals, dedicated lovers of peace, who had in the Peace Ballot laid down the principles by which the nation's foreign policy was to be guided and, who, in the critical moment of the Hoare-Laval proposals, held their representatives responsible for upholding those principles.

Another dedicated pacifist, and the greatest idealist of his time in British politics, George Lansbury, later spoke the essential truth:

> In my judgment the greatest crime connected with the conquest of Abyssinia is that the governments forming the League of Nations allowed the Emperor to believe that the League would save his country, when all the time those at Geneva knew that effective sanctions could not be imposed without war, which the governments representing Great Powers were not prepared to risk. Had the League basically been quite honest, it would have told the Emperor the truth and done its utmost to secure him some better position than is his now.[6]

## Negus and Duce

In a morality play, it is essential that there be a hero and a villain. It was Europe's misfortune that at a critical episode of its history, the characters of hero and villain, the champions of good and evil, should have been so sharply drawn in colors so glaringly bright.

If the suggestion has been made that a compromise solution of the Italo-Abyssinian confrontation would have helped mightily to preserve the peace of Europe and the world, that detracts not at all from the sterling qualities that Haile Selassie displayed. His impassive dignity, his stoic courage in the face of impossible odds, and the pathos of his appeal for justice indelibly impressed and profoundly moved the world-wide audience. In his character and bearing, he was a worthy bearer of the ancient crown of the Negus Negusti, the King of Kings, the Conquering Lion of Judah. Two millennia later, there was once again waged the unequal struggle between Jerusalem and Rome.

His personal qualities tended to obscure other facts. His power was as absolute as Mussolini's and his country labored under savage conditions which he had attempted to ameliorate. To many of his subjects, the Emperor was a conqueror and an oppressor. Slavery indelibly stained Abyssinian society.

The Emperor's interests were not wholly impersonal. His dynastic position was a continuing element in the choices he made, whether to give direct battle to the Italians, or to refuse utterly to treat with a victorious Mussolini. Had he followed his precept and waged guerrilla war, saving his not inconsiderable warrior forces from a wholly unequal struggle, the end might have been different. But the frontal assault against odds was an essential part of the role he played in the drama. It is instructive to note that at the same time he obstinately refused to talk of a negotiated peace, he earnestly pleaded for Abyssinia to become a British dependency.

The villain of the piece was clearly the Fascist dictator who gloried in armed force and ferociously assaulted, with all the weapons that science had devised, including the most hated and the most horrible, the barefoot soldiers and innocent subjects of the Christian Emperor. Shattering the treaties which Italy had signed, contemptuous of the rule of law and the world organization which embodied it, he incurred almost universal odium. His love of war and glory repelled the British public which had had its full of both and longed most of all to preserve at least cost what war and glory had gained for them.

There was a certain compelling grandeur in the boldness, the decisiveness, and the clarity with which Mussolini created and executed the plan that his dreams of a second Roman Empire had inspired. He took grave risks, he staked his country and his own career, he eschewed half measures, and he won decisively.

Yet, if this was Mussolini at the zenith, he came to the zenith reluctantly. He recognized the threat of Hitler clearly, he judged Hitler perceptively, he led the effort to contain Nazi Germany. With Laval at Rome, with Britain and France at Stresa, he worked diligently to spur them both to save the peace of Europe.

He had no quarrel with Britain, and from the first attempted to reassure it that he wished in no way to trench on British interests. Victorious in the end, he renewed those assurances and his desire to collaborate in achieving safety and stability in Europe. To this the answer was the continuation of sanctions which could hurt Italy but no longer alter the result.

He clearly distinguished between a European war and a colonial war and thought that history, especially British history, warranted the distinction. Grounding his policy firmly on the interests of Italy as he saw them, he was baffled by the inconsistencies of British policy. Impervious to the appreciation of morality as the basis of foreign policy, he could in the end only conclude that British policy was driven by hypocrisy and conspiracy.

In his hour of triumph, he gloomily concluded that the weakness Britain had displayed offered little support and less hope to resist Hitler. If events were inevitable, then it was better to face the inevitable with them rather than against, a conclusion that echoed the fatalistic strain ingrained in his nature.

## The Führer

In these years, Hitler's policy was clear and consistent. To achieve the goals which a diabolical imagination had created and an iron will would strive to achieve, brute force was the essential tool, whether it succeeded by intimidation or war. Immediately on becoming Chancellor, he framed his goals and set to work to build that force, sweeping aside all opposition on the way.

In the earliest years, he was constrained by the limits of Germany's economic capacity. Concealing what he could, he parleyed for attainable goals within the limits of that capacity.

As the capacity of Germany to sustain war grew beyond concealment, he pushed brutally forward with the building of his war machine, and, unveiling it to the world, did not hesitate to exaggerate its power precisely to strike fear in the hearts of his adversaries.

It was his uncanny gift to assess the emotions of the French and above all the British peoples that helped to pave the way. "Circumstances forced me," he ruminated in 1938,

> to speak almost entirely of peace these last ten years and more. It was only by harping on Germany's desire and search for peace that I managed, little by little, to secure the freedom of action and the armaments that we needed to take each successive step.[7]

Each warlike move was accompanied by peace plans and protestations. Thus, the *Times* could conclude that the Blood Purge of 1934 was evidence of Hitler's democratic tendencies and that the reoccupation of the Rhineland was a constructive move that offered a chance to rebuild.

Faced with the choice of judging Hitler by his acts or his words, large segments of the British people were eager to accept the words and ignore the deadly consequences which might follow from his acts. When the words had long since been proven false, Britain was left to face the consequences.

For Hitler, the Abyssinian war was providential. Astutely playing a neutral role, sensitively playing on Mussolini's needs and psyche, and the impact upon Mussolini of the sanctions policy he correctly identified with Britain, Hitler achieved two vital aims. He secured Italy as an ally and used the cover of the Abyssinian crisis to achieve his then greatest triumph, the reoccupation of the Rhineland.

## France

France had no illusions. The perception of the threat of Hitler's Germany was both visceral and intellectual. From the start, French statesmen clearly appraised Hitler and German policy. France, the victor of 1918, had nothing to gain and everything to defend. Deprived of the British and American guarantees for which she had bargained in 1919, relegated to a League of Nations which enshrined British and American principles rather than French realities, France was compelled to stand on the continuing enforcement of the Versailles settlement. For this, Britain had little taste and was often found ranged on the side of Germany in weakening and eliminating key parts of that settlement, both before and after Hitler took power. As Hitler's power grew, and his armed forces strengthened, Britain was more inclined to find reasons to accept the power of the new Germany and seek an accommodation which, however appealing in British eyes, might well seem to France to put the nation in deadly peril.

When Laval went to Rome and Moscow to enlist Italy and the Soviet Union in a defensive front, he was carrying out the policy that Barthou had designed. The Pact of Rome was as well received in France as in Italy and in February, 1935, gained British endorsement.

Faced with a choice between Italy and Abyssinia, Laval unhesitatingly chose Italy. Morals are one thing he observed to Hoare, and the interests of the nation quite another. He understood the importance of the League of Nations and strove desperately to create a compromise that would preserve the League's authority. After his hopes of compromise had failed, his challenge to the French Parliament was this: Have I defended the interests of France? He gained then, as he had before, the support of Parliament and his successors carried on his policy.

Laval played no lone hand in framing French policy. Nor did he conspire. To the contrary, he faced the issues with blunt honesty. From the start, he wished to make public the limitations on collective action to which he had agreed with Hoare on the eve of Hoare's Geneva speech. He did in fact make clear both those limitations and the bases from which he was operating.

Laval faced multiple and complex problems with courage and agility. Lacking Baldwin's comfortable Parliamentary margin, he simultaneously dealt with fiscal pressures, a profound division between Left and Right, and the Abyssinian crisis. To attempt to resolve the Abyssinian crisis, he had to deal effectively with his other two crises.

He studied Mussolini and, an astute negotiator, he maintained his lines of communication and his personal rapport. His method always was to induce the parties to a dispute to come to the table, to find a fundamental basis for discussion, whereupon he had confidence a compromise could be found.

The record lends no support to the once-popular theory that Laval tricked and overbore Hoare. Hoare knew clearly why he had come to Paris, negotiated as an equal, and in the end it was Laval who acceded to Hoare's plan rather than the reverse.

France did not possess Germany's strength. It must, then, find strength in combination with others. This was Laval's goal. If he could find a solution to the Abyssinian crisis which, however imperfect, was acceptable, he could build on that combination. Appalled by the prospect of war, he was ready to negotiate with Germany, but it was the essence of his policy that France he should negotiate from a position of strength and not, as happened in the aftermath of his fall, from a position of weakness.

Mussolini's war on Abyssinia, and Britain's response seemed to offer the opportunity for which France had always waited. If covenants and treaties were to be enforced by sanctions, then the gap in the post-Versailles arrangements might be filled. Britain demanded France's support in enforcement of the Covenant in Africa and this France gave. In the supreme moment of crisis, when the interests of France were critically at stake, there was no support in Britain for France or for the Locarno Treaty which was France's last safeguard.

In one respect, however, the failure lay in France. Firmly locked in the mentality of 1918, the aging leaders of the military which France had lavishly provided had neither the suitable force nor the will to act when Germany marched into the Rhineland. Led by an interim government, with a general election approaching, with a military insisting upon a general mobilization, France was compelled, if she acted, to act alone. That she should have acted alone is precisely what British critics have ever since insisted. Eden was more generous. Had France marched, he said years later,

> World opinion would have regarded it as scarcely less blameworthy than Hitler's action and France would have been told two wrongs do not make a right. Over all this contention and hesitation loomed the gravest of all dangers, proclaimed Anglo-French differences. A military operation by France could have divided her from her British ally as deeply as the occupation of the Ruhr and more deeply if blood had flowed. It must have weakened the alliance, it might have reduced the need for it. That was all veiled in the mists of uncertainty.[8]

Hitler, Eden concluded long years after, should have been called to order: "But nobody was prepared to do it, in this country, literally nobody."[9]

The French strove once more to turn the reoccupation of the Rhineland and the obvious degeneration of the European scene to advantage by building a stronger alliance with Britain and obtaining such guarantees as she could. Was this not, then, an example of the realism which was so conspicuous an element of French policy?

## Britain

If from January, 1933, Hitler's plans and programs were the driving force of European international relations, it was to Britain that the world looked for a lead in framing a response. Unlike Germany, Britain was a true world power, and it was incontestably the leader of the League of Nations that it had done so much to create.

Unhappily, Britain was loath to lead. By 1935, Hitler was firmly in command of the German people, their economy, and their armed forces. When Mussolini, planning an African empire, approached the Foreign Office in January 1935, there was literally no response. Britain responded to Hitler's March strokes, his army and his air force, his defiance of the peace treaties, and his calculated snub with Sir John Simon's visit to Berlin, his protestations of British friendship and the smiles of a man to whom smiles did not come easily.

At Stresa, British diplomats had evaded not only the Abyssinian issue, but the far broader issues raised by unilateral breach of treaties, and the mechanisms by which the treaties might be enforced and the affairs of Europe arranged other than by the mailed fist and the fait accompli. Always Britain stood aloof from the critical affairs of Eastern Europe and distanced itself as best it could from the affairs of Austria, Hitler's first target.

In a startling reversal, Britain proclaimed itself in Hoare's speech at Geneva as the universal enforcer of the Covenant of the League of Nations, at the same time furiously backpedaling at the suggestion that the sanctions she called for in the Mediterranean should be enforced in Europe. In the end, there was a fatal divergence between the two branches of the double policy; what Hoare negotiated, Baldwin, Parliament, and the British people rejected. The day came on March 7, 1936 when the policy so boldly proclaimed in Geneva in September and so emotionally upheld in December might, if followed through, have stemmed for a moment the Nazi tide. In that moment there was only apathy, inaction, and futility.

Underneath all this lay the failure to rearm to the degree the clear and present danger required. This put Britain, in all these transactions, at an irretrievable disadvantage; what Hitler achieved by force and the threat of force there were neither the means nor the will to counter.

The most grievous failure lay in the relationship with France. In January, 1935, the British Cabinet concluded that the Rhineland was not a vital British interest. Thus the fate of France was put to the hazard, but none thought to inform the French. After Hitler's dramatic revelations of armed might in March, 1935, ignoring completely the joint declarations of Britain, France, and Italy of the month before condemning unilateral violation of treaties, British statesmen traveled to Berlin to parley with Hitler without notice or consultation with France whose interests were vitally engaged.

At Stresa, Britain resisted cooperative action to maintain the European settlement and the Covenant of the League of Nations.

More critical still was Britain's open condonation of German rearmament in the Anglo-German Naval Treaty of June, 1935, deliberately concluded in the face of French opposition without French consultation or participation.

While the ink on the Naval agreement was scarcely dry, Eden went to Rome to offer the Zeila compromise to Mussolini, again quite deliberately behind the back of France whose vital interests were once more at risk.

There was an arrogance and a self-centeredness in British policy which found its ultimate expression in the demands for French support of the Royal Navy, unilaterally deployed in the Mediterranean without French forewarning or assent, at the same time rebuffing French pleas for at least equal support in Europe.

France followed Britain's lead; France proclaimed its support for the Covenant; France embarked upon sanctions that would hazard the dearly bought treaty with Mussolini, the primary aim of which was to shore up French defenses against Germany. Jointly with Britain, France negotiated a compromise settlement of the Abyssinian affair to avoid a European debacle only to see the agreement Sir Samuel Hoare had negotiated abandoned by his Government and his people, robbing France of its intended benefits.

When all these things had come to pass, Britain sought primarily its own security and an air pact which would defend from the skies the Britain that was protected, as France was not, by the seas around it from the immediate onslaught of the German Wehrmacht. In the climactic moment, the day before Hitler struck, the British Government was attempting, without French knowledge or assent, to trade the security of France, the demilitarized Rhineland, for the security of Britain, the air pact. This lamentable catalog of inaction, ineptitude, and betrayal brought forth in its time the bitter consequences of the Second World War.

## The Reason Why

Lord Cecil had proclaimed that the ultimate power lay in public opinion. In this he was proved unerringly right. From Hitler's ascent to power, the British Government was continually well informed of his goals and his progress in attaining them. Churchill was not alone in his knowledge or in his warnings.

But public opinion in 1933 and 1934, captivated by the Disarmament Conference and, swayed by dreams of disarmament, was in no mood to face the hard facts and the harder burdens of rearming. However large the Government's majority in Parliament, it was not only the East Fulham election, but a whole series of Parliamentary contests in which to proclaim oneself the peace candidate seemed to assure victory, that raised real issues about the Government's ability to survive a rearmament program.

Baldwin early proclaimed that the bomber would indeed get through, that Britain's frontier was on the Rhine, that Britain could not afford to be inferior in air power to any nation within striking distance of Britain's shores, adding solemnly from time to time that he could not continue to bear the heavy responsibility for the well-being and survival of Britain if he were not given the means to defend it.

He did in fact establish important committees to study the evidence and to propose the response. The results were the White Papers of 1935 and 1936, each timed uncannily within days of a German stroke. Real progress was made, and if, to be sure, it was not enough, then perhaps it represented the limit of what public opinion would accept. It is paradoxical that in the bitter years of the war, none reviled Baldwin more than those that had preached disarmament and fought every measure, however timid, of adequate defense.

The Labour Party, grounded in an internationalist philosophy, diagnosing capitalism as the primary cause of war, inherently suspicious of the integrity of its own Government, which it was inclined chiefly to blame for all the world's ills, Hitler included, offered no support to a realistic response to the German threat. To the contrary, it preached disarmament, scorned war as an instrument of national policy, and was on principle in active opposition to the provision of an adequate defense.

The Labour Party was, nonetheless, a distinct minority in Parliament. Facing the critical decisions of 1935, the British Government was confronted with a far more massive, broad-based force that seemed to it to speak in peremptory tones. This was public opinion, as Lord Cecil had conceived and organized it, and it spoke, in an election year, with the voices of eleven million electors.

These were the Peace Balloters. They voted for peace. They voted for disarmament. They voted for the League of Nations as the vehicle by which British foreign policy was to be conducted. There were, of course, inherent contradictions in the Peace Ballot, and there were conditions and clauses that all may not have appreciated or weighed equally. The results could be most easily judged using the lowest common denominator.

Churchill later wrote that Lord Cecil and his colleagues came to understand the need for arms and, as events showed, would fight for a righteous cause. But, Churchill said, the Peace Ballot's "name overshadowed its purpose...in the meanwhile, the Peace Ballot was a heavy deterrent upon necessary action both in military preparations and foreign policy."[10]

Of Baldwin it was said that he feared equally losing an election and returning to the trenches. He heard the voice of eleven million electors and assured Lord Cecil and his deputation that the League of Nations was indeed and would be the sheet anchor of British policy. At Geneva, Hoare specifically referred to the Peace Ballot in endorsing its results and applying them without limit to the upholding of the Covenant of the League of Nations. Prudence immediately thereafter dictated a less ambitious policy, but the influence of the Peace Ballot continued unabated. In the General Election of 1935, the Peace Ballot was incorporated in almost literal terms into the Government's electoral program, which was garnished with symbols, words, and phrases ringingly reminiscent of what its adherents had dubbed "the Cause."

Here then was the vital force that doomed the Hoare-Laval proposals to defeat. It has been suggested that the public response was less overwhelming than had been perceived at the time, that instead it was the attitudes and actions of the members of Parliament that produced the verdict. Lord Cecil had anticipated this. Each prospective member of Parliament had been carefully interrogated by the League of Nations Union on the issues of the Peace Ballot, on the League of Nations and on its place in British policy, and forcibly reminded of what eleven million electors had said.

When the proposals were before Parliament, Lord Cecil's forces took vigorous action to remind the members of Parliament of their answers and pledges and appealed effectively to the sense of honor that those pledges evoked a scant month later. Whether in the last analysis the rejection of the proposals had its fundamental origin in mass public opinion, or in the reaction of individual members of Parliament to the positions they had declared and on which they had secured election, the role of the League of Nations Union in orchestrating the result is clear to see.

On March 7, 1936 there was, as Eden reported, literally no one willing to respond to Hitler. If Hoare-Laval was seen as a betrayal of the Peace Ballot and the election pledges it inspired, if Italy was seen as the Covenant breaker, the warmonger, and the ultimate foe of the moral order, then by this very comparison, Hitler's coup evoked no response. Germany was, after all, not a member of the League of Nations; its action had taken place on its own territory and, as it happened, totally peacefully. Neither the principles of the Peace Ballot nor the moral commitment that inspired it seemed to the British public to be offended by the remilitarization of the Rhineland. It was, after all, only the vital interests of the British Empire that were at stake.

Perhaps Toynbee was perceptive when he wrote his review of 1935 and asked if the Peace Balloters had not voted for "a contingency for which they had no stomach, in the hope that 'something would turn up' to save them from the necessity of having to make the painful choice between honoring their words and eating them."[11]

But the Peace Ballot did not spring full blown from the forehead of Lord Cecil. He did not write on a clean slate. Behind the Peace Ballot were the attitudes, the ideas, and the passions that the years since the war had nourished.

There was, at the bottom of it all, the horror of war, both war as the generation of the thirties had known it and the even more terrible war they feared. Amid the economic storms and political stresses of the thirties, the awful sacrifices of 1914–18 seemed quite out of proportion to the results, or, indeed all in vain when one compared contemporary life to the years before the war, shining as they did with a golden glow that existed perhaps more in memory than in reality.

What loomed ahead was more terrible than the trenches—the assurance that another war meant the end of civilization, great cities obliterated in instants, the earth smothered in poison gas and racked with high explosives raining down from the sky. The fear of war was a potent force in making the war that came inevitable.

To the generation which had been instructed that the causes of war were economic, that they were instigated and fought to enrich the Merchants of Death and that there was no way that the gains of war could compensate for the losses of war, peace at any price might seem a practical bargain. Morality counseled this. Wars and the arms that sustain them were an unmitigated evil. The still influential voice of the churches preached in this vein and was heard by the faithful.

The public was gulled by the master confidence man, Adolf Hitler, his cries of injustice and protestations of peace. They believed what they wanted desperately to believe.

"Who could in 1934–37 have foreseen Hitler's development?"[12] The question would have lain better in the mouth of an ordinary man in the street, concerned for his daily bread, his attention distracted from the struggle by the sporting pages and lurid reports of popular sensations. The question came instead, in 1940, from Tom Jones, the confidant of Prime Ministers, the perennial guest at Blickling and Cliveden, the ultimate insider.

Toynbee castigated those "who merely wished to make a gesture so long as they could be certain of making it without seriously imperiling their own comfort."[13] But his own analysis of the Abyssinian crisis was equally impaired by his ultimate conclusion that British policy suffered because of "the prevailing lack of a lively faith in ultimate spiritual principles."[14]

There was, too, the undue reliance on the League of Nations, which Lord Cecil and LNU so assiduously propagated. There was a logic in this; in 1914 the balance of power had failed and the consequences had been cataclysmic. But the League was novel, it was incomplete, it had no guiding executive and for means of enforcement only what its members volunteered. National sovereignty remained unimpaired and national interests untouched. There was faith, too, in the power of economic sanctions to curb warlike appetites and this had been another of Lord Cecil's guiding lights.

To Lord Cecil there were only two choices: full enforcement of the Covenant by the League of Nations or a return to the naked balance of power. The perspective of time indicates perhaps a third way, a way that Pierre Laval sensed and tried to work. The League was an enormously useful forum for the expression of international opinion, for the venting of grievances, and for the resolution of disputes within the limits of its power and processes. All this was, of course, in addition to its mighty accomplishments in dealing with the less political issues of labor, health, and international administration. It could speak with some authority to the smaller powers and often bring about the coincidence between their self-interest and acceptable dispute resolution.

With the Great Powers, the League was in a far weaker position. Yet it was not without merits and opportunities. The League could offer the Great Powers a decent cover for the clash of interests, a device which they could use to arrange their affairs, to save face, to keep up appearances, all of which are vital aspects of diplomacy. It could be a cloak for compromises which, if they reflected the realities of power, made of the balance of power not just a shoot-out at high noon but an acceptable part of a system of international law, a system, moreover, which might grow and strengthen as the League resolved conflicts, not perhaps on the basis of perfect justice or the literal application of the words of the Covenant, but without utterly denying the principles on which the Covenant was based.

The choice lay, then, not solely between the Covenant and the balance of power. The balance of power operating within the structure of the League and paying lip service to the Covenant might have been a better way.

The Hoare-Laval proposals surely rewarded aggression, and surely bore heavily on the innocent to the profit of the guilty. But a compromise, sponsored by the League of Nations, and accepted, however reluctantly by the parties to the dispute, might have enhanced the League, saved Italy for the front against Hitler and advanced the cause of international conciliation, all the while preserving to Haile Selassie his throne. As it happened, the results were quite the opposite and an unmitigated disaster.

War came. It did not end civilization. The weapon that evoked the greatest horror, that was most feared was, in the end, never used. London survived, even Berlin and Tokyo, and civilization, in Europe and in the world, has recorded creditable progress since. Economic sanctions in the form of the British blockade had not broken Germany in the First World War but only the defeat of the Germany armies in the field. In the Second World War German armaments factories reached their peak production in the summer of 1944 under the hail of Allied bombing and were stopped only when the Allied armies occupied the ground on which those plants stood.

Thus were the hopes and illusions of the British people frustrated and the principles for which they voted in the Peace Ballot became the instruments of the consequences they most feared.

Britain knew the nature and extent of the threat. Its leaders knew, its people had ample evidence before them had they wished to know, as many did. France always knew and always tried desperately to act on that knowledge. Baldwin stated the danger clearly. He pushed for rearmament to the extent that seemed possible within the limits of that public opinion which Lord Cecil had so carefully gauged as the ultimate sanction.

The lapses of British diplomacy are plain. But it operated under limits that the public imposed. The confusion engendered by morality and its place in international affairs and the conflict between principle and interest were brilliantly illustrated in the Peace Ballot of which the fatal providence was to address the wrong issues at the wrong time.

So Britain, in response to the overwhelming voice of the British people, chose Abyssinia over Austria. Indicting Italy and losing sight of Germany, Britain proceeded to push a reluctant Mussolini into alliance with Germany, completely failing to respond to the greatest crisis from which Hitler emerged, the Rhineland in hand, to carry out a plan far more criminal and infinitely more damaging than the Italian aggression in Africa. All this it did, sadly enough, betraying its French ally at critical steps along the way.

But, it is said, the duty of leaders is to lead; and with a powerful Government majority in hand, Baldwin should have led the public to the policy the times required. Could he have survived Hoare-Laval, backing it to a conclusion? Many who sat in the seats of power thought not, and Baldwin agreed. No one spoke up for a counter-thrust in the Rhineland.

A comparison is instructive. President Roosevelt had incomparable popularity, authority, and large majorities in Congress. Alert to the danger, he did what lay within his power, trading, in a critical moment, destroyers for bases, sending American troops to Iceland, and the American Navy to guard the flow of shipping to Britain. Yet, in the summer of 1940, an unarmed America was only a distant spectator in Britain's finest hour, and the destruction of the Soviet armies and the conquest of Russia could have been attained without an American response. The American public wanted peace and war came only when the Japanese attacked Pearl Harbor. On December 8, the United States declared war on Japan, and on Japan only. It was left to Hitler and Mussolini to declare war on the United States on December 11, and then, and only then, did America become fully engaged in the war it had sought to avoid. In all this, Roosevelt has received a different judgment of history then has been awarded to Stanley Baldwin.

## Some Enigmas of History

The story of the years 1933–36 contains fascinating problems for the historian. What, indeed, was the bargain Laval made with Mussolini in Rome in January, 1935, and did Laval give Mussolini the signal for war in Africa? Laval vehemently denied this. His own and the evidence of others, and especially his final exchange of letters with Mussolini weigh the balance in Laval's favor; surely he gave a free hand economically to Italy, waiving French interests in Italy's favor, but without sanctioning war.

What happened at Stresa, and did Mussolini make clear there his intentions in Africa? It is an oft told tale that in reviewing the final communique, Mussolini read these words:

> The three powers, the object of whose policy is the collective maintenance of peace within the framework of the League of Nations find themselves in complete agreement in opposing by all practicable means the unilateral repudiation of treaties which may endanger the peace.

and paused, inquiring significantly, whether it was not necessary to add after "endanger the peace" the words "of Europe." So the final communiqué appeared.

Documents now available show the words "of Europe" appeared in earlier drafts.[15] If the story is less dramatic, nevertheless the words retain their significance and, by any canon of legal interpretation, exclude their application outside Europe. In all events, Abyssinia was carefully ignored by the British representatives at Stresa.

Would the oil sanction have forced Mussolini's capitulation? This is another well known story told by Hitler's interpreter, Dr. Schmidt. In 1938, he reported, Mussolini told Hitler that had the oil sanction been put into effect "I would have had to withdraw from Abyssinia within a week. That would have been an incalculable disaster for me."[16]

Among his many skills, Mussolini was a practiced actor. Keeping face with Hitler was a necessity in 1938. Was this a literal statement of fact or the gossip of dictators and the proud boast of a vain man how nerve and bluff had succeeded over timidity and weakness? Such an anecdote might have been timely on the eve of Munich.

The testimony of experts leads to different conclusions. The League's Committee of Experts reported in February, 1936, that an oil sanction could become effective if all major producers joined in it, and only after a period of three and one-half months. If it be granted that Laval's parliamentary difficulties in early December were genuine, of which there should be little doubt, and if the December 12 meeting date of the Committee of Eighteen to consider the oil sanction is taken as an index date, then it will be seen that within two and one-half months of that date, Italy had won decisive victories at Amba Aradam and in Shire, utterly destroying the armies of Ras Mulugeta, Ras Kassa, and Ras Imru, leaving the road to Addis Ababa barred only by the Emperor's last army facing overwhelming odds.

Would all of the oil producing nations have, in that time, joined in an effective oil sanction, and if they had, would Mussolini, victory in sight, have reembarked his victorious armies for Italy, leaving the Abyssinians in possession of the field for a second time? Eden rests his case on Schmidt's anecdote, and perhaps that anecdote led him to Suez. The facts are not quite so clear as Eden makes them.

Would Mussolini have gone to war with Britain if an oil sanction had been imposed? The only answer here is that it was not and we will never know.

Would Mussolini have accepted the Hoare-Laval proposals? With his armies minimally inside Abyssinian borders, the uncertainties of the campaign, including the Abyssinian offensive yet to come, and the European situation vexed, Mussolini was in December in a compromising mood, as he clearly signaled. He had, of course, at the same time and in public to maintain the bellicose stance which had placed the Italian armies at war in Africa.

The Hoare-Laval proposals had much to offer Italy: recognition of land already conquered and imposing opportunities for development in the South under terms which amounted to Italian hegemony if not sovereignty. Mussolini clearly had the voice and skills to proclaim this a major triumph.

There is ample evidence that he convened a meeting of the Fascist Grand Council timely to act upon the proposals and even that announcements had been prepared indicating that Italy was prepared to negotiate on their basis.

Again, we cannot know because, on the eve of the Italian reply, word was received in Rome of Hoare's resignation. Compromise was clearly out and Mussolini gloomily pursued the path on which he had embarked, through Abyssinian battles to ultimate victory.

The sanctions imposed, and they were early and meaningful, had not diverted or delayed Mussolini. In the end sanctions were maintained after the Italian victory was complete, indicating, perhaps, that an important function of sanctions is to vent the indignation and outraged morality of the sanctionists.

Would Hitler have retreated before a French riposte in the Rhineland? The estimable Dr. Schmidt who reported that Mussolini would have yielded to the oil sanction also records Hitler's assertion that he would have been forced to retreat.[17] Historians today are not so sure. "[W]e now know," one of the most eminent has concluded, "that Hitler would at least have tried to fight—he was quite mad enough for that."[18]

The stakes were overwhelming and Hitler's determination and conviction are well known. Perhaps, like Mussolini, his table talk was intended to glorify his own daring and emphasize what he came increasingly to believe, the cravenness of the military officers who served his will. At all events, he was not put to the test.

## How It All Ended

By mid-1936, there was a new constellation of power in Europe. Italy, instigator of the Stresa Front, was becoming and would become Germany's partner and ally. The German army was firmly established in the Rhineland where the work of fortification and military preparation went on at a fevered pace. France's Eastern allies were isolated from the hope of effective French aid. Germany's military and economic power instead increasingly dominated Central and Southeastern Europe.

All this took place without any really compensating gains in collaboration between Britain and France; instead, the reversion to neutrality of Belgium in the fall was a severe setback to Allied cooperation.

Now came the familiar historical landmarks of the second half of the thirties—the Spanish Civil War, the Anschluss, Munich, Prague, and Hitler's war. Hitler had played a shrewd and risky game and he had won resoundingly. He had been farsighted, decisive, and had appealed with remarkable success to the weaknesses and illusions of his adversaries. Behind it all was the threat of the military force he had built and continued to build.

Mussolini, too, had taken great risks, had displayed great courage, boldness, and his usual flair for public utterance. He won an empire in Africa but the century was out of joint for colonial aggrandizement.

Hitler was intensely single-minded. Mussolini saw both sides. Hitler did not choose between alternatives; like a sleepwalker he proceeded in utter assurance. Mussolini faced his choices and in the end, the choice he made was not the one he preferred, but the one he saw thrust upon him by circumstances. If he could not do business with the British and the French, then to gain an empire he would do business with Hitler.

The results, of course, were disastrous for both Mussolini and Hitler and led only to suicide in the Berlin bunker and the sordid spectacle of the corpses of Mussolini and Clara Petacci hanging by their heels in the public square of Milan.

Haile Selassie lived on in impoverished exile in England, an embarrassment to the government which had promised what it failed to perform. In Abyssinia, Graziani ruled by murder and terror for the first year of the Italian victory, attempting to liquidate the Abyssinian intelligentsia and exacting bloody revenge for an attempt on his life.

His successor was as humane and just as Graziani had been cruel and repressive. He was Amadeo, Duke of Aosta, cousin of the King. His short tenure of four years was marked by an effective administration and by an immense outpouring of Italian investment and energy for which there could be no short-term return. The roads, the schools, the hospitals, the public works and institutions which Italy built in Abyssinia had never been before and the benefit was inestimable. Truly, the Emperor later remarked, the genius of the Italians was not to fight but to build.

While resistance continued in Abyssinia, the embittered Emperor wondered whether he had not erred in refusing an Italian protectorate.[19] He negotiated with the Vatican and Italy for his abdication, declining an offer of a million pounds because the parties could not reach agreement on all of the terms. A year later he sought to reopen negotiations, but it was too late.[20]

In 1941, the Emperor returned to Africa, a figurehead for a motley collection of British and native troops and old Africa hands of whom Orde Wingate was by no means the most colorful. In a short, sharp campaign, together with the Free French they defeated the Italian armies not only in Abyssinia but in the sometime Italian colonies of Somaliland and Eritrea.

Five years to the day after he had fled, the Emperor returned to Addis Ababa. He counseled humanity to the Italians, lest victory be tarnished, and the picture of Haile Selassie restored and the Italians routed was an important symbol, while the war remained wholly at issue, of the triumph of justice over the aggressor.

As always, behind the symbol there was the reality, and the reality was a bitter one for Haile Selassie. Rather than liberation he found the British in firm control of Abyssinia, military and civil, and the King of Kings was pressed "to agree to abide in all important matters, internal and external, by the advice tendered to them by His Majesty's Government in the United Kingdom."[21]

When he attempted to appoint cabinet ministers and a governor of the central province of Shoa, the British commander instructed him that he could not resume his status and powers as Emperor until a peace treaty with Italy was signed, adding, remarkably, "Until that happens the King of Italy remains the legal ruler of Ethiopia."[22]

When an Anglo-Ethiopian agreement was signed in January, 1942, Sir Phillip Mitchell and his staff arrived first and received the humiliated Emperor on the steps of his own palace.[23] When Rommel stood at El Alamein later in the year, the Emperor intrigued with the Italian underground to undermine the British occupation forces in Abyssinia.[24]

Long after the war, far into the fifties, as the winds of change blew across Africa and the bonds of Empire loosened, British projects were continually pressed for the inclusion of the Ogaden into British Somaliland, as foreshadowed by Colonel Stewart's 1934 march to the wells of Wal Wal.[25] The Empire died hard in the Horn of Africa and in its dealings with Abyssinia did not act out of the pure and disinterested motives that Eden, Hoare, and Baldwin had so fervently proclaimed.

Haile Selassie remained at heart and in practice an absolute monarch. In the postwar years there was progress in education and administration as Abyssinia advanced toward a more modern society. But there was never any question of democracy or political parties; the Emperor's goal remained what it had been since 1930—the centralization of power.

As he aged, he became erratic. After a coup failed in 1960, the traditional Abyssinian struggle for power continued as the Emperor verged on senility An Abyssinian observer later remarked that "the palace had become an empty house, free for its taking."[26]

Taken it was by a military junta called the Derg. First using the Emperor as a front, they consolidated power, and in November, 1974, machine-gunned down sixty ministers and leaders of the former regime, recording the bloody scene on film under floodlights.[27]

Haile Selassie remained a prisoner in his palace, living the senile dream that he was still Emperor, until in August 1975, he disappeared. No one knows how he died; few noted his passing.[28]

Pierre Laval was the statesman who had seen most clearly, after Barthou's assassination, the need for a working combination to curb the German threat. With realism and skill he set out to build that combination and in the process displayed candor, persistence, and courage to an uncommon degree. He also displayed the flexibility for which he has been so universally condemned. It is perhaps better to be flexible in pursuit of realistic goals than inflexible in pursuit of unrealistic goals. Thus, for instance, could the diplomacy of Pierre Laval be contrasted to the diplomacy of Neville Chamberlain.

That is, of course, another story, the story of the years from mid-1936 to September 1, 1939. Pierre Laval took no active role in French politics after his resignation in January 1936, nor indeed, until France collapsed in June 1940.

In March, 1940, just before the deluge, Robert Boothby, a British member of Parliament who had fervently opposed the Hoare-Laval compromise, called on Laval in Paris. Laval asked if he might speak seriously about the situation:

> We are all agreed now that the best chance of stopping Hitler was when he sent his troops into the Rhineland; and that we failed. I know that you think that the last chance was at Munich. I disagree. The last chance was at Stresa. Austria, not Czechoslovakia, was the essential bastion of central Europe. Only one power could have saved Austria and that was Italy. We could have had Italy. But the price was Abyssinia. It was well worth paying; and, believe me, it would have been of benefit, not harm, to the Ethiopians.

Stresa, Laval said, had been the critical moment. Boothby commented on MacDonald's reluctance to face facts, for which very reason, he said, the MacDonald government suited the British so admirably. "Well," Laval said,

> it was unfortunate for us all that he refused to face the unpalatable fact of Abyssinia at Stresa, because Mussolini mistook his silence for agreement instead of imbecility; and his subsequent disillusion threw him into the arms of Germany, with the result that we lost Austria, and with it the whole of central Europe.

With Italy, Germany could have been contained. "Not now," Laval said,

> We have given most of Europe to Hitler, let us try to hold on to what we have got left. I am a peasant from the Auvergne. I want to keep my farm, and I want to keep France. Nothing else matters now.

The French army, Laval said, was badly led, and demoralized in its defensive positions. Armor was needed. The heart of France was not in the war. The Germans, he predicted, would attack and defeat French in three weeks. What would be left? Only to come to terms.[29]

The role of Pierre Laval in wartime France is outside the scope of this work. Conversely, his performance as Foreign Minister and Prime Minister in 1934–36 must be judged by the record he made then, and not by what he did or failed to do years later or the reputation he acquired thereby.

For his role in the Pétain government he was promptly indicted on the day of victory. His trial was less a judicial proceeding than a calculated act of vengeance. The pretrial examination which is an integral part of criminal proceedings in France was cut short, depriving Laval of vital opportunities to make his record. His personal papers and the official documents needed for his defense were sequestered and withheld, nor was he able to call witnesses in his defense. So deprived was he of the opportunity to prepare for trial that his lawyers, with the assent of the Batonnier of the Paris bar, declined to participate in the trial. Alone, Laval conducted a fierce but well-argued defense until, in the face of the naked hostility of judge and jury, he boycotted the trial as hopeless, refusing, he said, to become an accomplice in a judicial crime.

The trial opened on October 4, 1945. Judgment of death was rendered on October 10 and the execution set for October 15. Laval bore all this with immense courage and spiritual grace. De Gaulle refused any appeal but granted that, at the hands of the firing squad, Laval had "died bravely"[30] while the judge and the prosecutor who were required by law to attend the execution cowered out of sight.

These were among the last words he wrote:

> I ask that my tricolor scarf be left with me. I want to keep it for the long journey....
>
> I give my last salute to the France that I have served. My last thought is for her.[31]

Britain reserves a kindlier fate for her statesmen, especially when they have failed. Sir John Simon, having been succeeded by Hoare as Foreign Secretary, remained a leading figure in the Government as Home Secretary and then Lord Chancellor, a post to which his talents were eminently more suited than diplomacy. He entered the House of Lords as Viscount Simon and his honors matched his years.

Not long after his resignation as Foreign Secretary, Sir Samuel Hoare returned to the Cabinet as First Lord of the Admiralty. Like Simon, he was a member of the Big Four that under Chamberlain dominated government. In wartime he served usefully as Ambassador to Spain. A grateful government rewarded his services to the state with a peerage and as Viscount Templewood, he lived elegantly and devoted himself to literature and sport.

To his credit, he resigned when his and Laval's compromise settlement was rejected by his Government, and he never ceased to pronounce, firmly and cogently, that his policy had been right.

His problem was to have spoken in two voices. If Hoare-Laval was right, then he was clearly wrong to have spoken so ardently and seemingly so unambiguously in Geneva in September. If the policy of September was right, then the policy of December was wrong. In defense, he pleaded that more had been read into his speech than he had said or meant to say. The public is not so sophisticated or critically adept in parsing the pronouncements of statesmen and is burdened with a tendency to hear what it wishes to hear.

Baldwin did not resign, incurred an immense loss of prestige over his management of Hoare-Laval, then retrieved much of it by his adroit handling of the abdication of Edward VIII. In wartime he was adjudged chief among the Guilty Men. This was unjust.

Eden had profited from Hoare's dismissal and added luster to his reputation when he was forced by Chamberlain to resign in 1938. At last Prime Minister in succession to Churchill, he tried to apply the lessons he had learned in the 1930s to a very different world of the 1950s. He regarded the appropriate use of force against an overreaching and fundamentally weak dictator as a lesson learned. There was another lesson, and this he had failed to learn. Polls showed that no more than half the British people approved the use of military force at Suez.[32] Though Eden, like Baldwin held his party majority, he was very shortly compelled to change his policy, retreat, and not long after resign.

Mr. Boorman, whose Ilford poll had inspired the Peace Ballot, gained public notice once more. The January 14, 1937 *Times* reported the award to him as Hon. Secretary of the Ilford branch of the Royal National Lifeboat Institution of a statuette of a lifeboatman.

In 1937, Lord Cecil was awarded the Nobel Peace Prize. His presenter, Christian Louis Lange, a member of the selection committee, aptly sketched his character:

> [C]learly, Lord Cecil is of a fundamentally religious temperament—of the High Church Episcopalian stamp. Listening to him speak from the rostrum is often like listening to a venerable Bishop preaching the revealed truth. But he also has other strings to his bow in addition to that of the preacher; he is a skillful lawyer, a quick-witted debater, and, when the occasion demands, a shrewd tactician. His tall, now somewhat bowed figure is imposing. But, even when he just smiles, one can always sense the underlying earnestness of purpose. The conversion from his youthful indifference to the problem of peace, to the profound conviction of its central importance which he now holds in maturity has been perhaps the most momentous experience of his life.[33]

He was never a pacifist. He saw more clearly than the Peace Balloters the need, if belated, for arms and opposed Munich.

At his age, he found no new employment in the Second World War. He appeared once more on the world stage at the final meeting of the Assembly of the League of Nations, in Geneva on April 8, 1946. Lord Cecil had conceived the plan for a League of Nations and the League as it emerged bore the stamp of his hand and mind. He had been its greatest champion, as a delegate, as an advocate, and as the chief promoter of that mass support which he saw as the essential condition of success.

Wilson, Clemenceau, Lloyd George, Streseman, Briand, the apostles of the postwar order were long dead, long absent from the world arena. At eighty, Lord Cecil looked back, not at the failures and the shattered hopes of the past but at the constructive work that had been done by the League which would make possible a better organization in a wiser world. His last salute was as eloquent and timely as it was simple: "The League is dead. Long live the United Nations."[34]

In the sunset of the Empire over which his father had presided, Lord Cecil lived to a ripe and serene old age. Concerned with the disharmonies he found between the King James Bible and the Revised Version, he produced a characteristic solution. He wrote his own Bible, a collated text which, he hoped, would combine the poetry and inspiration of the old with the clarity and scholarship of the new. His manuscript found no publisher, but Lord Cecil had never been daunted by disappointment.[35]

At ninety-one, he was at work on a memorandum entitled "The Condition of Europe." With his wife, he celebrated their seventieth wedding anniversary. Childless, they were devoted to the end, which for him came on November 24, 1958 and for her, mercifully, five months later.

From his life and work, useful lessons may be drawn. Morality alone is an inadequate guide to the policy of nations. National interests, however hard to quantify and define, are an essential component of that policy. Principles are helpful, but wrongly applied can mislead. Perhaps, as in the common law, the law of nations will be better built by the painful resolution of hard cases establishing precedents for the future than by recourse to sweeping principles and the slogans in which they sometimes masquerade.

This puts a premium on leadership which must analyze, define, explain, and exhort. But in democracies, the more so as channels of communication and access to information proliferate, Lord Cecil's message retains its validity. Public opinion retains its ultimate authority, enjoining upon the public the heavy responsibility to listen, to think, and, as free of passion and moral posturing as may be humanly possible, to pass upon leaders and policies judgments that combine, in Pierre Laval's words, prudence and principle[36] and that recognize that the clash of national interests is seldom solved by absolutes.

# Epilogue

*"The veils of the future are lifted one by one, and mortals must act day by day."*
—Winston Churchill[1]

## Man and History

Shortly after men began to record history, they started to ask themselves—and each other—What Does It All Mean? Was there some system, some rule, some Grand Design to history? So the perennial question was raised—Do men make history? Or does history make men? This raised another series of questions. Were historians philosophers? Or did philosophers need to be historians?

There was a seductive charm in the pursuit of an all-purpose explanation of how history worked. It appealed not only to the professionals, but also to the laymen, like Adolf Hitler who was nothing if not a system maker. There was an added attraction. If you knew the laws of history, if you deduced how history worked, you could then with some assurance predict the future. This would raise historians to a level far above the tarot cards and the crystal ball.

So it came to the German philosopher Hegel that there was a whole which, in all of its complexity he called the Absolute, or sometimes the Idea: "The world of intelligence and conscious volition is not abandoned to chance, but must show itself in the light of the self-cognizant Idea."[2]

Hegel then invented a process he called the dialectic which, if it were properly followed, would reveal the whole in so far as it then existed and—this was the goal—as it must in the future exist in accordance with the inexorable denouement of the dialectic.

From all of this he deduced that there were three phases of historical development. There were the Oriental, in which *one* is free and the Greek and Roman in which *some* were free.

The reader will not be surprised to learn that the highest phase of historical development, which Hegel believed inevitable, was the German. In this climactic phase, *all* would be free though Bertrand Russell warns that Hegel's freedom might not be what you would suppose freedom to be.

Hegel's Determinism (which is also called Historicism), the idea that every event has its causes and is indeed fully determined by its causes and that you can predict the future if you know and understand the causes that will produce it, found favor among nineteenth-century historians. This was especially true as the laws of science were increasingly revealed, raising the issue whether similarly inexorable laws did not govern history. That there was a law of progress operating in history was in an optimistic era an increasingly compelling theory.

Karl Marx liberally imbibed his Hegel. He substituted class for nations in the operation of the dialectic which, he concluded, must work its way from feudalism to capitalism and inevitably to the dictatorship of the proletariat, followed by the freedom that would reign when the state withered away. He was, as Bertrand Russell has aphorized, not the salesman of socialism (he didn't need to sell the inevitable) but only its prophet.

In *War and Peace* Tolstoy created an epic history of the convulsions of Europe in the Napoleonic era, the vast tides of history flowing once eastward to Moscow, then reversing course and flowing westward to Paris. He peopled his epic with real historical personages, Napoleon and Czar Alexander I, and added to them the fictional characters to whom he imparted life and showed in all their humanity. When he had done all this, he retired to ponder the perennial question—What Did It All Mean? The answers he propounded are found in the essay on history which is the Epilogue to *War and Peace*.

Writing history, the life of peoples and of humanity, Tolstoy declared is "impossible." This didn't stop him from trying. Could it be, he asked, that Chance and Genius rule history? Or were not Napoleon and Alexander, far from acting of their own wills and their own determination, acting instead in response to the forces that produced them, the French Revolution and Mother Russia. Were they controlling or controlled by history?

Tolstoy paints a haunting picture. The Napoleonic drama is over:

> The act is performed.
>
> The last part is played. The actor is bidden to undress, to wash off his powder and paint; he will be needed no more.
>
> And for several years this man in solitude on his island plays his pitiful

farce to himself, intrigues and lies justifying his conduct when a justification is no longer needed and shows all the world what the thing was that men took for power when an unseen hand guided it.

The stage manager, when the drama is over, and the puppets stripped showed him to us.

Look what you believed in. Here he is. Do you not see that it was not he but I that moved you?

But, blinded by the force of the moment, men could not perceive that.[3]

There was bound to be another view. Its nineteenth-century champion was Thomas Carlyle who proposed the Hero as the motivating force of history and who concluded that,

> the history of what man has accomplished in this world is at bottom the History of Great Men who have worked here. They were leaders of men, these Great Men, the modellers, patterns, and in a wide sense creators of whatsoever the general mass of men contrived to do or to attain; all things that we see accomplished in the world are properly the outer material result, the practical realization and embodiment of thoughts that dwelled in Great Men sent into the world; the soul of the whole world's history it may be justly conceived, were the history of these.[4]

Later historians gradually began to see that the issue might not be so simple as whether history made men or men made history. They began to understand that instead of discovering history and its mechanisms as objective facts, the historian selects, edits, and refines the facts, interpreting them as he will, out of his own culture, his education and out of the resources available to him. In that light far from being on the sidelines as an observer and scorekeeper, the historian was actively engaged in and a part of the process he called history.

It is neither within the scope of this work nor the ability of its author to resolve these hardy perennial questions of history and philosophy. But there is here an extraordinary, a stunning example of what one man could and did accomplish that historians and philosophers would do well to consider in parsing the claims of Determinism, of Historicism, and of the autonomy, the primacy of the individual.

Lord Cecil's persona did not seem to be determined by his upbringing in one of the stateliest of stately homes, the son of Queen Victoria's Prime Minister. Instead, he was the Eton boy who wouldn't properly roll his umbrella, the young man who hated parties, went to the races once and never again, and roundly condemned the moral position of his numerous brothers-in-law, all pillars of the Establishment, an Establishment, by the way where he and his wife felt like fish out of water.

He was by his own admission an uncomfortable colleague and nothing in his career in public office so distinguished him as his repeated resignations on grounds, as he saw it, of principle.

When he saw the League of Nations, of which he had been a prime mover, faltering, when he saw the Disarmament Conference, for which he had worked and planned for a decade and of which he was a luminary fail, he decided to take matters into his own two hands.

His aim was as simple as it was grandiose—to compel the British government to reverse its course one hundred and eighty degrees and convert its tepid participation in the League of Nations, its ingrained and long-standing horror of foreign commitments including those inherent in the League, into full-blown and active support for collective security under the mantle and leadership of the League.

To achieve his aim, Cecil acted as a private citizen. The Peace Ballot was to be determinedly nonpartisan, though it would gather support from political factions wherever it could. He ran the Peace Ballot off the base of a private association, the League of Nations Union, which he had long led and nurtured for just such a purpose. He sounded his trumpet and raised an army of five hundred thousand, all of them acting like himself, as private citizens and it was they who, one by one, by shoe leather, sweat and persistence, gathered in the votes, one by one, that in the end surpassed eleven million, more than had ever voted in a Parliamentary election.

All of this Cecil did with private funds of which he was the chief solicitor and fund raiser, and based on a wholly private organization which he quickly created and shaped to his ends.

He acted from no official position and without the benefits or attributes of power as it is generally understood. Of Hitler it may be asked whether he was the leader or instead the reflection of the German people, the German past, and the German condition. Indeed it is often remarked how uncannily he addressed the German people in terms that they themselves most deeply felt and thought. The Churchill who stood alone, a figure of criticism and even ridicule in the thirties, was also the Churchill who was the voice of the British people in 1940, raising the issue whether Churchill formed the will of the nation or whether the nation expressed itself through Churchill.

Cecil raised and led his army without fear or concern of officialdom and his reward was to hear his aim and his goal adopted and endorsed by the Prime Minister who said in direct response to the Peace Ballot that the League of Nations was and would be the sheet anchor of British policy. This declaration was seconded in even more ringing terms by Sir Samuel Hoare before the League Assembly in Geneva and what is more adopted as the platform on which Baldwin and his government secured a massive election victory.

In the titanic explosion of public emotion and public policy that the Hoare-Laval proposals brought about, it was the forces that Lord Cecil had raised, the ideas he had promoted, the morality he had taught, and the electoral tactics he had so brilliantly orchestrated, that in the end won the day and determined the policy that was in its time to bear its bitter fruit.

It was, as Arnold Toynbee observed, with a ludicrously frank precipitancy that Baldwin bent to Lord Cecil's bow and his spear although in the aftermath the results, which profoundly affected all of the equations of European power, were hardly what Cecil had contemplated in carrying on his campaign. It would be difficult to find other historical examples of an individual—excluding perhaps religious figures—who, operating without the authority and trappings of power, out of his own heart and spirit, out of his own mind and will, imagined, created and led a mighty force to change his country's policy and thereby the course of history. It is an episode of history in which students of historical determinism would do well to study.

## The Avoidable War

If we observe that men can move nations, that nations can move history, and that the course of history is not wholly determined, then it is fair to ask to what extent the Second World War was truly the Avoidable War.

For this thesis there is an eminent authority. Churchill has given us the history of the Second World War in six captivating volumes, to each of which he attaches a theme. This is the theme[5] of the first volume, *The Gathering Storm,* which recounts the origins, the outbreak, and the progress of the war until he took power in 1940:

*How the English-speaking peoples*
*through their unwisdom,*
*carelessness, and good nature*
*allowed the wicked*
*to rearm.*

Had the wicked not been permitted to rearm, they could hardly have waged war. And if it was carelessness and unwisdom that allowed them to do so, then it follows that a wise and careful policy would have avoided the war.

Churchill makes his opinion explicit:

> One day President Roosevelt told me that he was asking publicly for suggestions about what the war should be called. I said at once: The Unnecessary War.
>
> There never was a war more easy to stop than that which has just wrecked what was left of the world from the previous struggle.[6]

It is easy to be seduced by Churchillian eloquence and wise rigorously to examine into the issue.

A pedestrian steps off the curb into the path of an approaching car. The accident was not inevitable and by the exercise of ordinary caution could have been avoided. The homeowner who buys an insurance policy will have avoided loss up to the policy limits should his house burn. If instead of fire his house falls victim to an earthquake, he will anxiously scan his policy to see if he has avoided that loss. Perhaps he thought the premium so high and the risk so improbable that he made a deliberate decision. The lessons are that prudence has its rewards and carelessness and unwisdom their penalties. In foreign policy to combine, in the words of Pierre Laval, prudence and principle is an art.

In foreign policy, as in business or the law, it is important to know your adversary. Carelessness or unwisdom here can exact heavy penalties. Yet the adversary, or potential adversary, may speak with forked tongue. He may talk of peace while preparing for war. In such a case the statesman should take counsel from the experienced chess player who always expects his opponent to make the strongest possible move. The statesman may hope for the best case, but he must be prepared for the worst; to do less is to invite unhappy, perhaps tragic results.

In formulating foreign policy, the relative strength of the parties is a critical consideration. Conciliation and negotiation are vital, but whether in law, business, or foreign policy, one negotiates most effectively from a position of strength. Thus appropriate military force is supremely important and only the careless and unwise will neglect their defenses or suffer their adversaries or potential adversaries to outmatch them.

A country's strength is limited by its population, resources, and industrial base among other considerations. Countries who are overmatched by the resources and manpower of their adversaries will join together in alliances to multiply their strength.

Foreign policy is also based on strategic positions. They made be borderlines or bastions, rivers or harbors, islands or continents. The combination of strength and strategic position is the measure of what is possible in foreign policy and where potency and where weakness lie.

A nation may possess great military strength. It may occupy critical strategic positions. These will avail little or nothing if it lacks the will, the determination to use those forces and to take advantage of those positions.

Both Britain and France were well informed about Hitler, his character, his regime, its goals, and its progress toward those goals. Sir Horace Rumbold, the British Ambassador in Berlin, had read *Mein Kampf* and believed it. Both countries knew about Germany's illegal rearmament in 1933 and 1934 and Germany's military buildup was announced for all the world to see in 1935.

However Hitler talked of peace—and he often did—it was prudent to act upon the facts rather than the words and it was unwise not to prepare for the day when Hitler might disavow his words and thrust forward on the basis of his armed might on the ground and in the skies.

After the failure of the Disarmament Conference, France decided in April, 1934, that she would ensure her security by her own means. It was important that those means should correspond to the threat they faced and that they should take advantage of the available strategic positions. It was not careless, but it was certainly unwise for France to invest all of its defense capital, financial, military, and intellectual, in a purely defensive system that could neither protect its long borders nor by its offensive capability redeem the strategic position that was the Rhineland.

The voices that cried for peace and disarmament in Britain in 1933, 1934 and 1935 were loud and insistent and generated massive support. But it was unwise for Britain to respond to the threat of Hitler with disarmament and when the necessity for rearmament became clear, Britain was always perennially behind Germany in its military strength and that disparity drove Britain to unwise policies.

Mussolini early understood the fatal threat of Nazi Germany and proclaimed himself the protector and defender of Austria which Hitler named his first target outside Germany. He made it his business to rally forces which could and would deter the march of Nazi Germany. Pierre

Laval understood this and composed long-standing issues with Italy. Such an understanding would add the strength of Italy to that of France, make Italian troops available on the Franco-German border and French troops on Italy's Austrian border under circumstances where neither country would have to stand watch on their mutual frontier. Pierre Laval entered into pacts with the Soviet Union and rallied the countries of the Little Entente to the containment of the German threat.

These were wise and careful policies, measuring and meeting the threat. France understood the critical strategic nature of the demilitarized Rhineland which barred Germany from the attack on France and gave France, if it would, the opportunity to invade Germany in support of its central and Eastern European allies. France had recognized the key importance of the demilitarized zone at Versailles and it served its purpose as long as France had the will to defend it.

What was required here was the close adherence of Britain, greatest of the world powers, and its close cooperation in containing a clear and present danger. That was the wise and prudent course and it was precisely the course Britain did not take. Instead, its Cabinet declared, in January, 1935, that the demilitarized Rhineland was not a vital British interest. Mussolini, alarmed by the looming danger of Hitler and Nazi Germany, convened Britain and France at Stresa, as he said, to propound concrete solutions to concrete cases. The Rhineland was such a case. This, too, was both a wise and careful program, but Britain would have none of it, mounting an elaborate deception to avoid any commitment. Immediately following this wasted effort, Britain, far from supporting its allies, entered into a bilateral naval pact with Germany that showed total disregard for the limitations of Versailles which were the safeguards of European peace.

Italy's aggression in Abyssinia created harrowing problems. There were reasons why Britain so often adopted a policy that was both laggard and conflicted. These included the pressures of public opinion, not least of which was its gigantic manifestation, under Lord Cecil's tutelage, in the Peace Ballot. The moral outrage was genuine. It reeked of what Churchill saw as British good nature. That did not make for wise and careful policy.

In this critical juncture of events Sir Samuel Hoare and Pierre Laval labored to resolve the tangled complex of issues—the war in Abyssinia, the defense of Austria, the preservation of the demilitarized zone of the Rhineland. It was, as recounted in these pages, a wise and prudent policy that had its focus not in Africa but on the critical pressure points in Europe: Austria and the Rhineland.

In rejecting the Hoare-Laval pact, the British people put moral considerations, considerations of honor, above the national interest. History rarely records this as wise policy. One fateful day when Germany reoccupied the Rhineland, Britain's vital interests were at stake but there was no support in Britain for France and as a result no determination in France to act on its own. More important, Italy, smarting under the sanctions imposed by the League of Nations under British leadership, backed by France, supported Hitler's Rhineland coup, and disaffected and disconsolate, moved into Hitler's orbit and thereby became his ally—the ally Hitler had always coveted. Hitler had a keener sense of the value of alliances than his adversaries.

Maurice Baumont, the eminent French historian of the Second World War has written,

> Between April 17, 1934, and March 7, 1936, the situation in Europe had completely changed, going from a state of balance, which contained Germany, to the supremacy of the hegemony of Hitler and this in less than two brief years. In 1934 he had been at the mercy of outside forces; with calculated moves he had passed through the most cryptical period of his rearmament. He had broken up the elements assembled to maintain balance.[7]

The consequences were tragic:

> Since the challenge of March 7, 1936, the entire structure of 1919 had been collapsing; the edifice of Versailles was now just a historical memory. It was a terrible blow to French policy and also to British policy though this would only become apparent later. The 'gathering storm' was absolutely certain after March, 1936.[8]

It is not given to us to know the answers to the what ifs of history. They abound in the history of the Second World War. What if Hitler had not ordered his panzers to stop on the line of the Aa River affording a desperately needed breathing space to the Allied forces at Dunkirk? What if Goering had not switched his 1940 bomber offensive from the British fighter bases to London? What if Hitler had started his Russian campaign a month earlier, or concentrated his forces on Moscow? But a mastery of the facts and the application of common sense can begin to suggest some answers. A Britain that wisely appraised the German threat could have rearmed timely to the level that would have permitted it to deal with Germany out of strength rather than fecklessly pursue a bilateral solution with Germany out of weakness. A wise policy would have been to cooperate closely with France and resolve the Abyssinian tangle in a manner that preserved Italy for the defense of Austria and the containment of Germany, at the same time taking concrete steps to preserve and protect the strategic bridgehead on the Rhine. The height of unwisdom was to thrust Italy into the arms of Hitler and present to him, in the disarray of the moment, the golden opportunity to remilitarize the Rhineland. In this moment Britain betrayed a France which, having failed to prepare a military force adequate to the long foreseen crisis, was paralyzed into submission.

Effects have causes and actions beget reactions. Had Britain and France adopted wise policies of strength and unity, combining appropriate military forces, alliances and strategic advantages, they could have acted constructively to protect the peace. By disunity and faithlessness, by naivete and good nature on the part of the British people and their leaders, by carelessness and unwisdom they produced an opposite result. And if Britain and France had based their policies on wisdom and care, Hitler may well have faced a different Germany. A Führer curbed, restrained, shorn of the golden mantle of success that his adversaries draped across his shoulders, might have followed a very different course than that which history records.

If, as Hitler once remarked, with dictators nothing succeeds like success, then the reverse will also be true of failure.

A.J.P. Taylor speculates that the war could have been avoided "by greater firmness or by greater conciliation" but not by the failure consistently to pursue either. A careful review of the actions and omissions of French and especially of British policy in the years from Hitler's ascent to power to the remilitarization of the Rhineland lends substance to Churchill's theme and firm support to his conclusion that the war was as unnecessary as it was avoidable.

## A Fundamental Misunderstanding

Perhaps the prime root of the failure of British and French policy in the thirties was the pervasive misunderstanding that bedeviled both the British and French people and their leaders. Vansittart remarked on their mutual misunderstanding about sex and gastronomy. They had, it was said, a different scale of values which they assigned to stupidity and dishonesty in their statesmen. If the British, in that period, mistook Frenchmen for Germans and Germans for Englishmen, this was a serious obstacle to enlightened policy. There was more truth than jocularity in all these observations which signaled far greater gaps in sympathy and knowledge.

The British found it difficult, if not impossible, to understand the French need for security. If they were not as detached from Europe as they had once been—the bomber, Baldwin told them, will always get through—still when they thought of security, they thought of a threat from the skies and not from the German army rolling across the border. These states of mind inspired radically different responses. Appraising Germany in one phase, where France saw a menace, Britain saw a market. British statesmen found it congenial to ascribe only the highest motives to British policy, and tended to assume that the French were both corrupt and unreliable. In a climatic moment, when French policy was guided by stern practical considerations, British policy was governed by an exalted concept of morality and a massive emotional catharsis. All this was encapsulated in Pierre Laval's lapidary phrase: morals are one thing; the interests of a country are another.

The drama is played out. History has happened. The statesmen and the generals, the citizens and the soldiers, depart the stage. *Exeunt omnes.* It is a new generation. The historians, faithful to their calling, go busily about their work. They are, all of them, inspired by the lofty purpose of learning—and indeed teaching—from the history they write. You might suppose that in the process they would draw conclusions that approximate and even harmonize with the conclusions of their fellows. This, alas, doesn't necessarily follow.

Tolstoy once observed that a historian might offer an explanation of history that seemed perfectly plausible to his reader until he read about the same events as told by another historian of another nationality. The truth of this proposition is amply illustrated by the histories of the years 1933–1936. Two leading historians, one British, A.J.P. Taylor, and one French, Maurice Baumont, have addressed these years and the succeeding years of which the climax came in September, 1939, with the German war on Poland. Each has chosen the same title: *The Origins of the Second World War.*

To Baumont it was not difficult to locate the war's cause. Adolf Hitler was the deus ex machina, the true and proximate cause of the Second World War:

> The drama, stripped of its main characters and of the scenery obscuring it, has the simplicity of an action in which a few characters clash in a conflict of wills. The strongest will remains that of a crafty being filled with demonical guile: Adolf Hitler who plunged Germany into a tragedy beyond measure.[8]

And it was Adolf Hitler who,

> Having grown into the most important figure of the 1930's...provoked the worst catastrophe in European history. He brought more calamities to the world than any other man of modern times.[10]

Quite the contrary, says A.J.P. Taylor. For him Hitler was largely a passive figure, patiently awaiting the turn of events: "Hitler did not plan for world conquest or for anything else. He assumed that others would provide opportunities and that he would seize them."[11] If a once-hostile Mussolini was propelled into Hitler's arms, then he welcomed and profited by that. In Taylor's view, the British offered first Austria, then Czechoslovakia to Hitler and he accepted these gifts. In the end when war came, it was more by blunders than by wickedness. So Taylor is able to conclude: "In international affairs there was nothing wrong with Hitler except that he was a German."[12]

The same kind of split vision is apparent in the treatment by British and French historians of the Hoare-Laval Pact. It was, of course, as easily approved by the French Parliament as it was heatedly disowned in Britain. The French had viewed the pact as logical and rational calculations of the national interest. Baumont measures it by a practical standard: "The Hoare-Laval Plan was not feasible."[13] Laval's more recent French biographers, Jean-Paul Contet[14] and Fred Kupferman[15] outline the substance of the plan and its ultimate fate, but they eschew any analysis or opinion. It was and it failed. For Claude Paillat,[16] the whole incident merits only a passing footnote.

How different is the treatment accorded by the English historians. Not all can match the moral fervor of Arnold Toynbee in his characterization of a tale of sin and retribution. Typical is the epithet by Halifax's biographer, "the Hoare-Laval Pact of evil memory'[17] and Eden's portrait of the "wily" Laval and description of "the full depth of Laval's scheme."[18]

Geoffrey Warner in his biography of Laval and Frank Hardie in his history of the Abyssinian War, put forth fair statements of the issues, the benefits, and the detriments of the plan. Warner concludes it was, like Laval's overall policy, a total failure[19] and his presentation of Leon Blum's grand philippic against Laval in the French Parliament amply portrays the thinking and the flavor of the fervent condemnation of Laval on moral grounds.

In the same vein, Hardie sets out in compelling terms the argument against the plan that it was "plainly immoral." [20] The reasons for this spread of opinion may be found in the times out of which the opinions arose. The subsequent career of Pierre Laval has cast a shadow upon his policies and his acts, his successes and his failures in the 1930s. It has made it difficult, at least up to the present, to put him center stage, more difficult perhaps to praise him. To the contrary the British experience of Hoare-Laval was based on a moral and ethical tempest in which so many had reason to take pride for so long that a balanced appraisal today does not flow easily from the historian's pen.

Except, of course, from the pen of that veteran contrarian A.J.P. Taylor:

> Yet this was a perfectly sensible plan, in the line of the League's previous acts of conciliation from Corfu to Manchuria. It would have ended the war, satisfied Italy, and left Abyssinia with a far more workable national territory. The common sense of the plan was in the circumstances of the time, its vital defect.[21]

Time may prove kindly to this view. Earlier standard histories of the Second World War refer to "the notorious Hoare-Laval plan"[22] and one of Churchill's biographers calls it "opera bouffe."[23] More recently Henry Kissinger has accorded the plan his highest accolade—Realpolitik.[24] That the plan and its failure were a critical stage on the road to the Second World War is the firm conclusion of this work and the contribution it offers to history.

## Some Lessons of History

If historians discharge the weighty task of writing history and readers accomplish the weighty and sometimes tedious task of reading it, then there ought to be some benefit, some dividend flowing from these processes. It does happen from time to time that history warns, illuminates, and advises, even if it can hardly dispose of the future. It is appropriate to consider in this regard the usefulness of polling public opinion on matters of foreign policy and the power and limits of the United Nations.

The Peace Ballot was a pioneer venture in public opinion polling. It was a mass referendum not a scientific sample. This was deliberate because the Peace Ballot was meant to be a mandate to government rather than a tool in the process of statecraft.

It tackled issues of foreign policy which are apt to be the most difficult and the least accessible. The public can decide whether to vote for a sales tax, and how much, or whether to build new prisons or schools. The issues are relatively close to home, take place in a circumscribed system, and are based on readily available information. The issues are reasonably static, at least throughout the referendum or the political process.

To the contrary, issues of foreign policy usually contain substantial amounts of information, military, scientific, economic, not available to the public and often shrouded in classified confidentiality. There is a fluidity in issues of foreign policy which requires that the questions and the answers remain closely tied to the issues at hand. And they must be the right questions. It was the fatal defect of the Peace Ballot to ask the wrong questions at the wrong time. A crisis developed and the answers to the ballot were read to make policy in a crisis which had not existed when many of the ballots were cast.

Not only must the right questions be asked but they must produce responsive answers. Often there can be competing explanations to the same answers. What did the answers to the Peace Ballot mean? Lord Cecil and Stanley Baldwin read them very differently.

Foreign policy is not a matter of a tax here or a bond issue there. It is a continuous process in which give and take will create fast changing questions and twists and turns along the way to a fruitful conclusion. Polling and sampling are highly developed today, not to mention everyday. Questions and responses are rapid. The tallies are found in the pockets of most politicians and statesman.

But foreign policy is a matter of negotiation. Peremptory instructions of any kind can inhibit the process or cut off the path to a solution that a poll could not have envisioned. The public's choices may be based on passions or prejudices. They may be based on exalted ideals. It is less likely that they will be based upon careful calculation of the national interest supported by the knowledge required for such calculations. That was why, as Sir Samuel Hoare ruefully observed, the public were more likely to be attracted to the gallant and dashing figure of Anthony Eden and the ideal he propounded than to his own more pedestrian person and policy. To the extent that public opinion polls can aid statesman in determining the breadth and depth of support for various policies or positions, public opinion polls can be useful, but they can become dangerous when they are used to direct rather than to advise on policy.

Another lesson illuminates the power and limitations of international organizations. The League of Nations was a pioneering venture. Tasks were thrust upon it which it had neither the power nor the ability to perform. In crucial moments of its history great powers, the United States for one, Germany for another, were not, members. The League had no military staff or force nor any provision for one. The concept of collective security seemed to negate the application of military power and in the application of economic power, as in all other things, the rule of unanimity held good.

The United Nations sought to, and indeed did profit from the experience of the League. It was meant to be universal and it was intended to give the Security Council a primacy and powers broader than the League had conferred on its Council. But in the end, there was the veto, which meant, in the clash of the super powers, or indeed in the case of any member of the Security Council possessing the veto, that the U.N.'s power was curtailed or negated.

The U.N. could and did raise observer and peacekeeping forces which have done useful work. But the job of observers is to observe and the job of peacekeeping forces is to separate adversaries and not to impose the U.N.'s will on them.

On two occasions the U.N. rallied impressive military forces to fight a hot war. It could achieve this in Korea because of the Soviet Union's absence when the use of force was approved to repel North Korea's invasion of South Korea. Again, in the Persian Gulf, there was no veto and the campaign was fought under a U.N. banner. That could and did happen on these two occasions by either the absence or the concurrence of the superpowers.

Yet there was a Cold War, when the superpowers faced each other with increasingly massive arsenals of increasingly powerful, not to say apocalyptic weapons. There were agonizing and costly wars on the fringes but, on a larger view, the general peace was kept until one day one of the superpower adversaries underwent a total change of regime that ended, after half a century, what we called the Cold War.

The history of the second half of the twentieth century was far different from the history of the first half. For all of its constructive work, the U.N. could no more keep the peace than the League could in its day. There was a vital difference.

To many of the League's founders, Wilson among them, and for much of its history, collective security and the balance of power were thought to be mutually incompatible not to say antithetical. The North Atlantic Treaty Organization addressed this dichotomy. It provided a cohesive, concerted bloc, a balance of military force on the ground ready to act or react and a balance, too, in weapons of deterrence. If the nations of the Warsaw Pact viewed their combination of forces in the same light, this then was the balance of power acting outside but also within the ambit of the U.N., different functions discharged by different organizations, each indispensable to the other in achieving what neither the League nor the U.N. alone could. This had been the intuitive vision of Sir Samuel Hoare and Pierre Laval, the balance of power acting within and parallel to the framework of the League of Nations. The policy that might have avoided the Second World War was replayed to the world's benefit in its aftermath, avoiding the worst and leading to a more constructive future.

Napoleon bitterly remarked that history is written by the victors. It sometimes happens that makers of history, like Caesar, become historians. It was, perhaps, in both these qualities that Churchill concludes the Preface to his history of the Second World War:

> It is my earnest hope that pondering upon the past may give guidance in days to come, enable a new generation to repair some of the errors of former years and thus govern, in accordance with the needs and glory of man, the awful unfolding scene of the future.[25]

# Notes

Abbreviations used in these Notes:

CAB: British Cabinet Minutes
DBFP: Documents on British Foreign Policy
DDF: Documents Diplomatiques Francais
DGFP: Documents on German Foreign Policy
DIA: Documents on International Affairs
*MG*: *Manchester Guardian*
*MK*: *Mein Kampf*
*NYT*: *New York Times*
*SIA*: *Survey of International Affairs*
*Times*: *London Times*

## Chapter 2: A Most Inconvenient Dilemma

1. Carr, *Crisis*, 93.
2. *Times*, 8 July 1935.
3. *Times*, 19 July 1935.
4. *Times*, 24 July 1935.
5. CAB 23/82 35(35).
6. *Headway*, August 1935, 148.
7. *Times*, 20 August 1935.
8. *Times*, 26 August 1935.
9. *MG*, 18 October 1935, cited at Carr, *Crisis*, 77.
10. *SIA* 1935, Vol 2.
11. Churchill, 165–6.
12. Winston S. Churchill, *Maxims and Reflections*, 84, citing *The River War.*
13. Eden, 249.
14. *Times*, 22 July 1935.
15. DBFP 2d, XIV, no. 564.
16. Vansittart, *Procession*, 522.
17. CAB 23/82 35(35).
18. *Times*, 12 July 1935.
19. DBFP 2d, XIV, no. 354.

20. DBFP 2d, XIV, no. 371.
21. DBFP 2d, XIV, no. 372.
22. DBFP 2d, XIV, no. 377.
23. DBFP 2d, XIV, no. 384.
24. CAB 23/82 39(35).
25. CAB 23/82 40(35).
26. DBFP 2d, XIV, no. 392.
27. DBFP 2d, XIV, no. 402.
28. DBFP 2d, XIV, no. 403.
29. CAB 23/82 41(35).
30. Torres, 65.
31. DBFP 2d, XIV, no. 376.
32. *Times*, 2 July 1935.
33. Eden, 246.
34. DBFP 2d, XIV, no. 407.
35. DBFP 2d, XIV, no. 412.
36. *Times*, 5 August 1935.
37. *Times*, 5 August 1935.
38. Eden, 248.
39. DBFP 2d, XIV, no. 423.
40. CAB 53/25 COS 388.
41. DBFP 2d, XIV, no. 427.
42. DBFP 2d, XIV, no. 426, CP 159(35).
43. Eden, 249.
44. DBFP 2d, XIV, no. 428, 432.
45. DBFP 2d, XIV, no. 429.
46. DDF 1st, XI, no. 416.
47. DBFP 2d, XIV, no. 430.
48. DBFP 2d, XIV, no. 431.
49. DBFP 2d, XIV, no. 442.
50. DBFP 2d, XIV, no. 443.
51. DBFP 2d, XIV, no. 446.
52. DBFP 2d, XIV, no. 451.
53. DBFP 2d, XIV, no. 452.
54. DBFP 2d, XIV, no. 458.
55. DBFP 2d, XIV, no. 456.
56. DBFP 2d, XIV, no. 461.
57. DBFP 2d, XIV, no. 465.
58. DBFP 2d, XIV, no. 472.
59. *Headway*, August 1935, 148.
60. *Times*, 16 August 1935.
61. *Times*, 19 August 1935.
62. *Times*, 23 August 1935.
63. *Times*, 26 August 1935.
64. *Times*, 26 August 1935.
65. *Times*, 27 August 1935.

66. *Times*, 27 August 1935.
67. Baer, *Coming*, 267.
68. DBFP 2d, XIV, no. 476.
69. DBFP 2d, XIV, no. 477.
70. DBFP 2d, XIV, no. 480.
71. DBFP 2d, XIV, no. 483.
72. DBFP 2d, XIV, no. 481.
73. DBFP 2d, XIV, no. 483.
74. DBFP 2d, XIV, no. 484.
75. CAB 23/82 F.A./H/7, 21 August 1935.
76. CAB 23/82 42(35).
77. DBFP 2d, XIV, no. 493.
78. DBFP 2d, XIV, no. 493.
79. Vansittart, *Lessons*, 42.
80. 2 *SIA* 1935, 240–1.
81. DBFP 2d, XIV, no. 498.
82. DDF 1st XII, no. 77.
83. *Times*, 19 August 1935.
84. Baer, *Coming*, 296–8.
85. Mussolini, *Opera Omnia*, XXVII, 277; de Bono, *Anno XIII*, 191, cited at Baer, *Coming*, 278.
86. *Times*, 29 August 1935.
87. DDF 1st, XII, no. 87.

## Chapter 3: The Die is Cast

1. Thompson, 6.
2. *Times*, 2 September 1935.
3. *Times*, 4 September 1935.
4. DBFP 2d, XIV, no. 520, Eden, 258.
5. DBFP 2d, XIV, no. 520.
6. DDF 1st, XII, no. 79.
7. DDF 1st, XII, no. 103.
8. DBFP 2d, XIV, no. 526.
9. DBFP 2d, XIV, no. 528.
10. 2 DIA 1935, 55–61.
11. 2 DIA 1935, 60–84.
12. 2 DIA 1935, 84–86.
13. 2 DIA 1935, 86–7.
14. 2 *SIA* 1935, 181.
15. DDF 1st, XII, no. 130.
16. DDF 1st, XII, no. 125.
17. DDF 1st, XII, no. 124, DBFP 2d, XIV, no. 541.
18. *Times*, 9 September 1935.
19. DDF 1st, XII, no. 132.
20. DDF 1st, XIII, no. 132.

21. *Times*, 10 September 1935.
22. *Times*, 11 September 1935.
23. Viscount Templewood (Sir Samuel Hoare), *Nine Troubled Years*, 166.
24. Templewood, *Nine Troubled Years*, 167.
25. Eden, 260–1.
26. DBFP 2d, XIV, no. 553.
27. DDF 1st, XII, no. 150.
28. DBFP 2d, XIV, no. 554.
29. DDF 1st, XII, no. 150, DBFP 2d, XIV, no. 554.
30. Neither the British nor the French record attributes any statement to Eden.
31. Hoare, 168–9.
32. 2 *SIA* 1935, 184.
33. *Times*, 12 September 1935.
34. *Headway*, October 1935, 189.
35. *Headway*, October 1935, 191.
36. *Headway*, October 1935, 192.
37. *Headway*, October 1935, 192.
38. *Times*, 12 September 1935.
39. Baer, *Coming*, 329.
40. Harold Butler, *The Lost Peace*, 43.
41. *Times*, 12 September 1935.
42. *Times*, 13 September 1935.
43. *Times*, 19 September 1935.
44. *Times*, 13 September 1935.
45. *Times*, 12 September 1935.
46. Colvin, 70.
47. *Headway*, August 1935, 148.
48. Maurice Cowling, *The Impact of Hitler*, 81.
49. *Headway*, October 1935, 182.
50. *Times*, 13 September 1935.
51. DBFP 2d, XIV, no. 564.
52. DDF 1st, XII, no. 155.
53. Hoare, 166.
54. Eden, 261.
55. *Times*, 13 September 1935.
56. 1 DIA 1935, 243.
57. *Times*, 14 September 1935.
58. 1 DIA 1935, 244–245.
59. *Times*, 16 September, 23 September 1935.
60. *MG*, 13 September 1935.
61. *NYT*, 13 September 1935.
62. *Times*, 16 September 1935.
63. DDF 1st, XII, no. 171.
64. DBFP 2d, XIV, no. 588, DDF 1st, XII, no. 183.
65. DBFP 2d, XIV, no. 591.

66. DBFP 2d, XIV, no. 595.
67. 2 *SIA* 1935, 192.
68. *Times*, 18 September, 19 September 1935.
69. 2 DIA 1935, 106–10.
70. 2 *SIA* 1935, 195–6.
71. DDF 1st, XII, no. 206.
72. DDF 1st, XII, no. 206.
73. DDF 1st, XII, no. 206.
74. 2 DIA 1935, 114–17.
75. *Times*, 23 September 1935.
76. *Times*, 27 September 1935.
77. DBFP 2d, XIV, no. 620.
78. DBFP 2d, XIV, no. 630.
79. *Times*, 6 September 1935.
80. *Times*, 21 September 1935.
81. *Times*, 21 September 1935.
82. *Times*, 22 September 1935.
83. CAB 23/82 42(35).
84. CAB 23/82 43(35).
85. DBFP 2d, XIV, no. 640.
86. DBFP 2d, XIV, no. 235.
87. DBFP 2d, XiV, Annex to no. 650.
88. DDF 1st, XII, no. 241.
89. *Times*, 28 September 1935.
90. *Times*, 30 September 1935.
91. DBFP 2d, XIV, no. 658.
92. DBFP 2d, XIV, no. 662.
93. *Times*, 30 September 1935.
94. *Times*, 1 October 1935.
95. CAB 23/82 44(35).
96. *Times*, 3 October 1935.
97. *Times*, 4 October 1935.
98. *Times*, 4 October 1935.
99. *Times*, 4 October 1935.

## Chapter 4: The Double Policy

1. DBFP 2d, XV, no. 65.
2. *Times*, 8 October 1935.
3. *Times*, 7 October, 8 October 1935.
4. *Times*, 12 October 1935.
5. *Times*, 14 October 1935.
6. *Times*, 16 October 1935.
7. *Times*, 16 October 1935.
8. *Times*, 18 October 1935.
9. *Times*, 21 October 1935.

10. *Times*, 16 October 1935.
11. *Times*, 18 October 1935.
12. *Times*, 23 October 1935.
13. DBFP 2d, XV, no. 4.
14. DBFP 2d, XV, no. 10.
15. DBFP 2d, XV, no. 7.
16. DBFP 2d, XV, Enclosure in no. 27.
17. DBFP 2d, XV, no. 15.
18. DBFP 2d, XV, no. 29.
19. *Times*, 4 October, 5 October 1935.
20. *Times*, 4 October 1935.
21. 2 DIA 1935, 149–50.
22. 2 DIA 1935, 149–50.
23. 2 *SIA* 1935, 201.
24. 2 *SIA* 1935, 204.
25. Covenant of the League of Nations, Article 16, Walters 51–2.
26. 2 *SIA* 1935, 209.
27. 2 DIA 1935, 187–8.
28. 2 DIA 1935, 188–9.
29. *Times*, 12 October 1935.
30. *Times*, 12 October 1935.
31. 2 *SIA* 1935, 224.
32. 2 DIA 1935, 204–5.
33. 2 DIA 1935, 205–6.
34. 2 DIA 1935, 206–7.
35. 2 DIA 1935, 207–9.
36. 2 *SIA* 1935, 230.
37. *Times*, 25 October 1935.
38. Sydney F.K. Nettleton, *Times*, 2 October 1935.
39. L.S. Amery, *Times*, 4 October 1935.
40. *Times*, 7 October 1935.
41. *Times*, 7 October 1935.
42. *Times*, 11 October 1935.
43. *Times*, 11 October 1935.
44. *Times*, 11 October 1935.
45. *Times*, 12 October 1935.
46. *Times*, 16 October 1935.
47. *Times*, 22 October 1935.
48. *Times*, 24 October 1935.
49. *Times*, 18 October 1935.
50. *Times*, 17 October 1935.
51. 2 *SIA* 1935, 1.
52. 2 *SIA* 1935, 219.
53. 2 *SIA* 1935, 220.
54. DBFP 2d, XV, no. 20.
55. DBFP 2d, XV, no. 43.

56. 2 *SIA* 1935, 255–6.
57. CAB 23/81 45(35).
58. DBFP 2d, XV, no. 74.
59. *Headway*, November 1935, 210.
60. DBFP 2d, XV, no. 79.
61. DBFP 2d, XV, no. 81.
62. CAB 23/81 47(35).
63. DBFP 2d, XV, no. 87.
64. DBFP 2d, XV, no. 91, 95.
65. *Times*, 14 October 1935.
66. DBFP 2d, XV, no. 115.
67. DBFP 2d, XV, no. 115, fn. 12.
68. CAB 23/81 48(35).
69. George W. Baer, *Test Case*, 89.
70. DDF 1st, XII, no. 376.
71. DDF 1st, XII, no. 405.
72. DDF 1st, XII, no. 466.
73. DDF 1st, XIII, no. 1.
74. DDF 1st, XIII, no. 1, DBFP 2d, XV, no. 108.
75. DBFP 2d, XV, no. 108, fn. 3, 128.
76. DBFP 2d, XV, no. 108, fn. 3, 129.
77. DBFP 2d, XV, no. 98.
78. DBFP 2d, XV, no. 111.
79. DBFP 2d, XV, no. 122.
80. DBFP 2d, XV, no. 134.
81. CAB 23/81 48(35).
82. *Times*, 21 October 1935.
83. *Times*, 28 October 1935.
84. *Times*, 31 October 1935.
85. *Times*, 25 October 1935.
86. *Times*, 26 October 1935.
87. *Times*, 26 October 1935.
88. *Times*, 23 October 1935.
89. *Times*, 23 October 1935.
90. *Times*, 24 October 1935.
91. *Times*, 25 October 1935.
92. *Times*, 25 October 1935.
93. *Times*, 25 October 1935.
94. *Headway*, November 1935, 220.
95. *Headway*, November 1935, 218.
96. DBFP 2d, XV, no. 139.
97. DBFP 2d, XV, no. 139.
98. DBFP 2d, XV, no. 150.
99. DBFP 2d, XV, no. 151.
100. DBFP 2d, XV, no. 154.
101. DBFP 2d, XV, no. 155.

102. DBFP 2d, XV, no. 158.
103. DBFP 2d, XV, no. 160, 161.
104. DBFP 2d, XV, no. 162.
105. DBFP 2d, XV, no. 166.
106. DBFP 2d, XV, no. 171.
107. DBFP 2d, XV, no. 175.
108. DBFP 2d, XV, no. 149.
109. *Times*, 30 October 1935.
110. 2 *SIA* 1935, 285.
111. 2 *SIA* 1935, 285–6.
112. 2 *SIA* 1935, 286.
113. *Times*, 31 October 1935.
114. *Times*, 1 November 1935.
115. *Times*, 5 November 1935.
116. *Times*, 9 November 1935.
117. *Times*, 8 November 1935.
118. *Times*, 9 November 1935.
119. *Times*, 29 October 1935.
120. *Times*, 21 November 1935.
121. *Times*, 24 October 1935.
122. *Times*, 2 November 1935.
123. Jones, 155.
124. 2 DIA 1935, 214–15.
125. DDF 1st, XIII, no. 128.
126. DBFP 2d, XV, no. 188, 189.
127. DBFP 2d, XV, no. 197, 198, 206.
128. DDF 1st, XIII, no. 209.
129. DBFP 2d, XIV, no. 210.
130. DBFP 2d, XV, no. 215.
131. DBFP 2d, XV, no. 219.
132. DBFP 2d, XV, no. 220.
133. DDF 1st, XIII, no. 214.
134. DDF 1st, XIII, no. 224.
135. *Times*, 18 November 1935.
136. DBFP 2d, XV, no. 222.
137. DBFP 2d, XV, no. 224.
138. DBFP 2d, XV, no. 231.
139. DBFP 2d, XV, no. 233.
140. *Times*, 31 October 1935.
141. *Times*, 16 October 1935.
142. DBFP 2d, XV, no. 237.
143. *Times*, 23 November 1935.
144. DBFP 2d, XV, no. 244.
145. DBFP 2d, XV, no. 247.
146. DBFP 2d, XV, no. 248.
147. DIA 1935, vol. 2, 342.

148. DDF 1st, XIII, no. 286.
149. DDF 1st, XIII, no. 295.
150. 2 DIA 1935, 343–344.
151. *Times*, 29 November 1935.
152. *Times*, 30 November 1935.
153. DBFP 2d, XV, no. 253.
154. DBFP 2d, XV, no. 254.
155. DBFP 2d, XV, no. 273.
156. DDF 1st, XIII, no. 318.
157. DBFP 2d, XV, no. 283.
158. DBFP 2d, XV, no. 258, 269.
159. Salvemini, 378.
160. DBFP 2d, XV, no. 256.
161. DBFP 2d, XV, no. 269.
162. DBFP 2d, XV, no. 274.
163. DBFP 2d, XV, no. 277.
164. DBFP 2d, XV, no. 280.
165. DBFP 2d, XV, no. 274.
166. Stephen Roskill, *Hankey, Man of Secrets*, vol. III, 189.
167. Eden, 297.
168. DBFP 2d, XV, no. 286.
169. DBFP 2d, XV, no. 213.
170. DBFP 2d, XV, no. 235.
171. DBFP 2d, XV, no. 271.
172. *Times*, 9 November 1935.
173. Gamelin, *Servir*, vol. II, cited at Adamthwaite, *The Making of the Second World War*, 148.

## Chapter 5: Hoare-Laval

1. Vansittart, *Procession*, 544.
2. *NYT*, 12 December 1935.
3. CAB 23/81 50(35).
4. *Times*, 3 December 1935.
5. *Times*, 4 December 1935.
6. CAB 23/81 51(35).
7. *Times*, 6 December 1935.
8. *Times*, 6 December 1935.
9. *Times*, 7 December 1935.
10. *Times*, 7 December 1935.
11. Warner, 115.
12. *Times*, 6 December 1935.
13. Cranborn Private Papers, F.O. 800/296 cited at Baer, *Test Case*, 49.
14. DDF 1st, XIII, no. 347.
15. *Times*, 6 December 1935.
16. *Times*, 9 December 1935.

17. *Times*, 9 December 1935.
18. DBFP 2d, XV, nos. 254, 278, 292.
19. DDF 1st, XIII, no. 318.
20. DBFP 2d, XV, no. 280.
21. DBFP 2d, XV, no. 283.
22. DBFP 2d, XV, no. 295.
23. DBFP 2d, XV, nos. 307, 308.
24. *Times*, 4 December 1935.
25. *Times*, 6 December 1935.
26. *NYT*, 5 December 1935.
27. DBFP 2d, XV, no. 314.
28. DBFP 2d, XV, no. 293.
29. Eden, 298.
30. Vansittart, *Procession*, 539.
31. DBFP 2d, XV, no. 290.
32. Vansittart, *Procession*, 543, Jones, 159.
33. DDF 1st, XIII, no. 340.
34. DDF 1st, XIII, no. 348, DBFP 2d, XV, no. 328.
35. DBFP 2d, XV, nos. 330, 338, 337, DDF 1st, XIII, no. 352.
36. DBFP 2d, XV, no. 329.
37. DBFP 2d, XV, no. 336.
38. DBFP 2d, XV, no. 337.
39. DBFP 2d, XV, no. 337.
40. DBFP 2d, XV, no. 337.
41. Baer, *Test Case*, 127.
42. DBFP 2d, XV, no. 335.
43. DBFP 2d, XV, no. 292.
44. DBFP 2d, XV, no. 337.
45. Genevieve Tabouis, *They Called Me Cassandra*, 267–9.
46. Eden, 300–2.
47. CAB 23/81 52(35).
48. *Times*, 10 December 1935.
49. *Times*, 10 December 1935.
50. *Times*, 11 December 1935.
51. *Times*, 11 December 1935.
52. *Times*, 11 December 1935.
53. *Times*, 11 December 1935.
54. Rowse, 23.
55. DBFP 2d, XV, nos. 347, 349, 350.
56. DBFP 2d, XV, no. 352.
57. DBFP 2d, XV, no. 355.
58. DBFP 2d, XV, no. 355.
59. DBFP 2d, XV, no. 353.
60. DDF 1st, XIII, no. 368.
61. DBFP 2d, XV, nos. 354, 356, DDF 1st, XIII, no. 371.
62. *Times*, 11 December 1935.

63. *Times*, 11 December 1935, 12 December 1935.
64. *Times*, 12 December 1935.
65. *Times*, 11 December 1935.
66. *Times*, 11 December 1935.
67. All excerpts are from *Times*, 11 December 1935.
68. *Times*, 13 December 1935.
69. *Times*, 13 December 1935.
70. CAB 23/82 54(35).
71. DBFP 2d, XV, no. 373.
72. DBFP 2d, XV, no. 371.
73. *Times*, 13 December 1935.
74. Warner, 125.
75. 2 DIA 1935, 366–7, DDF 1st, XIII, no. 410.
76. *Times*, 13 December 1935.
77. *Times*, 16 December 1935.
78. *Times*, 17 December 1935.
79. *Times*, 18 December 1935.
80. Keith Feiling, *The Life of Neville Chamberlain*, 274.
81. *Times*, 14 December 1935.
82. *Times*, 14 December 1935.
83. *Times*, 14 December 1935.
84. *Times*, 14 December 1935.
85. *Times*, 16 December 1935.
86. CAB 23/81 56(35).
87. Waley, chapter 2.
88. DBFP 2d, XV, no. 381.
89. DDF 1st, XIII, no. 427.
90. DBFP 2d, XV, no. 385.
91. DBFP 2d, XV, no. 389.
92. 2 DIA 1935, 382.
93. Eden, 309.
94. Templewood, *Nine Troubled Years*, 185.
95. DBFP 2d, XV, no. 390.
96. Eden, 309.
97. 2 DIA 1935, 382.
98. 2 DIA 1935, 367.
99. 2 DIA 1935, 371–81.
100. 2 DIA 1935, 383.
101. CAB 23/82 56(35).
102. Daniel P. Waley, *British Public Opinion and the Abyssinian War*, 41.
103. Angelo de Boca, *The Ethiopian War, 1935–41*, 76.
104. *Times*, 19 December 1935.
105. Baer, *Test Case*, 142.
106. DDF 1st, XIII, no. 415.
107. *Times*, 19 December 1935.
108. *Times*, 20 December 1935.

109. *Times*, 20 December 1935.
110. *Times*, 20 December 1935.
111. Templewood, *Nine Troubled Years*, 188.
112. *Times*, 20 December 1935.
113. *Times*, 20 December 1935.
114. *Times*, 20 December 1935.
115. *Times*, 20 December 1935.
116. *Times*, 20 December 1935.
117. *Times*, 20 December 1935.
118. *Times*, 20 December 1935.
119. *Times*, 20 December 1935.
120. *Times*, 20 December 1935.
121. Salvemini, 407.
122. *Times*, 20 December 1935.
123. DBFP 2d, XV, no. 411.
124. Observer, 6 February 1936, cited at Salvemini, 407.
125. Vansittart, *Procession*, 543.
126. DDF 1st, XIII, no. 475.
127. DDF 1st, XIII, no. 493.
128. Max Gallo, *L'affaire d'Ethiopie*, 59–9.
129. *Times*, 28 December 1935.
130. *Times*, 25 December 1935.
131. Gallo, 208.
132. 2 *SIA* 1935, 323.
133. 2 *SIA* 1935, 324.
134. *Times*, 30 December 1935.
135. *Times*, 30 December 1935.
136. *Times*, 27 December 1935.
137. *Times*, 31 December 1935.
138. *Times*, 31 December 1935.
139. DBFP 2d, XV, no. 383.
140. DBFP 2d, XV, no. 404.
141. André François-Poncet, *The Fateful Years*, 241.
142. Colvin, 74.
143. Vansittart, *Procession*, 541.
144. 2 *SIA* 1935, 46.
145. Young, 217.
146. *Headway*, July 1935, 130.
147. Jones, 228.

## Chapter 6: Hitler Bides His Time

1. James T. Emmerson, *The Rhineland Crisis*, 39.
2. *Times*.
3. DGFP, C-IV, no. 480.
4. DGFP, C-IV, no. 485.

5. DGFP, C-IV, no. 487.
6. DDF 2d I, no. 34.
7 . DDF 2d, I, no. 36.
8. DBFP 2d, XV, no. 404.
9. DDF 2d, I, no. 1.
10. DDF 2d, I, no. 30.
11. DDF 2d, I, no. 32.
12. DDF 2d, I, no. 57.
13. DDF 2d, I, no. 53.
14. DDF 2d, I, no. 63, no. 75.
15. DDF 2d, I, no. 82.
16. DDF 2d, I, no. 83.
17. 2 DIA 1935, 416–17.
18. DBFP 2d, XV, no. 463.
19. *Times*, 23 January 1936.
20. DBFP 2d, XV, no. 464.
21. *Times*, 23 January 1936.
22. DBFP 2d, XV, no. 433.
23. DBFP 2d, XV, no. 443.
24. DBFP 2d, XV, no. 452.
25. DBFP 2d, XV, no. 446.
26. DBFP 2d, XV, no. 461.
27. DBFP 2d, XV, no. 455.
28. Supra 420–1.
29. DBFP 2d, XV, appendix I, memorandum by Sargent and Wigram.
30. DBFP 2d, XV, appendix I, comments by Collier.
31. DBFP 2d, XV, appendix I, comments by Vansittart.
32. DBFP 2d, XV, no. 460.
33. DBFP 2d, XV, enclosure in no. 482.
34. DBFP 2d, XV, no. 475.
35. DBFP 2d, XV, enclosure in no. 483.
36. DBFP 2d, XV, no. 486.
37. DBFP 2d, XV, no. 484.
38. DDF 2d, I, no. 112.
39. DGFP, C-IV, no. 531.
40. CAB 23/83, 3(36).
41. DBFP 2d XV, no. 490.
42. Del Boca, 120–1.
43. Del Boca, 100–11.
44. DBFP 2d, XV, no. 491.
45. DBFP 2d, C-IV, no. 525.
46. DGFP, C-IV, no. 544.
47. DGFP, C-IV, no. 545.
48. DGFP, C-IV, 553.
49. *Times*, 13 February 1936.
50. DGFP, C-IV, no. 564.

51. Emmerson, 82–3.
52. DGFP, C-IV, no. 538.
53. DGFP, C-IV, no. 562.
54. DGFP, C-IV, no. 568.
55. DGFP, C-IV, no. 575.
56. DGFP, C-IV, no. 579.
57. DGFP, C-IV, no. 592.
58. DGFP, C-IV, no. 603.
59. Namier, 17.
60. DDF 2d, I, no. 126.
61. DDF 2d, I, no. 125.
62. DDF 2d, I, no. 143.
63. DDF 2d, I, no. 155.
64. Flandin, 195, cited at Emmerson, *Crisis*, 44.
65. DDF 2d, I, no. 170.
66. DDF 2d, I, no. 186.
67. DDF 2d, I, no. 184.
68. DDF 2d, I, no. 196.
69. DDF 2d, I, no. 202.
70. DDF 2d, I, no. 203.
71. DDF 2d, I, no. 211.
72. DDF 2d, I, no. 223.
73. DIA, 1935, vol. 2, 223–30, *Times.*
74. DDF 2d, I, no. 224.
75. DDF 2d, I, no. 239.
76. DDF 2d, I, no. 241.
77. *SIA*, 1936, 256.
78. *SIA*, 1936, 256.
79. *SIA*, 1936, 257.
80. DBFP 2d, XV, no. 493.
81. DBFP 2d, XV, no. 509.
82. DBFP 2d, XV, no. 517.
83. DBFP 2d, XV, no. 521.
84. DBFP 2d, XV, no. 522.
85. DBFP 2d, XV, no. 524.
86. DGFP, C-IV, no. 583.
87. CAB 23/83 7(36).
88. Middlemas and Barnes, 909.
89. Middlemas and Barnes, 910.
90. Churchill, 181.
91. Del Boca, 126.
92. Del Boca, 128.
93. Del Boca, 134–5.
94. DBFP 2d, XV, no. 531.
95. DBFP 2d, XV, no. 532.
96. DBFP 2d, XV, 540 CAB.

97. *Times*, 25 February 1936.
98. *Times*, 25 February 1936.
99. *Times*, 25 February 1936.
100. CAB 23/83 10(36).
101. DBFP 2d, XV, no. 546.
102. DBFP 2d, XV, no. 551.
103. DBFP 2d, XV, no. 552.
104. DBFP 2d, XV, no. 556.
105. Del Boca, 136–43.
106. *Times*, 2 March 1936.
107. DDF 2d, I, no. 265, DGFP, C-IV, no. 604.
108. DDF 2d, I, no. 272.
109. DGFP, C-IV, 603, C-V, no. 5.
110. DGFP, C-V, no. 3.
111. Toynbee, *Acquaintances*, 285.
112. Toynbee, *Acquaintances*, 279–81.
113. Toynbee, *Acquaintances*, 288.
114. DBFP 2d, XVI, no. 3.
115. DBFP 2d, XVI, no. 14, DDF 2d, I, no. 264.
116. DBFP 2d, XVI, no. 13.
117. DDF 2d, I, no. 283 annex.
118. DBFP 2d, XVI, no. 20.
119. DBFP 2d, XVI, no. 22.
120. DBFP 2d, XVI, no. 15.
121. *Times*, 4 March 1936.
122. Young, 221.
123. *Times*, 6 March 1936.
124. DBFP 2d, XVI, no. 26.
125. DDF 2d, I, no. 295.
126. CAB 23/83 15(36).
127. DGFP, C-V, no. 8, DBFP 2d, XVI, no. 29.
128. DGFP, C-V, no. 9.

## Chapter 7: Hitler Strikes

1. Namier, 5.
2. *NYT*, 9 March 1936.
3. *Times*, 9 March 1936.
4. DBFP 2d, XVI, no. 33, 34.
5. DBFP 2d, XVI, no. 42.
6. DGFP, C-V, no. 21.
7. DBFP 2d, XVI, no. 37.
8. DDF 2d, I, no. 301.
9. DBFP 2d, XVI, no. 37.
10. DDF 2d, I, no. 316.
11. DDF 2d, I, no. 298.

12. DDF 2d, I, no. 299.
13. DBFP 2d, XVI, no. 39.
14. DDF 2d, I, no. 317.
15. Emmerson, 105.
16. DDF 2d, I, no. 334.
17. DDF 2d, I, no. 321.
18. *Times*, 9 March 1936.
19. DBFP 2d, XVI, no. 39, 48.
20. Eden, 243–4, 347.
21. DBFP 2d, XVI, no. 56.
22. Jones, 180–1.
23. DBFP 2d, XVI, no. 48.
24. *Times*, 9 March 1936.
25. CAB 23/81 16(36), *Times*, 10 March 1936.
26. *Morning Post* cited in *Times*, 10 March 1936.
27. *Daily Mail* cited in *Times*, 10 March 1936.
28. *Nottingham Guardian* cited in *Times*, 10 March 1936.
29. *Sheffield Telegraph, Northern Mail* cited in *Times*, 10 March 1936.
30. *Daily Herald* cited in *Times*, 10 March 1936.
31. *Evening Standard* cited in *Times*, 10 March 1936.
32. *Daily Express* cited in *Times*, 10 March 1936.
33. *News Chronicle* cited in *Times*, 10 March 1936.
34. *Sussex Daily News* cited in *Times*, 10 March 1936.
35. *Headway*, April 1936, 64.
36. Churchill, 194.
37. Taylor, 386.
38. *Times*, 23 March 1936.
39. *Times*, 24 March 1936.
40. Eden, 346.
41. Barnett, 384.
42. Colvin, 97.
43. Gibbs, 171, 174.
44. *Northern Mail* cited in *Times*, 10 March 1936.
45. Carlton, 82.
46. *Headway*, April 1936 cited at Thompson, 103.
47. 2 *SIA*, 1935, 340.
48. Norwich, 195.
49. Eden, 338.
50. Eden, 366–7.
51. DBFP 2d, XVI, no. 61, 63.
52. DBFP 2d, XVI, no. 62.
53. CAB 33/83 18(36).
54. DGFP, C-V, no. 85.
55. DGFP, C-V, no. 84.
56. DGFP, C-V, no. 84.
57. DDF 2d, I, no. 390, 391, 392.

58. DBFP 2d, XVI, no. 78.
59. DDF 2d, I, no. 407.
60. DBFP 2d, XVI, no. 82.
61. DBFP 2d, XII, no. 91.
62. DBFP 2d, XVI, no. 95, 99.
63. DBFP 2d, XVI, no. 94.
64. DBFP 2d, XVI, no. 94.
65. Paul Schmidt, *Hitler's Interpreter*, 47.
66. Baynes, III, 1307–10.
67. Churchill, 197; Middlemas and Barnes, 919–20, Emmerson, 183–4.
68. Colvin, 98–9.
69. Harold Nicholson, *Diaries and Letters, 1930–39*, 250.
70. DBFP 2d, XVI, no. 108.
71. *SIA* 1936, 297.
72. DBFP 2d, XVI, no. 110.
73. DBFP 2d, XVI, no. 119.
74. DBFP 2d, XVI, no. 110.
75. DBFP 2d, XVI, no. 134.
76. CAB 23/83 21(36).
77. DBFP 2d, XVI, no. 132.
78. DBFP 2d, XVI, no. 144.
79. Churchill, 198.
80. DBFP 2d, XVI, no. 142.
81. DGFP, C-V, nos. 170, 174.
82. *Times*, 21 March 1936.
83. 2 DIA 1935.
84. Del Boca, 149–55.
85. 2 DIA 1935, 422–3.
86. 2 DIA 1936, 424.
87. DBFP 2d, XVI, no. 149, 155.
88. *Times*, 23 March 1936.
89. *Times*, 24 March 1936.
90. DDF 2d, I, no. 489.
91. *Times*, 25 March 1936.
92. *SIA* 1936, 319.
93. *SIA* 1936, 320.
94. CAB 23/83 24(36).
95. DBFP 2d, XVI, no. 168.
96. *Times*, 27 March 1936.
97. *Times*, 30 March 1936.
98. Dalton Diaries, 11 March 1936, cited at Emmerson, 147.
99. *Times*, 28 March 1936, cited at Emmerson, 215.

## Chapter 8: The Triumph of the Dictators

1. 2 *SIA* 1935, 499–500.

2. Mockler, 114, del Boca, 163.
3. Mockler, 114–16.
4. Mockler, 117–18, del Boca, 166–73.
5. Del Boca, 179–81.
6. DBFP 2d, XVI, no. 193, 198.
7. *Times*, 4 April 1936.
8. *Times*, 4 April 1936.
9. *Times*, 2 April 1936.
10. *Economist*, 4 April 1936.
11. *New Statesmen*, 4 April 1936.
12. DBFP 2d, XVI, no. 204.
13. DDF 2d, II, no. 85.
14. DBFP 2d, XVI, no. 222.
15. DBFP 2d, XVI, no. 223.
16. DDF 2d, II, no. 37A, DIA 1936, 171–5.
17. DDF 2d, II, no. 37B.
18. DBFP 2d, XVI, no. 233.
19. DBFP 2d, XVI, no. 231.
20. DBFP 2d, XVI, no. 269.
21. DBFP 2d, XVI, no. 291.
22. DBFP 2d, XVI, no. 307.
23. DBFP 2d, XVI, no. 328.
24. DBFP 2d, XVI, no. 326.
25. DBFP 2d, XVI, no. 328.
26. Salvemini, 502–3.
27. DBFP 2d, XVI, no. 336.
28. DBFP 2d, XVI, no. 363.
29. DBFP 2d, XVI, no. 393.
30. DBFP 2d, XVI, no. 404.
31. DBFP 2d, XVI, no. 407.
32. DBFP 2d, XVI, no. 454.
33. DBFP 2d, XVI, no. 454.
34. DBFP 2d, XVI, annex to no. 464.
35. DIA 1936, 218–19.
36. *SIA* 1936, 345.
37. DIA 1936, 219–20.
38. *SIA* 1936, 350.
39. *SIA* 1936, 350.
40. *SIA* 1936, 947.
41. DIA 1936, 223–27.
42. DBFP 2d, XVI, no. 278.
43. DGFP C-V, nos. 66 and 85.
44. DBFP 2d, XVI, no. 203.
45. DBFP 2d, XVI, no. 207.
46. DBFP 2d, XVI, no. 207 fn. 2.
47. DDF 2d, II, no. 17.
48. DDF 2d, II, no. 17.

49. DDF 2d, II, no. 17.
50. DDF 2d, II, no. 17.
51. DBFP 2d, XVI, no. 213.
52. DBFP 2d, XVI, no. 218.
53. DBFP 2d, XVI, no. 221.
54. DDF 2d, II, no. 61.
55. DDF 2d, II, no. 46.
56. 2 *SIA* 1935, 348.
57. 2 DIA 1935, 435–44.
58. 2 DIA 1935, 444–52.
59. 2 *SIA* 1935, 353.
60. 2 DIA 1935, 459–60.
61. DDF 2d, II, no. 90.
62. *Times*, 20 April 1936.
63. DBFP 2d, XVI, no. 259.
64. DBFP 2d, XVI, no. 284.
65. 2 *SIA* 1935, 356–7.
66. DBFP 2d, XVI, no. 287.
67. *Times*, 6 May 1936.
68. *Times*, 5 May 1936.
69. DDF 2d, II, no. 150.
70. DDF 2d, II, no. 161.
71. *Times*, 5 May 1936.
72. *Times*, 7 May 1936.
73. *Times*, 7 May 1936.
74. DBFP 2d, XVI, no. 280.
75. *Times*, 22 April 1936.
76. *Times*, 23 April 1936.
77. *Times*, 24 April 1936.
78. *Times*, 25 April 1936.
79. *Headway*, May 1936, 100.
80. *Times*, 9 May 1936.
81. *Times*, 13 May 1936.
82. *Times*, 20 April 1936.
83. *Times*, 20 April 1936.
84. *Times*, 12 May 1936.
85. *Times*, 30 April 1936.
86. *Times*, 9 May 1936.
87. *Times*, 28 May 1936.
88. Baer, *Test Case*, 278.
89. Baer, *Test Case*, 282.
90. Baer, *Test Case*, 281.
91. DBFP 2d, XVI, no. 321.
92. *Headway*, June 1936, 120.
93. *Times*, 4 June 1936.
94. DBFP 2d, XVI, no. 352.
95. Sir Maurice Peterson, *Both Sides of the Curtain*, 123.

96. Baer, *Test Case*, 262.
97. Baer, *Test Case*, 288.
98. Baer, *Test Case*, 289.
99. DBFP 2d, XVI, no. 347.
100. Baer, *Test Case*, 289.
101. *Times*, 11 June 1936.
102. *Times*, 19 June 1936.
103. *Times*, 19 June 1936.
104. *Times*, 22 June 1936.
105. *Times*, 22 June 1936.
106. *Times*, 22 June 1936.
107. *Times*, 23 June 1936.
108. *Times*, 24 June 1936.
109. 2 DIA 1935, 520–1.
110. 2 DIA 1935, 528.
111. 2 DIA 1935, 523–4.
112. 2 DIA 1935, 530.
113. 2 DIA 1935, 542–3.
114. 2 DIA 1935, 542.
115. 2 DIA 1935, 544–5, 545–7.
116. *Headway*, August 1936, 160.
117. *Headway*, August 1936, 160.
118. Kirkpatrick, 321.
119. DBFP 2d, XVI, no. 176.
120. DBFP 2d, XVI, no. 347.
121. Salvemini, 459.
122. Supra, 969.
123. DGFP, C-V, 756–9.
124. DDF 2d, II, no. 432.
125. DGFP, C-V, 756–9.
126. DGFP, C-V, no. 553.
127. *Popolo d'Italia*, 14 July 1936, cited at *SIA* 1936, 455.
128. François-Poncet, 247.
129. DGFP, C-V, no. 553.
130. DGFP, C-V, nos. 562, 588.
131. DGFP, C-V, nos. 597, 624.
132. DIA 1936, 343.
133. DIA 1936, 344–5.
134. DGFP, C-V, 1138–9, DIA 1936, 297–9.
135. DIA 1937, 306–7.
136. DIA 1936, 290.
137. DIA 1936, 583.

## Chapter 9: Paradoxes of Peace

1. Arnold J. Toynbee and G.R. Urban, *Toynbee on Toynbee*, 68.
2. John E. Dreifort, *Yvon Delbos at the Quai D'Orsay*, 83.

3. F.D. Laurens, *France and the Italo-Ethiopian Crisis*, 323.
4. Jones, 19 May 1936.
5. Beverly Nichols, *News of England*, 11.
6. Lansbury.
7. Irving, 60.
8. Eden, 353–4.
9. Eden, 367.
10. Martin Gilbert, *Winston Churchill*, vol. V, 1202–3.
11. 2 *SIA* 1935, 448–9.
12. Jones, 448.
13. 2 *SIA* 1935, 449.
14. 2 *SIA* 1935, 449.
15. DBFP 2d, XII, 910, fn. 43, 914.
16. Schmidt, 60.
17. Schmidt, 41.
18. Weinberg, 263.
19. John H. Spencer, *Ethiopia at Bay*, 84.
20. Spencer, 94.
21. Spencer, 97.
22. Spencer, 96.
23. Spencer, 98.
24. Spencer, 112.
25. Spencer, 142, 148–52, 271–2.
26. Spencer, 336.
27. Spencer, 342.
28. Spencer, 342–3.
29. Boothby, 137–8.
30. Charles de Gaulle, *Le Salut,* cited at Warner, 416.
31. Josée Laval, *The Diary of Pierre Laval*, 237.
32. Nobel Lectures, *Peace 1926–1950*, 237.

## Epilogue

104. Winston S. Churchill, *The Second World War, The Gathering Storm*. Boston: Houghton Mifflin, 1948.
105. G.N.F. Hegel, quoted at page 736, Bertrand Russell, *A History of Western Philosophy*.
106. Leo Tolstoy, *War and Peace*, 1057.
107. Thomas Carlyle, quoted at page 188, *Ideas.*
108. Churchill, *The Gathering Storm*, ix.
109. Churchill, *The Gathering Storm*, iv.
110. Maurice Baumont, *The Origins of the Second World War*, 199.
111. Baumont, *The Origins of the Second World War*, 204.
112. Baumont, *The Origins of the Second World War*, 313.
113. Baumont, *The Origins of the Second World War*, 314.
114. A.J.P. Taylor, *The Origins of the Second World War*, 131.
115. Taylor, *The Origins of the Second World War*, 293.

116. Baumont, *The Origins of the Second World War*, 170.
117. Jean-Paul Contet, *Pierre Laval.*
118. Fred Kupferman, *Laval, 1883–1945.*
119. Claude Paillat, *La Guerre a L'Horizon, 1930–1938.*
120. Earl of Birkenhead, *Halifax*, 346.
121. Eden, *Facing the Dictators*, 298, 304.
122. Warner, 130.
123. Frank Hardie, *The Abyssinian Crisis*, 170.
124. Taylor, *The Origins of the Second World War*, 96.
125. Louis L. Snyder, *The War, A Concise History, 1939–1945*, 30.
126. William Manchester, *The Last Lion*, 162.
127. Henry Kissinger, *Diplomacy*, 300.
128. Churchill, *The Gathering Storm*, v.

# Bibliography

## Documents


Documents on British Foreign Policy, 1919–1939, Ser. 2, vols. I–XVI, edited by W.N. Medlicott, Douglas Dakin, and M.E. Lambert. Her Majesty's Stationery Office, London: 1947– (cited as DBFP).

Documents Diplomatiques Français, 1932–1939, Ser. 1, vols. I–XIII, Ser. 2, vols. I–II, edited by Maurice Baumont and Pierre Renouvin. Paris: Imprimerie National, 1963–1966 (cited as DDF).

Documents on German Foreign Policy, 1918–1945, Ser. C, vols. I–V, edited by Margaret Lambert et al. Department of State. Washington, D.C.: 1962 (cited as DGFP).

Documents on International Affairs, 1933, 1934, 1935, 1936, edited by Steven Heald. Oxford University Press. Public Record Office, London: Cabinet Documents.

*The Treaty of Versailles and After.* Department of State. Washington, D.C.: 1947.

Adamthwaite, Anthony. *The Lost Peace.* New York: St. Martin's Press, 1981.

———. *The Making of the Second World War.* London: George Allen & Unwin, 1977.

Baynes, Norman H. *The Speeches of Adolf Hitler,* 3 vols, London: Oxford University Press, 1942.

Langsam, Walter. *Documents and Readings in the History of Europe Since 1918.* Philadelphia and New York: Lippincott, 1951.

Remak, Joachim. *The Nazi Years.* Englewood Cliffs, N.J.: Prentice Hall, 1969.


## General


Avon, Earl of (Anthony Eden). *The Eden Memoirs, Facing the Dictators.* London: Cassell, 1962.

Baer, George W. *The Coming of the Italo-Ethiopian War.* Cambridge, Mass.: Harvard University Press, 1967.

———. *Test Case.* Stanford, Cal.: Hoover Institution Press, 1976. Barnett, Corelli. *The Collapse of British Power.* New York: William Morrow, 1972.

Baumont, Maurice. *The Origins of the Second World War.* New Haven, Conn.: Yale University Press, 1978.

Bechtel, Guy. *Laval vignt ans apres.* Paris: Laffont, 1963.

Birkenhead, Earl of. *Halifax.* Boston: Houghton Mifflin, 1966.

Birn, Donald S. *The League of Nations Union.* Oxford: Clarendon Press, 1981.

Bloch, Marc. *Strange Defeat.* New York: W.W. Norton, 1968.

Bonnet, Georges. *Quai D'Orsay.* Isle of Man: Times Press and Anthony Gibbs & Phillips, 1965.

Boothby, Lord (Sir Robert Boothby). *Boothby, Recollections of a Rebel.* London: Hutchinson, 1978.

Bullock, Alan. *Hitler, A Study in Tyranny.* New York: Harper & Row, 1962.

Butler, Harold. *The Lost Peace.* New York: Harcourt Brace, 1942.

Butler, J.R.M. *Lord Lothian.* London: Macmillan, 1960.

Carlton, David. *Anthony Eden.* London: Allen Lane, 1981.

Carr, E.H. *International Relations Between the Wars, 1919–1939.* Harper Torchbooks, New York: Harper & Row, 1966.

———. *The Twenty Years' Crisis, 1919–1939.* Harper Torchbooks, New York: Harper & Row, 1964.

Carr, William. *Arms, Autarky and Aggression.* New York: W.W. Norton, 1973.

"Cato." *Guilty Men.* New York: Frederick A. Stokes, 1940.

Cecil of Chelwood, Viscount (Lord Robert Cecil). *All the Way.* London: Hodder & Stoughton, 1949.

———. *A Great Experiment.* New York: Oxford University Press, 1941.

Churchill, Winston S. *The Second World War, The Gathering Storm.* Boston: Houghton Mifflin, 1948.

———. *The River War.* New York: Award Books, 1964.

Clemenceau, Georges. *Grandeur and Misery of Victory.* New York: Harcourt Brace, 1930.

Cockburn, Claud. *The Devil's Decade.* New York: Mason & Lipscomb,1973.

Colvin, Ian. *None So Blind.* New York: Harcourt, Brace & World, 1965.

Contet, Jean-Paul. *Pierre Laval.* Paris: Fayard, 1993.

Coote, Colin and Batchelor, Denzil. *Winston S. Churchill's Maxims and Reflections*,Boston: Houghton Mifflin, 1949.

Cowling, Maurice. *The Impact of Hitler, British Politics and British Policy, 1933–1940.* Chicago: University of Chicago Press, 1977.

Craig, Gordon A. and Felix Gilbert. *The Diplomats, 1919–1939,*vol 2. New York: Atheneum, 1977.

Czernin, Ferdinand. *Versailles, 1919.* New York: Capricorn Books, 1965.

De Chambrun, Comte René. *Mission and Betrayal.* Stanford, Cal.: Hoover, 1993.

———. *Pierre Laval Devant L'Histoire.* Paris: France-Empire, 1983.

Del Boca, Angelo. *The Ethiopian War.* Chicago: University of Chicago Press, 1969.

*Dictionary of National Biography.* Oxford: Oxford University Press.
Dreifort, John E. *Yvon Delbos at the Quai D'Orsay.* Lawrence: University of Kansas Press, 1973.
Dugan, James and Lawrence LaFore. *Days of Emperor and Clown.* Garden City, N.Y.: Doubleday, 1973.
Emmerson, James T. *The Rhineland Crisis.* Ames: Iowa State University Press, 1977.
Epstein, Leon D. *British Politics and the Suez Crisis.* Urbana: University of Illinois Press, 1964.
Feiling, Keith. *The Life of Neville Chamberlain.* London: Macmillan, 1947.
Ferrell, Robert H. *Woodrow Wilson and World War I.* New York: Harper & Row, 1985.
François-Poncet, André. *The Fateful Years.* New York: Harcourt Brace, 1949.
Furnia, Arthur H. *The Diplomacy of Appeasement.* Washington, D.C.: University Press of Washington, D.C., 1960.
Gallo, Max. *L'Affaire d'Ethiopie.* Paris: Editions du Centurion, 1967.
Gathorne-Hardy, Geoffrey M. *A Short History of International Affairs, 1920 to 1938,* London: Oxford University Press, 1938.
Gatzke, Hans W. *European Diplomacy Between Two Wars.* Chicago: Quadrangle Books, 1972.
George, Margaret. *The Warped Vision: British Foreign Policy, 1933–1939.* Pittsburgh: University of Pittsburgh Press, 1965.
Gibbs, Sir Philip. *Across the Frontiers.* New York: Doubleday Doran, 1938.
Gilbert, Martin. *Plow My Own Furrow.* London: Longmans, 1965.
———. *Winston Churchill, 1922–1939.* vol 5. Boston: Houghton Mifflin, 1977.
———. *The Roots of Appeasement.* New York: New American Library, 1970.
Gilbert, Martin and Richard Gott. *The Appeasers.* Boston: Houghton Mifflin, 1963.
Graves, Robert and Alan Hodge. *The Long Weekend.* New York: W.W. Norton, 1963.
Haines, C. Grove and Ross J.S. Hoffman. *The Origins and Background of the Second World War.* New York: Oxford University Press, 1947.
Halifax, Lord. *Fullness of Days.* New York: Dodd Mead, 1957.
Hardie, Frank. *The Abyssinian Crisis.* Hamden, Conn.: Archon Books, 1974.
Harris, Kenneth. *Attlee.* New York: W.W. Norton, 1982.
Havighurst, Alfred H. *Britain in Transition.* Chicago: University of Chicago Press, 1979.
Henderson, Sir Nevile. *Failure of a Mission.* New York: G.P. Putnam, 1940.
Hitler, Adolf. *Hitler's Secret Book.* New York: Grove Press, 1961.
———. *Mein Kampf.* Boston: Houghton Mifflin, 1943.
Holborn, Hajo. *The Political Collapse of Europe.* New York: Alfred A. Knopf, 1962.

Irving, David. *The War Path.* New York: Viking, 1978.

James, Robert Rhodes. *Anthony Eden, A Biography*. New York: McGraw Hill, 1987.

———. *Winston Churchill, His Complete Speeches, 1897–1963.* New York: Chelsea Books, 1983.

———. *Memoirs of a Conservative.* New York: Macmillan, 1970.

Jones, Thomas. *A Diary with Letters.* London: Oxford University Press, 1954.

Kapuscinski, Ryszard. *The Emperor.* New York: Harcourt Brace Jovanovich, 1978.

Kissinger, Henry. *Diplomacy*, New York: Simon & Schuster, 1994.

Kupferman, Fred. *Laval, 1883–1945.* Paris: Champs Flammarion, 1988.

LaFore, Lawrence. *The End of Glory.* Philadelphia and New York: Lippincott, 1970.

Lange, Walter C. *The Mind of Adolf Hitler.* New York and London: Basic Books, 1972.

Lansbury, George. *My Pilgrimage for Peace.* New York: Henry Holt,1938.

Laurens, F.D. *France and the Italo-Ethiopian Crisis, 1935–1936.* The Hague and Paris: Mouton, 1967.

Laval, Pierre. *The Diary of Pierre Laval.* New York: Charles Scribners, 1948.

*Le proces Laval.* Paris: Albin Michel, 1946.

Lawford, Valentine. *Bound for Diplomacy.* Boston: Little Brown, 1963.

Livingston, Dame Adelaide. *The Peace Ballot, An Official History.* London: Gollancz, 1935.

Manchester, William. *The Last Lion: Alone, 1932–1940.* Boston: Little Brown, 1988.

Marwick, Arthur. *Clifford Allen: Open Conspirator.* Edinburgh: Olwer and Boyd, 1964.

Macmillan, Harold. *Winds of Change, 1914–1939.* New York: Harper University Press, 1989.

Medlicott, W.N. *British Foreign Policy Since Versailles.* London: Methuen, 1940.

Meehan, E.G. *The British Left Wing and Foreign Policy.* New Brunswick, N.J.: Rutgers University Press, 1960.

Middlemas, Keith and John Barnes. *Baldwin, A Biography.* New York: Macmillan, 1969.

Milne, A.A. *Peace with Honour.* New York: E.P. Dutton, 1934.

Mockler, Anthony. *Haile Selassie's War.* New York: Random House, 1984.

Mowat, Charles L. *Britain Between the Wars, 1918–1940.* London: Methuen, 1955.

Muggeridge, Malcolm. *Things Past.* New York: William Morrow, 1979.

Murray, Gilbert. *The Ordeal of This Generation.* London: Allen & Unwin, 1929.

Mussolini, Benito. *My Autobiography.* New York: Charles Scribners, 1928.
Namier, Sir L.B. *Europe in Decay.* London: Macmillan, 1950.
Nichols, Beverley. *Cry Havoc.* New York: Doubleday Doran, 1933.
———. *News of England.* New York: Doubleday Doran, 1938.
Nicholson, Harold. *Diaries and Letters, 1930–1939.* New York: Atheneum, 1966.
———. *Peacemaking, 1919.* Universal Library Edition, New York: Grosset & Dunlap, 1965.
Nobel Lectures. *Peace, 1926–1950.* Amsterdam: Elsevier, 1972.
Northedge, F.S. *The Troubled Giant.* London: G. Bell, 1966.
Norwich, Earl of (Alfred Duff Cooper). *Old Men Forget.* New York: E.P. Dutton, 1954.
Paillat, Claude. *La Guerre A L'Horizon.* Paris: Laffont, 1981.
Papen, Franz von. *Memoirs.* London: Andre Deutsch, 1952.
Peterson, Sir Maurice. *Both Sides of the Curtain.* London: Constable, 1950.
Popper, Karl R. *The Poverty of Historicism.* Boston: Beacon Press, 1957.
Remak, Joachim. *The Origins of the Second World War.* Englewood Cliffs, N.J.: Prentice-Hall, 1976.
Renwick, Robin. *Economic Sanctions.* Cambridge: Center for International Affairs, 1981.
Reynaud, Paul. *In the Thick of the Fight.* New York: Simon & Schuster, 1955.
Robertson, E.M. *Hitler's Prewar Policy and Military Plans.* New York: The Citadel Press, 1967.
Rose, Kenneth. *The Later Cecils.* London: Weidenfeld & Nicholson, 1975.
Roskill, Stephen. *Hankey, Man of Secrets,* vol III. London: Collins, 1974.
Rowse, A.L. *Appeasement.* New York: W.W. Norton, 1963.
Russell, Bertrand. *A History of Western Philosophy.* New York: Modern Library, 1945.
Salvemini, Gaetano. *Prelude to World War II.* London: Gollancz, 1953.
Schmidt, Paul. *Hitler's Interpreter.* New York: Macmillan, 1951.
Scott, William Evans. *Alliance Against Hitler, the Origins of the Franco-Soviet Pact.* Durham, N.C.: Duke University Press, 1962.
Seton-Watson, R.W. *Britain and the Dictators.* New York: Macmillan, 1938.
Shirer, William. *The Collapse of the Third Republic.* New York: Simon & Schuster, 1969.
Simon, Viscount (Sir John Simon). *Retrospect.* London: Hutchinson, 1952.
Simon, Yves. *The Road to Vichy, 1918–1938.* New York: Sheed & Ward, 1942.
Smith, Denis Mack. *Mussolini, A Biography.* Vintage Books Edition, New York: Random House, 1983.
———. *Mussolini's Roman Empire.* New York: Viking, 1976.
Spencer, John H. *Ethiopia At Bay.* Algomac, Mich.: Reference Publications, 1984.

Swinton, Earl of (Phillip Cunliffe-Lister). *Sixty Years of Power*. London: Hutchinson, 1966.

Tabouis, Genevieve. *They Called Me Cassandra*. New York: Charles Scribners, 1942.

Taylor, A.J.P. *English History, 1914–1945*. London: Oxford University Press, 1965.

———. *The Origins of the Second World War.* New York: Fawcett Premier, 1961.

Templewood, Viscount (Sir Samuel Hoare). *Nine Troubled Years*. London: Collins, 1954.

———. *The Unbroken Thread*. New York: Alfred A. Knopf, 1950.

Thompson, Geoffrey. *Front Line Diplomat*. London: Hutchinson, 1959.

Thompson, Neville. *The Anti-Appeasers*. Oxford: Clarendon Press, 1971.

Tolstoy, Leo. *War and Peace*. New York: The Modern Library.

Torres, Henri. *Pierre Laval*. London: Gollancz, 1941.

Toynbee, Arnold. *Acquaintances*. New York: Oxford University Press, 1967.

———. *Experiences*. New York and London: Oxford University Press, 1969.

———. *Survey of International Affairs*. 1932, 1933, 1934, 1935, 1936. London: Oxford University Press.

Toynbee, Arnold and G.M. Urban. *Toynbee on Toynbee*. New York: Oxford University Press, 1974.

Vansittart, Lord (Sir Robert Vansittart). *Lessons of My Life*. New York: Alfred A. Knopf, 1943.

———. *The Mist Procession*. London: Hutchinson, 1958.

Villari, Luigi. *Italian Foreign Policy Under Mussolini*. New York: Devin-Adair, 1956.

Voigt, F.A. *Unto Caesar.* New York: G.P. Putnam, 1938.

Waley, Daniel P. *British Public Opinion and the Abyssinian War.* London: Maurice Temple Smith, 1975.

Walters, F.P. *A History of the League of Nations*. London:Oxford University Press, 1952.

Warner, Geoffrey. *Pierre Laval and the Eclipse of France*. New York: Macmillan, 1968.

Watt, D.C. "The Anglo-German Naval Agreement of 1935, An Interim Assessment." *Journal of Modern History,* June, 1956.

———. "The Secret Laval-Mussolini Agreement of 1935 on Ethiopia." *The Middle East Journal*, Winter, 1961.

Weinberg, Gerald. *The Foreign Policy of Hitler's Germany.* Chicago: University of Chicago Press, 1970.

Wilson, Duncan. *Leonard Woolf, A Political Biography.* New York: St. Martin's Press, 1978.

Williams, Frances. *A Prime Minister Remembers*. London: Heineman, 1961.

Windrich, Elaine. *British Labour's Foreign Policy.* Stanford, Cal.: Stanford University Press, 1952.

Wiskeman, Elizabeth. *Europe of the Dictators.* New York: Harper & Row, 1966.

Wolfers, Arnold. *Britain and France Between Two Wars.* New York: W.W. Norton, 1966.

Woolf, Leonard. *The Intelligent Man's Guide to Peace.* London: Gollancz, 1933.

Yates, Louis R. *United States and French Security.* New York: Twayne Publications, 1957.

Young, G.M. *Stanley Baldwin.* London: Rupert Hart-Davis, 1952.

# Index